New Choices for Writers

HOW TO GET PUBISHED IN THE NEW AGE MARKET

WRITER'S RESOURCES

15 MARGARET'S WAY, NANTUCKET, MA 02554

New Choices for Writers

Published by Writer's Resources, 15 Margaret's Way, Nantucket, MA 02554
508-325-0041, Fax: 508-325-0667

Elizabeth Gould, Editor
Editorial Staff: Barbara Cauper, Annie Laskey, Kimberly Sellers, Rie Traub

International Standard Serial Number
ISSN 1077-324X

International Standard Book Number
ISBN 0-9637387-1-2

CONTENTS

NEW TIMES, NEW CHOICES

Times are changing, and, if you were drawn to this book, you know what we mean. Our planet is experiencing an awakening of consciousness, a new creativity, and a change in the way experiences are expressed. We felt that it was time to respond to this change and create a guide for writers whose work reflects these sensibilities. *New Choices for Writers* is dedicated entirely to magazines and book publishers committed to exploring the evolving new age consciousness.

We view the term "new age" as inclusive and growing, not subject to a particular definition. We began by actively researching the market for publishers who espoused non-traditional and alternative views of positive planetary and personal growth and change. Our sights never narrowed; in fact, they were broadened and surprised by the variety of unique and creative ways in which people strive to understand our world and things beyond.

Rather than limit your view, we've listed almost every book publisher and magazine that wanted to be part of *New Choices for Writers*. It is a deliciously eclectic mix. Therefore, you will find markets seeking articles about politics, feminism, parenting and lifestyle alongside those interested in UFOs, channeling, astrology, and the occult. We encourage you to explore—you may be surprised at what you have to offer and to whom.

To acquaint yourself with the scope of the market, turn to the Subject Indexes (p. 16 for magazines; p. 146 for book publishers) where editors' interests are indexed under more than 50 categories. Within these categories, too, interests are wide and varied, so it important to read an individual listing to ascertain a market's particular slant and needs. Using the Listings (pp. 15 and 145) will show you how to get the most out of each listing.

In addition to the listings, we wanted you to have as much information as possible about the publishing industry and submissions process. The article, "Thirteen Reasons Why Most Writers Fail to Get Published and What You Can Do to Succeed," on page 5 will guide you through common mistakes writers make in the publishing process and show you how to avoid them. Beginning on page 12, you will find tips on manuscript presentation and how to write queries and cover letters. A postage chart shows you an easy way to calculate first-class postage for your manuscript. On page 14, we have listed proofreaders symbols and examples of their usage. The Glossary on page 201 will answer any questions you have about terms and abbreviations used in *New Choices*.

We also hope you will use this book as a networking tool. To help you connect with others who share your interests, we've provided, when possible, information on workshops, conferences, seminars, and retreats offered by the publishers or affiliated organizations. Often these events can be springboards into new opportunities. You'll also find information on advertising availability and rates, subscription costs, and a variety of writing contests for prose and poetry.

For some, this book may be a beginning—a place to be inspired, to discover what's out there, where your interests lay, and which magazines and publishers share your concerns. If you are a seasoned writer, you'll find new avenues for your work. Whatever your purpose, we hope that you will be inspired and enlightened by the information, the magazines, and the publishers listed within these pages.

This book was written with you in mind, and, in that light, we welcome suggestions, comments, and questions. You can write to the editor, Elizabeth Gould, at Writer's Resources, 15 Margaret's Way, Nantucket, MA 02554, or call 508-325-0041 (fax: 508-325-0667).

Thirteen Reasons Why Most Writers Fail to Get Published and What You Can Do to Succeed

by Elizabeth Gould

You write for many different reasons—to teach, to share, to inform, to entertain, to inspire—but above all you write to get published. You want to see your words in print, you want your talent recognized, and your hard work rewarded. You should. There is no reason you can't do what you love to do and even get paid for it. You already do the hard part—the writing. The rest is easy. The following paragraphs discuss thirteen reasons why most writers fail to get published and what you can do to succeed. Read through all thirteen reasons, even if you think that some of them don't apply to you. Be honest with yourself in assessing your weak spots, and then read through those sections again.

Next make a commitment to follow through and get your work published; to actively work to correct anything that is keeping you from your goal. At the end of your life you will be the only person you have to answer to. Don't have regrets about who you could have been and what you might have done. Do it now. You might be a prize-winning author. Don't you think that's worth finding out?

Mistake #1: Not marketing your work.

If you send out an article to fifteen magazines and all are returned with the comment that it's not what the editor is looking for, you haven't done your market research. There is no shortage of writers in this country, but there is a shortage of writers who take the time to research a magazine's or book publisher's interests before submitting a manuscript. Most editors are swamped with material and don't have time to read manuscripts on topics that are not of interest to their readers. Even if yours is the most brilliant piece ever written, it won't get published if it is not what the editor is looking for. If you want to sell your work, you need to produce something that people will buy.

Define the market before you write. The most efficient way to assure that your work is of interest to an editor is to research the market *before* you start to write. Begin by looking through the listings in *New Choices for Writers* and choose magazines or book publishers that share your interests. Note what the editors are looking for and what they have no interest in seeing. Then review several recent issues or catalogues to assess the editorial slant, audience, general focus and tone, and previously covered topics. If your topic is similar to recently published material, make sure that you are approaching the topic from a different angle, or find another market for that piece. Once you have targeted several markets, and you have a solid grasp of the audience and their interests, then you begin to write.

Tailor your existing work to fit an editor's needs. You need to move away from writing that satisfies you alone and move towards writing what people want to read. Take the time to tailor you work so that it is more in line with existing editorial needs. Your piece on dolphin family units could be refocused to become dolphin sexuality or dolphin habitats depending on a particular editorial focus. Perhaps you can make a lengthy article into a series of shorter pieces, or change the tone or slant of an article to fit a particular magazine's approach. This may take extra research or simply time to refocus and rewrite. But it's worth the effort. You took the time to write it, why not take the time to get it published?

The prospect of assessing the market before you write may seem unappealing if you think of writing as an inspired creative act, not a form of production and marketing. Yet, your marketing savvy need not interfere with your muse. Your having a focus before you set pen to paper does not make your creation any less inspired, just more saleable.

Mistake #2: Not promoting your work.

You've written an article that guarantees personal happiness, and it comes back with a rejection slip. Your short story that offers incredible insight into human consciousness remains unpublished. Why? Because you didn't tell the editor up front why it was so great. Out of the fifty articles most editors receive each day, what makes yours different? What do you have to offer to their readers?

Your cover letter is your pitch. An editor will often quickly assess whether or not your piece will be read based on the content of your cover letter. (You will find the mechanics of a cover letter defined in *How to Write a Cover Letter* on page 13.) Don't assume that editors will take the time to read an entire manuscript to ascertain its relevance to their needs. Tell them up front.

Show the editor that you've done your homework. You've done the research and you know that the readers of *Somnial Times* will be interested in "Musical Dreaming." Your tone fits the magazine, and your focus meets its interest in dream research. Put it in your cover letter.

Tell the editor why readers will be interested. Ask yourself what the readers will get out of your article. This may differ from what inspired you to write it. Readers won't care that the article is original in its application of music to the subconscious, but they will be interested in a way to control their dreams with music, a cure for their insomnia, and having more energy upon waking. The point is not what you know, but what you have to offer. If you find that you don't have anything to offer the readers, refocus your article.

For books, point out potential markets. You have assessed the market, seen the call for a book on Widget Spirituality, and written it. Yours is the only existing work on Widget Spirituality and you know there are 250,000 people practicing Widgetism in the country. You think it is important that the world understand the simplicity of the Widget lifestyle. Your editor will think it's important that a quarter of a million people will want a copy of *How to Attain Personal Happiness Through Widgetism: Traditions, Rituals, and Songs*. This is not to say that editors don't care about the content of a book and its intellectual merit, but, given the choice between two books, an editor is more likely to publish the one with a clear-cut market.

For fiction, write a "review" and use it in your cover letter. Marketing fiction is decidedly less straight-forward than marketing nonfiction. In general, fiction must speak for itself. However, you can identify your central theme and what it will mean to readers. In this way you will lead the editor into your manuscript—without having to retell the story—and show how readers will benefit from your work. To help focus, pretend you are a reviewer, and write a short blurb plugging your piece. Remember to keep the readers in mind: What they will they feel, learn, or experience from reading *Sara Goes to the Store?*

Don't write more than one or two sentences. The purpose of this exercise is to focus on the important parts: Your theme and what readers will get from it. Will they be touched? "You will laugh and cry with Sara as she discovers the truth about who she is when on her way to the store." Frightened? "You will be shocked and then terrified by the hidden past Sara discovers on her way to the store." Inspired? "You will learn the truth about yourself as Sara's walk to the store brings you into the past—a past that we all share."

Put it all together in your cover letter. Rather than the generic "I'm sure you will enjoy the enclosed manuscript, *Sara Goes to the Store*, about a girl discovering her past on the way to the market," your cover letter will read, "The enclosed *Sara Goes to the Store*, will inspire readers to the truth about themselves. As Sara uncovers her past on the way to the store, she discovers the truth about us all." In two sentences you have shown the editor the story's theme, plot, and interest to readers.

No one is ever going to be as knowledgeable and enthusiastic about your work, or care more about your success, than you. The time you take to lead an editor to your work can make the difference between publication and rejection.

Mistake #3: Not keeping abreast of the competition.

I know of a doctor who spent weeks writing an article for a prestigious medical journal. Although articulate and timely, the article was rejected. The reason? A competing journal had published an almost identical piece two months before. If the doctor had kept up with the developments in his field he would have saved himself time and professional embarrassment. An essential part of being a writer is knowing what is going on in your fields of interest.

Read what you like to write about. The market is ever-changing. You cannot expect your work to be timely and insightful if you don't know what's going on around you: What people are interested in, what is passé, what is changing, and what is being discovered and uncovered everyday. If you are interested in politics, you'd better be reading the daily paper. If you write about new age topics and you are not reading at least a few general new age magazines, it will be difficult to write relevant and timely pieces. By keeping current, you will be in a position to assess what subjects have been sufficiently covered, and which subjects need to be covered or covered in more detail.

For fiction, read the magazines you are interested in submitting to. Contemporary fiction is a wide and varied field and the only way you can match your style to the market is to read. There is a big difference between the fiction in *The New Yorker* and the fiction in *Omni Magazine* and you better know what that difference is before you submit. By reading recently published fiction you will also see what editors are buying—style, subject, genre, tone, character type, etc.

For books, read reviews. It is not necessary to read entire books to keep up with what other writers are doing. Read the book reviews. The book review section in your favorite magazines will review the kinds of books you are interested in reading and writing. Look at the Sunday book review section of your local newspaper or *The New York Times Book Review* for a more general look at what is being published. *Publishers Weekly*, available in libraries or on newsstands, also has an excellent book review section that is conveniently divided into categories of interest.

In addition, pay attention to what is being advertised. Looking at what products and services are being marketed to readers can give you valuable insight and inspiration.

Mistake #4: Not rewriting.

The quickest way to rejection is to present an editor with a sloppy manuscript. Even if your ideas are great, an editor will not take the time to plod through the first draft of a manuscript that clearly needs basic rewriting. If you want your work to be regarded on a professional level, you need to present it that way.

Proofreading your work is a given. Proofreading is editing for the technical aspects of your work—grammar, punctuation, spelling, and typographical errors. Not proofreading your work is inexcusable. There is no reason for a professional writer to ignore these fundamentals. If you are a shaky speller, invest in a spell check for your computer or use a dictionary. For help with grammar and punctuation, I recommend that you beg, borrow, or buy a copy of *The Elements of Style* by William Strunk, Jr. and E. B. White.

Rewriting is much more than proofreading. Rewriting involves checking your work for clarity and structure, and, for fiction, character development, plot, and dialogue. Always ask: Have I said what I wanted to say in the way I wanted to say it? Was it worth saying? Is it the best I can possibly do?

Everybody has a different method of rewriting. If you have one that works for you, stick with it. If you don't have a method that suits you, I suggest the following tools to help you develop your own system.

1. **Proofread first.** Technical errors are distracting to the rewriting process. Get them out of the way.
2. **Read the article (or chapter) aloud.** Reading aloud points out any glaring errors in clarity, structure, and flow. Chances are if you stumble over something when you say it, readers will stumble, too.
3. **Cut the verbiage.** Most writers over-write in the first draft. This is as it should be. You need to get all your ideas out. Naturally you will use more words, sentences, and even paragraphs than necessary. Now it is time to refine what you have written. Read through each paragraph and cut words or sentences that do not contribute to the whole. Deleting parts of your creation is difficult, but necessary. A clever sentence loses its wit if it doesn't fit.
4. **Check for clarity and flow.** Read from your audience's perspective. Will they understand everything you have written? You may need to add transitional paragraphs or rearrange them altogether in order for your piece to follow a logical path.
5. **Write a second draft.** Rewrite the entire piece (or print up the edited version) and go through the process again beginning with proofing. Continue to rewrite, starting with a fresh copy each time, until you are satisfied that it is done. Obviously, each draft will require less rewriting, and the refining is worth the effort.
6. **Put it aside.** By the time you have written your third or fourth draft you may never want to see your work again. Put it away for a few days. Distance will give you clarity and a fresh perspective.
7. **Proofread the final piece.** Give it a final read for remaining technical errors.

By rewriting you will be submitting your best work. This translates into the editor regarding you and your manuscript on a professional level.

Mistake #5: Failure to deliver the goods.

Your cover letter and presentation are professional and intriguing, and the editor eagerly turns to page one of your manuscript. She will never get to the end of the first chapter if your manuscript does not meet the expectations you set. Market research and a solid cover letter cannot compensate for a weak manuscript. Your work can shine in its professional polish, your clarity and character development may be impeccable, but did you deliver the goods? In *Sara Goes to the Store*, do readers really learn a truth about themselves, or is it just a story about a girl taking a walk? Does "Musical Dreaming" explicitly show people how to control their dreams with music, or is it only loosely implied? There is nothing more disappointing than a build-up to nothing.

If you lose your focus, you'll lose your audience. Zeroing in on your audience and purpose from the onset will help you stay focused as you write. Make a list of your intentions. Ask yourself what you are writing about, who you are writing for, what purpose it serves, and how it will benefit your readers. Write down a sentence or two for each question. When I conceived of this article my answers were as follows:

1. **What am I writing about?** How to get published.
2. **Who am I writing it for?** Writers who are having trouble getting published or who would like to get more of their work published.
3. **What purpose does it serve?** To help writers succeed.
4. **How will it benefit the readers?** Help them recognize common mistakes and pitfalls, and give them ways to correct these errors in order to succeed.

If you think you may have lost your focus as you were writing, you can refocus as you review your first draft. Return to your list of intentions, and create a list of follow-up questions to ask as you read through your first draft. (If you don't have a list of intentions, create one now.) When I reviewed the first draft of this article I asked: Did I give them good reasons? Did I explain the problems? Did I offer solutions to the problems? If they follow this advice, will it point toward their publishing success? Did I leave anything out? Could I say it any better? I asked these questions for each of the thirteen points I have listed. You may want to ask your questions with each paragraph, page, or chapter, depending on the length and format of your piece.

As always, this process is a bit more of a challenge if you are writing fiction. However, the exercise does apply, as good fiction always has purpose beyond telling a story. For the novel, *Sara Goes to the Store,* the original intentions may have looked like this:

1. **What am I writing about?** A girl who uncovers her past.
2. **Who am I writing it for?** Readers of inspirational fiction and people interested in universal truths.
3. **What purpose does it serve?** To enlighten and entertain.
4. **How will it benefit the readers?** An adventure that will bring them to a better understanding of themselves.

Among the follow-up questions you might ask are: Was her past worth uncovering? Did it explain a universal truth? Is her story inspiring, enlightening, and entertaining? Is Sara's going to the store an adventure? Is Sara believable? Do we care?

The truly creative part of being a writer is not the idea or plot, but the execution. A great writer can make a simple trip to the store a thing of inspiration and beauty. Ninety-nine percent of the time that beauty and inspiration do not spontaneously pour forth from a writer's pen; they are painstakingly crafted with conscious purpose. Here lies the difference between talent and success.

Mistake #6: Failure to utilize available resources.

We live in the age of information. There is more available on every subject out there than we know what to do with. So why are you using a three-year-old market guide? How come you are still stuck on the mechanics of writing when there are hundreds of books available on grammar? Thousands of writers' groups meet every night of the week, why do you sit at home wishing you had a peer group? Everything you ever wanted to know about writing—from how to diagram a complex sentence to left-brain writing—is available to you now. Besides books, magazines, newsletters, videos, and audio tapes, there are workshops, conferences, seminars, and writer's groups.

You can't afford all those books and magazines. Go to the library. Swap them with your new friend from the Tuesday night writers' group you started attending. Decide to review a series of how-to-write books and request free review copies from the publisher. Save your pennies. You're a writer, be creative.

There is no writers' group in your town. Start one. Pick a time and a place, and put an ad in the newspaper or hang a flier on the community bulletin board announcing that you will be starting a group. If you connect with only one other writer, it's one more than you knew before.

Take advantage of all the resources that are available to you. Writing can be creative and fulfilling, but it can also be frustrating and lonely. Sharing with kindred spirits, reading about writing, and seeking the knowledge and help of others who have gone before you can be uplifting, motivating, and inspiring.

Mistake #7: Failure to query for nonfiction ideas.

You spend a lot of time and energy writing articles and hoping that the markets you have researched will be interested. Why not find out if they are interested before you write? Send a query. As a writer, a query letter can be your greatest tool. (The components of how to write a query letter are detailed on p.12.)

A query does not mean you can skip the preliminary research. Most editors would buy an article on the First Lady's sex life, but could you get the interview? A query is a waste of both the editor's and your time if you can't follow through. For the article, "Musical Dreaming," some preliminary research might include locating several professionals in both the music and medical fields willing to be interviewed, testimonies from former insomniacs who were cured through music, and friends who are willing to find out how their dreams are affected by the music they listen to as they sleep.

An effective query letter is focused, enticing, and brief. As when writing an article, define what it is you are writing about, who you are writing for, what purpose it serves, and how it will benefit readers. Describe how and where you will get your information, list any relevant credentials, and close. Don't forget to slant your query to each magazine's editorial needs. The main focus of your article will change from dreams for *Somnial Times* to music for *Take Note! Music Magazine.*

Of course a positive response on a query does not guarantee that the piece will be published, but if you follow through in every way, your chances are pretty good.

Mistake #8: Ignoring non-paying markets.

A part of the satisfaction of getting published is getting paid. Unfortunately, there are thousands of writers vying for every paying job out there. Do not be discouraged. There is no reason why you shouldn't get one of those paid assignments. However, if you have few-to-no publishing credits, you are less likely to get an editor's attention than an apparently more experienced writer. Non-paying markets may be what you need to get your foot in the door.

Some things to keep in mind about non-paying markets:
1. They can be just as professional (read "competitive") as those that pay. However, they are often smaller, and more open to working with new writers.
2. You are more likely to have personal contact with an editor and gain valuable experience with the submission process.
3. You can establish publishing credits that can lead to paid assignments.
4. Often, these are the editors who will take the time to tell you exactly why they rejected your manuscript. This information can be invaluable to your growth as a writer.

Remember: A journey of a thousand miles begins with one step, and you usually don't get paid for taking it.

Mistake #9: Doing tons of research for only one project.

You spend a month doing research and you write one article on dolphin family units. A month of research and all the editor wants is thirty column inches! But since you have a wealth of information at your finger tips, why not put it to use?

You are an expert. If you have spent a week, a month, or a year researching dolphin family units, you probably know more about them than ninety-nine percent of the population. Write another article on a different aspect of dolphin family units. Or propose a series following the dolphin family as it develops from the single dolphin, to the dolphin couple, to the dolphin family of three. If you've written a book on the subject, write articles. This is an excellent way to promote your book.

Mistake #10: Blaming editors for your rejection.

No doubt about it: rejection stinks. When you send in a manuscript with great anticipation and get it back two months later with a rejection slip, it is easy to blame the editor who rejected it. But blaming the editor won't get you published. What will get you published is taking a look at why your manuscript was turned down.

Pay attention to editor's comments: It is rare, but there are editors who will take the time to explain the reason for a manuscript's rejection. These comments have validity. Read your manuscript through, keeping the editor's comments in mind, and rework it accordingly. Holding your ground and ignoring the input of a busy professional will not get you published.

Be honest with yourself: Often the only comments you will receive will be a form letter with one or more reasons for your manuscript's rejection checked off on a list. If the comments are specific enough, take heed. However, these checklists are often vague, and it is therefore up to you to assess your manuscript. Go through each of the thirteen points listed in this article and note any that apply to your manuscript's rejection. Follow through, make the necessary changes, and then resubmit your work.

Mistake #11: Not trying to get published because you are afraid of rejection.

You are afraid of public opinion, of failing, of being rejected and feeling foolish. These fears are valid and are experienced by every living soul who has ever risked exposing a part of themselves for public review. Laurence Olivier had stage fright to the point of vomiting before each performance, and yet he was one of the greatest actors of our time. And like Mr. Olivier, the only way you will overcome your fears is to do it anyway. Take a deep breath and submit your work.

It may help you to know that most writers get many rejection slips before a manuscript is accepted. With your first rejection slip you can count yourself as one among such writers as Edgar Allan Poe, Leo Tolstoy and Stephen King. Rejection is practically unavoidable. It is part of the learning process. (And it is likely that the reason for your rejection and how to correct it is on this list).

Mistake #12: Laziness.

You have half-finished articles and stories taking up space on your computer or wasting pages in your journal or notebook. You are excited and motivated at the onset of a project but lose steam somewhere in the middle. And if you do finish a piece, and take the time to edit and rewrite, the idea of writing a cover letter and submitting your work seems overwhelming. You would rather do two weeks worth of laundry and clean the scum around the base of your toilet than open a market guide to see who might be interested in your work. Most likely you are also incredibly talented, and it is a shame that your pet gerbil is using your masterpiece to nest in.

There is no cure for laziness—if there were, parents of teenagers all over the world would rejoice—but with a little effort you can fight your natural sluggish tendencies. Moving beyond laziness boils down to three things:

1. Making a list
2. Dedicating time
3. Taking action

The first step is to make a list of all the things you want to accomplish that are *relevant to your writing and getting published* (laundry and toilet scum do not apply). Depending on how detailed you want to get, the list might begin with "turn on the computer" and end with "walk to the post box." You are wise to get as detailed as you need to be. Next, break down the list into four phases: writing, editing, marketing, and submitting. Then list specifics under the relevant headings. Your final lists may resemble these:

Writing	Editing	Marketing	Submitting
1. develop an idea	1. proof: grammar, spelling, punctuation	1. research magazines	1. make copies
2. do research	2. read for clarity, development, style	2. write cover letters	2. double check editor names and addresses
3. create outline	3. second draft	3. proof and re-read cover letters	3. address & stamp envelopes, include SASE.
4. write first draft	4. proofread	4. final drafts of covers	4. mail
	5. final draft		

The next step is to dedicate a *realistic* amount of time per day to the completion of your project. It is probably not realistic to think that you will wake up every morning at five o'clock and write for three hours, but scheduling thirty minutes of writing after dinner each night might be something that you can commit to.

The final step is to take action. No matter how much you want to re-grout your bathroom or wash the dog, don't. Sit down and spend the time you have dedicated to attaining your goal and do it! You will be amazed at how easily you will be swept up in your creation and how quickly the time will pass. The hardest part is getting yourself to sit down at your desk.

Mistake #13: Having a negative attitude.

Attitude may not get you everywhere, but it can point you in the right direction. If you don't believe that you will get published, you probably won't.

Look where you are headed. Energy and effort follow intent. If you intend to get published, then focus on that goal. In professional car racing there are many obstacles and distractions set up on the track. To avoid crashing, the drivers are trained to focus on where they are going and never to look at the obstacles because they will unconsciously steer the car in that direction. There is a difference between being aware of the obstacles and focusing on them. If all you think about is the competitive market, the long and often frustrating submissions process, the tedium of rewriting the same article three times, you won't write. If you focus, instead, on the creative process, on getting published, and on the satisfaction of attaining your goal, you will be motivated and inspired.

Editors are not always right. Editors often have to make difficult choices about what to publish and what to reject. They base their decisions on the market, their readers, and a host of other criterion. And they don't always make the right choice. You probably have heard of rejected book manuscripts that have gone on to be best sellers. James Redfield, the author of *The Celestine Prophecy* received so many rejections that he published the book himself. It sold hundreds of thousands of copies. The rights were bought by Warner Books. Well-known philosopher Wayne Dyer bought the entire first print run of his book, *Your Erroneous Zones,* and sold them himself. The book is so well-known now that it is an answer in *Trivial Pursuit.* If your work is well-written, focused, and relevant to a specific audience, and you are willing to do what it takes to get it published, don't give up. There are many self-publishing books available to help you. I recommend *The Self-Publishing Manual* by Dan Poynter, *1001 Ways to Market Your Books* by John Kremer, and for any nonfiction work, *How to Make a Whole Lot More than $1,000,000 Writing, Commissioning, Publishing, and Selling "How-To" Information* by Jeffrey Lant. Check your library or bookstore for others.

Some Final Words.

At this point getting your work published may seem like an overwhelming task. But while your first few attempts may be a bit frustrating and time consuming, the process will soon be a natural part of your writing. There is nothing like seeing your words in print for the first time. Not only does it signify the achievement of your goal, it is recognition of you as a writer and a professional. Above all, be patient with yourself and with the process. Remember that it's not how far you go, but how you go far.

HOW TO SUBMIT YOUR WORK

The market listings that follow are tools of the trade. They will help you choose which few among the hundreds of book publishers and magazines are best suited to your work. Your options will narrow and focus as you consider the interests, audience, payment policies, and concerns of each. Using our listings to target appropriate markets can save you hours of research time. They also provide general information on how, when, and to whom you submit your material. They are not, however, a substitute for hands-on knowledge of the book publishers and magazines you select. It is often impossible to fit the full range of editorial needs and requirements into our analysis.

Most editors request that perspective writers send for contributor's guidelines and a sample magazine or catalogue before submitting material. Writer's guidelines will differ greatly in scope and content. Some consist simply of one or two paragraphs of suggested topics; others run several pages and detail very specific editorial and submission requirements that guarantee rejection if not followed. All contain information that will help you present an article, proposal, or book that is well thought out and professional.

HOW TO WRITE A QUERY LETTER

A query letter is a one page, single-spaced business letter, the purpose of which is to interest an editor in your article or book idea. Generally, query letters are used to propose nonfiction articles. This may apply to nonfiction books, as well, depending on the publisher. As a rule, editors prefer to review fiction in its entirety.

The goal of your query is to convince an editor that not only is your idea a good one, but that you are the writer to bring it to life. Remember that this is an editor's first impression of you and your work. Therefore, your letter should be well written and edited. If in the query you demonstrate your ability as a writer and a thinker, you are more likely to get an assignment.

Query Format

A query generally consists of four parts:

1. *The Lead* (1 paragraph). An enticing lead-in that conveys clearly the nature of your article or book and your ability to write.

2. *Description* (1–2 paragraphs). A clear and concise description of your idea. Explain your focus, how you will cover the subject, and why your approach is unique or valuable. List any elements you plan to use as supplements or resources: interviews, expert opinions, informative sidebars, bibliography, and/or resource lists. State the availability of photos or artwork that will illustrate your text. If an article, demonstrate your knowledge of the magazine and why your idea will appeal to its audience. If proposing a book, explain why it would fit in with the publisher's existing list.

3. *Experience* (1 paragraph). Describe your qualifications. List any relevant experience or expertise such as educational background, professional experience, or volunteer work that qualifies you to write the article or book, along with previous publishing credits, if any. If you have not been published, there is no need to mention it. Remember to stress the positive, but do not overdo it. If you have enclosed a resume, clips, writing samples, or other relevant materials, mention them here.

4. *Closing* (1 paragraph). State the proposed word length and when the finished manuscript can be available. Do not discuss payment. If you have submitted the same manuscript to another magazine or book publisher, mention it here (many editors accept simultaneous submissions; some wish to be notified). Note that you have enclosed a self-addressed, stamped envelope for a response. End cordially and professionally.

Common Mistakes

The following are common mistakes or oversights that lead to rejection:

1. *Lack of research.* A query should imply your knowledge of the magazine or book publisher and its editorial needs. Studying back issues, writer's guidelines, or book catalogues for style and content will tell you if your idea is appropriate. If a company has recently published something similar to what you are proposing, you may want to consider refocusing your idea or submitting elsewhere. Your research will minimize the risk of proposing articles that are overdone or a book that is ill-suited to the publisher's needs.

2. *Too long or too informal.* Editors usually do not have time to weed through pages of irrelevant, wordy material. Keep your query brief and focused. Avoid being too friendly, sentimental, or chatty. A query letter is a business proposal and

deserves professional treatment.

3. *Careless writing.* Poorly written and edited letters do not entice editors. Proofread your letter for spelling errors and typos. Double check the editor's name and be sure it is spelled correctly.

4. *Sloppy presentation.* Presentation is important. Use quality bond paper, cream or white, and be sure that the type is clean and legible.

It is good practice to include a self-addressed, postage-paid envelope for materials you want returned and/or a self-addressed, stamped postcard for confirmation of receipt. Many editors will not contact you without one. Keep a copy of all query letters for your files. Finally, a positive, confident attitude is an asset. Be yourself, and be professional.

HOW TO WRITE A COVER LETTER

Some publishers would rather review a complete manuscript. As mentioned earlier, this is often the case for fiction. In these cases it is common practice to enclose a cover letter as an accompaniment to your manuscript. A cover letter is similar to a query in form, but even more concise, allowing the manuscript to speak for itself.

Cover Letter Format

A cover letter should be a one-page business letter addressed to the appropriate editor. It can include the following:

1. *Lead.* Introduce the manuscript enclosed. State its title, word length, intended audience, and potential market appeal.

2. *Description.* Again, be brief. State the focus and slant of your work and how it fits publisher's interests. If not enclosed, state the availability of artwork and/or photos.

3. *Experience.* Mention any relevant experience and/or publishing credits. Refer to any additional enclosures such as a resume, author biography, published clips, or bibliography.

4. *Closing.* Indicate a simultaneous submission if applicable. Refer to the enclosed self-addressed, stamped envelope for response.

As with a query, a good cover letter is well written, neatly presented, and error free. It reflects your knowledge of the publisher and its interests.

HOW TO SUBMIT A MANUSCRIPT

Most editors will accept manuscripts that follow the standard format outlined below. Some, however, require a particular set-up or request additional information. Check the writer's guidelines and market listings for any special requirements before submitting your work.

Manuscript Format

Manuscripts should be neatly typed and double spaced. Allow generous top, bottom, and side margins—at least one inch—for editor's comments. On the first page, type your name, address, phone number, and social security number, single spaced, in the upper left corner. Type the approximate word length in the upper right corner. Center your title (and byline, if desired though not necessary) one-third of the way down the page. Begin your text two or three lines below the title. On subsequent pages, type your last name and the page number in the upper right corner. Space down three or four lines to continue your text.

A note about word lengths: There are several ways to divine the number of words in your manuscript. If you do your writing on a computer, most programs will provide word counts. If not, count the number of words in five lines and divide it by five. This will give you the average number of words per line. Then count the number of lines on a page and multiply to find your per-page word count. Multiply this by the total number of pages for your total word count.

Presentation and Mailing

As with any business proposal, manuscript presentation counts, so be professional. Use heavy-weight 8.5x11 white bond paper that allows for minimal show-through. Erasable paper is flimsy and sloppy—avoid using it. Whether typewritten or computer printed, check that your manuscript type is dark, clean, and very legible. Many editors accept clear dot-matrix printouts and photocopies, but letter-quality originals are always preferred. Be sure your manuscript is neat and smudge free. Always keep a copy for your files.

Short manuscripts, usually less than five pages, can be folded and mailed in a business-size envelope. Longer articles should be mailed flat, unstapled, in a 9x12 or 10x13 envelope. Book-length manuscripts should be mailed flat, unstapled, in a 9x12 box. Include a SASE marked First Class with sufficient return postage (see page 14 for rates) or International Reply Coupons (IRCs) if submitting to a foreign publication. Enclose a SAS postcard if you wish the editor to acknowledge receipt.

Wait the predetermined response time before following up on your submission, and then contact the editor by mail. Above all, be patient.

FIRST CLASS POSTAGE RATES

The chart below will help you determine the amount of postage needed to mail manuscripts to prospective publishers in the U.S. and Canada, as well as return postage for self-addressed, stamped envelopes. When mailing to foreign countries, check with the Post Office for International Reply Coupon (IRC) rates and requirements.

The number of pages per ounce are based on using standard 20 lb. paper and standard-weight 9x12 envelopes. Costs may vary according to the quality and weight of the paper and envelopes used. A query or short manuscript can be mailed in a #10 business-size envelope with a $.29 stamp. A self-addressed postcard requires $.19 postage.

First-class pieces weighing over 11 ounces are considered Priority Mail and are priced according to geographical zone as well as weight. Check with the Post Office for rates and requirements.

Ounces	Number of pages plus 9x12 envelope and 9x12 SASE	First-class postage rates	Rates to Canada from U.S.
1	1–2 pages	$.39	$.63
2	3–7 pages	$.52	$.73
3	8–14 pages	$.75	$.86
4	15–20 pages	$.98	$1.09
5	21–27 pages	$1.21	$1.32
6	28–34 pages	$1.44	$1.55
7	35–40 pages	$1.67	$1.78
8	41–47 pages	$1.90	$2.01
9	48–54 pages	$2.13	$2.24
10	55–60 pages	$2.36	$2.47
11	61–66 pages	$2.59	$2.70

PROOFREADER'S SYMBOLS

Correction	Symbol	Correction	Symbol	Correction	Symbol
Insert character	the white house	Delete word	ask any questions	New paragraph	brightly. The new
Insert period	away She saw it	Delete and close space	tommorrow night	No new paragraph; run text in	in his way. no¶ The next day
Insert comma	with them but he	Close space	his text book	Move left	nearly ten feet
Insert semicolon	this time however	Replace word	In the evening morning	Move right	nearly ten feet
Insert colon	as follows	Transpose letters	at the widow	Move up	a dark sky above
Insert hyphen	well known dog	Transpose words	heard the ring bell	Move down	sharp rocks below
Insert EM dash	this day a day	Spell out	at least 10 sp	Move text	as he drove Suddenly the wheel shifted. He heard a crackling sound.
Insert EN dash	12 4 years	Lowercase	choose Wisely		
Insert space	today they went	Uppercase	rev. Jonas cap	Return to original	the only one stet
Insert quotation	said, Come back.	Set in italics	entitled Roots ital	More than one correction per line	He left without a word #/ ∩/ ⊙
Insert apostrophe	Elizabeths room	Set in boldface	in Chapter 1 bf		
Delete character	the churchn door	Set in small capitals	a limited time sc		

14

PUBLICATIONS: USING THE LISTINGS

Your research into the new age market can begin with a careful study of the listings that follow. The listings are divided into two groups: Publications, beginning on page 28, and Book Publishers, beginning on page 152. Both sections are organized in alphabetical order. For a complete index of all the publications and book publishers in the guide, turn to the Index of Publishers, on page 203.

Both the Publications and Book Publishers sections are preceded by a subject index of publishers listed alphabetically under various headings. Some are general categories of writing, others are topics specific to new age markets. Scan the subject headings for interests that match your own and you will find a list of likely markets. If your particular interests are not reflected, consider related subjects, or turn directly to the market listings for a complete assessment of editorial needs.

Our market listings are designed to help you make informed choices about the best opportunities for your work. The sample listing and outline that follow introduces the format and type of information presented under each subheading.

Common Boundary
Anne Simpkinson, Editor, 4304 East-West Highway, Bethesda, MD 20814   Phone: 301-652-9495, Fax: 301-652-0579

1   **Profile:** A national magazine exploring the connection between spirituality and psychology. Established in 1988. Issued bimonthly. Circ: 30,000. Trim size: 8.5x11. Glossy color cover; 4-color; coated paper; saddle stitched. 74 pages. Subscription cost: $22. Sample copy cost: $5. Guidelines available with SASE.
2   **Focus and Tips:** *Common Boundary* is dedicated to exploring the sources of meaning in human experience. Readers are those interested in the interface between spirituality, creativity, and psychology. The magazine offers thoughtful discussions of transformational processes such as dreamwork, storytelling, meditation, and creative expression. Prefers journalistic reporting to academic styles and grounded prose to inflated writing.
3   **Editorial Interests**
Psychology, spirituality, bodywork, dreams, feminism, healing, holistic health, inspiration, lifestyle, meditation, men's issues, mysticism, mythology, philosophy, prayer, psychology, recovery, religion, self-help, and women's issues.
• *Nonfiction:* Features, 1,500–3,000 words. Articles, 1,500 words. Interviews and profiles, 1,500–2,000 words. Essays, personal experiences, and opinion pieces, 1,000 words. News items, 500 words. Reviews, 750 words. Departments include Innovations, Book Reviews, and In Your Own Words. Accepts submissions for End Page column.
• *Illustrations:* Photo essays.
4   **Submission Policy:** Query with outline, writing samples, and resume. Include SASE. Accepts photocopies, computer printouts, and WordPerfect disks. Simultaneous submissions okay. Reports in 3 months. If accepted, expect publication in 3 months.
5   **Terms and Payment:** One-time rights. Pays on publication. Offers a varied per word rate for articles. Authors receive copies of the issue.
6   **Advertising:** Rates: B/W full-page, $ 1,080; 4-color full-page, $1,550; back cover 4-color; $1,825. Contact Grace Ogden, 301-652-9495. List rental available. Contact Pacific Lists, 413-381-0826.
7   **Other Interests:** Offers a $1,000 Thesis/Dissertation Award for the best psychospiritual MA thesis or Ph.D. dissertation. Deadline is December 31 in the year thesis/dissertation was accepted. Essay based on winning entry is published. Contact Charles H. Simpkinson, 301-652-9495. Sponsors an annual conference on interface between spirituality, creativity, and psychology. Held in Arlington, Virginia in November. Contact Mary Jane Casavant, 301-652-9495.

1. **Profile:** A general description of the publication, including its publishing house, frequency, circulation, size, physical characteristics, page length, and subscription and sample copy costs.
2. **Focus and Tips:** The flavor of the publication including advice for writers on the publication's philosophy and interests, the types of articles most in demand, and those topics, writing styles, viewpoints, or literary forms to avoid.
3. **Editorial Interests:** Specific topics of interest to the publication and areas such as fiction, nonfiction, articles, stories, personal experiences, etc., open to freelance writing. Also included are word lengths.
4. **Submission and Payment Policy:** Details on how to approach a publication: whether to query first or send a complete manuscript; what to include with submissions, i.e., cover letter, resume, writing samples, etc.; acceptable submissions forms, i.e., photocopies, computer printouts and disks, or fax submissions; and special submissions restrictions or deadlines. Also includes whether the publication accepts reprints and simultaneous submissions. Finally, the average time it will take for an editor to respond to submissions and the average time between acceptance and publication are noted.
5. **Terms and Payment:** An outline of general publication terms: the type of rights the publisher requests; whether payment is made on acceptance or publication; rates per word or per piece; the number of contributor's copies offered; and any special policies regarding compensation.
6. **Advertising:** The magazine's advertising policies including per page rates for black and white or color ads and whether subscriber/mailing list rental is available.
7. **Other Interests:** Listed here are any school or organizational affiliations; the sponsorship of writing contests; and connections to conferences, workshops, seminars, retreats, or other programs.

PUBLICATION SUBJECT INDEX

ASTROLOGY
Aqua Terra
Baltimore Resources
The Cosmic Family Newsletter
Crone Chronicles
Diamond Fire
Exceptional Human Experience
Fate Magazine
International UFO Library Magazine
Lightworks
Llewellyn's New Worlds
The Monthly Aspectarian
The New Times
New Visions
Night Roses
Of A Like Mind
Panegyria
Planetary Connections
Rays from the Rose Cross
Tarot News
Unique Magazine
Whole Life Times
Wholistic Alternatives

BODYWORK
Ascension
Balanced Living
Bliss
Brain/Mind
Common Boundary
Conscious Choice
Constructive Action Newsletter
Free Spirit--California
Free Spirit--New York
Health News and Review
Massage
The Mirror
The Muscle News
Natural Health
Nexus
Qi
Rainbow Network
TRANS Quarterly
Tantra
Yoga Journal

BOOK EXCERPTS
Afrique
Asian Pacific American Journal
Bliss
Button

Chiron Review
Crone Chronicles
Diamond Fire
Encore Magazine
The Evergreen Chronicles
Familiars
InnerSelf
Modern Shaman Magazine
New Thought Journal
The Psychic Reader
Womyn's Press

BUDDHISM
Fish Drum Magazine
Heaven Bone
Mountain Record
Shambhala Sun
Tricycle
Turning Wheel
Wheel of Dharma

CHANNELING
Attain
Coming Out Pagan
Convergence
The Cosmic Family Newsletter
Dream International Quarterly
Exceptional Human Experience
The Faithist Journal
International UFO Library Magazine
Intuitive Explorations
The New Age Reporter
Pathfinder
Santa Fe Sun
The Shaman Papers
Sweet Fern
Sword of Dyrnwyn
TRANS Quarterly
Temple Doors
Trends & Predictions Analyst
The Unexplained Magazine
WE: Walk-ins for Evolution

CRYSTALS
The Cosmic Family Newsletter
Diamond Fire
The Faithist Journal
The New Age Reporter
New Mexico Light
Red Clay
Reflections Directory

The Shaman Papers
Sweet Fern
Sword of Dyrnwyn
Temple Doors
The Unexplained Magazine

CULTURAL AND ETHNIC
AIM
Black Bear Review
Bohemian Chronicle
The Compleat Mother
Cultural Survival Quarterly
Dwelling Portably
The Eagle
Explanasion
Heart & Soul
Hinduism Today
Illahee
India Currents
Indiana Review
Men As We Are
Modern Shaman Magazine
Mother Jones
New Moon
New Moon Parenting
New Pages
The Other Paper
Pacific Coast Journal
Pan-American Indian Association News
PDXS
The Peace Newsletter
Plain Brown Wrapper
The San Francisco Bay Guardian
Santa Fe Sun
Sipapu
Skipping Stones
Struggle
The Sun
Teaching Tolerance
Thema
Third Force
Tricycle
The Voice and the Vision
Whispering Wind Magazine
Wildfire
Women Artists News
Womyn's Press
World Rainforest Report

DISABILITY
Constructive Action Newsletter

Exceptional Parent
Expressions
Kaleidoscope

DRAMA
American Writing
The Arizona Light
Bohemian Chronicle
Crystal Tower
Earth's Daughters
The Evergreen Chronicles
Expressions
Familiars
Fish Drum Magazine
Kids Lib News
Macrobiotics Today
New Mexico Light
Pacific Coast Journal
The Portable Wall
Shambhala Sun
Spirit Magazine
Struggle

DREAMS
American Writing
Angel's Wings
Avatar
Brain/Mind
Common Boundary
Convergence
Dream International Quarterly
Dynamic Life New Times
Encore Magazine
The Faithist Journal
Llewellyn's New Worlds
The Mirror
Modern Shaman Magazine
The New Age Reporter
Night Roses
Plain Brown Wrapper
Plainsong
Potato Eyes
Rainbow City Express
Reclaiming
Shaman's Drum
Somatics
Sominal Times
Spirit Magazine
Thresholds Quarterly
Trends & Predictions Analyst
Venture Inward
Winners

ECOSYSTEMS
Alternatives
American Writing
Anima
Aqua Terra
Conscious Choice
Family Earth
Green Fuse Poetry
Heaven Bone
How on Earth!
Illahee
Natural Foods Merchandiser
New Lifestyles Newspaper
New Visions
Next Phase
Nexus
The Oregon PeaceWorker
Organica Quarterly
Planetary Connections
The Suspicious Humanist
Talking Leaves
Vegetarian Journal
Voices of Women
Whole Life Times
The Wild Foods Forum
World Rainforest Report

ENVIRONMENT
Alternatives
Aqua Terra
Arizona Networking News
Baltimore Resources
Celebrate Life!
Color Wheel
Community Service Newsletter
Conscious Choice
Creation Spirituality
Crystal Tower
Dwelling Portably
E: The Environmental Magazine
Earthwatch Oregon
Eco-Notes Magazine
Electronic Green Journal
Family Earth
Forefront--Health Investigations
Heart Dance
High Country News
Illahee
Living Off the Land
Men As We Are
Mother Jones
Mothers Resource Guide

Mountain Luminary
Networker Magazine
New Lifestyles Newspaper
New Pages
New Texas Magazine
The New Times
Next Phase
Odyssey
Organica Quarterly
Pan-American Indian Association News
The Peace Newsletter
Perceptions
Planetary Connections
The Psychic Reader
Sequoia
S.L.U.G.fest, Ltd.
Struggle
Take Note! Music Magazine
Talking Leaves
Tricycle
Turning the Tide
Turning Wheel
Vegetarian Journal
Vegetarian Times
Vegetarian Voice
The Wild Foods Forum
Wildfire
World Rainforest Report

EXTRATERRESTRIALS
Borderlands
The Cosmic Family Newsletter
Final Frontier
The Gate
Infinite Onion
International UFO Library Magazine
Intuitive Explorations
Omega New Age Directory
Omni Magazine
Perceptions
The Psychic Reader
The Shaman Papers
The Skeptical Inquirer
Star Wars Collection Trading Post
Time Pilot
Trends & Predictions Analyst
UFO Review
Unexplainable Universe
The Unexplained Magazine
Unique Magazine
Unsolved UFO Sightings

FEMINISM

American Writing
Anima
Birth Gazette
The Compleat Mother
Crone Chronicles
Daughter of Nyx
Earth's Daughters
Encore Magazine
The Evergreen Chronicles
The Fire Fly and Fire Fly, Jr.
Heresies
Herspectives
Hysteria
Mother Jones
New Moon
New Pages
On The Issues
The Oregon PeaceWorker
The Other Paper
The Peace Newsletter
Peacework
Plain Brown Wrapper
The Red Queen
SageWoman
Sequoia
SingleMOTHER
Single Mothers by Choice
Sipapu
S.L.U.G.fest, Ltd.
Struggle
Turning the Tide
The Unforgettable Fire
Voices of Women
Windy City Times
The Wise Woman
Woman of Power
Woman's Way
Women Artists News
Women & Recovery
Womyn's Press

FOLKLORE

AIM
Afrique
Alberta History
Angel's Wings
Anima
Explanasian
Familiars
FireHeart
The Gate

Green Egg
Keltria
Magic Realism
New Moon
New Moon Parenting
North Dakota Quarterly
Ocean Gypsy
Pan-American Indian Association News
Parabola
Plain Brown Wrapper
Plainsong
Potato Eyes
The Red Queen
Skipping Stones
Talking Leaves
Unexplainable Universe
Whispering Wind Magazine
The Wild Foods Forum

GAY AND LESBIAN

The Advocate
Backspace
Bohemian Chronicle
Chiron Review
Church & State
Coming Out Pagan
Common Lives/Lesbian Lives
The Evergreen Chronicles
Hysteria
Infinite Onion
Men As We Are
Mother Jones
Off Our Backs
Open Hands
The Oregon PeaceWorker
The Other Paper
The Peace Newsletter
Peacework
Potato Eyes
RFD
The San Francisco Bay Guardian
Sequoia
Spring
Struggle
Teaching Tolerance
Truth Seeker
Turning the Tide
The Unforgettable Fire
Village Voice
Windy City Times
Woman's Way
Womyn's Press

HEALING

Angel's Wings
Baltimore Resources
Both Sides Now
The Civil Abolitionist
Color Wheel
Constructive Action Newsletter
Creation Spirituality
Creations Magazine
Crystal Tower
Delicious!
Diamond Fire
Dynamic Life New Times
The Eagle's Cry
The Edge
Free Spirit--California
Free Spirit--New York
Health Consciousness
Health News and Review
Heart Dance
Herspectives
InnerSelf
Kids Lib News
Lightworks
Massage
Midwifery Today
The Mirror
Modern Shaman Magazine
The Muscle News
The National Spiritualist--Summit
Natural Health
Networker Magazine
New Age Journal
New Editions Health World
New Visions
The Northeast Recovery Networker
Odyssey
The Phoenix
Potato Eyes
The Psychic Reader
Qi
Rainbow Network
Rays from the Rose Cross
Recovery Times
Reiki News
SageWoman
Second Mile
Shambhala Sun
Smart Drug News
Spirit Magazine
Spirit of Change Magazine
Spirit of the Times

Sproutletter
Unity Magazine
Vegetarian Voice
Women & Recovery

HEALTH
The Advocate
Alternatives
Arizona Networking News
Attain
Birth Gazette
Borderlands
Brain/Mind
Brickwall Bulletin & Bulletin Too
The Civil Abolitionist
Community Service Newsletter
Delicious!
Diet & Health Series
E: The Environmental Magazine
Endless Possibilities
Energy Times
Family Life Educator
Forefront--Health Investigations
Forever Alive
Health Consciousness
Health Foods Business
Health News and Review
Heart & Soul
Inside Kung Fu
It's Your Choice
Lightworks
Massage
Maui'arna Magazine
The Muscle News
Natural Foods Merchandiser
The Networker
New Editions Health World
New Pages
Omni Magazine
On The Issues
Outpost Exchange
Perceptions
The Phoenix
The Portable Wall
Priority Parenting
Rainbow Network
Recovery Times
Reflections Directory
Reiki News
Science of Mind
Smart Drug News
Somatics

Spirit of the Times
Sproutletter
The Suspicious Humanist
Tai Chi
Three Rivers Wellness Directory
Thresholds Quarterly
Vegetarian Journal
Vegetarian Times
Vegetarian Voice
Veggie Life
Welcome Home
Whole Earth Review

HOLISTIC HEALTH
Alt/Alternative Press
Alternatives
The Arizona Light
Arizona Networking News
Ascension
Balanced Living
Body, Mind & Spirit
Brain/Mind
Catalist
Conscious Choice
Convergence
Creations Magazine
Delicious!
The Eagle's Cry
Free Spirit--California
Free Spirit--New York
Health Consciousness
Herbal Gram
How on Earth!
Kids Lib News
Macrobiotics Today
The Muscle News
Natural Health
Networker Magazine
New Age Journal
New Editions Health World
New Frontier Magazine
New Lifestyles Newspaper
New Mexico Light
New Texas Magazine
New Visions
Nexus
The Northeast Recovery Networker
Odyssey
Organica Quarterly
Pathfinder
Qi
Rainbow Network

Reflections Directory
Sharing Spirit
Stepping Up
Symposium
Tantra
TRANS Quarterly
Uptown Express
Vegetarian Journal
Venture Inward
Visions Magazine
Whole Life Times
Yoga Journal

INSPIRATIONAL
Catalist
Constructive Action Newsletter
The Cosmic Family Newsletter
Endless Possibilities
Expressions
The Faithist Journal
The Fire Fly and Fire Fly, Jr.
Free Spirit--California
Free Spirit--New York
Heart Dance
Integral Yoga
The National Spirituality--Summit
The New Age Reporter
The New Press Literary Quarterly
Next Phase
Ocean Gypsy
On Course
Open Hands
Recovery Times
Science of Mind
Skipping Stones

JUVENILE AND TEEN
AIM
Brilliant Star
Familiars
Family Life Educator
How on Earth!
Kids Lib News
New Moon
New Moon Parenting
PDXS
Priority Parenting
SingleMOTHER
Skipping Stones
Teaching Tolerance
Venture Inward

LIFESTYLE
Afrique
Angle's Wings
Asian Pacific American Journal
Baltimore Resources
Birth Gazette
Bliss
Changes
CoHousing
Communities
Community Service Newsletter
Creations Magazine
Diet & Health Series
Dwelling Portably
Dynamic Life New Times
Encore Magazine
The Evergreen Chronicles
Explanasian
Farm Family America
Farm and Ranch Living
FEMALE Forum
The Fire Fly and Fire Fly, Jr.
Forever Alive
Infinite Onion
Intergral Yoga
It's Your Choice
The Networker
New Age Journal
New Lifestyles Newspaper
New Mexico Light
The New Press Literary Quarterly
New Texas Magazine
Omni Magazine
Outpost Exchange
Pathfinder
PDXS
Potato Eyes
RFD
The San Francisco Bay Guardian
Santa Fe Sun
Single Mothers by Choice
S.L.U.G.fest, Ltd.
Spirit of the Times
Star Wars Collection Trading Post
Take Note! Music Magazine
Three Rivers Wellness Directory
Vegetarian Times
Whispering Wind Magazine
Wholistic Alternatives
The Wild Foods Forum
Windy City Times

LITERARY
American Writing
Backspace
Black Bear Review
Calyx
Chiron Review
Half Tones to Jubilee
The Heartlight Journal
Indiana Review
Kaleidoscope
The Ledge Poetry and Fiction Magazine
Magic Realism
New Letters
The New Press Literary Quarterly
NorthEast Arts
Plainsong
Potato Eyes
Story Quarterly
Thema
Willow Springs
Women Artists News

MAGIC
Diamond Fire
Dream International Quarterly
FireHeart
Green Egg
Intuitive Explorations
Keltria
Llewellyn's New Worlds
New Moon Rising
Ocean Gypsy
Panegyria
The Personal Magnetism Home Study
The Skeptical Inquirer
Spirit Magazine
Tarot News
Thema
Whole Life Times

MEDITATION
Arizona Networking News
Balanced Living
Bliss
Color Wheel
Diamond Fire
Dynamic Life New Times
The Eagle's Cry
Health Consciousness
InnerSelf
The National Spiritualist--Summit
Qi

The Quest
Rainbow City Express
Shambhala Sun
Sharing Spirit Newsletter
Somatics
Sproutletter
Tricycle
Turning Wheel
Unity Magazine
Yoga Journal

MEN'S ISSUES
The Evergreen Chronicles
Exceptional Parent
Full-Time Dads
Heart & Soul
Men As We Are
Mentor
New Texas Magazine
PDXS
Sipapu
Snake River Reflections
Spring
Village Voice

METAPHYSICS
Aqua Terra
Borderlands
Celebrate Life!
Convergence
Crystal Tower
Diamond Fire
The Eagle's Cry
Friend's Review
Heaven Bone
Intuitive Explorations
Light of Consciousness
Massage
The Monthly Aspectarian
New Frontier Magazine
Next Phase
North Dakota Quarterly
Omega New Age Directory
Perceptions
Plainsong
The Quest
Rosicrucian Digest
Science of Mind
The Shaman Papers
Sharing Spirit Newsletter
Spirit Magazine
Stepping Up

Sword of Dyrnwyn
Temple Doors
Three Rivers Wellness Directory
Thresholds Quarterly
TRANS Quarterly
Unity Magazine
Visions Magazine
WE: Walk-ins for Evolution
Whole Life Times
Wholistic Alternatives
Winners

MYSTICISM
Aqua Terra
Avatar
Creation Spirituality
Dream International Quarterly
Earth's Daughters
Gnosis
Hinduism Today
Light of Consciousness
The Mirror
New Thought Journal
Omega New Age Directory
Otisian Directory
Red Clay
Rosicrucian Digest
Shaman's Drum
Shambhala Sun
Tantra
Temple Doors
Unexplainable Universe
Unique Magazine
Venture Inward

MYTHOLOGY
American Writing
Anima
Asian Pacific American Journal
Color Wheel
Common Boundary
Daughter of Nyx
Earth's Daughters
Familiars
Fate Magazine
FireHeart
The Gate
Gnosis
Green Egg
Heaven Bone
Keltria
Magic Realism

The Monthly Aspectarian
New Visions
North Dakota Quarterly
Ocean Gypsy
Otisian Directory
Pan-American Indian Association News
Parabola
Plainsong
Red Clay
The Red Queen
Samsara
Snake River Reflections
Spring
Symposium
TRANS Quarterly
Unique Magazine
The Wise Woman

NATIVE AMERICAN
Alberta History
Crystal Tower
The Eagle
North Dakota Quarterly
Pan-American Indian Association News
The Portable Wall
Whispering Wind Magazine
Wildfire

NATURAL HEALTH
Alt/Alternative Press
Alternatives
Ascension
Baltimore Resources
Bohemian Chronicle
Celebrate Life!
The Civil Abolitionist
Conscious Choice
Delicious!
The Doula
Dwelling Portably
Eco-Notes Magazine
The Edge
Health Foods Business
Health News and Review
Heart & Soul
Herbal Gram
Macrobiotics Today
Massage
Midwifery Today
Mothers Resource Guide
Natural Foods Merchandiser
Natural Health

New Editions Health World
New Lifestyles Newspaper
Organica Quarterly
Outpost Exchange
Pan-American Indian Association News
Science Journal and Newsletter
Sharing Spirit Newsletter
Spirit of Change Magazine
Tai Chi
Vegetarian Journal
Vegetarian Times
Veggie Life
Voices of Women
Wholistic Alternatives
The Wild Foods Forum
Wildfire

NEW AGE
Afrique
The Arizona Light
Arizona Networking News
Ascension
Attain
Avatar
Balanced Living
The Beacon
Bliss
Body, Mind & Spirit
Borderlands
Both Sides Now
Brickwall Bulletin & Bulletin Too
Button
Christian*New Age Quarterly
Coming Out Pagan
Creations Magazine
Crystal Tower
Dynamic Life New Times
The Eagle's Cry
Earth's Daughters
Eco-Notes Magazine
The Edge
Encore Magazine
Exceptional Human Experience
The Faithist Journal
Familiars
Fate Magazine
Friend's Review
Heart Dance
Herspectives
Inner Light
InnerSelf
International UFO Library Magazine

NUTRITION—PARENTING

Intuitive Explorations
Kids Lib News
Light of Consciousness
Lightworks
Maui'arna Magazine
The Monthly Aspectarian
Mountain Luminary
NAPRA Trade Journal
The Networker
Networker Magazine
New Age Journal
New Age Marketing Opportunities
The New Age Reporter
New Frontier Magazine
New Lifestyles Newspaper
New Mexico Light
New Pages
New Thought Journal
The New Times
New Visions
Next Phase
Night Roses
Odyssey
Of A Like Mind
Omega New Age Directory
Outpost Exchange
Pathfinder
The Personal Magnetism Home Study
Plainsong
Planetary Connections
The Quest
Rainbow City Express
Red Clay
Reflections Directory
SageWoman
Santa Fe Sun
The Shaman Papers
Sharing Spirit Newsletter
Snake River Reflections
Spirit Magazine
Spirit of Change Magazine
Sweet Fern
Sword of Dyrnwyn
Symposium
Synthesis
Tarot News
TRANS Quarterly
Unexplainable Universe
The Unexplained Magazine
Uptown Express
Vegetarian Voice
Visions Magazine

WE: Walk-ins for Evolution
Whole Earth Review
Whole Life Times
Wholistic Alternatives

NUTRITION
Arizona Networking News
Ascension
Balanced Living
Birth Gazette
Body, Mind & Spirit
Changes
Delicious!
Diet & Health Series
The Doula
Dwelling Portably
E: The Environmental Magazine
Eco-Notes Magazine
Energy Times
Health Foods Business
Health News and Review
How on Earth!
Midwifery Today
The Muscle News
Natural Foods Merchandiser
Natural Health
New Age Journal
New Editions Health World
Organica Quarterly
Outpost Exchange
Priority Parenting
Sproutletter
Vegetarian Journal
Vegetarian Times
Vegetarian Voice
Veggie Life
The Wild Foods Forum

OCCULT
Fate Magazine
FireHeart
The Gate
Gnosis
Green Egg
Keltria
Llewellyn's New Worlds
New Moon Rising
Otisian Directory
Panegyria
The Personal Magnetism Home Study
Reclaiming
The Red Queen

The Skeptical Inquirer
Sword of Dyrnwyn
Tarot News
Temple Doors
Trends & Predictions Analyst
Village Voice
Winners

PARAPSYCHOLOGY
Attain
Exceptional Human Experience
Fate Magazine
The Gate
Ghost Trackers Newsletter
Infinite Onion
Llewellyn's New Worlds
Modern Shaman Magazine
The Psychic Reader
Shaman's Drum
The Skeptical Inquirer
Thema
Trends & Predictions Analyst
UFO Review
UFO Universe
The Unexplained Magazine
Unsolved UFO Sightings
Venture Inward

PARENTING
Birth Gazette
CoHousing
Community Service Newsletter
The Compleat Mother
The Doula
Dwelling Portably
Eco-Notes Magazine
Exceptional Parent
FEMALE Forum
The Fire Fly and Fire Fly, Jr.
Forefront--Health Investigations
Full-Time Dads
Heart & Soul
It's Your Choice
Kids Lib News
Men As We Are
Midwifery Today
Mothers Resource Guide
New Moon Parenting
Priority Parenting
SingleMOTHER
Single Mothers by Choice
Third Force

Time Pilot
Welcome Home

PHILOSOPHY
The Animal's Agenda
The Beacon
Brain/Mind
Button
Celebrate Life!
The Civil Abolitionist
Earth's Daughters
Hinduism Today
Illahee
India Currents
Integral Yoga
Journal of Philosophy
Live and Let Live
Macrobiotics Today
New Age Journal
The New Press Literary Quarterly
New Thought Journal
Off Our Backs
On Course
On The Issues
The Other Paper
Otisian Directory
Plain Brown Wrapper
The Quest
Rosicrucian Digest
Science Journal and Newsletter
Science of Mind
S.L.U.G.fest, Ltd.
The Sun
The Suspicious Humanist
Tai Chi
Tantra
Time Pilot
Tricycle
Truth Seeker
Turning Wheel
Unity Magazine

POETRY
American Writing
Angel's Wings
Anima
The Arizona Light
Black Bear Review
Bohemian Chronicle
Both Sides Now
Brickwall Bulletin & Bulletin Too
Button

Chiron Review
Color Wheel
Coming Out Pagan
Common Lives/Lesbian Lives
Crone Chronicles
Dream International Quarterly
The Eagle
Earth's Daughters
Encore Magazine
Ethereal Dances
Expressions
Family Earth
Full-Time Dads
Green Fuse Poetry
Half Tones to Jubilee
Heresies
Herspectives
Kaleidoscope
Keltria
Light of Consciousness
Macrobiotics Today
Magic Realism
Maui'arna Magazine
Modren Shaman Magazine
Mountain Luminary
Mountain Record
New Moon
The New Press Literary Quarterly
New Texas Magazine
New Thought Journal
Night Roses
North Dakota Quarterly
NorthEast Arts
The Northeast Recovery Networker
On Course
Open Hands
Pacific Coast Journal
Pan-American Indian Association News
The Portable Wall
Potato Eyes
The Red Queen
Samsara
Science of Mind
S.L.U.G.fest, Ltd.
Spirit Magazine
Struggle
The Suspicious Humanist
Symposium
Thresholds Quarterly
TRANS Quarterly
Turning the Tide
Turning Wheel

The Unforgettable Fire
Wildfire
Woman's Way
Women Artists News
Women & Recovery
Womyn's Press

POLITICS
Active Voice
The Advocate
AIM
The Animal's Agenda
Black Bear Review
Church & State
The Civil Abolitionist
Conscious Choice
Eco-Notes Magazine
Explanasian
The Fire Fly and Fire Fly, Jr.
Forefront--Health Investigations
Forever Alive
Green Fuse Poetry
Heresies
Illahee
Indiana Review
Infinity Forum
It's Your Choice
Live and Let Live
Mother Jones
The Neighborhood Works
Off Our Backs
On The Issues
The Oregon PeaceWorker
Organica Quarterly
The Other Paper
PDXS
The Peace Newsletter
Peacework
Perceptions
Reclaiming
The San Francisco Bay Guardian
Struggle
The Sun
The Suspicious Humanist
Talking Leaves
Teaching Tolerance
Third Force
Time Pilot
Truth Seeker
Turning the Tide
Turning Wheel
The Voice and the Vision

Science of Mind
Second Mile
Sequoia
Skipping Stones
Snake River Reflections
Thema
Thresholds Quarterly
Truth Seeker
Unity Magazine
Wholistic Magazine

SELF-HELP
Afrique
Avatar
Body, Mind & Spirit
Brickwall Bulletin & Bulletin Too
Catalist
Celebrate Life!
Changes
Constructive Action Newsletter
Endless Possibilities
Forefront--Health Investigations
Friend's Review
Heart Dance
Intuitive Explorations
Living Off the Land
Maui'arna Magazine
The Monthly Aspectarian
Mothers Resource Guide
Mountain Luminary
Natural Foods Merchandiser
The Networker
Networker Magazine
New Mexico Light
New Thought Journal
The New Times
Night Roses
The Northeast Recovery Networker
Outpost Exchange
The Personal Magnetism Home Study
The Phoenix
Planetary Connections
Priority Parenting
Rainbow Network
Rays from the Rose Cross
Recovery Times
Reflections Directory
Santa Fe Sun
SingleMOTHER
Smart Drug News
Somatics
Spirit of the Times

Sproutletter
Stepping Up
Sweet Fern
Symposium
Take Note! Music Magazine
Three Rivers Wellness Directory
Thresholds Quarterly
Uptown Express
Visions Magazine
Voices of Women
Whole Earth Review
Winners
Woman's Way
Women & Recovery

SENIORS
CoHousing
Crone Chronicles
Encore Magazine
Personal & Family History Newsletter
Reflections Directory
Santa Fe Sun
Third Force

SEXUALITY
Bliss
New Frontier Magazine
Tantra

SHORT STORIES
Afrique
AIM
Angel's Wings
Anima
The Arizona Light
Asian Pacific American Journal
Brilliant Star
Button
Changes
Chiron Reivew
Coming Out Pagan
Common Lives/Lesbian Lives
Community Service Newsletter
Daughter of Nyx
Diamond Fire
Dream International Quarterly
Ethereal Dances
The Evergreen Chronicles
Familiars
FireHeart
Fish Drum Magazine
Full-Time Dads

Half Tones to Jubilee
Heresies
Herspectives
Illahee
India Currents
Indiana Review
Integral Yoga
Kaleidoscope
Macrobiotics Today
Magic Realism
Massage
Men As We Are
Modern Shaman Magazine
New Mexico Light
New Moon
New Moon Parenting
New Thought Journal
Next Phase
Nigth Roses
North Dakota Quarterly
The Northeast Recovery Networker
Ocean Gypsy
Open Hands
Otisian Directory
Panegyria
The Portable Wall
Potato Eyes
The Psychic Reader
Recovery Times
Red Clay
The Red Queen
Samsara
Shaman's Drum
Shambhala Sun
S.L.U.G.fest, Ltd.
Story Quarterly
Willow Springs
Womyn's Press

SOCIAL AND WORLD ISSUES
Active Voice
AIM
Alt/Alternative Press
Alternatives
The Animal's Agenda
Asian Pacific American Journal
Black Bear Review
Both Sides Now
Brilliant Star
Church & State
Community Service Newsletter
Creation Spirituality

SPIRITUALITY—WOMEN'S ISSUES

Cultural Survival Quarterly
The Eagle
Earthwatch Oregon
Family Earth
Forever Alive
Green Fuse Poetry
Illahee
India Currents
Infinite Onion
Infinity Forum
It's Your Choice
Living Off the Land
Mother Jones
Mountain Record
The Neighborhood Works
New Thought Journal
Next Phase
On The Issues
The Oregon PeaceWorker
The Other Paper
The Peace Newsletter
Peacework
Perceptions
Planetary Connections
RFD
The San Francisco Bay Guardian
Science of Mind
Sequoia
Sipapu
Skipping Stones
Smart Drug News
Snake River Reflections
Struggle
The Suspicious Humanist
Talking Leaves
Teaching Tolerance
Third Force
Three Rivers Wellness Directory
Time Pilot
Tricycle
Truth Seeker
Turning the Tide
Turning Wheel
The Unforgettable Fire
Village Voice
The Voice and the Vision
Whole Earth Review
Wildfire
Woman's Way
World Rainforest Report

SPIRITUALITY

The Arizona Light
Balanced Living
The Beacon
Body, Mind & Spirit
Both Sides Now
Brilliant Star
Catalist
Changes
Coming Out Pagan
Convergence
Creations Magazine
Crone Chronicles
Dream International Quarterly
Earth's Daughters
Endless Possibilities
The Faithist Journal
FireHeart
Free Spirit--California
Free Spirit--New York
Friend's Review
Health Consciousness
Heart Dance
Heart & Soul
Herspectives
India Currents
Indiana Review
InnerSelf
Integral Yoga
International UFO Library Magazine
Light of Consciousness
Macrobiotics Today
The Monthly Aspectarian
Mountain Luminary
The Networker
New Frontier Magazine
New Mexico Light
The New Press Literary Quarterly
The New Times
Nexus
North Dakota Quarterly
The Northeast Recovery Networker
Odyssey
On Course
Open Hands
Otisian Directory
The Phoenix
The Psychic Reader
The Quest
Rainbow City Express
Reclaiming
Recovery Times

Red Clay
Science Journal and Newsletter
Sharing Spirit Newsletter
Spirit Magazine
Spirit of Change Magazine
The Sun
Talking Leaves
Temple Doors
Thema
Thresholds Quarterly
Unity Magazine
Uptown Express
Visions Magazine
Whole Earth Review
Wildfire
The Wise Woman
Woman of Power
Women & Recovery
Yoga Journal

TRADE AND BUSINESS

Co-operative Grocer
Health Foods Business
The Muscle News
NAPRA Trade Journal
Natural Foods Merchandiser
New Age Marketing Opportunites

VEGETARIANISM

How on Earth!
Live and Let Live
Sproutletter
Vegetarian Journal
Vegetarian Times
Vegetarian Voice
Veggie Life

WITCHES

Green Egg
New Moon Rising
Of A Like Mind
Panegyria
Reclaiming
SageWoman
Sword of Dyrnwyn
The Wise Woman
Womyn's Press

WOMEN'S ISSUES

Baltimore Resources
Birth Gazette
Calyx

The Compleat Mother
Crone Chronicles
Daughter of Nyx
The Doula
Encore Magazine
The Evergreen Chronicles
FEMALE Forum
The Fire Fly and Fire Fly, Jr.
Fish Drum Magazine
Heresies
Herspectives
Indiana Review
Midwifery Today
Mothers Resource Guide
The Neighborhood Works
New Moon
New Moon Parenting
New Texas Magazine

Night Roses
Ocean Gypsy
Off Our Backs
On The Issues
Peacework
Plain Brown Wrapper
Priority Parenting
The Red Queen
SingleMOTHER
Single Mothers by Choice
Sipapu
Snake River Reflections
Spring
Truth Seeker
The Unforgettable Fire
Voices of Women
Windy City Times
Woman's Way

Women Artists News
Women & Recovery
Womyn's Press

YOGA
Avatar
Bliss
Brickwall Bulletin & Bulletin Too
Hinduism Today
India Currents
Integral Yoga
Light of Consciousness
New Frontier Magazine
Qi
Shambhala Sun
Somatics
Yoga Journal

Active Voice

Ron McEntee, Publisher, 19470 East Bagley Road, Middleburg Heights, OH 44130   Phone: 216-243-2189, Fax: 216-362-4623

Profile: A newspaper of public opinion. Published by Active Communications, Inc. Established in 1988. Issued monthly. Circ: 15,000. Trim size: Tabloid. Newsprint; folded. 8 pages. Subscription cost: $10. Sample copy cost: Free. No writer's guidelines.
Focus and Tips: *Active Voice* was created and exists to give the general public an outlet of mass communication with each other without being auditioned, edited, or evaluated by a "high-and-mighty media landlord." It strives to be a "genuine free press." There are no restrictions on subject matter, length, or viewpoint: readers are invited to respond to a previously published piece or to send original work.
Editorial Interests
Open to all topics.
• *Fiction and Nonfiction:* Accepts all types of writing. No length restrictions.
Submission Policy: Send complete manuscript. Accepts photocopies, computer printouts, and faxes. Simultaneous submissions okay. Reports in 1 month. Publication follows immediately.
Terms and Payment: One-time rights. No payment. Authors receive 3 copies of the issue; more upon request.
Advertising: Rates: B/W full-page, $600. Contact Ron McEntee, 216-243-2189.

The Advocate

J. V. McAuley, Associate Editor, 6922 Hollywood Boulevard, Los Angeles, CA 90028   Phone: 213-871-1225

Profile: A national gay and lesbian newsmagazine. Issued biweekly. Circ: 120,000. Subscription cost: N/A. Sample copy cost: N/A. Writer's guidelines available with SASE.
Focus and Tips: *The Advocate* publishes news, features, and interviews of interest to gay men and lesbians. Articles need to be interesting, factual, timely, well-sourced, and well-written. Does not publish fiction, poetry, recipes, humor pieces, cartoons, or personal essays.
Editorial Interests
Gay and lesbian issues, sexuality, community, arts and entertainment, health, and politics.
• *Nonfiction:* News features of interest to gay men and lesbians, 100–3,000 words.
Submission Policy: Query first with outline and clips. Include SASE. Accepts photocopies and computer printouts. No simultaneous submissions.
Terms and Payment: First North American serial rights. Pays on publication. $50–$1,500.

Afrique

Jalyne Strong, Editor-in-Chief, 4554 North Broadway, Suite 320, Chicago, IL 60640   Phone: 312-989-8138, Fax: 312-989-8148

Profile: A regional African-American newspaper. Issued monthly. Circ: 75,000. Trim size: Tabloid. Color cover; newsprint; folded. 40 pages. Subscription cost: $16. Sample copy cost: Free. Writer's guidelines available with SASE.
Focus and Tips: *Afrique* is geared toward a growing audience of immigrant Africans and Caribbeans in the Chicago area. All material must reflect the concerns of and issues relating to people of African descent. Avoid political articles.
Editorial Interests
African-American issues, lifestyle, history, education, cultural and ethnic concerns, crystals, feminism, folklore, healing, health, holistic health, inspiration, juvenile and teen issues, men's issues, mythology, natural health, new age, philosophy, psychology, regional issues, relationships, self-help, social and world issues, spirituality, and women's issues.
• *Fiction:* Short stories, 500 words. Book excerpts, 500 words and up.
• *Nonfiction:* Features, articles, interviews, profiles, personal experiences, opinion pieces, news items, and reviews, 900 words. Departments include Business, Thinking Globally, The Educational Edge, Focus on Finance, and Arts & Culture. The African Affairs section reports on local events.
Submission Policy: Query first with outline. Include SASE. Accepts photocopies, computer printouts, 3.5" computer disks, and faxes. Simultaneous submissions okay. Reports in 1 month. If accepted, expect publication in 2 weeks.
Terms and Payment: Rights vary. Pays $50 minimum per piece. Authors receive 1 copy of the issue.
Advertising: Rates: B/W full-page, $50; 4-color full-page, $500. Contact Advertising Office, 312-989-8138. List rental available. Contact Karen, 312-989-8138.
Other Interests: Sponsors The ETA Book Seminar, held in Chicago's Broadview Afro-wear Bookstores. For more information, contact Andrew Eperi, Publisher.

AIM: America's Intercultural Magazine

Ruth Apilado, Editor, 7308 South Eberhart, Chicago, IL 60619   Phone: 312-874-6184, Fax: 206-543-2441

Profile: A journal promoting racial harmony. Published by AIM Publication Association. Issued quarterly. Circ: 6,000. Trim size: 8.5x11. Glossy cover; B/W; saddle stitched. 48 pages. Subscription cost: $10. Sample copy cost: $4. Writer's guidelines available with SASE.

Focus and Tips: *AIM* strives to purge racism from the human bloodstream through the written word. All material submitted must show that people from different ethnic and racial backgrounds are more alike than they are different. Readers are teenagers and young adults.

Editorial Interests

Social and world issues, fiction of social import, cultural and ethnic concerns, folklore, teen issues, and politics.
• *Fiction:* Short stories, 3,500 words. Short-short stories and genre fiction, 1,500 words. Book excerpts, 1,000 words.
• *Nonfiction:* Articles, 1,500 words. Interviews, profiles, and essays, 600 words. Personal experiences and opinion pieces, 1,000 words. News items, 300 words. Filler, 150 words.

Submission Policy: Send complete manuscript with cover letter. Include SASE. Accepts photocopies, computer printouts, computer disks, and faxes. Simultaneous submissions okay. Reports in 2 months. If accepted, expect publication in 3 months.

Terms and Payment: One-time rights. Pays on publication. $15–$25 per piece. Authors receive 1 copy of the issue.

Advertising: Rates: B/W full-page, $350. Contact Ruth Apilado, 312-874-6184.

Alberta History

Hugh A. Dempsey, Editor, 95 Holmwood Avenue NW, Calgary, Alberta, T2K 2G7 Canada   Phone/Fax: 403-289-8149

Profile: A regional magazine. Published by the Historical Society of Alberta. Issued quarterly. Circ: 1,500. Trim size: 8.5x11. Coated paper; saddle stitched. 32 pages. Subscription cost: $20. Sample copy cost: Free. Writer's guidelines available with SASE/IRCs.

Focus and Tips: *Alberta History* is devoted to the history of Alberta, Canada, from its Native Peoples to the present era.

Editorial Interests

Western Canadian history, Native American culture, folklore, politics, and missionary work.
• *Nonfiction:* Articles and personal experiences, 3,000–5,000 words.

Submission Policy: Query with outline or send complete manuscript with cover letter. Include SASE/IRCs. Accepts photocopies, computer printouts, and WordPerfect disks. No simultaneous submissions. Reports in 2 months. If accepted, expect publication in 1 year.

Terms and Payment: One-time rights. No payment. Authors receive 12 copies of the issue.

Alt/Alternative Press

Joseph Schmidbauer, Publisher/Editor, P.O. Box 729, Buffalo, NY 14205   Phone/Fax: 716-845-6993

Profile: A regional, progressive new age newspaper. Published by Kullman Publishing. Issued 10 times a year. Circ: 15,000. Trim size: Tabloid. Newsprint; folded. 16–24 pages. Subscription cost: $10. Sample copy cost: $2. Writer's guidelines available with SASE.

Focus and Tips: *Alt/Alternative Press* is a progressive publication that offers an alternative perspective on health-related, environmental, social, and transformational issues. It presents what is possible in the future by showcasing those people who have committed their lives to positive change and transformation. Readers are Western New York-area adults, ages 25–45.

Editorial Interests

Personal transformation, bodywork, ecosystems, the environment, feminism, health, holistic health, meditation, men's issues, natural health, politics, relationships, social and world issues, and spirituality.
• *Nonfiction:* Features, 2,100–3,000 words. Articles, 700–1,800 words. Interviews, profiles, essays, and personal experiences, 1,000–1,200 words. Opinion pieces, 700–1,000 words. News items, 700–1,800 words. Reviews, 500 words.

Submission Policy: Query with outline and writing samples or send complete manuscript with cover letter. Include SASE. Accepts photocopies, computer printouts, and WordPerfect or Amipro disks. Simultaneous submissions okay. Reports in 3 months. If accepted, expect publication in 3 months.

Terms and Payment: Pays on publication. Rates vary, between $.02–$.05 per word. Authors receive copies of the issue.

Advertising: Rates: B/W full-page, $600; half-page, $350; quarter-page, $175. Contact Joe Schmidbauer, 716-845-6993. List rental available.

Alternatives

Rochelle Haigh Blehr, Editor, P.O. Box 566822, Atlanta, GA 30356   Phone: 404-303-1873

Profile: A regional health and lifestyle newsmagazine. Issued monthly. Circ: 45,000. Trim size: Tabloid. Newsprint; folded. 24 pages. Subscription cost: Free. Sample copy cost: $.52 postage with 11x14 SASE. Writer's guidelines available with SASE.

Focus and Tips: *Alternatives* addresses Atlanta-area readers looking for information on the environment, health, science, psychology, self-help, and alternative philosophies. Prefers well-researched, objective, "hard news" journalistic approaches with both pros and cons represented. Not interested in personal opinion, personal commentary, or personal experience.

Editorial Interests
Regional issues, cultural and ethnic issues, ecosystems, the environment, extraterrestrials, feminism, healing, health, holistic health, natural health, politics, social and world issues, and women's issues.
• *Nonfiction:* Articles and news pieces, 1,500 words. Reviews, 350 words.
Submission Policy: Send complete manuscript with cover letter. Include SASE. Accepts photocopies, computer printouts, and Macintosh disks. Simultaneous submissions okay. Reports in 1 month. If accepted, expect publication within 1 month.
Terms and Payment: First North American serial rights. Pays on publication. Articles and news, $35–$100 per piece. No payment for reviews. Authors receive 1 copy of the issue.
Advertising: Rates: B/W full-page, $938; spot-color, additional $200. Contact Rochelle Haigh Blehr, 404-303-1873.

American Writing: A Magazine
Alexandra Grilikhes, Editor, 4343 Manayunk Avenue, Philadelphia, PA 19128

Profile: A literary arts journal. Published by Nierika Editions. Issued 2 times a year. Circ: 3,000. Heavy bond cover; B/W inside; matte paper; perfect bound. 80 pages. Subscription cost: $10. Sample copy cost: $6. Writer's guidelines available with SASE.
Focus and Tips: *American Writing* is interested in "new writing that takes risks, explores new forms, writing that in the surrealist sense of seizure, seizes us." It is not a mainstream literary journal and writers are encouraged to review a sample copy.
Editorial Interests
Literary writing, the arts, creativity, shamanism, cultural and ethnic issues, dreams, ecosystems, the environment, feminism, folklore, gay and lesbian issues, magic, mysticism, mythology, psychology, social and world issues, spirituality, witches and women's issues.
• *Fiction:* Short stories, drama, and book excerpts, up to 3,500 words. Poetry, up to 3 pages per poem.
• *Nonfiction:* Essays, up to 3,500 words. Query for interviews and personal experiences.
Submission Policy: Send complete manuscript with brief author biography. Query for interviews and personal experience pieces. Include SASE. Accepts photocopies, computer printouts, and Macintosh submissions. Simultaneous submissions okay. Responds to queries in 3 weeks, to manuscripts in 1–3 months. If accepted, expect publication in up to 1 year.
Terms and Payment: First North American serial rights. No payment. Authors receive 2 copies of the issue.

Angel's Wings
Cheryl Padilla, Editor, 6250 Hargrove Avenue, No. 217, Las Vegas, NV 89107   Phone: 702-877-6930

Profile: A newsletter of angel experiences. Issued monthly. Circ: 800+. Trim size: 8.5x11. 20 lb. paper; stapled. 4 pages. Subscription cost: $12.95. Sample copy cost: $1.50. Writer's guidelines available with SASE.
Focus and Tips: *Angel's Wings* reports on angelic influences on modern-day life. Of special interest are testimonials of divine revelation, visions, or ideas on how a particular incident, experience, or individual changed a life and could be regarded as angelic. Focus on the lighter side of spirituality, such as self-help and positive issues for men and women. Not interested in occult, channeling, crystals, mysticism, witches, or specific religious viewpoints.
Editorial Interests
Angels, issues of morality, miracles, testimonies, dreams, folklore, healing, lifestyle, men's issues, natural health, rebirthing, relationships, religion, self-help, spirituality, and women's issues.
• *Fiction:* Short stories, 300 words. Poetry, 20 lines.
• *Nonfiction:* Features, 500 words. Articles and personal testimonies, 300 words. Books, lecture, and seminar reviews, 200 words. Filler in the form of inspirational quotes and notices of upcoming events.
• *Illustrations:* Accepts illustrations.
Submission Policy: Query with outline or send complete manuscript with cover letter. Include SASE. Accepts photocopies and computer printouts. Simultaneous submissions okay. Reports in 2 weeks. If accepted, expect publication in 30 days.
Terms and Payment: Rights negotiable. Pays on acceptance. Articles, testimonies, and reviews, $30. Filler, $15. Authors receive 12 copies of the issue.
Advertising: Rates: Business-card ads, $10. Contact Cheryl Padilla, 702-877-6930.
Other Interests: Sponsors angel workshops, support groups, and workshops on the empowerment of women and redirecting children's behavior in a positive manner. For more information, contact Cheryl Padilla, 702-877-6930.

Anima: The Journal of Human Experience
Harry Buck, Executive Editor, 1053 Wilson Avenue, Chambersburg, PA 17201   Phone/Fax: 717-267-0087

Profile: A journal of human spirituality and comparative religion. Published by Conococheague Associates, Inc. Issued 2 times per year. Circ: 1,000. Trim size: 8.5x8.5. Glossy cover; B/W; saddle stitched. 72 pages. Subscription cost: $9.95. Sample copy cost: $3.95. No writer's guidelines.

Focus and Tips: *Anima* explores the human spirit and mystery, informed by myth and ritual, Asian and Western spiritualities, Jungian thought, feminism, the Goddess, and the earth. Writers are advised to study previous issues.

Editorial Interests

Mythology, religion, folklore, feminism, and ecosystems.

• *Fiction:* Short stories and book excerpts, no length restrictions. Short poems.

• *Nonfiction:* Articles, interviews and profiles, essays, and personal experiences, no length restrictions.

Submission Policy: Query with outline or send complete manuscript with cover letter. Include SASE. Accepts computer printouts and IBM or Macintosh disks. No simultaneous submissions. Reports in 3 months. If accepted, expect publication in 1 year.

Terms and Payment: All rights. No payment. Authors receive 50 offprints.

Advertising: Rates: B/W full-page, $150. Contact Harry Buck, 717-267-0087.

The Animals' Agenda

Kim Stallwood, Editor-in-Chief, 3201 Elliott Street, Baltimore, MD 21224   Phone: 410-675-4566, Fax: 410-675-0066

Profile: An animal rights publication. Published by The Animal Rights Network, Inc., a nonprofit organization founded in 1979. Issued bimonthly. Circ: 20,000. Trim size: 8x11. Glossy color cover; B/W inside; saddle stitched. 45 pages. Subscription cost: $22. Sample copy cost: $1. Writer's guidelines available with SASE.

Focus and Tips: *The Animals' Agenda* is dedicated to informing the public about animal rights and cruelty-free living in hopes of inspiring action for animals. It is committed to serving a combined audience of animal advocates, interested individuals, and the entire animal-rights movement. Readers are young, progressive professionals, primarily women, who purchase cruelty-free products, clothes, and vegetarian/vegan food. Articles should focus solely on the animal-rights movement and associated current affairs, issues, ongoing problems and investigations, exploitation, and historical and sociological analysis. Avoid criticizing other animal-rights groups. Review writer's guidelines before submitting.

Editorial Interests

Animal-rights issues and related philosophy, history, and activism.

• *Nonfiction:* Cover Story, major investigatory piece with photos and sidebars, 2,500 words. Articles discussing strategy and offering in-depth coverage, 1,200 words. Perspectives, different opinions on one issue, 1,200 words. Toward Kinship, big picture or off-beat essay on one aspect of animal rights, 1,200 words. Reviews of significant books, videos, or resources, 750 words. Interviews and profiles, 750 words. Letters to the Editor, readers' feedback, 400 words. Headlines, action-oriented news shorts from organizations, 200 words. Resources, overview of newly released program materials, 200 words. News & Notes, news shorts with photo and caption, 100 words. Activities, lists of upcoming events with contact address and phone number, 50 words.

Submission Policy: Send complete manuscript with cover letter. Include SASE. Accepts photocopies, computer printouts, 3.5" computer disks, and faxes. Simultaneous submissions okay if noted. Reports in 1 month. Publication time varies.

Terms and Payment: No payment.

Advertising: Classifieds, $1 per word with a 20-word minimum. Contact publication for display ad rates.

Aqua Terra: Water Concepts for the Ecological Society

Barbara Harmony, Coordinator, Route 7, Box 720, Eureka Springs, AR 72632   Phone: 501-253-9431

Profile: A publication devoted to water experiences. Published by The Water Center. Issued irregularly. Circ: 3,000. Trim size: 6.75x11.5. Newsprint; folded. Subscription cost: $7.95. Sample copy cost: $7.95. No writer's guidelines.

Focus and Tips: *Aqua Terra* strives to be a participatory publication that examines the concepts surrounding and research on the blending of metaphysics and ecology. All material is centered around water concepts, particularly cultural, aesthetic, spiritual, and metaphysical approaches to water.

Editorial Interests

Water concepts. Open to astrology, ecosystems, the environment, metaphysics, and mysticism as related to water.

• *Fiction:* Short stories and poetry on water experiences. No length restrictions.

• *Nonfiction:* Articles, interviews, profiles, research, and ceremonies on technical and/or spiritual experiences with water. No length restrictions.

Submission Policy: Prefers complete manuscripts with cover letter. Accepts all types of submissions. Include SASE. Accepts photocopies, computer printouts, and Macintosh disks. Simultaneous submissions okay if noted. Reporting time varies.

Terms and Payment: One-time rights. No payment. Authors receive copies of the issue.

The Arizona Light

Jacqueline Pieters, Publisher, P.O. Box 55717, Phoenix, AZ 85078   Phone/Fax: 602-443-1964

Profile: A tabloid of new age thought and regional event promotion. Issued monthly. Circ: 30,000. Trim size: Tabloid.

Newsprint; folded. 24–28 pages. Subscription cost: $14.95. Sample copy cost: $1. Writer's guidelines available with SASE.

Focus and Tips: *The Arizona Light* provides news and information to promote well-being, natural living, and personal growth of the whole person. Aims to present alternative ideas for the benefit of its readers, who range from mainstream to new age enthusiasts primarily in the Arizona area. Does not accept self-promotional or commercial material.

Editorial Interests

New thought, astrology, bodywork, crystals, dreams, environment, extraterrestrials, feminism, healing, holistic and natural health, inspiration, juvenile and teen issues, meditation, metaphysics, parapsychology, parenting, psychic phenomenon, rebirthing, recovery, relationships, self-help, seniors, spirituality, yoga, and other new age topics.

• *Fiction:* Short stories, drama, and genre fiction, 800 words. Short-short stories, 600 words. Book excerpts, 600–700 words. Poetry, 200 words.

• *Nonfiction:* Features, articles, interviews, and profiles, 800 words. Essays, 600–800 words. Personal experiences and opinion pieces, 600 words. News items, 200–600 words. Reviews, 200–400 words. Filler, 200–300 words.

Submission Policy: Send complete manuscript with cover letter. Include SASE. Accepts photocopies, computer printouts, and WordPerfect or Word for Windows disks. Simultaneous submissions okay. Reports in 2–3 months. If accepted, expect publication within 2–4 months.

Terms and Payment: One-time rights. No payment. Authors receive copies of the issue.

Advertising: Rates: Full-page B/W, $650–$900; half-page B/W, $350. Contact Jacqueline Pieters, 602-443-1964.

Other Interests: Will sponsor the first annual Southwest Healthy Living Conference, on November 10–12, 1995. For information, contact Jacqueline Pieters, 602-443-1964.

Arizona Networking News

Joanne Henning Tedesco, Editor, P.O. Box 5477, Scottsdale, AZ 85261-5477   Phone: 602-951-1275, Fax: 602-951-1295

Profile: A regional new age/holistic health newspaper. Published by TRI Pyramid, Inc. Issued bimonthly. Circ: 50,000. Trim size: 11x17. Newsprint; folded. 20 pages. Subscription cost: $15. Sample copy cost: $3. Writer's guidelines available with SASE.

Focus and Tips: *Arizona Networking News* is a holistic living journal covering the Arizona, New Mexico, and Nevada areas.

Editorial Interests

New age, astrology, bodywork, channeling, crystals, cultural and ethnic issues, dreams, ecosystems, the environment, extraterrestrials, folklore, healing and health, holistic and natural health, inspiration, lifestyle, meditation, metaphysics, mysticism, nutrition, occult, parapsychology, parenting, philosophy, prayer, psychic phenomenon, psychology, rebirthing, recovery, relationships, self-help, social and world issues, spirituality, women's issues, and yoga.

• *Nonfiction:* Features, 1,100 words. Articles, 285, 550, or 1,100 words. Personal experiences, 285 or 550 words. Reviews, 70–100 words. Filler, 285 words. Columns include Vitamins, Herbs, and Health Hints.

Submission Policy: Query with outline. Include SASE. Accepts computer printouts, faxes, and Macintosh Microsoft Word or QuarkXpress disks. No simultaneous submissions. Reports in 1 month. If accepted, expect publication in 1–3 months.

Terms and Payment: First North American serial rights. No payment. Authors receive copies of the issue.

Advertising: Rates: B/W full-page, $573; half-page, $323; quarter-page, $179; Business Card, $45. Classified ads, $.25 per word with 20 word minimum. Contact Joanne Henning Tedesco, 602-951-1275.

Ascension

Claudia McNeely, Publisher/Editor, P.O. Box 1257, Gilmer, TX 75644   Phone: 903-734-5559/800-503-0984

Profile: A regional new age newsletter. Published by Warm Springs Enterprises. Issued monthly. Circ: 1,000. Trim size: 8.5x11. Stapled. 10 pages. Subscription cost: $12. Sample copy cost: Free. Writer's guidelines available with SASE.

Focus and Tips: Formerly *The Light*, *Ascension* is a holistic networking newsletter serving the Texas area, with plans to expand to Arkansas and Louisiana. Avoid Wicca, witchcraft, and Satanism.

Editorial Interests

New age, astrology, bodywork, channeling, crystals, cultural and ethnic issues, dreams, ecosystems, the environment, extraterrestrials, feminism, folklore, gay and lesbian issues, healing and health, holistic health, inspiration, juvenile and teen issues, lifestyle, magic, meditation, men's issues, metaphysics, mysticism, mythology, natural health, nutrition, occult, parapsychology, parenting, philosophy, politics, prayer, psychic phenomenon, psychology, rebirthing, recovery, relationships, religion, self-help, social and world issues, spirituality, women's issues, and yoga.

• *Nonfiction:* Features, articles, interviews, profiles, essays, personal experiences, opinion pieces, and news items, up to 2,000 words. Accepts reviews and filler.

Submission Policy: Query or send complete manuscript. Include SASE. Accepts photocopies, computer printouts, and faxes. Simultaneous submissions okay. Reports in 1 month. If accepted, expect publication in 1 month.

Terms and Payment: One-time rights. No payment. Authors receive up to 10 copies of the issue.

Advertising: Rates: B/W full-page, $60. Contact Claudia McNeely.

Other Interests: Sponsors various conferences and events. For more information, contact Claudia McNeely.

Asian Pacific American Journal

Julie Koo and Soo Mee Kwan, Co-editors, 296 Elizabeth Street, Second Floor, New York, NY 10012   Phone: 212-228-6718

Profile: A thematic journal of Asian American interest. Published by the Asian American Writer's Workshop. Issued 2 times a year. Circ: 1,500. Trim size: 5.5x8.5. 172 pages. Perfect bound. Subscription cost: $16. Sample copy cost: $10. Writer's guidelines available with SASE.

Focus and Tips: *Asian Pacific American Journal* serves as a survey of contemporary Asian American writing. It showcases poetry and prose of young and emerging Asian American authors. One-half of all issues are thematic. Upcoming themes include Super Heroes/Heroes, Travel, Poetry, History, and Living in Multicultural Society.

Editorial Interests

Asian American issues, cultural and ethnic concerns, travel, feminism, folklore, gay and lesbian issues, lifestyle, men's issues, mythology, politics, relationships, religion, social and world issues, spirituality, and women's issues.
• *Fiction:* Short stories, and book excerpts, up to 7,500 words. Poetry, up to 7 poems per submission.
• *Nonfiction:* Creative nonfiction such as autobiographical narratives and personal monologues, 7,500 words.

Submission Policy: Send complete manuscript with cover letter. Include SASE. Accepts photocopies and computer print-outs. Simultaneous submissions okay if noted. Reports in 4–5 months. If accepted, expect publication in 3 months.

Terms and Payment: First North American serial rights. Pays on publication. Offers a varied per page rate. Authors receive 2 copies of the issue.

Advertising: Rates: B/W full-page, $150. List rental available. Contact Douglas Lee, Business Manager, 212-228-6718.

Other Interests: Holds an annual Asian American Literary contest. Sponsors a variety of other literary activities. Contact Curtis Chin, Managing Director.

Attain

E. Arthur Winkler, Editor, 31916 University Circle, Springfield, LA 70462   Phone: 504-294-2129, Fax: 504-294-2157

Profile: A new age magazine. Published by St. John's University. Issued quarterly. Circ: 3,000. Trim size: 8.5x11. Self cover; B/W; saddle stitched. 20 pages. Subscription cost: $6. Sample copy cost: $1.50. Writer's guidelines available with SASE.

Focus and Tips: *Attain* is a new age magazine of health, happiness, and success. It is associated with The Congregational Church of Practical Theology, The American Counselors Society, and The National Society of Clinical Hypnotherapists. Readers include members of these groups along with students and alumni of St. John's University.

Editorial Interests

New age, channeling, healing, health, holistic health, inspiration, meditation, metaphysics, natural health, nutrition, parapsychology, prayer, psychic phenomenon, psychology, recovery, self-help, and social and world issues.
• *Nonfiction:* Articles, personal experiences, and opinion pieces, up to 400 words. News items and filler, up to 100 words. Departments include Thrift Time, Idea Exchange, Health Watch, Success, and Humor.

Submission Policy: Send complete manuscript with cover letter and clips. Include SASE. Accepts photocopies and computer printouts. Simultaneous submissions okay. Reporting time varies. If accepted, expect publication in 3–12 months.

Terms and Payment: One-time rights. No payment. Authors receive 10 copies of the issue.

Advertising: Accepts advertising. Contact Diana Albin, 504-294-2129.

Avatar

Miken Chappell, Editor, 237 North Westmonte Drive, Altamonte Springs, FL 32714
Phone: 407-788-3090, Fax: 407-788-1052

Profile: A publication of new consciousness. Published by Star's Edge, Inc. Issued twice a year. Circ: 100,000. Trim size: 8.5x11. Glossy color cover; full-color; saddle stitched. 34 pages. Subscription cost: N/A. Sample copy cost: 3.95.

Focus and Tips: *Avatar* publishes articles on self-development, awakening consciousness, and spiritual enlightenment. "Write about what you have experienced."

Editorial Interests

New age, dreams, healing, inspiration, lifestyle, meditation, metaphysics, mysticism, philosophy, psychology, rebirthing, relationships, self-help, and yoga.
• *Nonfiction:* Articles, personal experiences, and anecdotes with the theme of of obtaining enlightenment.

Submission Policy: Query with outline or send complete manuscript with cover letter. Include SASE. Accepts photocopies, computer printouts, DOS or Macintosh computer disks, and faxes. No simultaneous submissions. Reports in 3 months. If accepted, expect publication in 3–6 months.

Terms and Payment: Pays $100 per article.

Other Interests: Offers seminars in self-evolvement training.

Backspace

Kimberley Smith, Managing Editor, 33 Maplewood Avenue, Suite 201, Gloucester, MA 01930-6201   Phone/Fax: 508-283-3813

Profile: A gay and lesbian magazine. Published by Lock the Target. Issued quarterly. Circ: N/A. Trim size: 5.5x8.5. Self cover; B/W inside; saddle stitched. 28–36 pages. Subscription cost: $9. Sample copy cost: $2.50. Writer's guidelines available with SASE.
Focus and Tips: *Backspace* welcomes poetry, short fiction, art, and commentary from the gay, lesbian, bisexual, and transgender community. It is not interested in material portraying explicit sex and violence.
Editorial Interests
Gay and lesbian issues.
• *Fiction:* Short stories, 3,000 words. Short-short stories, 1,000–1,500 words. Poetry, 10–1,000 words.
• *Nonfiction:* Essays, 1,500 words. News items, 300 words.
• *Illustrations:* B/W artwork.
Submission Policy: Send complete manuscript with cover letter and short author biography. Include SASE. Accepts computer printouts, ASCII 3.5" disks, and faxes (call before attempting to send a fax). Simultaneous submissions okay. Reports in 3 weeks. If accepted, expect publication in 2 months.
Terms and Payment: One-time rights. No payment. Authors receive 1 copy of the issue.
Advertising: Rates: B/W full-page, $15.

Balanced Living

Ed Rocks, Publisher, 3770 Lalinda Drive, Concord, CA 94518   Phone: 510-676-5093, Fax: 510-945-0310

Profile: A newsletter on holistic health. Published by Stress Management Press. Issued bimonthly. Circ: 4,000. Trim size: 8.5x11. B/W; folded. 10 pages. Subscription cost: $10. Sample copy cost: $1. No writer's guidelines.
Focus and Tips: *Balanced Living* is written for people interested in the body-mind-spirit connection and a true holistic approach. Each issue features an article on health and alternative healing methods, positive-thinking/mental-health pieces, and an uplifting spiritual article. Writers should be fair, open, and non-dogmatic.
Editorial Interests
Holistic health, healing, bodywork, inspiration, meditation, metaphysics, natural health, nutrition, prayer, psychology, relationships, self-help, spirituality, and yoga.
• *Nonfiction:* Articles, 2,000–2,500 words.
Submission Policy: Query first with outline. Include SASE. Accepts photocopies, computer printouts, and 3.5" disks. No simultaneous submissions. Reports in 2 weeks. If accepted, expect publication in 4 months.
Terms and Payment: One-time rights. Pays on acceptance. $100 per piece. Authors receive 5 copies of the issue.
Advertising: One-time list rental available; $50/M. Contact Ed Rocks, 510-676-5093.

Baltimore Resources

Lora Hall, Editor, 602 Woodbine Terrace, Towson, MD 21204   Phone: 410-337-5525, Fax: 410-339-7716

Profile: A regional holistic resource guide. Issued quarterly. Circ: 40,000. Trim size: 10x16. Color cover; B/W newsprint inside; folded. 58 pages. Subscription cost: $15. Sample copy cost: $2. Writer's guidelines available with SASE.
Focus and Tips: *Baltimore Resources* is a resource guide for the Greater Baltimore area. It provides its readers with free access to local resources and specific tools for improving the quality of life environmentally, personally, mentally, emotionally, and spiritually. Its seeks articles on health and wellness that are holistic and progressive in approach. Its companion publication, *Voices of Women,* is dedicated to empowering and inspiring women.
Editorial Interests
Regional issues, holistic health and wellness, bodywork, cultural and ethnic issues, dreams, ecosystems, the environment, feminism, folklore, healing, health, inspiration, lifestyle, meditation, mysticism, natural health, nutrition, parenting, philosophy, prayer, recovery, relationships, self-help, seniors, social and world issues, spirituality, witches, women's issues, and yoga.
• *Nonfiction:* Holistic, progressive, research-based articles, 2,500 words.
Submission Policy: Query with outline and writing samples. Include SASE. Accepts photocopies, computer printouts, Macintosh disks, and faxes. Simultaneous submissions okay if competing markets are identified. Reports immediately. Publication time varies.
Terms and Payment: One-time rights. Pays on publication. $100–$150 per piece. Authors receive as many copies of the issue as requested.
Advertising: Rates: B/W full-page, $515; 4-color full-page, $715. List rental available. Contact Lora Hall, 410-337-5525.
Other Interests: Sponsors several conferences, expos, fairs, and weekend spirit circles. For more information, contact Lora Hall, 410-337-5525.

The Beacon

Sarah McKechnie, Editor, P.O. Box 722, Cooper Station, New York, NY 10276   Phone: 212-982-8770

Profile: A magazine of esoteric philosophy. Published by Lucis Publishing Co. Established in 1922. Issued bimonthly. Circ: 2,000. Trim size: 7x9. Heavy bond cover; B/W high-quality matte finish paper inside; saddle stitched. 32 pages. Subscription cost: $15. Sample copy cost: $2.75. No writer's guidelines.

Focus and Tips: Since its launch in 1922, *The Beacon* has strived to present the principles of the Ageless Wisdom as a contemporary way of life. "Its aim is to encourage the esotericist to apply his knowledge and spiritual resources to furthering the evolution of human consciousness." It explores the nature of humanity, of God, and of the universe; the "plan for humanity"; the "hierarchy of masters"; the reappearance of the Christ; and the emergence of new age principles. Writers should have a broad background of esoteric study, especially along Theosophical and Bailey line.

Editorial Interests

Spirituality and meditation. Cultural and ethnic concerns, healing, metaphysics, new age, philosophy, politics, prayer, psychology, religion, and social and world issues are appropriate if explored from an esoteric viewpoint.

• *Nonfiction:* Features and articles, up to 3,500 words.

Submission Policy: Query with outline and resume. Include SASE. Accepts photocopies and computer printouts. No simultaneous submissions. Reports in 1–2 months. If accepted, expect publication in 6–8 months.

Terms and Payment: Author retains right. Requests acknowledgement and appropriate attribution for Beacon articles reprinted in other magazines. No payment. Authors receive 2 copies of the issue.

Birth Gazette

Ina May Gaskin, Editor, 41 The Farm, Summertown, TN 38483   Phone: 615-964-2472, Fax: 615-964-3798

Profile: A magazine of childbirth issues. Published by The Second Foundation. Issued quarterly. Circ: N/A. Trim size: 8.5x11. 48 pages. Glossy color cover; B/W inside; saddle stitched. Subscription cost: $30. Sample copy cost: $6.95. Writer's guidelines available with SASE.

Focus and Tips: *Birth Gazette* is a women's magazine centered around childbirth. It is of interest to midwives, nurses, doctors, parents, and childbirth educators.

Editorial Interests

Childbirth, women's issues, feminism, the environment, healing, health, holistic and natural health, inspiration, lifestyle, nutrition, parenting, politics, and spirituality.

• *Nonfiction:* Features, articles, interviews, profiles, and personal experiences, 500–1,000 words.

Submission Policy: Query first with outline. Include SASE. Accepts photocopies, computer printouts, and computer disks. Simultaneous submissions okay. Reporting and publication time varies.

Terms and Payment: One-time rights. No payment. Offers a free 1-year subscription. Authors receive 3 copies of the issue.

Advertising: Accepts advertising. List rental available. Contact Pamela Hunt, 615-964-2472.

Other Interests: Sponsors the Birth Gazette Annual Conference on midwifery skills and issues. Held the first week in August. For more information, contact Carol Nelson, The Farm, Summertown, TN 38483, 615-964-2589.

Black Bear Review

Ave Jeanne, Editor, 1916 Lincoln Street, Croydon, PA 19021-8026

Profile: An international literary magazine. Published by Black Bear Publications. Issued 2 times a year. Circ: 500. Trim size: 5.5x8. Heavy bond cover; B/W; perfect bound. 64 pages. Subscription cost: $10. Sample copy cost: $5. Writer's guidelines available with SASE.

Focus and Tips: *Black Bear Review* is a forum for poetry and artwork emphasizing social, political, and environmental issues. Authors are advised to revise all work carefully and avoid traditional literary forms.

Editorial Interests

Poetry, social and world issues, politics, the environment, cultural and ethnic issues, and relationships.

• *Poetry:* No length restrictions.

• *Nonfiction:* Reviews, 500 words.

Submission Policy: Send complete manuscript with cover letter. Include SASE. Accepts computer printouts. No simultaneous submissions. Reports in 2 weeks. If accepted, expect publication in 6 months.

Terms and Payment: First North American serial rights. No payment. Authors receive 1 copy of the issue.

Advertising: Accepts advertising; rates negotiable.

Other Interests: Sponsors the annual Poems of Social Concern Competition. Deadline, November 1. Entry fee, $2 per poem. For more information, contact Ron Zettlemoyer, 1916 Lincoln Street, Croydon, PA 19021.

Bliss

Swami Virato, Publisher, 2229 Pemberton Street, Philadelphia, PA 19146   Phone: 215-772-0436

Profile: A magazine of Tantra sexuality. Published by New Frontier Education Society. Issued quarterly. Circ: 10,000. Trim size: 8.5x11. Perfect bound. 24 pages. Subscription cost: $25. Sample copy cost: $10. Writer's guidelines available with SASE.
Focus and Tips: *Bliss* presents "the cornucopia of dances of love and the sensual pleasure in all its dimensions." It also serves as a networking tool for those who embrace the Tantric lifestyle. Directed at those who see sexuality as spiritual, it provides stories of love and excitement, not pornography or vulgarity. "Be sexy and see the bliss in a spiritual and metaphysical sense."
Editorial Interests
Sexuality, Tantra, bodywork, holistic health, lifestyle, magic, meditation, mysticism, new age, and yoga.
• *Fiction:* Short stories, book excerpts, and genre fiction, 2,000 words. Short-short stories, 1,500 words.
• *Nonfiction:* Features, articles, and personal experiences, 2,000 words. Interviews and profiles, 3,000 words. Essays, 1,500 words. Opinion pieces, 1,000 words. News items, 500 words. Reviews, 750 words. Filler, 100 words.
Submission Policy: Send complete manuscript with cover letter. Include SASE. Accepts computer printouts, 3.5" or 5.25" IBM Microsoft Word or ASCII disks, and CompuServe modemed submissions, 73072, 2140. Simultaneous submissions okay. Responds to queries in 3 months, to manuscripts in 4 months. If accepted, expect publication in 2 months.
Terms and Payment: One-time rights. Pays on publication. $.10 per word. Authors receive 2 copies of the issue.
Advertising: Rates: B/W full-page, $300.

Body, Mind & Spirit

Jo-ann Langfeth, Associate Editor, 255 Hope Street, Providence, RI 02906   Phone: 401-351-4320, Fax: 401-272-5767

Profile: A national new age publication. Published by Island Publishing Company, Inc. Issued bimonthly. Circ: 150,000. Trim size: 8.25x11. Glossy color cover; full-color; saddle stitched. 110 pages. Subscription cost: $20. Sample copy cost: Free. Writer's guidelines available with SASE.
Focus and Tips: *Body, Mind & Spirit* covers the entire spectrum of the new age field, including diet and nutrition, spirituality, holistic healing, alternative therapies, self-improvement, whole foods, bodywork, psychic development, consciousness research, and the art of living. Articles should provide readers with practical tools they can use to make their lives happier, healthier, and more fulfilling. Avoid "far-out claims, sensationalism, and the occult."
Editorial Interests
New age, bodywork, dreams, the environment, healing, health, holistic health, inspiration, meditation, metaphysics, mysticism, natural health, nutrition, psychic phenomenon, psychology, relationships, self-help, spirituality, and prosperity.
• *Fiction:* Will accept new age-related fiction on occasion. No length restrictions.
• *Nonfiction:* Features, interviews, essays, and personal experiences, 1,000–3,000 words. Accepts news pieces on anything related to new age, natural living, and spirituality.
Submission Policy: Query with outline, resume, writing samples, and clips. Include SASE. Accepts photocopies, computer printouts, and faxes. Simultaneous submissions okay. Reports in 3–6 months.
Terms and Payment: First North American serial rights. Pays on publication. $.10 per word. Authors receive copies of the issue.
Advertising: Accepts advertising. List rental available. Contact Val Meleo, 401-351-4320.

Bohemian Chronicle

Emily Skinner, Publisher, P.O. Box 387, Largo, FL 34649-0387

Profile: An alternative arts/literary newsletter. Published by Bohemian Enterprises. Issued monthly. Circ: 500. Trim size: 5.5x8.5. Photocopied; stapled. 12 pages. Subscription cost: $12. Sample copy cost: $1 plus #10 SASE. Writer's guidelines available with SASE.
Focus and Tips: *Bohemian Chronicle* promotes sensitivity to the arts. It intends to be a forum to communities worldwide whose artistic voices have been quelled or lack an appreciative audience. Unpublished writers are welcome. It seeks different, original stories about people, circumstances, events, and real feelings written in a conversational style that communicates color, humor, emotion, and personality. Stay within appropriate word-length limits—"don't send long works or rambling letters and endless clips."
Editorial Interests
Experimental fiction, cultural and ethnic issues, environment, gay and lesbian issues, inspirational pieces, juvenile and teen stories, lifestyle, men's and women's issues, natural health, parenting, relationships, self-help, social and world issues, and spirituality.
• *Fiction:* Short stories and genre fiction, 1,000 words. Short-short stories, 500 words. Drama, 500–1,000 words. Poetry, up to 1 page.
• *Nonfiction:* Features, interviews, profiles, essays, personal experiences, and opinion, 1,000–1,500 words. Articles, 1,000 words.

Submission Policy: Send complete manuscript with cover letter. Include SASE. Accepts photocopies and computer print-outs. Responds to queries in 1 month, to manuscripts in 2 months. If accepted, expect publication within 6–10 months.
Terms and Payment: First North American serial rights or all rights. Pays on publication. $5 per piece. Authors receive 5 copies of the issue.
Advertising: Rates: B/W full-page, $25; half-page, $15. Contact Emily Skinner.

Borderlands

Tom Brown, Director, P.O. Box 429, Garberville, CA 95542   Phone: 707-986-7211, Fax: 707-986-7272

Profile: A journal of alternative scientific and medical theories. Published by Borderlands Sciences Research Foundation. Issued quarterly. Circ: 1,500. Trim size: 8.5x11. 50 pages. Stapled. Subscription cost: $25. Sample copy cost: Free. No writer's guidelines.
Focus and Tips: *Borderlands* serves as a forum for suppressed sciences, universal mysteries, alternative energies, etheric physics, UFOs, and advanced knowledge for a worldwide network of researchers and writers. While most of its material is written in-house, it is open to outside writers, especially columnists who can introduce an original idea.
Editorial Interests
Alternative sciences and health, etheric and pre-atomic theories, extraterrestrials, and alternative energies.
• *Nonfiction:* Features, articles, interviews, profiles, essays, personal experiences, reviews, and original columns. No length restrictions.
Submission Policy: Query first with outline. Include SASE. Accepts photocopies, computer printouts, computer disks, and faxes. Simultaneous submissions okay. Reporting time varies.
Terms and Payment: Rights negotiable. No payment. Authors receive copies of the issue.

Both Sides Now

Elihu Edelson, Editor/Publisher, 10457 State Highway 110N, Tyler, TX 75704-9537   Phone: 903-592-4263

Profile: An independent journal of spiritual and political alternatives. Published by Free People. Issued irregularly. Circ: 200. Trim size: 8.5x11. Photocopied; stapled. 16 pages. Subscription cost: $9 per 10 issues. Sample copy cost: $1. Writer's guidelines available with SASE.
Focus and Tips: *Both Sides Now* has a Green/New Age editorial policy, including ecology, nonviolence, social responsibility, grassroots democracy, and pluralistic spirituality. It hopes to share information, insights, opinions, and discoveries regarding the emerging new age. Readers are open-minded people who are willing to see things from a different perspective, or who already do. Keep articles concise and avoid using "big words," technical jargon, verbosity, and vulgarity.
Editorial Interests
New age, the environment, peace work, earth changes, prophecy, interfaith work, astrology, channeling, feminism, folklore, health and healing, inspiration, lifestyle, meditation, metaphysics, mysticism, mythology, occult, parapsychology, philosophy, politics, psychic phenomenon, psychology, comparative religion, social and world issues, and spirituality.
• *Fiction:* Short stories, fables, allegory, humor, satire, and poetry. No length restrictions, but keep it short.
• *Nonfiction:* Short articles, interviews, profiles, essays, personal experiences, opinion pieces, reviews, and filler.
• *Illustrations:* B/W artwork and cartoons.
Submission Policy: Send complete manuscript with cover letter and clips. Include SASE. Accepts photocopies and computer printouts. Simultaneous submissions okay. Reports in 1–3 months.
Terms and Payment: One-time and anthology rights. No payment. Authors receive 5 copies of the issue.
Advertising: Rates: B/W full-page, $50. Contact Elihu Edelson, 903-592-4263.

Brain/Mind

Eric Ferguson, Editor, 4717 North Figueroa, Los Angeles, CA 90042   Phone: 213-223-2500, Fax: 213-223-2519

Profile: A newsletter exploring human consciousness. Published by Marilyn Ferguson, Inc. Issued monthly. Circ: 3,500. Trim size: 8.5x11. B/W; folded. 8 pages. Subscription cost: $45. Sample copy cost: $4. No writer's guidelines.
Focus and Tips: *Brain/Mind* covers cutting-edge research in consciousness, neuroscience, psychology, health, learning, and human potential. Most material is staff-written, but will occasionally publish a freelance piece.
Editorial Interests
Neuroscience, bodywork, dreams, ecosystems, the environment, extraterrestrials, healing, health, holistic health, meditation, mysticism, parapsychology, philosophy, politics, psychology, social and world issues, and spirituality.
• *Nonfiction:* Considers articles. No length restrictions.
Submission Policy: Call first to determine editorial needs.
Terms and Payment: Payment varies depending on article. Authors receive copies of the issue.
Advertising: List rental available. $75/M. Contact Jason Keehn, 213-223-2500.

Brickwall Bulletin & Bulletin Too

Niel Rissler, Publisher, P.O. Box 10308, Scottsdale, AZ 85271-0308

Profile: A recovery-related directory. Published by Brickwall Publications. Issued monthly. Circ: 2,000. Trim size: 8.5x11. Photocopied; folded. 8–12 pages. Subscription cost: $30. Sample copy cost: Free. No writer's guidelines.

Focus and Tips: *Brickwall Bulletin & Bulletin Too* is an information guide and directory of companies and individuals that deal with health issues and primary chemical dependency and alcohol treatment. It is distributed free to over 350 locations. Use language carefully and watch judgmental attitudes.

Editorial Interests

Recovery, health, healing, bodywork, channeling, environment, feminism, folklore, holistic and natural health, inspiration, lifestyle, meditation, men's and women's issues, metaphysics, new age, nutrition, parenting, prayer, psychology, relationships, religion, self-help, spirituality, and yoga.
- *Fiction:* Real-life, 12-step recovery stories, 350 words. Book excerpts, 350 words. Poetry, up to 1 page.
- *Nonfiction:* Features, opinion pieces, and reviews, 350 words. Filler, up to 50 words. Assigns essays. Accepts personal experiences, serialized articles, and personal resumes.

Submission Policy: Query with outline, 2 sample chapters, writing samples, and resume; or send complete manuscript with cover letter, resume, and clips. Include SASE. Accepts photocopies and computer printouts. Simultaneous submissions okay. Responds to queries in 2 months, to manuscripts in 6 months. If accepted, expect publication in 6 months.

Terms and Payment: Rights negotiable. Pays on acceptance. $.05 per word unless otherwise arranged. Authors receive copies of the issue upon request.

Advertising: Rates: B/W full-page, $400; 2-color, $600. Contact Niel Rissler, 602-279-7713.

Other Interests: Brickwall Publications can arrange for group conferences, workshops, seminars, or retreats for 12–5,000 participants. Offers day, weekend, or longer programs. Contact Niel Rissler, 602-279-7713.

Brilliant Star

Pepper Oldziey, Managing Editor, Baha'i National Center, Wilmette, IL 60091

Profile: An international magazine for Baha'i children. Published by The National Spiritual Assembly of the Baha'is of the United States. Issued 6 times a year. Circ: 3,000. Glossy color cover; B/W inside; 60 lb. paper; saddle stitched. 36 pages. Subscription cost: $15. Sample copy cost: Free. Writer's guidelines available with SASE.

Focus and Tips: *Brilliant Star* serves the needs of English-speaking Baha'i children, ages 5–12, by confirming their Baha'i identity and helping them to become Baha'i teachers. Writers should be familiar with the Baha'i faith and its principles before submitting. Remember the audience and avoid "mature" subjects.

Editorial Interests

Baha'i religion, children's and teen issues, prayer, and social and world concerns from a spiritual perspective.
- *Fiction:* Short-short stories, drama, genre fiction, and poetry that help children develop a spiritual perspective, 500 words.
- *Nonfiction:* Short features and articles for children.

Submission Policy: Send complete manuscript with SASE. Include SASE. Accepts photocopies and computer printouts. Simultaneous submissions okay. Reports in 2–3 months. If accepted, expect publication in 2 years.

Terms and Payment: One-time rights or all rights. No payment. Authors receive 2 copies of the issue.

Button

Editor, Box 876, Lunenburg, MA 01462

Profile: A small-sized regional publication. Issued quarterly. Circ: 1,000. Trim size: 4x5. Photocopied; stapled. 26 pages. Subscription cost: $5. Sample copy cost: $1.50. Writer's guidelines available with SASE.

Focus and Tips: *Button* is New England's tiniest quarterly of fiction, poetry, and gracious living, aiming to bring cheer to a thoughtful, kindly audience. It looks for wit, brevity, and fresh, uncontrived writing. Avoid "whining, cheap sentimentality, egregious profanity, vampires, neuroses for neuroses' sake, most song lyrics passing as poetry, and anything overlong, over-dull, or overreaching."

Editorial Interests

New age, inspiration, astrology, philosophy.
- *Fiction:* Short-short stories, 1,500 words. Book excerpts, 1,500–3,000 words. Poetry, 200 words.
- *Nonfiction:* Cleverly-conceived of essays and recipes, 1,000 words. Practical how-to's, features, articles, interviews, and profiles, 1,000 words. Personal experiences and opinion, 500 words.

Submission Policy: Query with writing samples or send complete manuscript with cover letter and clips. Include SASE. Accepts photocopies, computer printouts, and MS DOS, Word Perfect, or ASCII disks. No simultaneous submissions. Responds to queries in 3 weeks, to manuscripts in 1 month. If accepted, expect publication in 4–8 months.

Terms and Payment: First North American serial rights. No payment. Offers a free one-year subscription. Authors receive

copies of the issue.
Advertising: Rates: B/W full-page, $45. Contact Sally Cragin, 617-776-0428.

Calyx

Beverly McFarland, Editor, P.O. Box B, Corvallis, OR 97339   Phone: 503-753-9384, Fax: 503-753-0515

Profile: A women's journal of art and literature. Established in 1976. Issued twice a year. Circ: 6,000. Trim size: 7x9. Glossy color cover; B/W inside; perfect bound. 128 pages. Subscription cost: $18. Sample copy cost: $8 plus $1.50 postage. Writer's guidelines available with SASE.
Focus and Tips: *Calyx* is a literary journal of poetry, fiction, prose, book reviews, and art by women.
Editorial Interests
Literary, feminism, gay and lesbian issues, and women's issues.
• *Fiction:* Short stories, up to 5,000 words.
• *Nonfiction:* Essays, up to 5,000 words. Book reviews, 800 words.
Submission Policy: Send complete manuscript with cover letter and resume. Query first for book reviews. Include SASE. Accepts photocopies and computer printouts. Simultaneous submissions okay. Reports in 3–8 months. If accepted, expect publication in 3–12 months.
Terms and Payment: First North American serial rights. Pays on publication. Rates vary. Authors receive copies of the issue.
Advertising: Rates: B/W full-page, $550. Contact Amy Agnello. List rental available; $80/M. Contact Micki Reaman.

Catalist

Cathy Richards, Editor, 42 Adrian Court, Burlingame, CA 94010   Phone: 415-692-4500

Profile: A magazine of personal transformation. Issued bimonthly. Circ: 37,000. Trim size: 8.5x11. Glossy color cover; full-color; saddle stitched. 64 pages. Subscription cost: $10. Sample copy cost: $1. No writer's guidelines.
Focus and Tips: *Catalist* provides health-enhancing, empowering material that encourages positive personal transformation. Readers are well-educated, professional women, ages 30–60, who are interested in personal and spiritual development. Subscribers receive $10 in coupons toward *Catalist* products.
Editorial Interests
Transformation, spirituality, self-help, women's issues, the environment, healing, holistic health, lifestyle, meditation, new age, nutrition, and psychology.
• *Nonfiction:* Articles, 700–2,000 words.
• *Illustrations:* Color prints and line drawings.
Submission Policy: Send complete manuscript with cover letter. Include SASE. Accepts photocopies, computer printouts, and Macintosh disks. Simultaneous submissions okay.
Terms and Payment: Rights vary. Pays on occasion. Authors receive 12 or more copies of the issue.
Advertising: Rates: 4-color full-page, $1,400. List rental available. Contact Michelle Salmon, 415-692-4500.

Celebrate Life!

Marty Johnson, Editor, P.O. Box 247, Indian Rocks Beach, FL 34635   Phone: 813-595-4141

Profile: A magazine of positive living. Published by Unimedia. Issued quarterly. Circ: 10,000. Trim size: 8.5x11. 60 lb. paper. 32–64 pages. Subscription cost: $18. Sample copy cost: $3 with SASE. Writer's guidelines available with SASE.
Focus and Tips: *Celebrate Life!* focuses on positive awareness, differing philosophical and religious viewpoints, the need for unity and transformation, environmental awareness, and natural living. After a brief hiatus, *Celebrate Life!* will be relaunched. Actively seeks personal interviews with spiritual or metaphysical leaders. Does not accept opinion pieces or personal experience pieces.
Editorial Interests
Transformation, positive living, ethics, bodywork, cultural and ethnic issues, ecosystems, the environment, healing, health, holistic health, inspiration, lifestyle, meditation, metaphysics, mysticism, natural health, nutrition, parapsychology, parenting, philosophy, prayer, relationships, Eastern and metaphysical religion, self-help, social and world issues, spirituality, and yoga.
• *Nonfiction:* Features, articles, interviews, and profiles, 400–2,500 words. News items, up to 1,000 words. Reviews, 50–200 words. Filler, up to 100 words. Departments and columns are open to freelancers.
Submission Policy: Query with outline and writing samples. Include SASE. Accepts photocopies, computer printouts, and Macintosh disks. Simultaneous submissions okay if noted. Reports in up to 4 months. If accepted, expect publication in 6 months.
Terms and Payment: First North American serial rights, one-time rights, or all rights. Pays on publication. Up to $100 per piece. Authors receive 1–3 copies of the issue.
Advertising: Accepts advertising. Contact Marty Johnson, 813-595-4141.

Other Interests: Plans to offer seminars and retreats in the future.

The Centennial Review

Cheryllee Finney, Managing Editor, 312 Linton Hall, East Lansing, MI 48824-1044   Phone: 517-355-1905, Fax: 517-336-1858

Profile: An interdisciplinary literary journal. Published by College of Arts and Letters, Michigan State University. Issued 3 times a year. Circ: 1,000. Trim size: 6x9. 200 pages. Subscription cost: $12. Sample copy cost: $6. Writer's guidelines available with SASE.

Focus and Tips: *The Centennial Review* is committed to reflection on intellectual work, particularly as set in the university and its environment. It seeks out literary and academic work on the various disciplines that speaks to and about the community of university experience.

Editorial Interests
Literary material about the different academic disciplines.
• *Poetry:* No length restrictions.
• *Nonfiction:* In-depth essays, interviews, and profiles, 10–30 manuscript pages.

Submission Policy: Send complete manuscript with cover letter. Include SASE. Accepts photocopies, computer printouts, and faxes. No simultaneous submissions. Responds to queries in 1 month, to manuscripts in 1–4 months. If accepted, expect publication in 3–12 months.

Terms and Payment: All rights and reprint rights. No payment. Offers a free 1-year subscription. Authors receive 2 copies of the issue.

Other Interests: Sponsors The Centennial Review Lecture on various subjects. Contact Cheryllee Finney, 517-355-1905.

Changes

Jeffrey Laign, Managing Editor, 3201 SW 15th Street, Deerfield Beach, FL 33442   Phone: 305-360-0909, Fax: 305-360-0034

Profile: A recovery lifestyle magazine. Published by U.S. Journal, Inc. and Health Communications, Inc. Issued bimonthly. Circ: 30,000. Trim size: 8.5x11. Glossy color cover; 4-color; perfect bound. 82 pages. Subscription cost: $18. Sample copy cost: $3.95. Writer's guidelines available with SASE.

Focus and Tips: *Changes* is aimed at people recovering from substance abuse or emotional traumas, and have chosen to change their lives. It offers information that can be used to cultivate inner well-being and physical health, develop intimate relationships, make responsible choices, and confront issues of dependence, and have fun. Seeks original, innovative tips on enhancing recovery; no sermons, however.

Editorial Interests
Recovery, healing, cultural and ethnic issues, dreams, feminism, holistic and natural health, inspiration, lifestyle, meditations, men's and women's issues, new age, nutrition, parapsychology, philosophy, prayer, psychology, rebirthing, relationships, self-help, and spirituality.
• *Fiction:* Short stories, 500–2,000 words.
• *Nonfiction:* Features, articles, interviews, and profiles, 1,500–2,000 words. Personal experiences, 500 words.

Submission Policy: Query first with outline. Include SASE. Accepts computer printouts, Macintosh 5.25" ASCII disks, and faxes. No simultaneous submissions. Responds to queries in 1 month, to manuscripts in 2–3 months. If accepted, expect publication within 6–12 months.

Terms and Payment: First North American serial rights. Pays on publication. Nonfiction, $.15 per word. Fiction, $100 per piece. Author receives 2 copies of the issue.

Advertising: Accepts advertising.

Chiron Review

Michael Hathaway, Editor, 522 East South Avenue, St. John, KS 67576-2212

Profile: A literary journal of poetry, prose, and reviews. Established in 1982. Issued quarterly. Circ: 1,000. Trim size: 10x13. Newsprint; folded. 32 pages. Subscription cost: $10. Sample copy cost: $3. Writer's guidelines available with SASE.

Focus and Tips: *Chiron Review* publishes a wide range of contemporary creative writing. Much of each issue is devoted to news and views of interest to writers and the literary community. It is always looking for intelligent nonfiction and talented reviewers to write in-depth literary reviews. All submissions are invited, traditional and off-beat. There are no taboos, but avoid didactic, religious, and political arguments.

Editorial Interests
Literary, poetry, reviews, and gay and lesbian issues.
• *Fiction:* Short stories and book excerpts, 3,000 words. Accepts shorter pieces. Poetry, no length restrictions.
• *Nonfiction:* Features, articles, interviews, profiles, essays, personal experiences, opinions, and news, 3,000 words. Book and magazine reviews, 700–1,000 words.

• *Illustrations:* Accepts artwork and photocopies.
Submission Policy: Query with outline for prose. Send up to 5 poems with cover letter. Include SASE. Accepts photocopies and computer printouts. No simultaneous submissions. No reprints. Reports in 1 month. If accepted, expect publication in 6–12 months.
Terms and Payment: One-time rights. No payment. Authors receive 1 copy of the issue.
Advertising: Rates: B/W full-page, $130; half-page, $65; quarter-page, $32.50. List rental available; $65 per 200 names. Contact Michael Hathaway, 316-549-3933.
Other Interests: Sponsors the Chiron Review Poetry Contest. Send a SASE for terms and deadlines. For more information, contact Jane Hathaway, 316-549-3933. Holds an annual Poetry Rendezvous during the first weekend in August. Includes workshops and poetry readings. Contact Terri Nye, 316-792-2409.

Christian*New Age Quarterly

Catherine Groves, Editor, P.O. Box 276, Clifton, NJ 07011-0276

Profile: A forum for dialogue between Christians and New Agers. Published by Bethsheva's Concern. Issued quarterly. Circ: N/A. Trim size: 7x8.5. Self cover; 20 lb. ivory paper; stapled. 24 pages. Subscription cost: $12.50. Sample copy cost: $3.50. Writer's guidelines available with SASE.
Focus and Tips: *Christian*New Age Quarterly* aims to serve as a bridge between Christianity and New Age thought. In a spirit of mutual appreciation, it explores both the differences and the common ground and features a diversity of viewpoints. Readers are Christians and New Agers, representing every possible degree of convergence with the practices and beliefs of the other. In that light, it seeks lively articles with "high-quality writing, sound scholarship, and a sparkle of good fun." Avoid patronizing or confusing subjective understanding with objective reality. Disrespect of either traditional Christianity or New Age alternatives brings immediate rejection.
Editorial Interests
New age, Christianity.
• *Nonfiction:* Features, articles, essays, and opinion pieces, 400–1,500 words. Columns include A Pensive Pause, personal experiences of Christian/New Age contact, 400–700 words. Filler, up to 50 words. Query first for interviews or profiles.
Submission Policy: Send complete manuscript with cover letter. Query first for interviews and profiles. Include SASE. Accepts photocopies and computer printouts. No simultaneous submissions. Responds to queries in 1 month, to manuscripts in 2 months. If accepted, expect publication in 6 months.
Terms and Payment: One-time rights. No payment. Offers a free one-year subscription to article/essay authors. Authors receive 1 copy of the issue.
Advertising: Rates: B/W full-page, $45. Contact Catherine Groves.

Church & State

Joe Conn, Managing Editor, 8120 Fenton Street, Silver Spring, MD 20910   Phone: 301-589-3707, Fax: 301-495-9173

Profile: A membership publication advocating church/state separation. Published by the Americans United for Separation of Church and State, a nonprofit corporation. Issued 11 times a year. Circ: 30,000. Trim size: 8.5x11. Self cover; perfect bound. 24 pages. Subscription cost: $18. Sample copy cost: $2. Writer's guidelines available with SASE.
Focus and Tips: *Church & State* promotes religious liberty and the separation of church and state. Its readership is from across religious, educational, and civil liberties spectrum. Articles must promise separation of church and state and be nonsectarian in approach. No proselytization—this is not a religious magazine.
Editorial Interests
Church/state separation, politics, social and world issues, prayer, and gay and lesbian issues.
• *Nonfiction:* Features and articles exploring church/state and constitutional issues, 2,000–3,000 words. Political and church/state reviews. Departments include Viewpoint, AU Bulletin, People and Events, and Editorial.
Submission Policy: Query with outline. Include SASE. Accepts photocopies, computer printouts, and faxes. Simultaneous submissions okay. Reports in 1–2 months.
Terms and Payment: All rights. Pays on publication. $150–$250 per piece. Authors receive copies of the issue.
Other Interests: Sponsors an annual Church-State Conference consisting of workshops, debates, dinner, and student seminars. Held in September or November at various location. Contact Regina Hayden, Conference Coordinator.

The Civil Abolitionist

Bina Robinson, Editor, P.O. Box 26, Swain, NY 14884-0026   Phone: 607-545-6213

Profile: An antivivisection newsletter. Issued quarterly. Circ: 2,500. Trim size: 8.5x11. Self cover; B/W; saddle stitched. 10 pages. Subscription cost: $5. Sample copy cost: Free with SASE. No writer's guidelines.
Focus and Tips: *The Civil Abolitionist* deals with human health issues and advancements in medical research that are not

dependent on animal research and vivisection. It is primarily an antivivisectionist publication rather than pro-animal rights, although it is sensitive to animal-rights issues. Aims to show that animal experimentation does not necessarily advance human health research. Its international audience includes health professionals, nurses, and individuals interested in health and opposed to animal cruelty. Writers should send for sample copies before submitting.

Editorial Interests

Antivivisection, animal rights, vaccines, legal drugs, health and medical research, the environment, politics, psychology, social and world issues, and women's issues.

• *Nonfiction:* Articles, interviews, profiles, essays, case studies, opinion pieces, news items, and book reviews. No length restrictions, but prefers short pieces.

Submission Policy: Send complete manuscript with cover letter. Include SASE. Accepts photocopies and computer print-outs. Simultaneous submissions okay if noted. Reports in up to 3 months. If accepted, expect publication in up to 1 year.

Terms and Payment: Authors retain rights. No payment. Authors receive 1 copy of the issue; more upon request.

CoHousing

Don Lindemann, Managing Editor, P.O. Box 2584, Berkeley, CA 94702   Phone: 510-526-6124

Profile: A journal of the CoHousing Movement of North America. Published by The CoHousing Network. Issued quarterly. Circ: 1,500. Trim size: 8.5x11. Stapled. 24 pages. Subscription cost: $25. Sample copy cost: $5.

Focus and Tips: *CoHousing* is aimed at people living in communities designed, developed, and managed by residents, along with potential residents, architects, and builders. It is most interested in writers who are well-connected to the CoHousing Movement. Preference given to articles that draw on experiences of more than one group. Avoid any topic that does not have an obvious, practical connection to the development or management of cohousing communities.

Editorial Interests

Co-op housing, parenting, and seniors.

• *Nonfiction:* Features, 1,000–3,000 words.

Submission Policy: Query first with outline and writing samples. Include SASE. Accepts photocopies, computer printouts, and IBM, Macintosh, ASCII, or Microsoft Word disks. Reports in 1–2 months. If accepted, expect publication in 3–6 months.

Terms and Payment: Pays $.05 per word. Authors receive 3 copies of the issue.

Advertising: Rates: B/W full-page, $250. Contact Don Lindemann, 510-526-6124.

Other Interests: Sponsors the National CoHousing Conference in Boulder, Colorado. Held annually each fall. For more information, contact Bill Paiss, 1705 14th Street, # 317, Boulder, CO 80302.

Color Wheel

Frederick Moe, Editor, R.R. 2, Box 806, Warner, NH 03278 Phone: 603-456-3036

Profile: A journal of poetry and prose exploring spiritual growth. Published by 700 Elves Press. Issued 3 times per year. Circ: 250+. Trim size: 8x11. Bond cover; B/W; flat bound. 32 pages. Subscription cost: $14. Sample copy cost: $6. Writer's guidelines available with SASE.

Focus and Tips: *Color Wheel* explores the interrelationships between one another and with the natural world through poetry, prose, mythology, and artwork. Geared toward writers and others interested in spiritual growth. Although it is a "homespun" publication, it seeks exceptional, insightful work. Writers are advised to review a sample copy to get a feel for editorial preferences. Avoid nihilistic, negative, narcissistic writing.

Editorial Interests

Creativity, mythology, spirituality, dreams, the environment, healing, magic, meditation, men's and women's issues, metaphysics, mysticism, new age, relationships, social and world issues, and witches.

• *Fiction:* Short-short stories, up to 1,200 words. Poetry, no length restrictions.

• *Nonfiction:* Essays and personal experiences, up to 1,500 words. Reviews, 100–200 words.

Submission Policy: Send complete manuscript with cover letter. Include SASE. Accepts photocopies. No simultaneous submissions. Reports in 2–4 weeks. If accepted, expect publication in 6 months.

Terms and Payment: First North American serial rights and one-time reprint rights. Pays on publication. Rates vary. Authors receive copies of the issue.

Advertising: Rates: Full-page B/W, $50. Contact Frederick Moe, 603-456-3036.

Coming Out Pagan

Magnolia Stuart, Editor, P.O. Box 12942, Tucson, AZ 85732-2942

Profile: A pagan publication of lesbian, gay, and bisexual spirituality. Published by Wordsmith Writing Services. Issued quarterly. Circ: 1,200. Trim size: 8.5x11. Card stock cover; B/W inside; saddle stitched. 24 pages. Subscription cost: $11. Sample copy cost: $3. Writer's guidelines available with SASE.

Focus and Tips: *Coming Out Pagan* is a "celebration of lesbian, gay, and bisexual spirituality promoting power from diversity and from within." It serves as a networking tool. Welcomes writers from all sexual orientations. Prefers positive writings with emphasis on "personal connection with the Divine, sacred sexuality, works of magic, and networking." No victim stories—"if you have a complaint, offer a solution." Avoid murder/crime stories and obscene, crude, or explicitly sexual language.

Editorial Interests

Gay and lesbian concerns, Buddhism, Wicca, astrology, bodywork, channeling, crystals, cultural and ethnic issues, dreams, ecosystems, the environment, feminism, folklore, healing, health, holistic health, inspiration, lifestyle, magic, meditation, men's issues, metaphysics, mysticism, mythology, natural health, new age, philosophy, prayer, psychic phenomenon, recovery, relationships, social and world issues, spirituality, witches, and women's issues.

• *Fiction:* Short stories, fantasy, and romance, up to 1,500 words. Poetry, up to 500 words.

• *Nonfiction:* Features on Goddess lore, historical articles, interviews, profiles, essays, opinion pieces, and positive personal experiences, 1,000–1,500 words. News items, reviews, and filler, 200 words. Columns: Tarot Advisor and Stone Circles, 200 words.

Submission Policy: Query with outline and writing samples, or send complete manuscript with cover letter and author biography. Include SASE. Accepts photocopies, computer printouts, and 3.5" Macintosh Microsoft Word or DOS WordPerfect 5.1 disks. No simultaneous submissions. Responds to queries in 1 month, to manuscripts in 3 months. If accepted, expect publication in 3 months.

Terms and Payment: Authors retain rights. No payment. Authors receive 1 copy of the issue.

Advertising: Rates: B/W full-page, $80. Discounts for multiple insertions. Contact Jo Sorgo.

Common Boundary

Anne Simpkinson, Editor, 4304 East-West Highway, Bethesda, MD 20814 Phone: 301-652-9495, Fax: 301-652-0579

Profile: A national magazine exploring the connection between spirituality and psychology. Established in 1988. Issued bimonthly. Circ: 30,000. Trim size: 8.5x11. Glossy color cover; 4-color; coated paper; saddle stitched. 74 pages. Subscription cost: $22. Sample copy cost: $5. Writer's guidelines available with SASE.

Focus and Tips: *Common Boundary* is dedicated to exploring the sources of meaning in human experience. Readers are those interested in the interface between spirituality, creativity, and psychology. The magazine offers thoughtful discussions of transformational processes such as dreamwork, storytelling, meditation, and creative expression. Prefers journalistic reporting to academic styles and grounded prose to inflated writing.

Editorial Interests

Psychology, spirituality, bodywork, dreams, feminism, healing, holistic health, inspiration, lifestyle, meditation, men's issues, mysticism, mythology, philosophy, prayer, psychology, recovery, religion, self-help, and women's issues.

• *Nonfiction:* Features, 1,500–3,000 words. Articles, 1,500 words. Interviews and profiles, 1,500–2,000 words. Essays, personal experiences, and opinion pieces, 1,000 words. News items, 500 words. Reviews, 750 words. Departments include Innovations, Book Reviews, and In Your Own Words. Accepts submissions for End Page column.

• *Illustrations:* Photo essays.

Submission Policy: Query with outline, writing samples, and resume. Include SASE. Accepts photocopies, computer printouts, and WordPerfect disks. Simultaneous submissions okay. Reports in 3 months. If accepted, expect publication in 3 months.

Terms and Payment: One-time rights. Pays on publication. Offers a varied per word rate for articles. Authors receive copies of the issue.

Advertising: Rates: B/W full-page, $ 1,080; 4-color full-page, $1,550; back cover 4-color; $1,825. Contact Grace Ogden, 301-652-9495. List rental available. Contact Pacific Lists, 413-381-0826.

Other Interests: Offers a $1,000 Thesis/Dissertation Award for the best psychospiritual MA thesis or Ph.D. dissertation. Deadline is December 31 in the year thesis/dissertation was accepted. Essay based on winning entry is published. Contact Charles H. Simpkinson, 301-652-9495. Sponsors an annual conference on interface between spirituality, creativity, and psychology. Held in Arlington, Virginia in November. For more information, contact Mary Jane Casavant, 301-652-9495.

Common Lives/Lesbian Lives

Editor, P.O. Box 1553, Iowa City, IA 52244

Profile: A lesbian journal. Issued quarterly. Circ: 1,000. Trim size: 5.5x8.5. Glossy cover; B/W; perfect bound. 128 pages. Subscription cost: $15. Sample copy cost: $5. No writer's guidelines.

Focus and Tips: *Common Lives/Lesbian Lives* seeks to document the experiences and thoughts of ordinary lesbians as it claims the past, names present conditions, and envisions an evolving future. It serves as a forum for developing and clarifying lesbian-defined social and political relationships. Committed to reflecting diversity, it solicits the work of "lesbians of color, Jewish lesbians, fat lesbians, lesbians over fifty and under twenty, physically challenged lesbians, poor and working-class lesbians, and lesbians of varying cultural backgrounds."

Editorial Interests
Lesbian issues.
• *Fiction:* Short stories, short-short stories, drama, science fiction, fantasy, and book excerpts, up to 4,000 words. Poetry, up to 5 pages.
• *Nonfiction:* Features and articles in the form of history, oral history, biography, autobiography, correspondence, journal entries, reminiscences, theory, and analysis, up to 4,000 words.
• *Illustrations:* Camera-ready or B/W photos and artwork. Model releases required.
Submission Policy: Send complete manuscript with cover letter and brief author biography. Include SASE. Accepts computer printouts. No simultaneous submissions. Reports in up to 3 months. If accepted, expect publication in 3–6 months.
Terms and Payment: No payment. Authors receive 2 copies of the issue.

Communities

Diana Christian, Managing Editor, 1118 Round Butte Drive, Fort Collins, CO 80524   Phone: 303-490-1550, Fax: 303-490-1469

Profile: A thematic journal of cooperative living. Published by the Fellowship for International Communities, a nonprofit organization. Issued quarterly. Circ: 4,000. Trim size: 8.5x11. Glossy 2-color cover; B/W inside; saddle stitched. 64–72 pages. Subscription cost: $18. Sample copy cost: $5. Writer's guidelines available with SASE.
Focus and Tips: *Communities* explores all aspects of international communities and cooperative living. Also offers up-to-date listings of existing and evolving communities. Each issue focuses on one theme. Past themes include adults who were raised in community as children and community living's affect on returning to mainstream society. Many manuscripts are rejected because they are on a totally unrelated subject.
Editorial Interests
Community living, international communities, worker-owned co-ops.
• *Nonfiction:* Features, articles, interviews, profiles, essays, personal experiences, opinion pieces, and reviews, 750–2,600 words. Columns include My Turn, opinion pieces.
Submission Policy: Query with outline and writing samples or send complete manuscript with clips. Include SASE. Prefers Macintosh MicroSoft Word disks with hard copy. Accepts IBM-compatible disks with hard copy, computer printouts, and typewritten manuscripts. Responds to queries in 1 month, to manuscripts in 1 week. If accepted, expect publication within 3–4 months.
Terms and Payment: First North American serial rights. Generally, no payment. May supply a free 1-year subscription or advertising exchange. Authors receive 1 copy of the issue.
Advertising: Rates: B/W full-page, $250; half-page, $145; quarter-page, $78. Contact Diana Christian, 303-490-1440. Considers list rental. Contact Laird Schaub, 816-883-5543.

Community Service Newsletter

Jane Morgan, Editor, P.O. Box 243, Yellow Springs, OH 45387   Phone: 513-767-2161

Profile: A newsletter on small community living. Published by Community Service, Inc. Issued bimonthly. Circ: 300. Trim size: 7x8.5. Self cover; B/W; stapled. 12 pages. Subscription cost: $25. Sample copy cost: $1. Writer's guidelines available with SASE.
Focus and Tips: *Community Service Newsletter* serves to promote the small community as a basic social institution involving organic units of economic, social, and spiritual development. Seeks practical articles that help inspire people to improve their own communities. Avoid "pie-in-the-sky articles about how people think things *might* be better."
Editorial Interests
Small community development, international communities, land trusts, education, the environment, health, lifestyle, parenting, philosophy, self-help, and social issues.
• *Fiction:* Short stories, up to 2,000 words.
• *Nonfiction:* Articles about communities, 2,100 words. Essays, personal experiences, opinion pieces, and book reviews, 700 words.
Submission Policy: Query or send complete manuscript. Include SASE. Accepts computer printouts. Reports promptly. If accepted, expect publication in 2 months.
Terms and Payment: No payment. Offers a free one-year subscription to contributors. Authors receive 12 copies of the issue.
Other Interests: Sponsors an annual conference in Yellow Springs, Ohio, on various aspects of community building. Held in October. For more information, contact Jane Morgan, 513-767-1461.

The Compleat Mother

Jody McLaughlin, Editor, Box 209, Minot, ND 58702   Phone/Fax: 701-852-2822

Profile: An international magazine of pregnancy, birth, and breastfeeding. Established in 1984. Issued quarterly. Circ: 14,000.

Trim size: 7.75x10.5. Self cover; newsprint; saddle stitched. 56 pages. Subscription cost: $12. Sample copy cost: $3. Writer's guidelines available with SASE.

Focus and Tips: *The Compleat Mother* is a reader's forum focusing on pregnancy, noninterventive childbirth, and breastfeeding. Readers are parents, teachers, midwives, and others in the health and helping professions. Writers are advised to "know your subject, speak from the heart—or ovaries, and don't sanitize your writing." Avoid sending long-winded narratives.

Editorial Interests

Pregnancy, birth, breastfeeding, home birth, midwifery, parenting, cultural and ethnic issues, feminism, healing and health, holistic and natural health, politics, rebirthing, relationships, self-help, social and world issues, and women's issues.

• *Nonfiction:* Articles, essays, personal experiences, and opinion pieces. Prefers short pieces.

• *Illustrations:* B/W cartoons.

Submission Policy: Query or send complete manuscript with cover letter. Include SASE. Accepts photocopies, computer printouts, and Macintosh 3.5" disks. Reports in 1–4 weeks. If accepted, expect publication in 3–12 months.

Terms and Payment: Offers free one-year subscription in lieu of payment. Authors receive 1–100 copies of the issue upon request.

Advertising: Rates: B/W full-page, $350; half-page, $225; quarter-page, $125. List rental available: $.05 per name, in state or zip code order. Contact Jody McLaughlin, 701-852-2822.

Other Interests: Affiliated with The Friends of Breastfeeding Society, Box 209, Minot, ND 58702.

Conscious Choice

Sheri Reda, Editor, 920 N. Franklin, Suite 301, Chicago, IL 60610-3119   Phone: 312-440-4373, Fax: 312-751-3973

Profile: A thematic journal of ecology and natural living. Published by Conscious Communications, Inc. Established in 1988. Issued 6 times a year. Circ: 50,000. Trim size: 10x13. Newsprint; saddle stitched. 56 pages. Subscription cost: $26. Sample copy cost: $6. Writer's guidelines available with SASE.

Focus and Tips: *Conscious Choice* encourages readers to take personal responsibility for their lives by offering information that describes and explores alternatives. Strong emphasis is placed on natural living, local community building, and developing a sense of place. Issues are thematic. Past themes include Rising Global Awareness, Building Community, The Healthy Home, Animals, Conscious Child Raising, Socially Responsible Business, Pursuit of Physical Perfection, and Careers. Avoid new age "airy-fairy" material.

Editorial Interests

Natural health, nutrition, the environment, sustainable economics, bodywork, ecosystems, healing and health, politics, and social and world issues.

• *Nonfiction:* Features, reviews, local news, and several columns. Columns include News from the Earth, timely news on environmental topics; Neighborhood Beat, profiles of community groups; Guide to Conscious Eating, reviews of local restaurants; Nutrition Insight, discussions on nutrition; Healing Foods, one food and its healing properties; and Humus, a regular page of comics. Query for word lengths.

Submission Policy: Query with outline and writing samples. Include SASE. Accepts computer printouts and Macintosh disks. Reports in 2 months. If accepted, expect publication in 6 months.

Terms and Payment: No payment as of yet. Authors receive 5 copies of the issue.

Advertising: Rates: B/W full-page, $1,010; half-page, $640; quarter-page, $365. Two-color full-page, $1,190; half-page, $805; quarter-page, $520. Four-color full-page, $1,565; half-page, $1,090. Contact Jim Slama.

Constructive Action Newsletter

Shirley Burghard, Editor, 417 Churchhill Avenue, No. 2306, Syracuse, NY 13205   Phone: 315-498-4117

Profile: A self-help publication. Issued monthly. Circ: 100. Trim size: 8.5x14. 8 pages. Subscription cost: $8. Sample copy cost: Free. No writer's guidelines.

Focus and Tips: *Constructive Action Newsletter* is an inspirational self-help publication designed to help people reach their full potential. Audience includes individuals with physical disabilities. Understand the self-help genre before submitting articles. Not interested in material on homosexuality.

Editorial Interests

Self-help, disability, bodywork, ecosystems, the environment, feminism, folklore, healing, health, holistic health, inspiration, lifestyle, meditation, natural health, nutrition, seniors, and social issues.

• *Nonfiction:* Self-help features and articles, interviews, profiles, essays, personal experiences, opinion pieces, news items, and book reviews, 1,000 words. Accepts recipes.

Submission Policy: Send complete manuscript. Include SASE. Accepts any typewritten material. Reports in 2 weeks. If accepted, expect publication in 2 weeks.

Terms and Payment: No payment. Authors receive 2 copies of the issue.

Convergence

Virginia Slayton, Editor, One Sanborn Road, Concord, NH 03301   Phone/Fax: 603-225-3720

Profile: A publication of holistic living. Published by Riverside Communications. Issued 5 times a year. Circ: 4,500. Trim size: 8.5x11. Glossy cover; B/W; saddle stitched. 40–48 pages. Subscription cost: $12.50. Sample copy cost: Free. Writer's guidelines available with SASE.

Focus and Tips: *Convergence* is a magazine for personal and spiritual growth and holistic health. It offers application of spiritual and holistic principles to everyday life. Audience consists mostly of college-educated professional, ages 30–65. Avoid using didactic styles and lecturing. "Stories with warmth, humor, or personal impact are best."

Editorial Interests

Astrology, bodywork, channeling, dreams, the environment, healing, health, holistic health, inspiration, metaphysics, mysticism, natural health, nutrition, psychic phenomenon, and spirituality.

• *Fiction:* Book excerpts, 1,000–2,400 words.

• *Nonfiction:* Features, 1,600–2,400 words. Articles, 1,000 words and up. Interviews and profiles, 1,200 words. Personal experiences, 1,200–2,400 words. News items, 400 words. Book reviews, 400–800 words. Filler, 30–100 words. Columns, 500 words.

Submission Policy: Query with outline and writing samples or send complete manuscript with cover letter. Include SASE. Accepts Macintosh Word disks with clean printout. Reports in 4–6 weeks. If accepted, expect publication in 4–6 months.

Terms and Payment: One-time rights. Pays on publication. $30–$60. Authors receive 5–10 copies of the issue.

Advertising: Rates: B/W full-page, $495. Contact Virginia Slayton, 603-225-3720.

Other Interests: Sponsors Convergence Conferences, workshops on spiritual growth. Contact Virginia Slayton, 603-225-3720, for more information.

Co-operative Grocer

Dave Gutknecht, Editor, P.O. Box 597, Athens, OH 45701   Phone: 800-878-7333, Fax: 614-594-4504

Profile: An industry publication for co-op managers. Issued bimonthly. Circ: 2,200. Trim size: 8.5x11. Stapled. 28 pages. Subscription cost: $22. Sample copy cost: Free. Writer's guidelines available with SASE.

Focus and Tips: *Co-operative Grocer* offers those who manage and work in grocery co-ops in the United States and Canada professional advice about co-op governing, management, marketing, leadership, and membership along with political and industrial trade issues.

Editorial Interests

Co-operative grocery management and operation.

• *Nonfiction:* Features, 2,000–3,000 words. Articles, 500–2,500 words. Interviews and profiles, 2,000 words. Essays, up to 2,500 words. Personal experiences, up to 1,500 words. Opinion pieces, 1,000 words. News items, up to 1,000 words. Reviews, up to 1,500 words. Columns include Retailing, practical hand-on information.

Submission Policy: Call for interests or query first with outline. Include SASE. Accepts photocopies, computer printouts, and Macintosh or IBM 3.5" disks. Simultaneous submissions okay. Reports in 2 months. If accepted, expect publication in 6 months.

Terms and Payment: Authors retain rights. Pays on publication. $50 for pieces under 1,000 words. $100 for pieces over 1,000 words. Authors receive 1 copy of the issue; additional copies available upon request.

Advertising: Rates: B/W full-page, $550; 4-color cover ads, $1,050.

The Cosmic Family Newsletter

Editor, 1885 Stockwell, Columbus, OH 43220   Phone: 614-442-1561

Profile: A newsletter of channeled information. Issued 5–6 issues a year. Circ: 1,500. Trim size: 8.5x11. 20 lb. paper; folded. 10 pages. Subscription cost: $29. Sample copy cost: Free. No writer's guidelines.

Focus and Tips: *The Cosmic Family Newsletter* devotes its pages to "space and the ascended masters," UFOs, and channeled material from "Lord Adrigon, Mother Mary, Isis, Lady Faith, and The Ashtar Command." Writing should be honest, truthful, and simple. No satanic, witches, or Wicca-related material.

Editorial Interests

Channeling, angels, astrology, crystals, cultural and ethnic issues, the environment, extraterrestrials, healing, health, holistic health, inspiration, meditation, natural health, philosophy, prayer, psychic phenomenon, relationships, self-help, social and world issues, spirituality, and women's issues.

• *Nonfiction:* Articles, personal experiences, opinion pieces, and channeled material, 1 manuscript page. Accepts book reviews.

Submission Policy: Send complete manuscript with cover letter. Include SASE. Accepts photocopies and computer printouts. Simultaneous submissions okay. Reporting and publication times vary.

Terms and Payment: Authors retain rights. No payment. Authors receive 1–2 copies of the issue.

Advertising: Rates: Camera-ready business-card ads, $25. Contact Nina Jenice, 614-442-1561.

Other Interests: Offers 3–4 retreats annually based on energy and a Lady Master as well as mini-retreats throughout the year. Contact Nina Jenice, 614-442-1561.

Creation Spirituality

John Mabry, Managing Editor, 4185 Park Boulevard, Oakland, CA 94619   Phone: 510-482-4984, Fax: 510-482-0387

Profile: A magazine of earth-centered spirituality. Published by the Friends of Creation Spirituality, Inc., a nonprofit corporation. Issued quarterly. Circ: 15,000. Trim size: 8.5x11. Glossy color cover; B/W inside; saddle stitched. 72 pages. Subscription cost: $24. Sample copy cost: $6. Writer's guidelines available with SASE.

Focus and Tips: Based on the work of Matthew Fox, *Creation Spirituality* strives to integrate the wisdom of Western spirituality and the global indigenous cultures. Its readers are interested in Earth-centered spirituality, the new cosmology, the arts and healing, and justice toward women, native peoples, and the Earth. Use a conversational tone—not too academic, but not simplistic either. Authors should be familiar with the writings of Matthew Fox. Knowledge of the Western mystical tradition is a plus. Not interested in channeled writings or articles on Eastern teachers.

Editorial Interests

Social justice, mysticism, ecumenism, spirituality, the environment, religion, holistic and natural health, social and world issues, feminism, gay and lesbian concerns, healing, philosophy, mythology, men's and women's issues, rebirthing, recovery, and dreams.

• *Nonfiction:* Features, 6,000 words. Articles, interviews, and profiles, 2,500–3,500 words. Essays and opinion pieces, 500–1,500 words. News items and reviews, 500 words. Departments include Ritual, Art-As-Meditation, and Deep Ecumenism.

Submission Policy: Send complete manuscript with cover letter and resume. Include SASE. Accepts photocopies, computer printouts, Macintosh disks, and faxes. Simultaneous submissions okay. Reports in 1–2 months. If accepted, expect publication in 6 months.

Terms and Payment: First North American serial rights. Pays on publication. $.02 per word. $20 per book review. Authors receive 5 copies of the issue.

Advertising: Rates per page: B/W, $440, 4-color, $680. Contact Julie Fretzin, 510-482-4984.

Other Interests: Offers Workshops in Creation Spirituality, week-long workshops featuring seminar classes and art-as-meditation. Dates are July 17–22 and August 7–12. Contact Sue Espinoza or Ken Caredo, 510-482-4984.

Creations Magazine

Vijay, Editor, P.O. Box 407, Sea Cliff, NY 11579   Phone: 516-674-3051, Fax: 516-671-7547

Profile: A regional new age magazine. Published by The InnerLight Center, Inc., a nonprofit organization. Established in 1987. Issued bimonthly. Circ: 40,000. Trim size: Tabloid. No writer's guidelines.

Focus and Tips: *Creations* serves the holistic, alternative, and artistic communities of Queens and Long Island, New York. It is distributed in nearly 475 locations and reaches 160,000 readers who are creative, health-conscious, growth-oriented, and quality-seeking. Writers are encouraged to "tap their creativity—their spirit, their godliness." Appreciates experiential pieces and sharing that comes from the heart. Avoid material that is too impersonal, text-like, and over-detailed.

Editorial Interests

New age, holistic health, astrology, bodywork, channeling, crystals, cultural and ethnic issues, ecosystems, the environment, extraterrestrials, healing, health, inspiration, magic, meditation, men's issues, metaphysics, mysticism, mythology, natural health, nutrition, occult, parapsychology, parenting, philosophy, politics, prayer, psychic phenomenon, psychology, rebirthing, recovery, relationships, self-help, spirituality, witches, women's issues, and yoga.

• *Fiction:* Short stories, 2,000 words. Short-short stories, 1,000 words. Book excerpts, 1,200 words.

• *Nonfiction:* Features, articles, interviews, profiles, essays, personal experiences, opinion pieces, and news, up to 2,000 words. Reviews, 1,200 words.

Submission Policy: Send complete manuscript with cover letter and bibliography. Include SASE. Accepts photocopies, computer printouts, and faxes. Simultaneous submissions okay. Reporting time varies. If accepted, expect publication in 3 months.

Terms and Payment: Rights vary. May offer small payment. Authors receive copies of the issue as requested.

Advertising: Rates: B/W full-page, $1,050; half-page, $685; quarter-page, $450. Directory, classified, and business card ads available. Camera-ready art required. List rental available. Contact Vijay, 516-674-3051.

Other Interests: Sponsors art contests and various conferences. Contact Vijay.

Crone Chronicles: A Journal of Conscious Aging

Ann Kreilkamp, Publisher, P.O. Box 81, Kelly, WY 83011   Phone: 307-733-5409, Fax: 307-733-1726

Profile: A spiritual magazine for older women. Published by Crone Corporation. Issued quarterly. Circ: 5,000. Trim size:

8.5x11. Glossy color cover; B/W inside; saddle stitched. 40 pages. Subscription cost: $18. Sample copy cost: $6.50. No writer's guidelines.

Focus and Tips: *Crone Chronicles* is dedicated to reactivating the archetype of the Crone within contemporary Western culture. It features women speaking to and for women as they share their own experiences and understanding. Currently, it is seeking a columnist to write on health issues for older women.

Editorial Interests

Women's issues, feminism, seniors, paganism, astrology, dreams, ecosystems, the environment, healing, holistic health, lifestyle, metaphysics, mysticism, mythology, nutrition, parapsychology, philosophy, psychic phenomenon, psychology, relationships, and spirituality.

• *Fiction:* Book excerpts, up to 5,000 words. Accepts poetry.

• *Nonfiction:* Articles and essays, 2,500 words. Interviews and profiles, 5,000 words. Personal experiences, 3,000 words. Opinion pieces, 750 words. Short news items, up to 200 words. Reviews, up to 500 words. Launching a column on health issues for older women.

Submission Policy: Query with outline and author biography, or send complete manuscript with cover letter and author biography. Include SASE. Accepts photocopies, computer printouts, faxes, and Macintosh disks. No simultaneous submissions. Reports in 1 month. If accepted, expect publication in 3 months.

Terms and Payment: One-time rights. No payment. Authors receive 1 copy of the issue.

Advertising: Rates: B/W full-page, $200. Contact Jane Folgeman, 307-739-8842. List rental available. Terms negotiable. Contact Ann Kreilkamp, 307-733-1726.

Other Interests: Sponsors the Crone Council, a gathering of Crones, in October. For more information, contact editor.

Crystal Tower

Sharon Dunbar, Editor, 10821 Douglas Avenue, No. 108, Urbandale, IA 50322   Phone: 515-254-0875, Fax: 515-254-9217

Profile: A magazine for the new age community in the Midlands. Issued quarterly. Circ: 3,500. Trim size: 8.5x11. Self cover; B/W; saddle stitched. 32 pages. Subscription cost: $5. Sample copy cost: Free. No writer's guidelines.

Focus and Tips: *Crystal Tower* reports on timely news and information of interest to a new age Midwestern readership. Prefers positive, new life, good news pieces.

Editorial Interests

New age, Native peoples, holistic health, metaphysics, astrology, bodywork, channeling, crystals, dreams, the environment, extraterrestrials, folklore, gay and lesbian issues, healing, meditation, men's and women's issues, occult, parapsychology, philosophy, psychic phenomenon, rebirthing, recovery, self-help, spirituality, witches, and yoga.

• *Fiction:* Short stories, short-short stories, genre fiction, drama, and book excerpts, 900–1,000 words. Poetry, 100–200 words.

• *Nonfiction:* Features, articles, interviews and profiles, essays, personal experiences, opinion, and news, 900–1,000 words. Reviews and filler, 500–1,000 words.

Submission Policy: Query with outline or send complete manuscript with cover letter. Include SASE. Accepts computer printouts and IBM-WordPerfect disks. Simultaneous submissions okay. Reports in 1 month. If accepted, expect publication within 2–4 months.

Terms and Payment: One-time rights. No payment. Authors receive copies of the issue upon request.

Advertising: Rates: B/W full-page, $125; half-page $75; quarter-page, $50. Contact Billy Dunbar, 515-254-0875.

Cultural Survival Quarterly

Maria Tocco, Managing Editor, 46 Brattle Street, Cambridge, MA 02138   Phone: 617-621-3818, Fax: 617-621-3814

Profile: A thematic human-rights membership journal. Published by Cultural Survival, a nonprofit organization. Issued quarterly. Circ: 20,000. Trim size: 8.5x11. 50 lb. paper; saddle stitched. 64–72 pages. Subscription cost: $45 membership fees. Sample copy cost: $5. Writer's guidelines available with SASE.

Focus and Tips: *Cultural Survival Quarterly* is an academic-oriented journal devoted to issues of human rights, land and resource rights, indigenous peoples, and world issues. Prefers documentation in the form of source lists, side bars, charts, and graphics. Issues are thematic; contact editor for upcoming themes. It is important to review guidelines before submitting.

Editorial Interests

Human rights, indigenous rights, land and resource rights, and world issues.

• *Nonfiction:* Human-rights features and essays related to theme, 1,000–4,000 words. Accepts news items for Briefly Noted column.

Submission Policy: Query first with outline and abstract. Include SASE. Accepts photocopies, computer printouts, and Macintosh Microsoft Word disks. No simultaneous submissions. Reports in 2 weeks. If accepted, expect publication in 2–12 months.

Terms and Payment: All rights; grants reprint rights for nominal charge. No payment.

Daughters of Nyx

Kim Antieau, Editor, Box 1187, White Salmon, WA 98672

Profile: A fiction magazine dedicated to matristic storytelling. Published by Ruby Rose's Fairy Tale Emporium. Issued quarterly. Circ: 1,000. Trim size: 8.5x11. Glossy cover; B/W inside; saddle-stitched. 32 pages. Subscription cost: $14. Sample copy cost: $4.50. Writer's guidelines available with SASE.

Focus and Tips: *Daughters of Nyx* strives to bring back a more female-centered culture through fiction dedicated to goddesses that celebrate the female and find alternatives to patriarchy. "Nyx is the Goddess of night, the ultimate mother, the one who birthed the cosmic egg." Writers are advised to learn about goddesses and matristic culture and to use imagination to break the bonds of patriarchal thinking. Great storytelling is a must. Avoid high fantasy and stories from a male perspective.

Editorial Interests

Fiction emphasizing feminism and/or goddesses.

• *Fiction:* Short stories, retold myths, fairy tales, and legends from a matristic viewpoint, 500–5,000 words.
• *Nonfiction:* Daughters Re-membered, 1,000 words. Reviews of matristic fiction or related resource books, 500 words.
• *Illustrations:* Profiles one artist each issue. Accepts B/W artwork.

Submission Policy: Send complete manuscript with cover letter. Include SASE. Accepts photocopies and computer printouts. Simultaneous submissions okay if noted. Reports in 1–3 months. If accepted, expect publication in 1 year.

Terms and Payment: First North American serial rights or one-time rights. Pays on publication. Fiction and nonfiction, $.25 per word with a $5 minimum. Artwork, $100 plus advertising space. Contributors receive 2 copies of the issue.

Advertising: Rates: B/W full-page, $225; half-page, $120; third-page, $85. Classified ads, $.50 per word with a 20-word minimum. Contact Kim Antieau.

Delicious!

Sue Frederick, Editor, 1301 Spruce Street, Boulder, CO 80302   Phone: 303-939-8440

Profile: A health and nutrition magazine. Issued monthly. Circ: 30,500.

Focus and Tips: *Delicious!* seeks health-related material about natural foods, nutrition, natural products, herbal medicines, homeopathy, fitness, and holistic or alternative healing methods. Personal-care articles—skin, hair, and natural beauty—are of current interest.

Editorial Interests

Health, natural and holistic health, nutrition, homeopathy, fitness, healing, and herbal medicines.

• *Nonfiction:* Features, 1,000–2,500 words.

Submission Policy: Query first with outline and resume or send complete manuscript with clips. Include SASE. Accepts photocopies and computer printouts. No simultaneous submissions.

Terms and Payment: First North American serial rights. Pays on acceptance. Rates are negotiable.

Diamond Fire

Joseph Polansky, Publisher/Editor, P.O. Box 20338, Sarasota, FL 34276   Phone/Fax: 813-921-5855

Profile: An esoteric review. Published by Malchitsedek Productions. Issued quarterly. Circ: 500. Trim size: 8.5x11. Heavy bond cover; spiral bound. 80–100 pages. Subscription cost: $30. Sample copy cost: $10. Writer's guidelines available with SASE.

Focus and Tips: *Diamond Fire* is aimed at the serious and sincere student of esoterism. Its focus is on astrology, spirituality, metaphysics, healing, dowsing, and meditation. Writers should keep it short, educate and enlighten readers, and offer new insights into esoteric subjects. Avoid political positions and political correctness—"just the truth."

Editorial Interests

Esoteric writing, Tarot, bio-electronics, dowsing, astrology, crystals, healing, inspiration, magic, meditation, metaphysics, mysticism, occult, parapsychology, prayer, psychic phenomenon, spirituality, and yoga.

• *Fiction:* Esoteric fiction and poetry. Short-short stories, up to 1,000 words. Book excerpts, 5,000 words. Short stories and drama, length depends on quality.
• *Nonfiction:* Features, articles, interviews, profiles, and personal experiences, 1,000 words.

Submission Policy: Send complete manuscript with cover letter. Include SASE. Accepts computer printouts and WordPerfect or ASCII disks. No simultaneous submissions. Reports in 1 month. If accepted, expect publication within 3–6 months.

Terms and Payment: All rights. Pays on publication. Material under 1,000 words, $.11 per word. Longer material, rates negotiable. Authors receive 1 copy of the issue.

Advertising: Rates: B/W full-page, $200. Contact Joseph Polansky, 813-921-5855.

Diet & Health Series

Editor, 2131 Hollywood Boulevard, No. 305, Hollywood, FL 33020   Phone: 305-925-5242, Fax: 305-925-5244

Profile: A health and fitness digest. Issued quarterly. Circ: 40,000. Trim size: Digest. Perfect bound. 120 pages. Available on newsstands. Sample copy cost: $4. Writer's guidelines available with SASE.

Focus and Tips: *Diet & Health Series* is designed for people concerned about diet and exercise. Its audience is health- and fitness-conscious seniors.

Editorial Interests

Nutrition, diet, fitness, exercise, and specialty foods.

• *Nonfiction:* Articles relating to nutrition.

Submission Policy: Query first with outline. Include SASE. Accepts WordPerfect disks. If accepted, expect publication in 6 weeks.

Terms and Payment: Pays on publication. Rates vary. Authors receive 1 copy of the issue.

The Doula

Michele Winkler, Editor, P.O. Box 71, Santa Cruz, CA 95063-0071   Phone/Fax: 408-464-9488

Profile: A thematic magazine covering pregnancy, childbirth, and early motherhood. Issued quarterly. Circ: 8,000. Trim size: 8.5x11. Self cover; 60 lb. recycled paper; spot color; saddle stitched. 40 pages. Subscription cost: $15. Sample copy cost: $4. Writer's guidelines and theme list available with SASE.

Focus and Tips: *The Doula* focuses on "mothering the mother" with information and inspiration on childbirth, breastfeeding, responsive parenting, homeschooling, and family-related topics. Looks specifically for first-person "mother to mother" stories, not parenting advice. There is no need to be an "expert"—writers should share their own experiences, joys, and sorrows, and write from the heart. Issues are thematic. Past themes include Beginnings and Endings, miscarriage, pregnancy, and post-partum; Family Relationships; and Natural Learning Rhythms in children.

Editorial Interests

Motherhood, childbirth, breast feeding, alternative schooling, mothering insights, family issues, environment, feminism, holistic and natural health, nutrition, relationships, and women's issues.

• *Nonfiction:* First-person, experiential pieces on mothering and related topics, 500–750 words. Reviews, 250–500 words. Hot Flashes, news bits on current family-related topics, 50–100 words.

• *Illustrations:* B/W photos and graphics.

Submission Policy: Send complete manuscript with cover letter and brief biography. Include SASE. Accepts photocopies, computer printouts, faxes, and Macintosh, PageMaker, MacWrite, or MS Word disks. Simultaneous submissions okay if noted. Reports in 1 month. If accepted, expect publication within 3–9 months.

Terms and Payment: One-time rights. No payment. Authors receive copies of the issue.

Advertising: Rates: B/W full-page, $675; half-page, $340; quarter-page, $170. One-time list rental available to earth- and family-friendly products. Contact Michele Winkler, 408-464-9488.

Dream International Quarterly

Tim Scott, Associate Editor, 4147 North Kedvale Avenue, Chicago, IL 60641   Phone: 312-794-0751

Profile: A publication dedicated to dreamwork. Established in 1980. Issued quarterly. Circ: 350. Trim size: 8.5x11. B/W; photocopied; stapled. 120 pages. Subscription cost: $30. Sample copy cost: $8. No writer's guidelines.

Focus and Tips: *Dream International Quarterly* emphasizes dream-related and dream-inspired fiction and nonfiction. Its audience is college-educated, intellectually inclined, and spiritual. Subscribers include libraries. Avoid dogmatic pieces that function to advance a particular ideological cause of any sort, including material specific to any one religion.

Editorial Interests

Dreams, channeling, cultural and ethnic concerns, magic, meditation, men's issues, metaphysics, mysticism, mythology, new age, occult, parapsychology, philosophy, psychic phenomenon, psychology, rebirthing, spirituality, and sexuality.

• *Fiction:* Short stories and genre fiction, 1,000–1,500 words. Short-short stories, 500–800 words. Book excerpts, 250 words. Poetry, 3–50 lines. Accepts drama, query first.

• *Nonfiction:* Dream accounts, 250–500 words. Features, articles, essays, personal experiences, and opinion pieces, 1,000–1,750 words. Reviews, 250 words. Filler, 100 words. Columns are assigned. Query for interviews and profiles.

Submission Policy: Query with outline. Include SASE. Accepts computer printouts. Simultaneous submissions okay. Reports in 1–2 months. If accepted, expect publication in 15 months.

Terms and Payment: First North American serial rights. No payment. Authors receive 1 copy of the issue.

Advertising: Rates: B/W full-page, $80. Contact Chuck Jones, 411 14th Street, No. N3, Ramona, CA 92065.

Dwelling Portably

Holly Davis, Co-editor, P.O. Box 190—WRS, Philomath, OR 97370

Profile: A newsletter for portable or mobile home dwellers. Published by Light Living Library. Established in 1980. Issued 3 times a year. Circ: 1,300. Trim size: 5.5x8.5. Self cover; stapled. 16 pages. Subscription cost: $3. Sample copy cost: $1. Writer's guidelines available with SASE.

Focus and Tips: *Dwelling Portably* offers how-to information for people living for long periods in portable homes such as tents, tepees, wickiups, vans, trailers, remote cabins, and boats. Seeks practical personal experience—"tell what you have done, how you did it, in what environment, for how long, and how well it worked." Avoid tourist guide pieces, environmental sermons, and outdoor sports.

Editorial Interests

Portable dwellings, low-cost shelters, camping, hiking, travel, cultural and ethnic issues, environment, health, lifestyle, natural health, nutrition, and parenting.

• *Nonfiction:* Articles, interviews, profiles, essays, personal experiences, and opinion pieces, 20–1,000 words. New items, 20–100 words. Plans for home-built shelters, 200–1,000 words. How-to tips, 20–400 words. Product reports, 20–200 words. Book and video reviews, 200–1,000 words, include quotes and paraphrasing.

Submission Policy: Query with writing samples or send complete manuscript with cover letter. Include SASE. Accepts photocopies and computer printouts. Simultaneous submissions okay. Reports in 2 months. If accepted, expect publication in 4 months.

Terms and Payment: One-time rights. Generally offers subscription in lieu of payment. Will pay $.01 per word on acceptance if requested. Authors receive 1–12 copies of the issue.

Advertising: Classified rates, $.25 per word.

Dynamic Life New Times

David Findlay, Editor, P.O. Box 6143, Clearwater, FL 34618-6143   Phone: 813-449-8964

Profile: A thematic new age magazine. Issued 6 times a year. Circ: 17,000. Trim size: 7.5x9.75. Self cover; newsprint; spot color; glued binding. 48 pages. Subscription cost: $8. Sample copy cost: $2. Writer's guidelines available with SASE.

Focus and Tips: *Dynamic Life New Times* is a holistic magazine dedicated to enhancing the union of body, mind, and spirit. Editorial has a self-help emphasis. Each issue focuses on one theme.

Editorial Interests

New age, holistic health, self-help, astrology, bodywork, channeling, crystals, cultural and ethnic issues, dreams, ecosystems, the environment, extraterrestrials, healing and health, natural health, inspiration, lifestyle, magic, meditation, metaphysics, mysticism, mythology, nutrition, parapsychology, philosophy, psychic phenomenon, psychology, rebirthing, recovery, relationships, seniors, spirituality, and yoga.

• *Nonfiction:* Theme-related articles, 650 words.

Submission Policy: Query for theme. Include SASE. Accepts photocopies, computer printouts, and Macintosh Word or PageMaker disks.

Terms and Payment: One-time rights. No payment. Offers a 25% discount on advertising in lieu of payment. Authors receive 1 copy of the issue.

Advertising: Rates: B/W full-page, $387. Four-color full-page, $464.40. Back cover, $600. Contact Dee Findlay, 813-449-8964.

E: The Environmental Magazine

Jim Motavalli, Managing Editor, 28 Knight Street, Norwalk, CT 06851   Phone: 203-854-5559, Fax: 203-866-0602

Profile: A resource of information on environmental issues. Published by Earth Action Network, Inc. Issued bimonthly. Circ: 50,000. Trim size: 8x11. Glossy color cover; 4-color; saddle stitched. 64 pages. Subscription cost: $20. Sample copy cost: $5. Writer's guidelines available with SASE.

Focus and Tips: *E Magazine* serves as a clearinghouse of news, information, and commentary on environmental issues for the benefit of the general public and in sufficient depth to involve dedicated environmentalists. Its goal is to inform those concerned about the environment and inspire them to take action. Write with a balanced tone; don't be strident or opinionated. Avoid scientific language or jargon.

Editorial Interests

Environmental issues and awareness.

• *Nonfiction:* Features, 2,400–4,000 words. Interviews and profiles, 2,000 words. News Items, 400–1,000 words. Reviews, 1,200 words. Departments include Environmentalist, 1,200 words; Food & Health, 1,200 words; and E-Notes, brief announcements of new books and publications, products and news, 50–100 words.

Submission Policy: Query with resume and clips. Include SASE. Accepts photocopies, computer printouts, and faxes. Simultaneous submissions okay. Reporting time varies.

Terms and Payment: First North American serial rights. Pays on publication. $.20 per word, but negotiable. No payment for E-Notes. Authors receives 1 copy of the issue, more upon request.

Advertising: Accepts advertising. Contact Alyssa Burger, Advertising Director, at 203-854-5559. List rental available. Contact Names in the News, 415-989-3350.

The Eagle

Richard Carlson, Editor, Box 579MO, Naugatuck, CT 06770-0579   Phone: 203-729-0035

Profile: A regional Native American publication. Published by Eagle Wing Press, Inc., a nonprofit American Indian corporation. Established in 1981. Issued bimonthly. Circ: 5,000. Trim size: Tabloid. Newsprint; folded. 28 pages. Subscription cost: $15. Sample copy cost: $2.50. Writer's guidelines available with SASE.

Focus and Tips: *The Eagle* concentrates on the positive aspects of Native American culture, presenting Native Americans as an important segment of American society past and present, practicing age-old traditions while participating fully in modern life. Focus is on the Native American communities of Connecticut, Rhode Island, Massachusetts, Vermont, New Hampshire, and Maine. Welcomes poetry. Also covers national and international Native American news. Avoid stereotyping.

Editorial Interests

Native American culture and arts, the environment, and social and world issues.

• *Poetry:* Up to 4 poems per submissions. No length restrictions.

• *Nonfiction:* Features, articles, interviews, profiles, essays, opinion pieces, and news items, 1,000–1,500 words. Book reviews and filler, 250–500 words.

Submission Policy: Query with outline, or send complete manuscript with cover letter. Include SASE. Accepts photocopies and computer printouts. Simultaneous submissions okay if noted. Reports in 2 months. Publication time varies.

Terms and Payment: One-time rights and reprint rights. No payment. Authors receive 5 copies of the issue.

Advertising: Rates: B/W full-page, $200. Contact Richard Carlson, 203-729-0035.

The Eagle's Cry

Wilma Paddock, Editor, P.O. Box 5110, Breckenridge, CO 80424   Phone: 303-453-6784, Fax: 303-453-0563

Profile: A publication of holistic experiences. Published by Sky Bright Enterprises. Established in 1988. Issued quarterly. Circ: 2,000. Trim size: 8.5x11. Self cover; B/W; saddle stitched. 16 pages. Subscription cost: $12. Sample copy cost: $3. No writer's guidelines.

Focus and Tips: *The Eagle's Cry* is dedicated to sharing holistic experiences, wisdom through growth, and educational knowledge to provide choices for life's direction. Open to all pieces that share holistic living and growth. Does not consider material that is political in nature or that is judgmental of people, ideas, or belief systems.

Editorial Interests

Holistic living, personal growth, astrology, bodywork, channeling, crystals, cultural and ethnic issues, dreams, ecosystems, the environment, extraterrestrials, feminism, folklore, gay and lesbian issues, healing, health, inspiration, juvenile and teen issues, lifestyle, magic, meditation, men's issues, metaphysics, mysticism, mythology, natural health, new age, nutrition, occult, parapsychology, parenting, philosophy, prayer, psychic phenomenon, psychology, rebirthing, recovery, relationships, self-help, seniors, spirituality, women's issues, and yoga.

• *Fiction:* Short stories and poetry. No length restrictions.

• *Nonfiction:* Articles, dreams, personal experiences, channeled material, and pieces of a holistic, healing, or wisdom orientation. No length restrictions.

Submission Policy: Send complete manuscript with cover letter. Include SASE. Accepts photocopies, computer printouts, faxes, and 3.5" or 5.25" disks. Simultaneous submissions okay. Reports in 3–6 months. If accepted, expect publication in 3 months.

Terms and Payment: No payment. Occasionally offers a free one-year subscription.

Earth's Daughters

Robin Willoughby, Co-editor, Box 41, Central Park Station, Buffalo, NY 14215-0041   Phone: 716-837-7778

Profile: A feminist arts journal. Established in 1971. Issued 3 times a year. Circ: 1,000. Trim size: varies. Heavy bond cover; B/W; perfect bound. Page count varies. Subscription cost: Individuals, $14; Libraries, $22. Sample copy cost: $5. Writer's guidelines available with SASE.

Focus and Tips: *Earth's Daughters* focuses on the experience and creative expression of women—in poetry, prose, and artwork. Looking for "incredibly good" poetry and prose. "We like to publish 'unknown' writers, but we require technical skill and artistic intensity." Avoid "Hallmark card" poetry and rhyming works. Stay within prescribed word limits.

Editorial Interests

Feminism, mysticism, mythology, new age, philosophy, and spirituality.

• *Fiction:* Short stories, short-short stories, drama, and genre fiction, up to 2,000 words. Poetry, 4 poems per submission.

• *Nonfiction:* Essays and personal experiences, 2,000 words.

• *Illustrations:* B/W artwork and photographs.

Submission Policy: Send complete manuscript with cover letter. Include SASE. Accepts photocopies and computer printouts. Simultaneous submissions okay if notified immediately upon acceptance elsewhere. Responds to queries in 1 month, to

manuscripts in 1–3 months. If accepted, expect publication in 6 months.
Terms and Payment: First North American serial rights. No payment. Authors receive 2 copies of the issue.

Earthwatch Oregon

Jane Haley, Editor, 027 SW Arthur Street, Portland, OR 97201   Phone: 503-222-1963, Fax: 503-222-1405

Profile: An environmental newsletter. Issued quarterly. Circ: 2,200. Trim size: 8.5x11. Stapled. 8 pages. Subscription cost: $40. Sample copy cost: Free. No writer's guidelines.
Focus and Tips: *Earthwatch Oregon* is a membership publication that focuses on environmental issues only. The newsletter is distributed to members, libraries, and policy makers.
Editorial Interests
Environmental issues.
• *Nonfiction:* Features, 1,400 words. Articles, 700–1,200 words. Interviews and profiles, 1,200–1,400 words. Opinion pieces, 800 words. News items, 400–800 words. Book reviews, 400–500 words. Columns: Eco-tips, 400–500 words.
Submission Policy: Call first for specific interests. Accepts photocopies, computer printouts, faxes, and WordPerfect disks. Simultaneous submissions okay. Reports in 1 month. If accepted, expect publication in 3 months.
Terms and Payment: All rights. Pays on publication. Authors receive 4 copies of the issue.
Advertising: List rental available.
Other Interests: Sponsors an environmental conference each year. For more information, contact Jane Haley, 503-222-1963.

Eco-Notes Magazine

Ms. P. J. Grimes, Publisher/Editor, P.O. Box 230542, Encinitas, CA 92023-0542   Phone/Fax: 619-632-0770

Profile: A newsletter of environmental education. Published by Imagination Station Communications. Issued quarterly. Circ: 1,500. Trim size: 8.5x11. 2-color; recycled paper; folded. 4 pages. Subscription cost: $10. Sample copy cost: $1. Writer's guidelines available with SASE.
Focus and Tips: *Eco-Notes Magazine* is an upbeat, community and environmental education publication. It welcomes unsolicited material, preferably self-help, positive change articles and tips. "Keep it short and to the point."
Editorial Interests
The environment, music, natural health, new age, nutrition, parenting, politics, self-help, social and world issues, women's issues, and yoga.
• *Nonfiction:* Open to all material, especially self-help articles, tips, resources, and event coverage, as well as reviews of Earth friendly products, music, videos, and books. No length restrictions.
• *Illustrations:* 5x7 or smaller B/W prints. Artwork with environmentally conscious themes.
Submission Policy: Query with outline, writing samples, resume, and clips. Do not send originals, submissions are not returned. Accepts computer printouts, computer disks, and faxes. No simultaneous submissions.
Terms and Payment: No payment. Offers advertising space in lieu of payment. Authors receive 2 copies of the issue.
Advertising: Accepts advertising. Contact P. J. Grimes, 619-632-0770.

The Edge

Lynn LaFroth, Editor, 318 South Fourth Street, Stillwater, MN 55082   Phone: 612-430-9646, Fax: 612-430-0517

Profile: A thematic, regional tabloid on alternative spirituality and natural health care. Published by LEAP Publications. Issued monthly. Circ: 20,000. Trim size: Tabloid. Newsprint; folded. 20–32 pages. Subscription cost: $18.50. Sample copy cost: $1.50. Writer's guidelines available with SASE.
Focus and Tips: *The Edge* publishes eclectic information about living spiritually in the '90s. Readers are primarily Midwest residents. Issues are thematic; monthly themes are listed in the magazine. Past themes include Parenting in the '90s, Earth Changes, What is Reality?, and Dreams, Myths, Storytelling, Ancients, and Ancestors. Prefers a feature-syle format, which includes a more informal type of journalism about a specific person, place, event, or idea.
Editorial Interests
Metaphysics, spirituality, self-empowerment, self-actualization, health and healing, spiritual art and dance, and related new age topics. Not interested in articles on magic, occult, politics, or witches.
• *Nonfiction:* All material must relate to monthly theme. Features, 600–850 words. Filler and news items, 400 words.
• *Photos:* Welcomes "action photos" that accompany articles.
Submission Policy: Call or write for monthly theme list. Query first with outline and 2–3 sentence biography. Include SASE. No unsolicited manuscripts. Accepts PC-DOS, ASCII, or WordPerfect 5.1 disks. Reporting time varies. If accepted, expect publication in 6 weeks.
Terms and Payment: One-time rights. No payment. Authors receive 1 copy of the issue.
Advertising: Accepts advertising, rates vary. Contact Gary Bechman, 612-427-7979.

Electronic Green Journal

Maria A. Jankowska, General Editor, University of Idaho Library, Moscow, ID 83844-2360
Phone: 208-885-6631, Fax: 208-885-6817

Profile: A professional environmental journal. Published by the University of Idaho Library. Issued irregularly. Circ: N/A. Subscription cost: Free. Sample copy cost: Free. Writer's guidelines available with SASE.

Focus and Tips: *Electronic Green Journal* is a professional refereed publication devoted to disseminating information concerning sources on international environmental topics. The journal serves as an educational environmental resource and includes both practical and scholarly articles.

Editorial Interests

The environment.

• *Nonfiction:* Articles, opinion pieces, and news items. No length restrictions.

Submission Policy: Query to E-mail address majanko@uidaho.edu. No simultaneous submissions. Reports in 2 months. If accepted, expect publication in 5 months.

Terms and Payment: All rights. No payment.

Advertising: Accepts advertising. Contact Maria Jankowska.

Encore Magazine

Joyce Cupps, Publisher/Editor, P.O. Box 1599, Mariposa, CA 95338   Phone: 209-966-1180, Fax: 209-745-0915

Profile: A magazine for women over forty. Issued 5 times a year. Circ: 1,000. Trim size: 8.5x11. B/W; saddled stitched. 40–48 pages. Subscription cost: $20. Sample copy cost: $5. Writer's guidelines available with SASE.

Focus and Tips: *Encore Magazine* celebrates the woman of age—as the crone, elder, matriarch, outrageous old woman, and grandmother—and her power and wisdom as she discovers her evolving purpose in the third phase of her life. It seeks to unite all older women, regardless of race, religion, philosophy, sexual orientation, education, or feminist commitment through the celebration of their similarities. Emphasis is given to dialogue among readers as they share experiences; material that inspires, educates, or informs; and material that explores possibilities and pathways for woman's spiritual and personal growth. Avoid "objective, advice-giving points of view."

Editorial Interests

Women of age, dreams, feminism, healing, lifestyle, meditation, mysticism, new age, spirituality, and women's issues.

• *Fiction:* Short-short stories, 500–1,500 words. Book excerpts, up to 2,000 words. Poetry, 50 lines.

• *Nonfiction:* Features, articles, interviews, profiles, essays, personal experiences, opinion pieces, and news, up to 4,000 words. Reviews, 250–500 words. Departments include Menopause and Death and Dying, 1,000 words. Accepts filler.

• *Illustrations:* Photos of older women accompanied by a 30-word biography about the subject. Line art and humorous cartoons are welcome.

Submission Policy: Query first. Include SASE. Accepts photocopies, computer printouts, and ASCII, DOS and Windows WordPerfect, and MS Word for Windows disks. Simultaneous submissions okay. Reports in 1 month. If accepted, expect publication within 1–6 months.

Terms and Payment: One-time rights. Offers advertising exchange in lieu of payment. Authors receive 1–4 copies of the issue.

Advertising: Rates: B/W full-page, $250; half-page, $130. Contact Joyce Cupps, 209-966-1180.

Other Interests: Sponsors a Poetry Contest in the Fall and an Essay Contest in the Spring. Entries must be on subjects related to women of age. Send SASE for guidelines.

Endless Possibilities

Sheri Olson, Editor, P.O. Box 8284, Long Beach, CA 90808   Phone: 310-930-0296

Profile: A self-improvement newsletter. Issued quarterly. Circ: 500. Trim size: 8.5x11. Glossy paper; folded. 4–8 pages. Subscription cost: $5. Sample copy cost: $1. Writer's guidelines available with SASE.

Focus and Tips: *Endless Possibilities* is geared toward helping people think of the positive things in life. Read by those who are in recovery or interested in self-help. It considers articles on self-improvement, how the mind affects the body, the power of positive self-talk, and how to view life in a positive way. Especially interested in pieces for its Life Has Endless Possibilities column, a first-person account about how an ordinary or not-so-ordinary event changed the author's life in a physical, mental, or spiritual way. Write for the general public and do not use technical jargon or trade lingo. Avoid preaching, articles with religious references, UFOs, channeling, and psychic phenomenon.

Editorial Interests

Positive thinking, self-help, recovery, feminism, health, inspiration, meditation, nutrition, psychology, relationships, spirituality, and women's issues.

• *Nonfiction:* Self-help and inspirational articles, 1,000–1,500 words. Interviews with and profiles of people who help others,

1,000–1,500 words. Life Has Endless Possibilities column, 300–500 words. Short affirmations geared toward season.

Submission Policy: Send complete manuscript with cover letter. Include SASE. Accepts photocopies, computer printouts, and IBM AmiPro or PageMaker disks. Simultaneous submissions okay. Reports in 1 month. If accepted, expect publication in 1–12 months.

Terms and Payment: One-time rights. Offers products in lieu of payment. Authors receive 10 copies of the issue.

Advertising: Rates: B/W 4.5x2, $30; 2x5, $25; 2x2, $15; business card, $20. Full-page flyer inserts, $50 (advertiser supplies flyers). Contact Sheri Olson, 310-930-0296.

Other Interests: Offers daily workshops on self-esteem, body image, and goal setting at various locations. For more information, contact Sheri Olson, 310-930-0296.

Energy Times

Gerard McIntee, Editor, 548 Broad Hollow Road, Melville, NY 11747-9806   Phone: 516-777-7773, Fax: 516-293-0349

Profile: A health food magazine. Issued bimonthly. Circ: 575,000. Trim size: 8x10.75. Saddle stitched. 76 pages. Subscription cost: $8.95. Sample copy cost: Free. Writer's guidelines available with SASE.

Focus and Tips: *Energy Times* is a database-driven publication geared toward health food consumers. All articles must be documented.

Editorial Interests

Health foods, vitamins, herbs, supplements, organic foods, health, and nutrition.

• *Nonfiction:* Features, articles, interviews, profiles, personal experiences, and news, 2,000–2,500 words. Reviews, 2,500 words.

Submission Policy: Query first with outline. Include SASE. Accepts computer printouts, faxes, and IBM disks. Simultaneous submissions okay. Reports in 1 month. If accepted, expect publication in 2 months.

Terms and Payment: All rights. Pays on publication. Authors receive 2 copies of the issue.

Advertising: Rates: B/W full-page, $7,440; 2-color full-page, $8,556; 4-color full-page, $9,671. Contact Gerard McIntee, 516-777-7773.

Ethereal Dances

Sara Hyatt Boyd, Editor, 509 Enterprise Drive, Rohnert Park, CA 94928

Profile: A compilation of fiction, poetry, and artwork. Published by Scream Press. Issued 3 times a year. Circ: 200. Trim size: 5.5x8.5. 60 lb. cover; 20 lb. stock; B/W; saddle stitched. 20–24 pages. Subscription cost: $5. Sample copy cost: $2. Writer's guidelines available with SASE.

Focus and Tips: *Ethereal Dances* is "a journal featuring poets, writers, and artists in an artistically simple way." Advises writers to be simple, honest, and provide a range of poetry for consideration. No pornography, gore, or "war, beer, or prostitute" stories. "Don't send form letters or lists of 300 publication credits!"

Editorial Interests

Fiction, poetry, romantic fantasy, and relationships.

• *Fiction:* Short stories, up to 1,000 words. Romantic poetry, up to 30 lines.

Submission Policy: Send complete manuscript or 3–6 poems with cover letter. Include SASE. Accepts photocopies and computer printouts. No simultaneous submissions. Responds to queries in 2 weeks, to manuscripts in 1 month. If accepted, expect publication in 2–8 months.

Terms and Payment: One-time rights. No payment. Authors receive 2 copies of the issue.

Advertising: Rates: B/W 5x4, $10. Contact Sara Hyatt Boyd.

The Evergreen Chronicles

Susan Raffo, Managing Editor, P.O. Box 8939, Minneapolis, MN 55408-0939   Phone: 612-724-0559

Profile: A journal of gay and lesbian literature. Issued 3 times a year. Circ: 1,800. Trim size: 5.5x8.5. Heavy bond 2-color cover; B/W inside; perfect bound. 125 pages. Subscription cost: $15. Sample copy cost: $8. Writer's guidelines available with SASE.

Focus and Tips: *The Evergreen Chronicles* is dedicated to exploring gay and lesbian arts and cultures through poetry, nonfiction, autobiography, short stories, and photography. While rooted in the Midwest, it draws its talents from a national audience of lesbian and gay writers and artists. Looks for works with deep sensitivity to the gay/lesbian experience. Review a sample copy for style and content.

Editorial Interests

Gay and lesbian concerns, cultural and ethnic issues, feminism, lifestyle, men's issues, politics, social and world issues, and women's issues.

• *Fiction:* Short stories, drama, book excerpts, and genre fiction, up to 25 typed, double-spaced pages. Poetry, up to 10 poems per submission.

• *Nonfiction:* Features, essays, personal experiences, and opinion pieces, up to 25 typed, double-spaced pages. Interviews and profiles, up to 15 typed, double-spaced pages. Reviews, up to 5 typed, double-spaced pages.
• *Illustrations:* 8x10 B/W glossy photos or B/W artwork. Do not submit originals.
Submission Policy: Send 4 copies of complete manuscript with cover letter and clips. Include SASE. Accepts photocopies and computer printouts. Responds to queries in 3–4 weeks, to manuscripts 6 weeks after deadline. If accepted, expect publication in 3 months.
Terms and Payment: One-time rights. Pays on publication. $50 per piece. Authors receive 1 copy of the issue.
Advertising: Rates: B/W full-page, $75. Contact Susan Raffo, 612-724-0559.
Other Interests: Sponsors a Novella Contest for novellas with gay/lesbian theme. Contact editor for guidelines.

Exceptional Human Experience

Rhea White, Editor, Two Plane Tree Lane, Dix Hills, NY 11746   Phone/Fax: 516-271-1243

Profile: A journal of psychic phenomenon. Issued twice a year. Circ: 350. Trim size: 8.5x11. Perfect bound. 150 pages. Subscription cost: $30. Sample copy cost: $15. Writer's guidelines available with SASE.
Focus and Tips: *Exceptional Human Experience* is a scholarly and mainstream journal of unusual or psychic human experience. It publishes accounts of experiences with commentary as well as the methodology and theories about the study of psychic experiences. Writers are encouraged to speak personally and from the heart, rather than from the head. "Look for feelings related to the the experience and how it was life-changing in both positive and negative ways." Avoid anything that is "too chatty."
Editorial Interests
Psychic phenomenon, near-death experiences, out-of-body experiences, unorthodox healings, astrology, channeling, dreams, extraterrestrials, feminism, folklore, inspiration, magic, meditation, mysticism, mythology, new age, parapsychology, philosophy, psychology, recovery, self-help, social and world issues, spirituality, and women's issues.
• *Nonfiction:* Features, articles, interviews, profiles, essays, personal experiences, opinion pieces, news items, and reviews. No length restrictions.
Submission Policy: Send complete manuscript with cover letter and article abstract. Include SASE. Accepts photocopies, computer printouts, and IBM-compatible disks. No simultaneous submissions. Reports in 1 month. If accepted, expect publication in 1–2 years.
Terms and Payment: All rights. No payment. Authors receive 1 copy of the issue.

Exceptional Parent

Kim Schive, Assistant Editor, 209 Harvard Street, Suite 303, Brookline, MA 02146   Phone: 617-730-5800, Fax: 617-730-8742

Profile: A magazine for parents of children with disabilities. Established in 1971. Issued monthly. Circ: 60,000. Trim size: 8.5x11. Glossy color cover; 4-color; saddle stitched. 68 pages. Subscription cost: $24. Sample copy cost: $6. Writer's guidelines available with SASE.
Focus and Tips: *Exceptional Parent* purposes to reach out to parents of children with disabilities and special health care needs and to empower parents by providing practical information and emotional support.
Editorial Interests
Disability, parenting, men's issues, and psychology.
• *Nonfiction:* Articles, 1,200 words.
Submission Policy: Query with outline. Include SASE. Accepts computer printouts, faxes, and Macintosh disks with hard copy. No simultaneous submissions. Reports in 6 months. Publication time varies.
Terms and Payment: All rights. Pays on publication. $25 per piece. Authors receive 10 copies of the issue.
Advertising: Rates: 4-color full-page, $3,500. Contact Kerry Cannon, 1-800-EPARENT. List rental available. Contact Mike Wilson, 1-800-445-2089.

Explanasian

Maria Antenorcruz and Aileen Cho, Coeditors, 296 Elizabeth Street, Second Floor, New York, NY 10012   Phone: 212-228-6718

Profile: A newsletter of the literary field. Published by the Asian American Writer's Workshop. Issued 3 times a year. Circ: 5,000. Trim size: 8.5x11. 16 pages. Stapled. Subscription cost: $20. Sample copy cost: $5.
Focus and Tips: *Explanasian* offers book reviews and personality profiles of the writing and writers of Asian American literature. Looks for in-depth material that will help writers grow artistically and professionally and inform them of the issues in the publishing and literary fields.
Editorial Interests
Asian American literature, cultural and ethnic concerns, feminism, folklore, gay and lesbian issues, lifestyle, men's issues, mythology, politics, relationships, religion, social and world issues, spirituality, and women's issues.

• *Nonfiction:* Features, interviews, profiles, opinion pieces, news and announcements, and book reviews, 2,500 words.
Submission Policy: Query with outline. Include SASE. Accepts photocopies and computer printouts. Simultaneous submissions okay if noted. Reports in 2 months. If accepted, expect publication in 4 months.
Terms and Payment: First North American serial rights. Pays on publication. Offers a varied per page rate. Authors receive 1 copy of the issue.
Advertising: Rates: B/W full-page, $150. List rental available. Contact Douglas Lee, Business Manager, 212-228-6718.
Other Interests: Sponsors a variety of other literary activities. Contact Curtis Chin, Managing Director, 212-228-6718.

Expressions

Sefra Kobrin Pitzele, Editor-in-Chief, P.O. Box 16294, St. Paul, MN 55116-0294   Phone: 612-451-1208, Fax: 612-559-1209

Profile: A nonprofit literary journal by people with disabilities and ongoing health problems. Published by Serendipity Press. Issued 2 times a year. Circ: 500. Trim size: 5.5x8.5. Glossy cover; B/W; perfect bound. 62–78 pages. Subscription cost: $10. Sample copy cost: $6. Writer's guidelines available with SASE.
Focus and Tips: *Expressions* features writers and artisans who may have limited energy due to disabilities or chronic illness. It aims to be a voice for many who have creative gifts to share. While contributors are chronically ill or disabled, submissions need not pertain to medical problems. *Expressions* is open to a variety of topics.
Editorial Interests
Poetry, fiction, essays, and art on any topic by writers with disabilities or chronic illnesses.
• *Fiction:* Short stories, genre fiction and memoirs, up to 1,500 words. Short-short stories, up to 1,000 words. Poetry, up to 60 lines. Accepts drama, query first.
• *Nonfiction:* Features, articles, essays, and personal experiences, up to 1,500 words. Reviews of books pertaining to illness and disability, 750 words.
• *Illustrations:* B/W artwork; color prints or reproducible slides.
Submission Policy: $2 reading per item submitted. For pieces under 1,500 words, send complete manuscript with short biography mentioning author's illness or disability. Query first for longer pieces and drama. Include SASE. Accepts photocopies and computer printouts. Simultaneous submissions okay if noted. Reports in 2 weeks. If accepted, expect publication within 2–4 months.
Terms and Payment: One-time rights. No payment. Authors receive 2 copies of the issue.
Advertising: Rates: B/W full-page, $120; half-page $60; quarter-page, $30. List rental available; $50 per 200 names. Contact Sefra Kobrin Pitzele, 612-451-1208.
Other Interests: Sponsors two contests: Serendipity Press Poetry Contest, Spring issue—open to poems up to 60 lines; Serendipity Press Fiction Contest, Fall issue—open to fiction up to 1,700 words. Winners receive $25. For more information, contact editor.

The Faithist Journal

K. Kares, Editor, P.O. Box 4670, Hualapai, AZ 86412

Profile: A new age, inspirational magazine. Published by Kosmon Publishing, Inc. Issued bimonthly. Circ: 3,000. Trim size: 5.5x8.5. B/W; 20 lb. paper; stapled. 57 pages. Subscription cost: $15. Sample copy cost: $1.50. Writer's guidelines available with SASE.
Focus and Tips: *The Faithist Journal* publishes material promoting world peace and liberty, with respect for all living creatures through the worship of the Creator of the Universe. Seeks inspirational material on life-after-death, vegetarianism, and kindness to all. Holds that "abortion is wrong, pacifism is right, and the way that hurts no one is the best." Avoid political pieces and articles about reincarnation unless to refute it.
Editorial Interests
New age, astrology, bodywork, channeling, crystals, dreams, the environment, extraterrestrials, folklore, healing, health, holistic health, inspiration, magic, meditation, metaphysics, mysticism, natural health, nutrition, occult, parapsychology, parenting, philosophy, prayer, psychic phenomenon, psychology, recovery, relationships, self-help, seniors, and spirituality.
• *Nonfiction:* Features and articles, 3–4 typed, double-spaced pages.
Submission Policy: Currently not accepting submissions. Query before sending manuscripts. Include SASE.
Terms and Payment: One-time rights. No payment. Authors receive up to 1–2 copies of the issue if requested.

Familiars

Winter Wren, Editor/Publisher, P.O. Box 247, Normal, IL 61761   Phone: 309-888-4689

Profile: A new age publication. Published by Mystic Link. Issued quarterly. Circ: 1,000. Trim size: 8.5x11. Stapled. 44–52 pages. Subscription cost: $22. Sample copy cost: $6.75. Writer's guidelines available with SASE.
Focus and Tips: *Familiars* is an educational and entertaining publication for pagans of all ages, including a children's section.

It invites writers to send "a good, readable piece, and we'll work with you." Avoid purposeful back-biting and negativity.

Editorial Interests

Paganism, new age, astrology, bodywork, channeling, crystals, cultural and ethnic issues, dreams ecosystems, the environment, feminism, folklore, gay and lesbian issues, healing, holistic health, juvenile and teen issues, magic, meditation, men's issues, metaphysics, mysticism, mythology, natural health, occult, parapsychology, parenting, philosophy, politics, psychic phenomenon, rebirthing, recovery, relationships, self-help, seniors, social and world issues, spirituality, witches, and women's issues.

• *Fiction:* Legends, pagan tales, children's tales and myths, ritual drama, divinational stories, poetry, and book excerpts. No length restrictions.

• *Nonfiction:* In-depth articles and features, retold myths, interviews with and profiles of pagan personalities, essays on current pagan events, personal experiences, Readers Forum opinion pieces, news of interest to pagans, recipes, children's articles, and book, music, and tarot reviews. Columns include Herbal Forum. No length restrictions.

Submission Policy: Send complete manuscript with cover letter. Include SASE. Accepts photocopies and computer printouts. Simultaneous submissions okay. Reports in 6 weeks. If accepted, expect publication in 3 months.

Terms and Payment: One-time rights. No payment. Authors receive 3 copies of the issue.

Advertising: Rates: B/W full-page, $40; 4-color full-page, $100. Contact Winter Wren, 309-888-4689.

Other Interests: Planning to hold an annual Pagan Yule Celebration contest. First deadline is August 1, 1995. No length restrictions. For more information, contact Winter Wren, 309-888-4689.

Family Earth

Denise Weldon-Siviy, Managing Editor, 129 West Lincoln Avenue, Gettysburg, PA 17325

Profile: A family magazine of environmental concerns. Published by Weldon-Siviy Consulting. Issued annually. Circ: 400. Trim size: 6x8.5. Folded; stapled. 28–32 pages. Subscription cost: $3. Sample copy cost: $3. Writer's guidelines available with SASE.

Focus and Tips: *Family Earth* focuses on environmental issues relevant to families with small children. Author should review a sample before submitting material. Not interested in articles that demean working mothers or are excessively religious.

Editorial Interests

Family, environment, parenting, ecosystems, and world issues.

• *Poetry:* Open to all styles. Prefers shorter poems.

• *Nonfiction:* Features, up to 1,000 words. Articles, 300–500 words. Essays and opinion pieces, 500 words. News items, to 800 words. Filler, puzzles and short humor, 50–300 words. Accepts book and magazine reviews.

• *Illustrations:* B/W line art and cartoons.

Submission Policy: Send complete manuscript with cover letter. Include SASE. Accepts photocopies and computer printouts. Simultaneous submissions okay. Reports in 1 month. If accepted, expect publication within 6–8 months.

Terms and Payment: One-time rights. Pays on acceptance. Articles, $2–$20. Poems, $1–$3. Filler, $1–$3. Authors receive 1 copy of the issue.

Advertising: Accepts classified advertising. $5 flat rate. Contact Denise Weldon-Siviy.

Family Life Educator

Kay Clark, Editor, P.O. Box 1830, Santa Cruz, CA 95061-1830   Phone: 408-438-4060, Fax: 408-438-4080

Profile: A magazine for health and education professionals. Published by ETR Associates. Issued quarterly. Circ: 4,000. Trim size: 8.5x11. Glossy color cover; B/W inside; saddle stitched. 40 pages. Subscription cost: $35. Writer's guidelines available.

Focus and Tips: *Family Life Educator* is an educational journal for middle and secondary school teachers and professionals who work with adolescents. Articles should be informative or be directly applicable to classroom use. Recent features have focused on eating disorders/body image, masturbation, teen fathers, sexuality education for high-risk adolescents, and teaching about sexual orientation. "We are an informative resource, not a research journal." Use clean language, free of jargon.

Editorial Interests

Middle and secondary school education and adolescent and teen issues.

• *Nonfiction:* Articles with classroom application, up to 4,000 words. News section includes information about successful and innovative programs in all types of learning environments, research reports, and updates on laws and public policy, up to 2,000 words. Teaching Tools, classroom and teaching ideas with information that is pertinent to successful adaptation.

Submission Policy: Send 2 copies of the complete manuscript with short author biography and bibliography if applicable. Include SASE. Prefers computer disk submissions with hard copy. Specify the software program used. No simultaneous submissions. Reports in 3 months.

Terms and Payment: All rights. Authors may request reprint rights.

Advertising: List rental available. Contact Melanie Oesterheld, 408-438-4060.

Farm Family America

George Ashfield, Editor, 190 Fifth Street East, Suite 121, St. Paul, MN 55101   Phone: 612-292-1747

Profile: A lifestyle magazine. Published by Fieldhagan Publishing. Issued 5 times a year. Circ: N/A. Trim size: 8x10.75. Saddled stitched. Page count varies. Subscription cost: N/A. Sample copy cost: N/A. Writers guidelines available with SASE.
Focus and Tips: *Farm Family America* is a publication for farm families, but not related to farming. Its seeks lifestyle pieces and articles on travel in the United States. Review guidelines before submitting material. Avoid fiction and first-person viewpoints.
Editorial Interests
Travel and lifestyle.
• *Nonfiction:* Features, articles, interviews, profiles, essays, personal experiences, opinion pieces, news, reviews, and filler, 1,200–1,500 words.
Submission Policy: Query with outline. Include SASE. Accepts photocopies and computer printouts. Simultaneous submissions okay. Reports in 1 month. If accepted, expect publication in up to 3 months.
Terms and Payment: First North American serial rights. Pays on publication. Authors receive 3 copies of the issue.

Farm and Ranch Living

Nick Pabst, Editor, 5400 South 60th Street, Greendale, WI 53129   Phone: 414-423-0100

Profile: A magazine dedicated to farming. Published by Reiman Publications. Issued 6 times a year. Circ: N/A. Trim size: 8.5x11. Saddle stitched. Subscription cost: $12.98. Sample copy cost: $2. Writer's guidelines available with SASE.
Focus and Tips: *Farm and Ranch Living* is distributed to farm families around the country. It prefers human-interest stories about farming that are "folksy and heartwarming." Audience is primarily seniors.
Editorial Interests
Farming and ranching.
• *Fiction:* Short stories, drama, books excerpts, genre fiction, and poetry, 1,500 words.
• *Nonfiction:* Features, articles, interviews, profiles, essays, personal experiences, opinion pieces, news, reviews, and filler, 1,500 words.
• *Illustrations:* Welcomes photos.
Submission Policy: Query with outline or send complete manuscript with cover letter and accompanying photos. Include SASE. Accepts photocopies and computer printouts. Simultaneous submissions okay. Reports in several months. If accepted, expect publication in up to 1 year.
Terms and Payment: One-time rights. Pays on publication. Rates vary. Authors receive 1 copy of the issue.
Advertising: List rental available. Contact Circulation Department, 414-423-0100.

Fate Magazine

Terry O'Neill, Editor, 84 South Wabasha, St. Paul, MN 55164   Phone: 612-291-1970, Fax: 612-291-1908

Profile: A publication of unusual phenomenon. Established in 1945. Issued monthly. Circ: 100,000. Trim size: 8.5x11. Glossy color cover; B/W inside; saddle stitched. 80 pages. Subscription cost: $21.50. Sample copy cost: $2.95. Writer's guidelines available with SASE.
Focus and Tips: *Fate Magazine* publishes fact-based true reports of "the strange and unknown." First-person accounts of unusual occurrences told in a straight, journalistic style are more likely to be accepted. Most of the material it publishes is unsolicited from first-time authors based on their true experiences. Articles should be lively, informative, play up the wonder of the subject matter, and develop practical benefits. Move beyond superficiality to a serious but popular presentation of the subject. Avoid dramatic or wordy approaches.
Editorial Interests
Unusual phenomenon, psychic phenomenon, extraterrestrials and UFOs, ghosts, near-death experiences, healing, spirituality, astrology, dreams, mysticism, mythology, and folklore.
• *Nonfiction:* True first-person accounts of unusual experiences. Full-length features, up to 5,000 words. Shorter pieces, 500–1,500 words. Filler, up to 500 words.
• *Illustrations:* Color or B/W prints to accompany article.
Submission Policy: Prefers receiving a complete manuscript with cover letter. Accepts a query with outline. Include SASE. Accepts photocopies, computer printouts, and Macintosh or IBM-compatible disks. No simultaneous submissions. Reports in 2 months. If accepted, expect publication in 2–3 months.
Terms and Payment: All rights. Pays up to 2 months after publication. Articles, $.10 per word. Photos, $10 each. Authors receive 3 copies of the issue.
Advertising: Rates: B/W full-page, $1,865. List rental available. Contact Amethyst MacGregor.

FEMALE Forum

Martha M. Bullen, Co-editor-in-Chief, P.O. Box 31, Elmhurst, IL 60126   Phone: 408-941-3551

Profile: A membership newsletter advocating women. Published by the nonprofit FEMALE, Formerly Employed Mothers at the Leading Edge. Issued 11 times per year. Circ: 2,500. Trim size: 8.5x11. Stapled. 8 pages. Subscription cost: $20 membership. Sample copy cost: $1. No writer's guidelines.

Focus and Tips: *FEMALE Forum* and its sponsoring organization support women who choose alternative to working out of the home while raising children. It looks for original pieces on the joys and trials of at-home parenting, personal growth while at home, legislative news affecting families, and pieces on how to combine some work with at-home motherhood. Focus on mothers' concerns, not on child development. Avoid judgmental pieces that blame mothers who work outside of the home or articles on "mommy wars."

Editorial Interests

At-home mothering, alternatives to out-of-the-home full-time work, family issues, lifestyle, parenting, and women's issues.

• *Nonfiction:* Features by at-home mothers, parenting articles, interviews with or profiles of authors or at-home mothers in the news, essays on at-home parenting issues, personal experiences, opinion pieces, news items, and relevant books reviews, 500–1,500 words. Departments and columns include Work & Family, Creative Ways to Work, News Briefs, Book Reviews, and On the Homefront.

Submission Policy: Query with writing samples or send complete manuscript with cover letter. Include SASE. Accepts photocopies and computer printouts. Simultaneous submissions okay. Responds to queries in 1–2 months, to manuscripts in 2–3 months. If accepted, expect publication in 3–6 months.

Terms and Payment: One-time rights. No payment. Authors receive up to 2 copies of the issue.

Other Interests: Sponsors an annual FEMALE Forum Writing/Art Contest. Categories include essays and personal experiences, humor, and cartoons and illustrations. Send an SASE to FEMALE Forum for guidelines.

Final Frontier

Leonard David, Editor, P.O. Box 15451, Washington, DC 20003-0451   Phone: 202-546-0363, Fax: 202-546-0132

Profile: A publication for those interested in outer space. Issued bimonthly. Circ: 87,000. Writer's guidelines available with SASE.

Focus and Tips: *Final Frontier* is devoted to space science, space technology, and the search for extraterrestrial life. Not interested in science fiction.

Editorial Interests

Extraterrestrials, space science, and space technology.

• *Nonfiction:* Features, 1,800–2,000 words. Departments include Notes from Earth.

• *Illustrations:* Accepts photos, illustrations, and cartoons.

Submission Policy: Query first with outline, writing samples, and author biography. Include SASE. Accepts faxes. No simultaneous submissions.

Terms and Payment: All rights for one year. Pays 30 days after publication. Features, $550–$750.

The Fire Fly and Fire Fly, Jr.

Jane Kirby, Editor, P.O. Box 133, Angle Inlet, MN 56711   Phone: 612-454-1317

Profile: An alternative family newsletter. Published by Fire Fly News. Issued bimonthly. Circ: 250. Trim size: 8.5x11. Photocopied; stapled. 8–12 pages. Subscription cost: $10. Sample copy cost: $2. No writer's guidelines.

Focus and Tips: *The Fire Fly* is a "leftist," anti-imperialist, environmental newsletter centered around family-related issues. Its companion publication, *Fire Fly, Jr.,* has the same slant but is written for children. Both seek concise, heart-felt articles and are open to a variety of subjects.

Editorial Interests

Family, parenting, home birth, breastfeeding, cultural and ethnic issues, ecosystems, the environment, feminism, juvenile and teen issues, lifestyle, natural health, politics, social and world issues, and women's issues.

• *Nonfiction:* Considers features, articles, interviews, profiles, essays, personal experiences, opinion, and news, 1,500 words.

Submission Policy: Send complete manuscript with cover letter and author biography. Include SASE. Accepts photocopies, computer printouts, and Macintosh Word disks. Simultaneous submissions okay. Reports in 2 weeks. If accepted, expect publication in 8–12 weeks.

Terms and Payment: No payment. Authors receive copies of the issue as requested.

Advertising: Rates: B/W full-page, $150. Contact Jane Kirby, 612-454-1317.

FireHeart

Editor, P.O. Box 365, Medford, MA 02155   Phone: 617-395-1023, Fax: 617-396-5066

Profile: A journal of magic and spiritual transformation. Published by The EarthSpirit Community, a nonprofit national network of Pagan and other Earth-centered groups. Issued annually. Circ: 6,000–7,000. Trim size: 8.5x11. Glossy color cover; B/W inside; perfect bound. 96 pages. Subscription cost: $6. Sample copy cost: $6.

Focus and Tips: *FireHeart* explores the spiritual process of transformation that brings people into contact with the mystery and wonder of creation. It seeks in-depth thought and research into the connections among people of different paths among all forms of life and between humanity and the Earth. Do not submit surface introductions or promotional materials.

Editorial Interests

Spirituality, Paganism, shamanism, Celtic culture, alternative relationships, astrology, bodywork, dreams, ecosystems, extraterrestrials, folklore, gay and lesbian spirituality, healing, magic, meditation, men's issues, metaphysics, mysticism, mythology, occult, philosophy, psychic phenomenon, recovery, witches, and women's issues.

• *Fiction:* Magical fiction, no length restrictions.

• *Nonfiction:* Features, in-depth articles, and book and music reviews, no length restrictions. Seeks songs for 20-voice chorus. Assigns interviews and profiles.

• *Illustrations:* B/W line drawings, photos, and any artwork reproducible in B/W.

Submission Policy: Prefers complete manuscript with cover letter and author biography stating qualifications. Accepts a query with outline and author biography. Include SASE. Accepts photocopies, computer printouts, and IBM Microsoft Word and ASCII disks. No simultaneous submissions. Reports in 2–3 months. Publication time varies.

Terms and Payment: Authors retain rights. No payment. Offers byline and author biography. Authors receive 1 copy of the issue.

Advertising: Accepts B/W ads. Contact Eric Leventhal, 617-395-1023.

Other Interests: Affiliated with The EarthSpirit Community, Deirdre Pulgrem Arthen and Andras Corban Arthen, Directors, 617-395-1023. Sponsors Rites of Spring Memorial Weekend, a 6-day Pagan celebration and Twilight Covening, a magical intensive weekend held in October. Also holds a variety of classes, workshops, and seasonal rituals. Contact The EarthSpirit Community.

Fish Drum Magazine

Robert Winson, Editor, 626 Kathryn Avenue, Santa Fe, NM 87501

Profile: An alternative literary arts magazine. Issued annually. Circ: 500. Trim size: 5.5x8.5. 100 pages. Subscription cost: N/A. Sample copy cost: $3. No writer's guidelines.

Focus and Tips: *Fish Drum Magazine* is a literary and arts publication with varied interests. It seeks, among other things, material on the practice of Buddhism in the form of first-person accounts, good lyric poetry, and translations. Welcomes lively language, personal experiences, and insight into "the maps the mind makes." No "flat" academic poetry or vague inspirational writing. Most readers are centered in Santa Fe.

Editorial Interests

Literary material, the arts, Buddhism, Zen Buddhism, and women's issues.

• *Fiction:* High-quality short stories, drama, and poetry. No length restrictions.

• *Nonfiction:* Articles, essays, interviews, and personal accounts, especially from Zen practitioners. Informed Buddhist book reviews. No length restrictions.

• *Illustrations:* B/W prints and line drawings.

Submission Policy: Send complete manuscript . Include SASE. Accepts photocopies and computer printouts. No simultaneous submissions. Reports in 1 month.

Terms and Payment: First North American serial rights. No payment. Authors receive 2–4 copies of the issue.

Forefront—Health Investigations

Steven Fowkes, Editor, P.O. Box 60637, Palo Alto, CA 94306   Phone: 415-321-CERI, Fax: 415-323-3864

Profile: A journal of theoretical and applied health technologies. Published by Cognitive Enhancement Research Institute. Issued 6 times a year. Circ: 1,000. Trim size: 10.5x13.25. B/W; folded. 8 pages. Subscription cost: $24. Sample copy cost: $4. No writer's guidelines.

Focus and Tips: *Forefront* is an eclectic health newsletter for technically sophisticated lay readers. It provides health-related information on life extension and biological technology.

Editorial Interests

Health, bio-rhythms, mind/body performance, science, the environment, healing and health, holistic health, juvenile and teen issues, lifestyle, men's issues, nutrition, parenting, politics, psychology, self-help, social and world issues, and women's issues.

• *Nonfiction:* Articles on updates in the health fields, 1,000–5,000 words. Interviews with authors, 1,000–5,000 words. Personal experiences, 200–1,000 words. Opinion pieces on policy, 1,000–2,000 words. Book reviews, 1,000–3,000 words.

Submission Policy: Query with outline. Include SASE. Accepts photocopies, computer printouts, faxes, and IBM ASCII disks. Simultaneous submissions okay. If accepted, expect publication in 1–2 months.

Terms and Payment: All rights unless otherwise negotiated. Pays on publication. Rates negotiable. Authors receive 2 copies of the issue.
Advertising: List rental available. Contact John Morgenthaler, 707-769-8078.

Forever Alive

Herb Bowie, Editor, P.O. Box 12305, Scottsdale, AZ 85267-2305   Phone: 602-922-0300, Fax: 602-922-0800

Profile: A magazine on physical immortality. Issued quarterly. Circ: 3,000. Trim size: 8.5x11. Glossy color cover; B/W inside; saddle stitched. 44 pages. Subscription cost: $24. Sample copy cost: $6. Writer's guidelines available with SASE.
Focus and Tips: *Forever Alive* investigates the theory of aliveness and physical immortality. It is interested in well-written contributions in all genres. View physical immortality as the "key to creating heaven on earth." Send for a sample copy to discern interests. Avoid negative portrayals.
Editorial Interests
Physical immortality, health, life extension, politics, science, relationships, social and world issues.
• *Fiction:* Short stories on physical immortality, 1,000–4,000 words. Accepts poetry.
• *Nonfiction:* Articles, essays, and interviews, 1,000–4,000 words.
• *Illustrations:* B/W prints and line drawings.
Submission Policy: Query with outline. Include SASE. Accepts photocopies, computer printouts, and faxes. Simultaneous submissions okay. Reports in 3 months.
Terms and Payment: Rights are negotiable. No payment. Authors receive 1 copy of the issue; more upon request.

Free Spirit

Stephany Evans, Editor, 300 San Juan Avenue, Venice, CA 90291   Phone: 310-581-6166

Profile: A regional magazine of personal transformation. Issued bimonthly. Circ: 50,000. Trim size: Tabloid. 60lb. glossy cover; newsprint; trim stitched. 90 pages. Subscription cost: $15. Sample copy cost: $2. No writer's guidelines.
Focus and Tips: *Free Spirit* is a regional new age publication serving the Southern California area. It focuses on regional issues as well as holistic living and physical, spiritual, and emotional wellness. Avoid poetry. Its East Coast sister publication, *Free Spirit*, offers similar editorial for New York City and Woodstock and Alster counties.
Editorial Interests
Regional issues, astrology, bodywork, cultural and ethnic issues, dreams, ecosystems, the environment, extraterrestrials, folklore, healing, health, holistic health, inspiration, meditation, metaphysics, mysticism, mythology, natural health, nutrition, occult, parapsychology, parenting, philosophy, prayer, psychic phenomenon, psychology, rebirthing, recovery, relationships, religion, self-help, social and world issues, spirituality, and vitamins.
• *Fiction:* Short stories, short-short stories, drama, book excerpts, and genre fiction, no length restrictions.
• *Nonfiction:* Articles, interviews, profiles, essays, personal experiences, opinion pieces, news items, and book and music reviews, no length restrictions.
Submission Policy: Query with outline or send complete manuscript with cover letter. Include SASE. Accepts photocopies, computer printouts, and faxes. Simultaneous submissions okay. Reporting and publication times vary.
Terms and Payment: One-time rights. Pays per piece on occasion. Rates vary. Authors receive 1 copy of the issue.
Advertising: Rates: B/W full-page, $1,000; 4-color full-page, $1,200–$1,300. Contact Rebecca Lay, 718-638-3733.

Free Spirit

Stephany Evans, Editor, 107 Sterling Place, Brooklyn, NY 11217   Phone: 718-638-3733, Fax: 718-230-3459

Profile: A regional magazine of personal transformation. Issued bimonthly. Circ: 50,000. Trim size: Tabloid. 60lb. glossy cover; newsprint; trim stitched. 90 pages. Subscription cost: $15. Sample copy cost: $2. No writer's guidelines.
Focus and Tips: *Free Spirit* is a regional new age publication serving the areas of New York City and Woodstock and Alster counties. It focuses on regional issues as well as holistic living and physical, spiritual, and emotional wellness. Avoid poetry. Its West Coast sister publication, *Free Spirit*, offers similar editorial for the Venice, California area.
Editorial Interests
Regional issues, astrology, bodywork, cultural and ethnic issues, dreams, ecosystems, the environment, extraterrestrials, folklore, healing, health, holistic health, inspiration, meditation, metaphysics, mysticism, mythology, natural health, nutrition, occult, parapsychology, parenting, philosophy, prayer, psychic phenomenon, psychology, rebirthing, recovery, relationships, religion, self-help, social and world issues, spirituality, and vitamins.
• *Fiction:* Short stories, short-short stories, drama, book excerpts, and genre fiction, no length restrictions.
• *Nonfiction:* Articles, interviews, profiles, essays, personal experiences, opinion pieces, news items, and book and music reviews, no length restrictions.
Submission Policy: Query with outline or send complete manuscript with cover letter. Include SASE. Accepts photocopies,

computer printouts, and faxes. Simultaneous submissions okay. Reporting and publication times vary.
Terms and Payment: One-time rights. Pays per piece on occasion. Rates vary. Authors receive 1 copy of the issue.
Advertising: Rates: B/W full-page, $1,000; 4-color full-page, $1,200–$1,300. Contact Rebecca Lay, 718-638-3733.

Friend's Review

Marie Friend, Publisher/Editor, 18018 NW Collins Road, Hillsboro, OR 97124   Phone/Fax: 503-647-5921

Profile: An independent review publication. Issued quarterly. Circ: 10,000. Trim size: 8.25x10.75. Glossy color cover; B/W; saddle stitched. 40 pages. Subscription cost: $8.50. Sample copy cost: $2.25. No writer's guidelines.
Focus and Tips: *Friend's Review* publishes independent reviews of spiritual and metaphysical books, videos, and tapes, as well as an occasional article. It reaches both readers and buyers of new age books and music. Self-publishers are welcome to submit their books for possible review, provided that they are professionally produced and well packaged.
Editorial Interests
New age, astrology, bodywork, channeling, crystals, cultural and ethnic issues, dreams, ecosystems, the environment, extraterrestrials, feminism, folklore, healing, health, holistic health, inspiration, juvenile and teen issues, magic, meditation, men's issues, metaphysics, mysticism, mythology, natural health, nutrition, occult, parapsychology, philosophy, prayer, psychic phenomenon, psychology, rebirthing, recovery, relationships, religion, self-help, spirituality, witches, and yoga.
• *Fiction:* Book excerpts, 400–500 words.
• *Nonfiction:* Features, articles, interviews, and profiles relating to book or music releases, 1,000–1,300 words. Opinion pieces, 400–500 words.
Submission Policy: Query with outline. Include SASE. Accepts photocopies, computer printouts, and faxes. Reporting time varies.
Terms and Payment: One-time rights. No payment. Offers advertising space in lieu of payment. Authors receive copies of the issue.
Advertising: Rates: B/W full-page, $745; 4-color full-page, $795. Contact Fran Khabundi, 503-647-2027, or David Austin, 503-647-5921.

Full-Time Dads

Stephen Harris, Editor/Publisher, P.O. Box 577, Cumberland, ME, 04021   Phone: 207-829-5260

Profile: A journal for caregiver fathers. Published by Big Daddy Publications. Issued bimonthly. Circ: 350. Trim size: 8.5x11. Self cover; B/W; saddle stitched. 24 pages. Subscription cost: $26. Sample copy cost: $5. Writer's guidelines available with SASE.
Focus and Tips: *Full-Time Dads* is for fathers who are active caregivers for their children. It provides a forum for fathers to share ideas, fund support, and discuss issues that will help them to be better parents. Avoid anything that is purposely offensive to good taste—sex, violence, etc.
Editorial Interests
Fathering, family life, parenting, and men's issues.
• *Fiction:* Short stories dealing with fatherhood, 600–1,200 words.
• *Nonfiction:* Articles relating to fatherhood, 600–1,200 words.
Submission Policy: Query with outline and send complete manuscript with cover letter. Include SASE. Accepts photocopies, computer printouts, faxes, and Macintosh Microsoft Word disks. No simultaneous submissions. Reports in 1–2 months. If accepted, expect publication in 4–6 months.
Terms and Payment: One-time rights. No payment. Authors receive 1 copy of the issue.
Advertising: Accepts advertising. List rental available. Contact Stephen Harris, 207-829-5260.

The Gate

Beth Robbins, Editor, P.O. Box 43516, Richmond Heights, OH 44143

Profile: A magazine of paranormal phenomenon. Issued quarterly. Circ: 200. Trim size: 5.5x8.5. Self cover; B/W; saddled stitched. Subscription cost: $8. Sample copy cost: $2. Writer's guidelines available with SASE.
Focus and Tips: *The Gate* is devoted to exploring paranormal mysteries such as UFOs, ghosts, Bigfoot, etc. Seeks factual articles; always query first for editorial approval. Avoid widely used topics that have been rehashed several times. "Don't be afraid to venture into a library for new research material. Originality is a big plus here."
Editorial Interests
Paranormal and psychic phenomenon, parapsychology, extraterrestrials, folklore, metaphysics, mysticism, mythology, occult, and unknown animals.
• *Nonfiction:* Factual articles.
Submission Policy: Query first with outline. Include SASE. Accepts photocopies and computer printouts. No simultaneous

submissions. Reports immediately. If accepted, expect publication in 2–6 months.
Terms and Payment: No payment. Authors receive copies of the issue.

Ghost Trackers Newsletter

Dale Kaczmarek, President, P.O. Box 205, Oak Lawn, IL 60454-0205   Phone: 708-425-5163

Profile: A membership newsletter reporting paranormal phenomenon. Published by the Ghost Research Society. Issued 3 times per year. Circ: 200. Trim size: 8.5x11. Photocopied; stapled. 25 pages. Subscription cost: $12. Sample copy cost: $4. Writer's guidelines available with SASE.

Focus and Tips: *Ghost Trackers Newsletter* is an official paranormal publication that deals with stories of ghosts, haunting, poltergeists, and life-after-death. It is only interested in these topics; avoid channeling, crystals, UFOs, new age, metaphysics, witchcraft, and Satanism. Readers are members of the Ghost Research Society, which is devoted to collecting, analyzing, and researching all forms of the paranormal.

Editorial Interests
Ghosts, poltergeists, life after death, parapsychology, and psychic phenomenon.
• *Nonfiction:* Features, articles, personal experiences, and news items, no length restrictions. Accepts book reviews.

Submission Policy: Send complete manuscript with cover letter and bibliography. Include SASE. Accepts photocopies, computer printouts, and WordPerfect 3.5" disks. Simultaneous submissions okay. Reports in 2 weeks. If accepted, expect publication within 3–4 months.

Terms and Payment: One-time rights. No payment. Authors receive 1 copy of the issue.

Advertising: Rates: B/W full-page, $65. List rental available; $1 per name, 200 name minimum. Contact Dale Kaczmarek.

Gnosis

Richard Smoley, Editor, P.O. Box 14217, San Francisco, CA 94114   Phone: 415-255-0400, Fax: 415-255-6329

Profile: A thematic journal of Western inner traditions. Published by Lumen Foundation. Issued quarterly. Circ: 14,000. Trim size: 8.5x11. Glossy color cover; 50 lb. offset paper; B/W; saddle stitched. 88 pages. Subscription cost: $20. Sample copy cost: $6 plus $1.50 postage. Writer's guidelines and theme list available with SASE.

Focus and Tips: *Gnosis* is dedicated to the spiritual traditions of Western civilization, particularly its esoteric, mystical, and occult traditions. It is nonsectarian and provides a forum for diverse views. Readers tend to be intelligent, thoughtful people with interests in these fields. Issues are thematic and strong preference is given to articles relating to these themes. In the past, *Gnosis* has covered Dreams, Holy War, Sufism, The Dark Side, Ritual, and Sacred Art & Music. It is not interested in fiction, poetry, personal experiences, or promotional material.

Editorial Interests
Spirituality, Western religions, magic, meditation, metaphysics, mysticism, mythology, occult, parapsychology, philosophy, prayer, psychic phenomenon, psychology, and witches.
• *Fiction:* Book excerpts, 1,000–4,000 words.
• *Nonfiction:* Features, articles, interviews and profiles, and essays, 1,000–4,000 words. News items, 500–1,000 words. Book reviews, 500–1,000 words.

Submission Policy: Query with outline, writing samples and resume; or send complete manuscript with cover letter. Include SASE. Accepts photocopies, computer printouts, and 3.5" disks, preferably Macintosh. No simultaneous submissions. Reports in 1–2 months. If accepted, expect publication in 5 months.

Terms and Payment: First North American serial rights. Pays on publication. Features, $200. Book reviews, $40. Authors receive 4 copies of the issue.

Advertising: Rates: B/W full-page, $805. List rental available; $100/M. Contact Jeff Chitouras, 415-255-0400.

Green Egg

Diane Darling, Editor, P.O. Box 1542, Ukiah, CA 95482   Phone: 707-485-0772, Fax: 707-468-3874

Profile: A magazine of Gaian spirituality. Established in 1968. Published by the Church of All Worlds, a nonprofit organization. Issued quarterly. Circ: 10,000+. Trim size: 8.5x11. Glossy color cover; B/W inside; saddle stitched. 76+ pages. Subscription cost: $18. Sample copy cost: $6. Writer's guidelines available with SASE.

Focus and Tips: *Green Egg* is the official journal of the Church of All Worlds, whose mission is to evolve a network of information, mythology, and experience that provides a context and stimulus for reawakening Gaia, and reuniting her children through tribal community dedicated to responsible stewardship and evolving consciousness. It prefers Neopagan and magical themes. Avoid personal attacks, channeled pieces, and time-specific material.

Editorial Interests
Paganism, Gaia, goddesses, deep ecology, eco-feminism, ecosophy, folklore, magic, metaphysics, mysticism, mythology, occult, and witches.

• *Fiction:* Short-short stories, 700–2,100 words. Poetry, 50–1,000 words.
• *Nonfiction:* Features, articles, interviews, profiles, essays, personal experiences, and opinion pieces, 1,000–3,000 words. Reviews, 500–1,000 words.
Submission Policy: Send complete manuscript with cover letter and accompanying computer disk, if available. Include SASE. Accepts photocopies, computer printouts, and Macintosh disks. Simultaneous submissions okay. Responds to queries in 1 month, to manuscripts in 3 months. If accepted, expect publication in 6 months.
Terms and Payment: One-time rights. Offers advertising space in lieu of payment. Authors receive up to 5 copies of the issue.
Advertising: Rates: B/W full-page, $456; half-page, $257; quarter-page, $144. Four-color full-page, $925; half-page, $486; quarter page, $254. Contact Richard Johnson, 707-459-5490. One-time list rental available. Contact Ottar Zell, 707-485-0772.
Other Interests: Holds seasonal festivals eight times a year. For more information, contact Diane Darling, 707-485-0772.

Green Fuse Poetry

Brian Boldt, Editor, 3365 Holland Drive, Santa Rosa, CA 95404 Phone: 707-544-8303

Profile: A journal of environmental poetry. Established in 1984. Issued twice a year. Circ: 600. Trim size: 5.5x8.5. Heavy bond cover; B/W; perfect bound. 56 pages. Subscription cost: $14 for 3 issues. Sample copy cost: $4. Writer's guidelines available with SASE.
Focus and Tips: *Green Fuse Poetry* publishes poetry with environmental, social justice, and war-and-peace themes. It presents a poetic alternative to a toxic and militaristic culture. It seeks accessible free verse that celebrates the natural beauty and mystery of the planet and the power of poetic truth in an age of prosaic lies and madness. Readers are environmentalists, peace activists, academics, and radicals. Avoid sentimentality, clichés, rhymed verse, and institutionally religious themes.
Editorial Interests
Poetry, the environment, peace work, social justice, ecosystems, politics, social and world issues.
• *Poetry:* Free verse, up to 70 lines.
Submission Policy: Send complete manuscript with cover letter. Include SASE. Accepts photocopies and computer printouts. No simultaneous submissions. Responds to queries in 1 week, to manuscripts in 3 months. If accepted, expect publication within 2–3 months.
Terms and Payment: One-time rights. No payment. Authors receive 1 copy of the issue; featured poets receive additional copies.

Half Tones to Jubilee

Allan Peterson, Co-editor, 1000 College Boulevard, Pensacola, FL 35604 Phone: 904-484-2554, Fax: 904-484-1826

Profile: A literary journal. Published by the Department of English, Pensacola Junior College. Issued annually. Circ: 500. Trim size: 6x9. Bond cover; B/W; 70 lb. recycled; perfect bound. 85–100 pages. Subscription cost: $4. Sample copy cost: $4. Writer's guidelines available with SASE.
Focus and Tips: *Half Tones to Jubilee* features poetry and short fiction. Writers should show an awareness of modern writing. No sing-song poetry or greeting-card verse. Avoid biases. "Take care and send your best work."
Editorial Interests
Literary material.
• *Fiction:* Short stories, 1,500 words. Short-short stories, up to 1,500 words. Poetry, no line limits.
Submission Policy: Send complete manuscript with cover letter. Include SASE. Accepts photocopies, computer printouts, and faxes. No simultaneous submissions. Reports in 3 months. If accepted, expect publication in 5 months.
Terms and Payment: One-time rights. No payment. Authors receive 2 copies of the issue.
Other Interests: Sponsors the annual *Half Tones to Jubilee* National Poetry Competition. Deadline is May 15. Entry fee, $2 per poem. Prizes: $300, $200, $100. Contact Allan Peterson, 904-484-2554. Also sponsors an annual Winnie McManus Seminar, a two-day conference on various subjects of interest to writers and teachers. Contact the English Department, 904-484-1403.

Health Consciousness

Roy B. Kupsinel, Editor-in-Chief, P.O. Box 550, Oviero, FL 32765 Phone: 407-365-6681, Fax: 407-365-1834

Profile: A new age, holistic health magazine and advertising vehicle. Issued bimonthly. Circ: 1,200. Trim size: 8.5x11. Glossy color cover; B/W inside; saddle stitched. 60 pages. Subscription cost: $18. Sample copy cost: $3. Writer's guidelines available with SASE.
Focus and Tips: *Health Consciousness* seeks to raise the awareness, understanding, and knowledge of health-related issues for its readers who are select health-oriented people, lay and professional, in 38 countries. It explores the physical, mental, emotional, and spiritual frontiers of medicine, offers alternative viewpoints, and provides a forum for various health-related advertisers.

Editorial Interests
Holistic health, the environment, healing, meditation, natural health, nutrition, philosophy, prayer, relationships, self-help, seniors, and spirituality.
• *Nonfiction:* Publishes holistic and alternative health-related articles and promotional material. No length restrictions.
Submission Policy: Send complete manuscript with cover letter. Include SASE. Accepts photocopies, computer printouts, and disk submissions.
Terms and Payment: No payment.
Advertising: Rates: B/W full-page, $800; half-page, $450; quarter-page, $250. Contact Roy Kupsinel, 407-365-6681.

Health Foods Business

Gina Geslewitz, Editor, 567 Morris Avenue, Elizabeth, NJ 07208   Phone: 908-353-7373, Fax: 908-353-5652

Profile: A trade magazine for the health food industry. Published by PTN Publishing. Issued monthly. Circ: 11,600. Trim size: 8.5x11. Glossy color cover; 4-color; perfect bound. 72 pages. Subscription cost: $33. Sample copy cost: $3. Writer's guidelines available with SASE.
Focus and Tips: *Health Food Business* covers the business, organizational, and legal issues of interest to owners of health/natural food stores.
Editorial Interests
Business, health, natural foods, and nutrition.
• *Nonfiction:* Profiles of successful health food stores, 1,500–2,000 words.
Submission Policy: Query with outline. Include SASE. Accepts photocopies, computer printouts, and WordPerfect or ASCII disks. No simultaneous submissions. Reports in 1 month. If accepted, expect publication within 3–6 months.
Terms and Payment: First North American serial rights. Pays on publication. $125 per piece. Authors receive 3 copies of the issue.
Advertising: Accepts advertising. Contact Ross Fields, 908-353-7373.

Health News and Review

Editor, 27 Pine Street, P.O. Box 876, New Canaan, CT 06840-0876

Profile: A natural health newspaper. Published by Keats Publishing. Issued quarterly. Circ: 120,000. Trim size: Tabloid. Newsprint; folded. Subscription cost: $11.80. Sample copy cost: $2.95. No writer's guidelines.
Focus and Tips: *Health News and Review* is a general-interest health newspaper for consumers interested in nutrition and nutritional supplements. Its focus is on the natural health field and related issues of diet, nutrition, and vitamins. Not interested in material on drugs or surgical techniques.
Editorial Interests
Health, natural health, nutrition, diet, fitness and exercise, bodywork, healing, and holistic health.
• *Nonfiction:* Features, articles, interviews, profiles, and news items, 750–1,250 words.
Submission Policy: Query with outline and resume. No unsolicited manuscripts. Include SASE. No simultaneous submissions. Reports in 2 weeks. If accepted, expect publication in 3–6 months.
Terms and Payment: All rights. Pays on acceptance. $25–$50 per piece. Authors receive 3 copies of the issue.
Advertising: Accepts advertising. Contact Norman Goldfind.

Heart Dance

Randy Peyser, Editor, 473 Miller Avenue, Mill Valley, CA 94941   Phone: 415-383-2525, Fax: 415-383-7500

Profile: A regional new age calendar of events. Issued monthly. Circ: 50,000. Trim size: 8.5x11. Color cover; B/W inside; recycled paper; glued. 64 pages. Subscription cost: $20. Sample copy cost: $1.21. Writer's guidelines available with SASE.
Focus and Tips: *Heart Dance* serves the Bay area of California and beyond. Allows readers to communicate their ideas and visions about personal growth, healing, spirituality, the exploration of consciousness, and the positive transformation of life on Earth. It is distributed at 1,500 sites in the Bay area. Looks for positive and inspiring writing that comes from the heart. Avoid referring to a specific deity or religion." No UFO or Bigfoot sightings. Elvis is dead—let's not see him either."
Editorial Interests
New age, healing, holistic health, lifestyle, self-help, the environment, and spirituality.
• *Nonfiction:* Personal experiences and insights. First-person accounts of near-death experiences. Experiences of having been "touched by a greater presence." Up to 1,200 words.
• *Illustrations:* Interested in visionary art, images that are uplifting and life-affirming. Color artwork for cover and B/W drawings inside.
Submission Policy: Send complete manuscript with cover letter. Include SASE. Accepts photocopies and computer printouts. No simultaneous submissions. Reports in 1 week. If accepted, expect publication in 3–6 months.

Terms and Payment: One-time rights. Pays on publication. $10–$25 per piece. Authors receive up to 25 copies of the issue.
Advertising: Rates: B/W full-page, $950. Contact advertising department, 415-383-2500.

Heart & Soul

Stephanie Stokes Oliver, Executive Editor, 33 East Minor Street, Emmaus, PA 18098   Phone: 610-967-5171/800-666-1716

Profile: A health and fitness publication. Published by Rodale Press, Inc. Issued quarterly. Circ: 125,000. Trim size: 8.5x11. Subscription cost: $15. Sample copy cost: free. No writer's guidelines.
Focus and Tips: *Heart & Soul* is a health and fitness magazine for African Americans. Its audience is predominately female. Writers are advised to send clear, focused queries that are tailored to the magazine and offer ideas that fit the magazine's needs.
Editorial Interests
Health, men's issues, natural health, nutrition, parenting, relationships, and spirituality.
• *Nonfiction:* Health, fitness, beauty, and nutrition features, 2,000 words. Interviews and profiles, 500–1,500 words. Personal experiences, 200 words. News items, 50–100 words. Columns include Natural Beauty, Healthy Kids, Healthy Eating, Fitness, Heart & Soul Cuisine, For Men Only, and Mind & Body, 750–1,000 words.
Submission Policy: Query with outline, writing samples, resume, or send complete manscript with cover letter and resume. Include SASE. Accepts photocopies. No simultaneous submissions. Reports immediately. If accepted, expect publication in 2 months.
Terms and Payment: First North American serial rights or all rights. Pays on acceptance. $.75 per word.
Advertising: Accepts advertising. Contact Reginald Wave, 312-696-4106.

The Heartlight Journal

Marilyn Bolden, Managing Editor, 42015 Ford Road, Box 232, Canton, MI 48187   Phone: 800-432-8309

Profile: A journal on writing for writers. Published by Nobel Communications. Issued quarterly. Circ: N/A. Trim size: 8.5x11. Heavy bond cover; B/W; 60 lb. paper; saddle stitched. 28 pages. Subscription cost: $18. Sample copy cost: $5. Writer's guidelines available with SASE.
Focus and Tips: *The Heartlight Journal* is a comprehensive journal featuring poetry, prose, and helpful information for writers such as writing tips, competition announcements, and products and services. Writers are advised to edit carefully and check grammar and punctuation. Avoid overtly sexual language. *Heartlight*'s editors offer comments on rejection notices.
Editorial Interests
Writing and literary material. Open to all topics and subject matter.
• *Fiction:* Short stories, 5 manuscript pages. Poetry, no length restrictions.
• *Nonfiction:* Features, 1,000–1,500 words. Interviews and profiles, 1,000 words. Considers personal experiences, opinion, and news pieces. Columns include Poet's Resource Gallery.
Submission Policy: Prose, query first. Poetry, send complete works. Include SASE. Accepts photocopies, computer printouts, and Macintosh disks. Simultaneous submissions okay. Reports in 1–3 months. If accepted, expect publication in 1–3 months.
Terms and Payment: One-time rights. Pays per word on occasion. Rates are negotiable. Authors receive 1 copy of the issue.
Advertising: Rates: B/W one-eighth-page display, $24. Contact Marilyn Bolden, 800-432-8309.
Other Interests: Runs quarterly poetry contests and thematic poetry, prose, short story, and chapbook competitions throughout the year. Send an SASE for guidelines.

Heaven Bone

Steven Hirsch, Editor/Publisher, P.O. Box 486, Chester, NY 10918

Profile: A magazine of spiritual expression. Published by Heaven Bone Press. Established in 1986. Issued quarterly. Circ: N/A. Trim size: 8.5x11. Glossy color cover; B/W inside; saddle stitched. 96 pages. Subscription cost: $16.95. Sample copy cost: $6. Writer's guidelines available with SASE.
Focus and Tips: *Heaven Bone* is a literary magazine that publishes "philosophically speculative and spiritually inquiring writing." While spiritual in tone, it is not traditionally religious. It seeks to inspire and bring "something of the gods down into the flesh and bone of our normal, spectacularly ordinary experiences." Avoid sensationalism and "blind theocratic rants for or against one deity or another." Submissions accompanied by a subscription request are well received.
Editorial Interests
Spirituality, philosophy, alternative cultural, the arts, the environment, and social and world issues.
• *Fiction:* Stories that are alternative cultural, post-beat, and yogic/anti-paranoiac in nature, up to 4,500 words.
• *Nonfiction:* Essays on surrealist, futurist, dada, ecological, social, artistic, and esoteric topics. Book and magazine reviews, 500–2,500 words.
• *Illustrations:* Accepts prints, slides, veloxes, or other representations. Prefers eclectic work.

Submission Policy: Query with outline. Include SASE. Accepts CompuServe modemed submissions, 71340,520. Reports in 3–16 weeks.
Terms and Payment: No payment. Authors receive copies of the issue.
Advertising: Accepts advertising; rates available upon request.

Herbal Gram

Mark Blumenthal, Editor, P.O. Box 201660, Austin, TX 78720   Phone: 512-331-8868, Fax: 512-331-1924

Profile: A publication on herbs and medicinal plants. Published by the American Botanical Council and the Herb Research Foundation. Issued quarterly. Circ: 20,000. Trim size: 8.5x11. Glossy color cover; full-color; saddle stitched. 80 pages. Subscription cost: $25. Sample copy cost: $5. No writer's guidelines.
Focus and Tips: *Herbal Gram* is an educational, peer-reviewed journal on herbs and medicinal plants. Prefers writers with backgrounds in scientific, medical, or other semi-technical fields. All material must be referenced. Not interested in fiction or chatty articles.
Editorial Interests
Herbs, natural medicine, health, and holistic health.
• *Nonfiction:* Features and essays on herbs and medicinal plants, 1,250–3,000 words.
• *Illustrations:* Color photos and artwork.
Submission Policy: Query with outline. Include SASE. Accepts photocopies, computer printouts, and WordPerfect or Microsoft Word 3.5" or 5.25" disks. Simultaneous submissions okay. Reports in 1 month.
Terms and Payment: First North American serial rights. No payment. Authors receive 24 copies of the issue.

Heresies: A Feminist Publication on Art & Politics

Jean Casella, Managing Editor, Box 1306, Canal Street Station, New York, NY 10013   Phone: 212-227-2108

Profile: A thematic journal of feminist thought. Established in 1977. Issued 1–2 times a year. Circ: 18,000. Trim size: 8.5x11. Glossy cover; B/W; 60 lb. paper; perfect bound. 96 pages. Subscription cost: Individual, $27; Institution, $38. Sample copy cost: $6. Writer's guidelines and theme list available with SASE.
Focus and Tips: *Heresies* is an idea-oriented journal devoted to the examination of art and politics from a feminist perspective. It publishes feminist work by women centered around a specific theme for each issue. Aims to stimulate dialogue around radical, political, and aesthetic theory, as well as generate new creative energies among women. "It is important to look at a back issue to get a sense of our magazine before submitting." It does not accept reviews or monographs on contemporary women.
Editorial Interests
Feminism, politics, the arts, and women's issues.
• *Fiction:* Accepts experimental writing, short stories, short-short stories, drama, book excerpts, genre fiction, and poetry that relates to issue themes. No length restrictions. Considers no more than six poems and two works of fiction per submission.
• *Nonfiction:* Accepts political and cultural commentary, features, articles, essays, personal experiences, opinion pieces, and news related to issue themes. No length restrictions.
Submission Policy: Query first for upcoming themes. Then send complete manuscript. Include SASE. Accepts photocopies and computer printouts. Simultaneous submissions okay. Reports in up to 12 months.
Terms and Payment: Pays on publication. $15 honorarium. Authors receive 3 copies of the issue; additional copies available at discounted prices.
Advertising: Rates: B/W full-page, $500. Contact Jean Casella, Managing Editor.

Herspectives

Mary Billy, Editor, P.O. Box 2047, Squamish, BC, V0N 3G0 Canada   Phone: 604-892-5723, Fax: 604-892-5749

Profile: A feminist forum of expression. Published by Her Productions. Issued quarterly. Circ: 200. Trim size: 8x11. Photocopies; stapled. 50–60 pages. Subscription cost: $25–$40. Sample copy cost: $6. Writer's guidelines and theme list available with SASE/IRCs.
Focus and Tips: For wise women, strong women, healers, and peacemakers, *Herspectives* is a feminist magazine of common women's dialogue that crosses all lines of communication. It addresses sexism, racism, homophobia, and other issues that divide people. Welcomes new and inexperienced writers who have a need to share their thoughts and ideas and to be read. Prefers short, tightly written material. No man-bashing or otherwise demeaning articles.
Editorial Interests
Feminism, women's issues, cultural and ethnic issues, dreams, environmental concerns, gay and lesbian concerns, healing, holistic health, inspiration, juvenile and teen material, lifestyle, magic, new age, philosophy, recovery, goddess worship, crones, and spirituality.

• *Fiction:* Short stories, 1,000–1,500 words. Short-short stories, 500–1,000 words. Book excerpts, 4 single-spaced pages. Genre fiction, 1,000–2,000 words. Poetry, up to 1 page.
• *Nonfiction:* Features, articles, essays, personal experiences, opinion, and news, up to 2,000 words. Reviews, up to 500 words. Filler, 100–200 words. Departments are by, for, or about women.
Submission Policy: Send complete manuscript with cover letter. Include SASE. U.S. authors must include IRCs for return. Accepts photocopies and computer printouts. Simultaneous submissions okay. Reports in 2–6 weeks. If accepted, expect publication within 3–12 months.
Terms and Payment: First North American serial rights. No payment. Authors receive 1–2 copies of the issue upon request.
Advertising: Rates per page: B/W, $75. Contact Mary Billy, 604-892-5723.

High Country News

Betsy Marston, Editor, P.O. Box 1090, Paonia, CO 81428   Phone: 303-527-4898

Profile: A nonprofit, regional environmental newspaper. Established in 1969. Issued biweekly. Circ: 15,000. Trim size: 10.25x16. Newsprint; folded. 16 pages. Subscription cost: $28. Sample copy cost: Free. Writers guidelines available with SASE.
Focus and Tips: *High Country News* is a natural resources newspaper covering the Rocky Mountain states—Colorado, Wyoming, Montana, Idaho, Utah, New Mexico, Arizona, and Nevada, as well as the Dakotas and the Pacific Northwest. Readers include grass-roots activists, executives, government policy makers, and educators. It considers material on any natural resource or environmental topic of regional interest. Analytical pieces that give the reader a sense of the importance of events and issues affecting the region are welcomed. New writers stand the best chance of acceptance with Roundups, short topical stories.
Editorial Interests
Regional issues, Western communities, natural resources, and the environment.
• *Nonfiction:* Features, up to 3,000 words. Interviews, profiles, essays, personal experiences, and news, 700–1,200 words. Roundups, 800–1,000 words.
• *Illustrations:* Unmounted B/W glossy prints, 5x7 or 8x10. Accepts color prints and slides, negatives, and contact sheets. Label and caption each photo.
Submission Policy: Query with outline or send complete manuscript with cover letter. Include SASE. Accepts photocopies, computer printouts, and Macintosh Microsoft Word disks. No simultaneous submissions. Reports in 1 month. If accepted, expect publication in 1–8 weeks.
Terms and Payment: First North American serial rights. Pays on publication. Articles, $.15 per word. Photos, $15–$50. Authors receive 1–2 copies of the issue.

Hinduism Today

Arumugaswami, Managing Editor, 107 Kaholalele Road, Kapaa, HI 96746   Phone: 800-890-1008

Profile: A newspaper on Hinduism. Established in 1979. Issued monthly. Circ: 150,000. Trim size: Tabloid. Color cover; B/W inside; folded. 24 pages. Subscription cost: $29. Sample copy cost: Free. Writer's guidelines available with SASE.
Focus and Tips: *Hinduism Today*, published in eight editions worldwide, covers all Hindu sects and news that is Dharma-related. Dedicated to sharing the philosophy, culture, and mysticism of the East and to dispelling myth and misinformation. It reports globally on the glories, failings, and insights of nearly a billion Hindus. Emphasis is placed on religion, family life, and current issues. It holds high standards and all major articles must have color photos. Avoid politics, criticism of other faiths, and fiction.
Editorial Interests
Hinduism, vegetarianism, yoga, nonviolence, philosophy, metaphysics, cultural and ethnic issues, religion, comparative religion, and family issues.
• *Nonfiction:* News items, opinion pieces, and biographical and institutional features, 100–2,000 words. Departments include My Turn. Accepts short pieces on interesting material.
• *Illustrations:* Color prints or slides to accompany major articles. Accepts B/W prints.
Submission Policy: Prefers a query with outline and resume. Accepts complete manuscript with cover letter. Include SASE. Accepts photocopies, computer printouts, and Macintosh disks. Simultaneous submissions okay. Reports in 2 months.
Terms and Payment: All rights unless otherwise negotiated. Pays on publication. $.06 per word plus expenses. Authors receive 1 copy of the issue.
Advertising: Accepts advertising. Contact Arumugaswami, 800-890-1008.

How On Earth!

Sally Clinton, Director, P.O. Box 3347, West Chester, PA 19381   Phone: 717-529-VNET, Fax: 717-529-8638

Profile: A national environmental publication for teens. Published by Vegetarian Education Network, a nonprofit organization. Issued quarterly. Circ: 12,000. Trim size: 8.5x11. Self cover; 2-color; saddle stitched. 32 pages. Subscription cost: $15. Sample copy cost: $4. Writer's guidelines available with SASE.

Focus and Tips: *How On Earth!* is written for and by youth interested in compassionate, ecologically sound living. It serves as a forum, offering support for alternative living and encouraging critical thinking.

Editorial Interests

Ecology, the environment, vegetarianism, teen issues, animal rights, bodywork, cultural and ethnic issues, feminism, gay and lesbian issues, healing and health, holistic and natural health, inspiration, meditation, metaphysics, nutrition, philosophy, politics, psychology, self-help, social and world issues, spirituality, and women's issues.

• *Poetry:* On appropriate topics. No length restrictions.

• *Nonfiction:* All written by teen authors. Articles, essays, profiles, recipes, and reviews. No length restrictions.

Submission Policy: Query or send complete manuscript. Include SASE. Accepts photocopies, computer printouts, Macintosh 3.5" disks, and faxes. Simultaneous submissions okay. Reports in 1–2 months.

Terms and Payment: One-time rights. No payment. Authors receive 3–10 copies of the issue.

Advertising: Accepts advertising appropriate to the publication's theme. Contact Sally Clinton, 717-529-VNET.

Other Interests: Sponsors youth workshops that are held at various locations. These are designed to empower and support youth who are concerned about the planet and all its inhabitants. For more information, contact Sally Clinton, 717-529-VNET.

Hysteria

Deborah Werksman, Editor, P.O. Box 8581, Brewster Station, Bridgeport, CT 06605 Phone: 203-333-9399, Fax: 203-335-6777

Profile: A quarterly magazine of women's humor. Published by Hysteria Publications. Issued quarterly. Circ: 8,000. Trim size: 8.5x11. Glossy cover; B/W; saddle stitched. 28 pages. Subscription cost: $18. Sample copy cost: $4.95. Writer's guidelines available with SASE.

Focus and Tips: *Hysteria* offers humor from a feminist perspective. Its audience is educated, thinking women, ranging in age from late 20s to late 50s. Especially interested in humor written by women about real life situations and profiles of women involved in unusual activities. Avoid articles about dieting and material that revolves solely around men.

Editorial Interests

Feminism, lesbian and women's issues, and humor.

• *Nonfiction:* Humorous and feminist features and articles, 750–1,000 words. Interviews and profiles of women doing unusual things, 750–1,000 words. Departments include Regular Menstruation, which covers menarche, menstruation, and menopause, 750–1,000 words. Short public service announcements of events of feminist interest, up to 200 words.

Submission Policy: Send complete manuscript with cover letter. Include SASE and author's phone number. Accepts photocopies, computer printouts, and faxes. Simultaneous submissions okay. Reports in 4–6 weeks. Publication time varies.

Terms and Payment: One-time rights. Pays 1–2 months after publication. Rates are negotiable. Authors receive 1 copy of the issue.

Advertising: Rates: B/W full-page, $600. List rental available. Contact Deborah Werksman, 203-333-9399.

Illahee: Journal for the Northwest Environment

Ellen W. Chu, Editor, Engineering Annex, FM-12, University of Washington, Seattle, WA 98195 Phone/Fax: 206-543-1812

Profile: A journal of environmental awareness. Published by the Institute for Environmental Studies at the University of Washington. Established in 1984. Issued quarterly. Circ: 1,000. Trim size: 8.5x11. Glossy color cover; B/W inside; recycled paper; perfect bound or saddle stitched. 72–104 pages. Subscription cost: $25. Sample copy cost: $8. Writers guidelines available with SASE.

Focus and Tips: Formerly the *Northwest Environmental Journal, Illahee* seeks to bridge the gap between scholars and consumers and foster environmental awareness of all regardless of viewpoint. It aims to increase public understanding of natural and cultural systems and the inextricable links among them; to stimulate innovative, flexible, and pragmatic thinking about environmental issues; and to promote interactions among scientists, policymakers, and citizens. Study a sample copy for style and content—knowledgeable, accurate information is a must. Especially interested in thoughtful book reviews. Not interested in anything "folksy or flaky. No new age-style submissions."

Editorial Interests

The environment, cultural and ethnic issues, philosophy, politics, regional Northwest issues, and social and world issues.

• *Nonfiction:* Thoughtful, serious, and factual pieces. Features and articles, up to 6,000 words. Interviews and profiles, 3,000 words. Essays and opinion pieces, 2,000 words. Book reviews, 750–1,000 words.

Submission Policy: Query with outline and 1 sample chapter or send complete manuscript with cover letter and brief author biography. Include SASE. Accepts photocopies, computer printouts, and computer disks with hard copy. Simultaneous submissions okay if identified. Reports in 2 months. If accepted, expect publication in 6–12 months.

Terms and Payment: First North American serial rights. No payment. Authors receive 2 copies of the issue.

Advertising: Rates: B/W, $100–$400. Considers 4-color ads. List rental available. Contact Ellen Chu, 206-543-1812.

Other Interests: Sponsors the Beyond Endangered Species: Governing for Ecological Health conference concerning endangered species. Contact Ellen Chu, 206-543-1812.

India Currents

Arvind Kumar, Editor, P.O. Box 21285, San Jose, CA 95151   Phone: 408-274-6966, Fax: 408-274-2733

Profile: A magazine on East Indian culture. Issued monthly. Circ: 27,000. Trim size: 8.4x10.5. Glossy color cover; B/W inside; saddle stitched. 88 pages. Subscription cost: $12.95. Sample copy cost: $1.95 for current issues, $3 for back issues. Writer's guidelines available with SASE.

Focus and Tips: *India Currents* is devoted to the culture, religions, thought, and people of India. It is targeted at American readers of Indian origin and others. Of interest are insightful articles about Indian systems of thought and belief: Hinduism, yoga, Vedanta, Buddhism, Jainism, Sikhism, and Indian Islam and Christianity. The magazine strives to portray India's true place in world culture—avoid treating India as mysterious, exotic, or impossible to understand.

Editorial Interests

India, Hinduism, yoga, Vedanta, Buddhism, Jainism, Sikhism, Indian Islam and Christianity, cultural and ethnic issues, the environment, health, philosophy, social and world issues, and spirituality.
- *Fiction:* Short stories, 1,500–2,000 words.
- *Nonfiction:* Features, essays, personal experiences, and opinion pieces, up to 800 words. Interviews and profiles, up to 2,000 words.
- *Illustration:* B/W or color 3x5 or 4x6 prints.

Submission Policy: Query with writing samples or send complete manuscript with cover letter, resume, and clips. Include SASE. Accepts photocopies, computer printouts, and computer disks. Simultaneous submissions okay. Reports in 2–3 months.

Terms and Payment: All rights. No payment. Offers up to 2 subscriptions per 1,000 words. Authors receive copies of the issue.

Advertising: Rates: B/W full-page, $300. List rental available. Contact Ashok Jethanandani, 408-274-6966.

Indiana Review

Cara Diaconoff, Editor, 316 North Jordon Avenue, Bloomington, IN 47405   Phone: 812-855-3439

Profile: A national literary magazine. Published by Indiana University. Issued twice a year. Circ: 2,000. Trim size: 6x9. Glossy color cover; B/W inside; perfect bound. 225 pages. Subscription cost: $12. Sample copy cost: $7. Writer's guidelines available with SASE.

Focus and Tips: *Indiana Review* publishes quality contemporary fiction, poetry, creative nonfiction, and book reviews for readers interested in literary writing. Authors are encouraged to read the publication before considering approaching it. It prizes stylistic innovation as well as control of craft. Avoid rhyming poetry and excessive sentimentality or gimmicks in either poetry or fiction.

Editorial Interests

Literary works, cultural and ethnic issues, the environment, feminism, folklore, gay and lesbian issues, mythology, politics, religion, social and world issues, spirituality, and women's issues.
- *Fiction:* Short stories, short-short stories, drama, unpublished novel excerpts, and poetry. No length restrictions.
- *Nonfiction:* Interviews, profiles, essays, and personal experiences, no length restrictions. Literary reviews, 500–1,500 words. Letters to the editor.

Submission Policy: Send complete manuscript with cover letter. Include SASE. Accepts photocopies, computer printouts, and IBM-compatible WordPerfect 5.0 disks. Simultaneous submissions okay. Responds to queries in 1 week, to manuscripts in 2–16 weeks. If accepted, expect publication in 4–10 months.

Terms and Payment: First North American serial rights. Pays on acceptance. $5 per page. Authors receive 2 copies of the issue.

Advertising: Rates: B/W full-page one-time, $150; two-times, $250. List rental available. Contact Mikki Smith 812-855-3439.

Infinite Onion

Dave Onion, Editor, P.O. Box 6445, Colorado Springs, CO 80934 Phone: 719-578-9167

Profile: An eclectic, counter-culture newspaper. Published by Osmosis. Issued twice a year. Circ: 2,500. Trim size: Tabloid. Newsprint; folded. 12 pages. Subscription cost: N/A. Sample copy cost: $1. No writer's guidelines.

Focus and Tips: *Infinite Onion* seeks to "change the world from the inside out." Advises writers to "build! Set yourself on fire! Build the next reality out of love and strength. Don't be afraid to let down your guard at times, but don't be naive." Avoid "Maoism, hippy-dippy writing, unnecessary punctuation, sexism, and mainstream assimilations."

Editorial Interests

Self-discovery, self-help, extraterrestrials, gay and lesbian issues, lifestyle, parapsychology, philosophy, psychic phenomenon, social and world issues, spirituality, and yoga.

• *Fiction and Nonfiction:* Open to anything relevant and interesting. No length restrictions.

Submission Policy: Query with outline and writing samples. Include SASE. Accepts photocopies, computer printouts, and Macintosh Word disks. Simultaneous submissions okay. Reports in 1 month. If accepted, expect publication in 1–9 months.

Terms and Payment: Rights negotiable. No payment. Authors receive 100 copies of the issue.

Advertising: Rates: B/W full-page, $250. Contact Marcie, 719-578-9167.

Infinity Forum

M. Colleen Owen, Publisher/Editor, 200 Mitchell Road, No. 77, Greenville, SC 29615   Phone: 803-322-5543

Profile: A social justice publication. Published by Brandy-Ben Productions. Issued bimonthly. Circ: 500. Trim size: 8.5x11. 65 lb. paper; stapled. Subscription cost: $10. Sample copy cost: $2. Writer's guidelines available with SASE.

Focus and Tips: *Infinity Forum* is aimed at creating wellness and positive social change with explorations of injustice, freedom, and social conditions. Reaches a humanistic audience with broad interests. No genre fiction.

Editorial Interests

Social and world issues, politics, injustice, freedoms, and current social conditions.

• *Nonfiction:* Features and opinion pieces with strong points of view that are supported by quotes and solid sources, 500–1,700 words.

Submission Policy: Query first with outline. Include SASE. Accepts E-Mail submissions at baish@aol.com. No simultaneous submissions. Reports in 2 weeks.

Terms and Payment: One-time rights. Pays 2 weeks after publication. $.02–$.30 per word. Authors receive 3 copies of the issue.

Advertising: Rates: B/W full-page, $67.50. Contact M. Colleen Owen, 803-322-5543.

Other Interests: Sponsors a Youth '95 contest for poetry, essays, and artwork. Contact M. Colleen Owen.

Inner Light—Voice of the New Age

Timothy Green Beckley, Publisher, 11 East 30th Street, Suite 4R, New York, NY 10016   Phone: 212-685-4080

Profile: A thematic new age tabloid. Published by Global Communications. Issued quarterly. Circ: 100,000+. Trim size: Tabloid. Distributed nationally on newsstands. Sample copy cost: $5. Writer's guidelines available with SASE.

Focus and Tips: *Inner Light* is one of the many UFO/new age publications put out by Global Communications. It serves as a promotional vehicle for other GC products and features articles on the new age, and spiritual and psychic fields. Issues are thematic. Companion publications include *UFO Universe, Unsolved UFO Sightings, Unexplainable Universe,* and *UFO Review.*

Editorial Interests

New age, psychic phenomenon, and spirituality.

• *Nonfiction:* Short articles that fit the issue's theme. Accepts book excerpts for promotional purposes.

Submission Policy: Send complete manuscript with author biography and photo. Include SASE. Accepts photocopies and computer printouts. Allow 4–5 month lead-time.

Terms and Payment: One-time rights and reprint rights. Pays on publication. Articles, $25–$50.

Advertising: Rates: full-page, $600; half-page, $375; quarter-page, $250. Classified ads, $1 per word with a 20-word minimum. List rental available: $70/M. Contact Tim Beckley, 212-685-4080.

InnerSelf

Miss Desmond, Assistant Editor, 915 South 21st Avenue, # 2A, Hollywood, FL 33020   Phone: 305-923-0730, Fax: 305-921-1221

Profile: A metaphysical and spiritual magazine. Issued monthly. Circ: 23,000. Trim size: 8.5x11. Glossy color cover; B/W inside; saddle stitched. 76 pages. Subscription cost: $28.50. Sample copy cost: $2.75. No writer's guidelines.

Focus and Tips: *InnerSelf* covers alternative lifestyle information. Its goal is to assist readers in rediscovering wisdom, peace, and joy within themselves. Committed to environmental awareness, it prints holistically oriented articles, stories, and poetry dealing with the positive side of life. Authors are encouraged to "let your inspiration and creativity express themselves on paper to be shared with others." Seeks informative, practical articles.

Editorial Interests

New age, holistic health, astrology, bodywork, channeling, crystals, dreams, ecosystems, the environment, healing and health, holistic health, inspiration, juvenile and teen issues, lifestyle, meditation, men's issues, metaphysics, natural health, nutrition, parapsychology, parenting, politics, psychology, rebirthing, recovery, relationships, religion, self-help, social and world issues, spirituality, women's issues, and yoga.

• *Fiction:* Book excerpts, 500 words and up.

• *Nonfiction:* Features, articles, essays, personal experiences, and opinion pieces, 700–750 words. Music and video reviews, 250 words. Columns: Earth Speaks, Sex Talk, Might Recipes, Money Talk, Tools for Healing, Herb's Corner, and Check It In.

Submission Policy: Send complete manuscript with cover letter and bibliography. Include SASE. Accepts computer print-outs and IBM-compatible disks. Simultaneous submissions okay. Reports in 3 weeks. If accepted, expect publication in 3–4 months.
Terms and Payment: One-time rights. Offers advertising exchange in lieu of payment. Authors receive 2 copies of the issue.
Advertising: Accepts advertising. Contact Sheila Caputo.

Inside Kung Fu

Dave Cater, Editor, 4201 Van Owen Place, Burbank, CA 91505   Phone: 818-845-2656

Profile: A martial-arts publication. Published by Unique Publications. Issued monthly. Circ: 60,000. Trim size: 8.5x11. Stapled. 120 pages. Subscription cost: $24. Sample copy cost: N/A. Writer's guidelines available with SASE.
Focus and Tips: As its name suggests, *Inside Kung Fu* provides informational articles on Kung Fu, other martial arts, and related health concerns.
Editorial Interests
Kung Fu, martial arts, and health.
• *Nonfiction:* Instructional articles, 500 words.
Submission Policy: Send complete manuscript with cover letter. Include SASE. Accepts photocopies, computer printouts, and Macintosh disks. Simultaneous submissions okay. Reports in 2 months. If accepted, expect publication in 3 months.
Terms and Payment: Pays on publication. Rates vary.
Advertising: Accepts advertising. Contact Advertising Department.

Integral Yoga

Kuorari de Sachy, Editor, Route 1, Box 1720, Buckingham, VA 23921   Phone: 804-969-1200, Fax: 804-969-1303

Profile: An ecumenical magazine of yoga technique. Issued quarterly. Circ: 700. Trim size: 6x9. 40 pages. Subscription cost: $15. Sample copy cost: $3.75. No writer's guidelines.
Focus and Tips: *Integral Yoga* is a spiritual journal based on the yoga teachings of Sri Swami Satchidananda. It reaches an audience interested in spirituality from a yogic and ecumenical point of view. Avoid occult and political writings and obscene language.
Editorial Interests
Yoga, healing, health, holistic health, inspiration, lifestyle, meditation, metaphysics, mysticism, natural health, nutrition, philosophy, relationships, religion, and spirituality.
• *Fiction:* Short stories and book excerpts, 250–1,000 words.
• *Nonfiction:* Features, 250–1,000 words. Articles and essays, 500–1,000 words. Reviews, 100–250 words.
Submission Policy: Query or send complete manuscript. Include SASE. Accepts photocopies, computer printouts, faxes, and Microsoft Word or Clarisworks disks. Reports in 1 month. If accepted, expect publication in 3 months.
Terms and Payment: No payment.
Other Interests: Sponsors several programs, workshops, and retreats on various branches of yoga, health and healing, and philosophy, including silent retreats and teacher training. Contact Ram Wiener, 804-969-3121.

International UFO Library Magazine

Joseph Randazzo, Publisher, 11684 Ventura Boulevard, # 708, Studio City, CA 91604   Phone: 818-769-2917

Profile: A clearinghouse of information on extraterrestrial life. Issued bimonthly. Circ: 100,000. Trim size: 8.5x10.5. Glossy color cover; 4-color; saddle stitched. 80 pages. Subscription cost: $19.95. Sample copy cost: $4.95. Writer's guidelines available with SASE.
Focus and Tips: *International UFO Library Magazine* seeks editorial that explores the possibility of UFOs and extraterrestrial life, as well as cutting-edge issues in science, art, spiritual awareness, discovery, and new thinking. Its readers are intelligent and well-read; therefore, articles should be short, concise, and very informative. Writer's are invited to call the publisher with article ideas.
Editorial Interests
Extraterrestrials, astrology, channeling, the environment, healing and health, holistic health, inspiration, meditation, new age, philosophy, politics, psychic phenomenon, psychology, spirituality, and yoga.
• *Nonfiction:* Features, 3,000–5,000 words. Articles, 1,250 words. Accepts celebrity interviews and profiles, personal experiences, opinion pieces, news items, book and video reviews, and filler.
• *Illustrations:* B/W and 4-color photos, slides, or drawings. Do not send originals.
Submission Policy: Query or call before submitting. Include SASE when querying. Accepts 3.5" IBM or Macintosh WordPerfect 5.0 disks with hard copy. Reports in 2 months.
Terms and Payment: Pays 1 month after press date.

Advertising: Rates: B/W full-page, $1,250; 4-color full-page, $1,740. Contact Suzie at J. E. Publishing, 310-572-7272.

Intuitive Explorations

Gloria Reiser, Editor, P.O. Box 561, Quincy, IL 62306-0561   Phone: 217-222-9082

Profile: A new age magazine. Issued bimonthly. Circ: 350. Trim size: 8.5x11. Heavy bond cover; B/W; stapled. 24+ pages. Subscription cost: $15. Sample copy cost: $2.50. No writer's guidelines.

Focus and Tips: *Intuitive Explorations* publishes material of broad-ranging metaphysical interest. It seeks articles that are of value and that stimulate free thought. Open to all subjects, it prefers good material written "from the heart" to formula writing that conforms to specific lengths or styles.

Editorial Interests

Metaphysics, human potential, planetary awareness, magic, astrology, bodywork, channeling, crystals, dreams, the environment, extraterrestrials, folklore, healing and health, holistic and natural health, inspiration, meditation, mysticism, mythology, new age, nutrition, occult, parapsychology, philosophy, psychic phenomenon, psychology, recovery, relationships, self-help, and spirituality.

• *Nonfiction:* Features and articles, up to 3,000 words. Interviews, profiles, and essays, 500–1,500 words. Personal experiences, opinion pieces, and news, up to 1,500 words. Reviews, up to 500 words. Departments include News & Notes and My Personal Experience. Accepts filler.

Submission Policy: Send complete manuscript with cover letter. Include SASE. Accepts photocopies, computer printouts and IBM WordPerfect disks. Simultaneous submissions okay. Reports in 2–4 months. If accepted, expect publication in 2–4 months.

Terms and Payment: One-time rights. No payment. Authors receive as many copies of the issues as needed.

Advertising: Rates: B/W full-page, $50; half-page, $30. Classified ads, $.30 per word. Contact Gloria Reiser, 217-222-9082.

Other Interests: Sister publications include *Tarot News* and *Somnial Times*.

It's Your Choice

Dr. James Rogers, Editor, P.O. Box 7135, Richmond, VA 23221

Profile: A newsletter of ethics and morality. Published by FutureWend Publications. Issued monthly. Circ: 2,000. Trim size: 8x11. Spot color; folded. 8–12 pages. Subscription cost: free. Sample copy cost: $2. Writer's guidelines available with SASE.

Focus and Tips: *It's Your Choice* researches through public opinion surveys and reports on current issues of ethical and moral import. It is distributed free to human service institutions and agencies by random selection. All articles must be related to ethic and morality in an essential way; don't just tack on a few related sentences. Regard ethics as a scientific study of the rightness or wrongness of human behavior in any context. Writers can address the larger social issues or personal actions. Do not use coarse language.

Editorial Interests

Ethics, morality, criminal justice, education, folklore, gay and lesbian issues, healing, health, lifestyle, new age, nutrition, parenting, philosophy, politics, psychology, relationships, religion, social and world issues, and witches.

• *Fiction:* Short stories, 1,000 words.

• *Nonfiction:* Features, articles, interviews and profiles, essays, personal experiences, and opinion pieces, 1,000 words.

Submission Policy: Send complete manuscript. Include SASE. Accepts computer printouts. Simultaneous submissions okay. Holding past 4 weeks indicated interest.

Terms and Payment: First North American serial rights and reprint rights. Pays on acceptance unless otherwise contracted. Pays up to $1 per word. Authors receive copies of the issue.

Other Interests: Sponsors *It's Your Choice* 1995 Writing Contests open to the general public. Deadline is March 31, 1995; awards announced May 31, 1995. First prize, $1,000 and publication; 4 runners-up, $250 and publication. Send for guidelines Also sponsors a Parent-Active College Scholarship Program (P-ACS-P), on raising and educating ethical children in unethical times. Contact editor for details.

Journal of Philosophy

M. Kelly, Managing Editor, 709 Philosophy Hall, New York, NY 10027   Phone: 212-666-4419, Fax: 212-932-3721

Profile: A university journal of philosophy. Published by Columbia University. Issued monthly. Circ: 4,000. Trim size: 4.25x7.75. Stapled. 64 pages. Subscription cost: $35. Sample copy cost: $5. Writer's guidelines available with SASE.

Focus and Tips: *Journal of Philosophy* publishes distinguished articles on issues of current interest. Its articles explore the relationship between philosophy and the special disciplines. Readers are philosophers, graduate students, professors, and other interested readers.

Editorial Interests

Philosophy.

• *Nonfiction:* Essays, 2,500 words.

Submission Policy: Send complete manuscript with cover letter. Include SASE. Accepts photocopies, computer printouts, computer disks, and faxes. No simultaneous submissions. Reports in 6 months. If accepted, expect publication in 3–6 months.

Terms and Payment: One-time rights. No payment. Authors receive copies of the issue.

Advertising: Rates: B/W full-page, $500. List rental available: $150/M. Contact Pamela Ward, 212-666-4419.

Kaleidoscope

Darshan Perusek, Editor-in-Chief, 326 Locust Street, Akron, OH 44302-1876   Phone: 216-762-9755, Fax: 216-762-0912

Profile: An international magazine of literature, fine arts, and disability. Established in 1979. Issued twice a year. Circ: 1,500. Trim size: 8.5x11. Glossy color cover; 4-color spread; B/W inside; saddle stitched. 64 pages. Subscription cost: Individual, $9; Institutional, $14. Sample copy cost: $4. Writer's guidelines available with SASE.

Focus and Tips: *Kaleidoscope* publishes well-crafted fiction, poetry, and visual arts related to the experience of disability along with critical essays, book reviews, and personal experience narratives. Each issue focuses on a different theme in relation to disability. The magazine features writers and artists both with and without disabilities. Readers include students, libraries, and health-care professionals. Avoid anything stereotypical or sentimental in regards to disability.

Editorial Interests

Disability, fine arts, and literature.

• *Fiction:* Short stories, 5,000 words. Poetry, up to 5 poems per submission. Accepts book excerpts.

• *Nonfiction:* Features, articles, interviews, profiles, essays, personal experiences, and opinion pieces, 5,000 words.

Submission Policy: Query or send complete manuscript with cover letter. Include SASE. Accepts photocopies, computer printouts, and faxes. Simultaneous submissions okay. Reports in 6 months. If accepted, expect publication in 2–12 months.

Terms and Payment: Pays on publication. $10–$125 per piece. Authors receive 2 copies of the issue.

Other Interests: Affiliated with United Disability Service, a not-for-profit United Way agency. For more information, contact Marian Kindell, 216-762-9755.

Keltria: Journal of Druidism and Celtic Magick

Tony Taylor, Editor-in-Chief, P.O. Box 33284, Minneapolis, MN 55433   Phone: 612-755-0773

Profile: A Neopagan journal. Published by the nonprofit Henge of Keltria. Issued quarterly. Circ: 750. Trim size: 8.5x11. Glossy cover; B/W; stapled. 24 pages. Subscription cost: $10. Sample copy cost: $3. Writer's guidelines available with SASE.

Focus and Tips: *Keltria* accepts materials on Druid and Celtic magick only. Writers are advised to read the journal for style, to use an active voice, and to avoid diatribes. Issues are thematic.

Editorial Interests

Druidism, Celtic magick, folklore, and mythology.

• *Fiction:* Mythological short stories and short-short stories, 500–1,000 words. Druid and Celtic poetry, 200 words.

• *Nonfiction:* Theme-related features, 500–1,000 words. Accepts articles, interviews, profiles, and essays. Reviews on Celtic, Druid, and Neopagan books, 50–150 words.

Submission Policy: Send complete manuscript with cover letter and bibliography. Include SASE. Accepts photocopies, computer printouts, and IBM ASCII disks. No simultaneous submissions. Reports in 2 months. If accepted, expect publication in 5 months.

Terms and Payment: One-time rights. Pays on publication. $.01 per word. No payment for poetry or reviews. Authors receive 1 copy of the issue.

Advertising: Accepts advertising, rates vary. Contact editor.

Kids Lib News

Michael Sunanda, Founder, P.O. Box 68, NaiLehn, HI 96772   Phone: 808-929-7311

Profile: A new age magazine for families with children. Published by Oness Press. Issued quarterly. Circ: 3,000. Trim size: 8.5x11. Newsprint; saddle stitched. 40 pages. Subscription cost: $12. Sample copy cost: $2–$4. No writer's guidelines.

Focus and Tips: *Kids Lib News* offers practical and humorous information for new age families on home education, children's rights, holistic parenting, natural healing, geo-toys, and cooperation. Material that helps readers "enjoy free family rites naturally" is welcome. Not interested in articles promoting "tough-love," conservation, scientific or religious morals, or domination of youth.

Editorial Interests

Family relationships, juvenile and teen issues, parenting, child birth, natural living, dreams, feminism, healing, meditation, natural health, nutrition, psychology, rebirthing, recovery, self-help, spirituality, women's issues, child abuse prevention, cooperation, and bonding.

• *Fiction:* Short stories about families and children, 300–500 words. Drama with cartoons and dialogue, 300 words. Deep feel-

ing genre fiction, 700 words. Jokes, 200 words.
• *Nonfiction:* Features, articles, interviews, and profiles concerning family liberation, 800 words. Essays, 700 words. Personal experiences of relating to children, 500 words. Opinion pieces and news on youth issues, 300 words. Book, music, and movie reviews, up to 200 words. Filler relating to nature, 200 words. Departments include Home Education, Health, Birthing, and Parenting.
Submission Policy: Query with outline and writing samples. Include SASE. Accepts photocopies and computer printouts. Simultaneous submissions okay. Responds to queries in 2 weeks, to manuscripts in 1 month. If accepted, expect publication in 3 months.
Terms and Payment: One-time rights. Payment negotiable. Offers advertising space in lieu of payment. Authors receive 1–10 copies of the issue.
Advertising: Rates: B/W full-page, $100. Ad trades available. Contact Michael Sunanda, 808-929-7311.
Other Interests: Sponsors a Kids Monkey writing contest, which is open to dramatic stories addressing the needs of family and children. Will organize Cooperative Parenting workshops and Geo-toys playshops upon request. For more contest or workshop information, contact Michael Sunanda, 808-929-7311.

The Ledge Poetry and Fiction Magazine

Timothy Monaghan, Editor/Publisher, 64-65 Cooper Avenue, Glendale, NY 11385

Profile: An eclectic literary journal. Issued 2 times a year. Circ: 700. Trim size: 5.5x8.5. Glossy cover; B/W; 60 lb. offset; perfect bound. 80 pages. Subscription cost: $15 for 2 years. Sample copy cost: $5. Writer's guidelines available with SASE.
Focus and Tips: *The Ledge* seeks cutting-edge, contemporary writing in the form of fiction and poetry that is gritty, arresting, and provocative. "Work that displays craft and heart stands the best shot here." It is eclectic and open to all schools and slants. Avoid "warmed-over workshop writing, uninspired academic bullshit, and punchline poetry or fiction. Shy away from rhyming poetry unless the poem resists or transcends the tradition."
Editorial Interests
Open to all subject matter.
• *Fiction:* Short stories, short-short stories, and poetry. No length restrictions.
Submission Policy: Send complete manuscript with cover letter. Include SASE. Accepts photocopies and computer printouts. Simultaneous submissions okay. Reports in up to 2 months. If accepted, expect publication in 6 months.
Terms and Payment: One-time rights. Pays on publication. Rates vary. Authors receive 1–3 copies of the issue.
Advertising: Rates: B/W full-page, $50. Contact Timothy Monaghan.
Other Interests: Sponsors The Ledge Annual Poetry Chapbook Contest and The Ledge Annual Poetry and Fiction Contest. Send SASE for guidelines. For more information, contact Timothy Monaghan.

Light of Consciousness

Sita Stuhlmiller, Editor, 3403 West Sweetwater Drive, Tucson, AZ 85745   Phone: 602-743-0384

Profile: A journal of metaphysics and inner awakening. Published by Truth Consciousness. Established in 1976. Issued 3 times a year. Circ: 4,000. Trim size: 8.5x11. Glossy color cover; spot color inside; saddle stitched. 72–80 pages. Subscription cost: $10. Sample copy cost: $2. No writer's guidelines.
Focus and Tips: *Light of Consciousness* is dedicated to the inner unfoldment of the soul and spiritual awakening. It seeks transformational articles celebrating the underlying unity of all spiritual paths and awakening consciousness on the planet. Prefers reader friendly pieces that use a "whole-brain" approach and offer something relevant to spiritual seekers. Avoid intellectual, dry, academic, political, or divisive writing.
Editorial Interests
Spirituality, sacred sites, saints, art and music, the environment, healing, holistic health, inspiration, meditation, metaphysics, mysticism, new age, prayer, universal religion, and yoga.
• *Fiction:* Short stories, short-short stories, drama, book excerpts, genre fiction, and poetry with spiritual, mystical, or transformational message. No length restrictions.
• *Nonfiction:* Features, articles, interviews, profiles, essays, personal experiences, opinion pieces, news, reviews, and filler of interest to spiritual seekers or related to spiritual awakening. No length restrictions.
Submission Policy: Query with outline or send complete manuscript with cover letter. Include SASE. Accepts photocopies, computer printouts, and Macintosh disks. Reports in 2 months. If accepted, expect publication in 4 months.
Terms and Payment: One-time rights. No payment. Occasionally considers ad trades. Authors receive copies of the issue.
Advertising: Rates: B/W full-page, $300; half-page, $170; quarter-page, $90. Full-color full-page, $1,500. Contact Marianne Martin, 602-743-0384.

Lightworks

Joanne Brandt, Editor, 405 South Fifth Avenue, West Reading, PA 19611-1301   Phone: 610-376-0589, Fax: 610-376-3063

Profile: A regional new age magazine. Issued 10 times a year. Circ: 15,000. Trim size: 8.5x11. Self cover; spot color; stapled. 24 pages. Subscription cost: $19.95. Sample copy cost: $2. Writer's guidelines available with SASE.
Focus and Tips: *Lightworks* publishes material that promotes health and peace of mind. It reaches an upscale, new age audience in the Pennsylvania-Maryland area. Special appeal is made to skeptics and new seekers, but articles address all with new age interests. Welcomes first-person narratives that offer a personal view of the topic. No lectures or preaching.
Editorial Interests
New age, health, business, economy, housing, urban renewal, organic gardening, astrology, channeling, dreams, the environment, gay and lesbian issues, healing, holistic and natural health, inspiration, juvenile and teen issues, lifestyle, magic, meditation, men's and women's issues, metaphysics, mysticism, mythology, nutrition, parenting, philosophy, politics, prayer, psychic phenomenon, psychology, rebirthing, recovery, relationships, self-help, spirituality, witches, and yoga.
• *Nonfiction:* Features, articles, essays, and personal experiences, 1,000–1,200 words. Interviews and profiles, 1,500 words. News items, 100–500 words. Reviews, 500–800 words.
Submission Policy: Query with outline and writing samples. Include SASE. Accepts photocopies and computer printouts. Simultaneous submissions okay. Responds to queries in 1 month, to manuscripts in 2 months. If accepted, expect publication within 1–3 months.
Terms and Payment: One-time rights. Pays on publication for interviews only. $20 per interview. Authors receive 1–10 copies of the issue.
Advertising: Rates: B/W full-page, $480; B/W half-page, $245; B/W quarter page, $120. Contact Joanne Brandt, 610-376-0589.
Other Interests: Sponsors monthly women's spiritual retreats. For more information, contact Joanne Brandt.

Live and Let Live

James Dawson, Publisher, P.O. Box 613, Redwood Valley, CA 95470

Profile: A libertarian, pro-life, animal-rights publication. Issued 2–4 times a year. Circ: 50. Trim size: 5.5x8. Photocopied; folded. 10–14 pages. Subscription cost: $3 for 4 issues. Sample copy cost: $.50 plus a first-class stamp. No writer's guidelines.
Focus and Tips: *Live and Let Live* seeks to explore and develop a theory and strategy of animal and fetal rights from a libertarian/individualist—as opposed to a left/collectivist—framework. Audience is either pro-life, libertarian, or pro-animal rights. Stresses content over quality. Avoid anything that is gratuitously inflammatory, racist, sexist, or insulting to particular religious groups.
Editorial Interests
Animal rights, fetal rights, libertarianism, vegetarianism, philosophy, politics, and religion.
• *Nonfiction:* Anything pertaining to magazine's theme, no length restrictions. Submissions are subject to editing.
Submission Policy: Send complete manuscript or query. Include SASE. Accepts photocopies and computer printouts. Simultaneous submissions okay.
Terms and Payment: Rights negotiable. No payment. Authors receive 2 copies of the issue.
Advertising: Rates: Classified ads, $.02 per word with a $1 minimum. Display ads, $.50 per inch. Contact James Dawson.

Living Off the Land

Marian Van Atta, Editor, P.O. Box 2131, Melbourne, FL 32902-2131   Phone: 407-723-5554

Profile: A subtropic newsletter. Published by Geraventure Corp. Issued 5 times a year. Circ: 600. Trim size: 8.5x11. B/W; folded. 6 pages. Subscription cost: $14. Sample copy cost: $1. No writer's guidelines.
Focus and Tips: *Living Off the Land* addresses the needs and interests of people who live in tropical climates and grow much of their own food. Accepts tropical gardening articles and recipes only. Welcomes the work of first-time authors.
Editorial Interests
Home gardening; exotic fruits, vegetables, and flowers; the environment; self-help; and social and world issues.
• *Nonfiction:* Features, 500 words. Accepts personal experience pieces about warm-weather growing.
• *Illustrations:* B/W line drawings.
Submission Policy: Query with outline. Include SASE. Simultaneous submissions okay. Reports in 1 month. If accepted, expect publication in 3–4 months.
Terms and Payment: All rights. Pays on publication. Articles, $10. Drawings, $5. Authors receive 12 copies of the issue.
Advertising: Rates: B/W, $10.
Other Interests: Holds an annual Rare Fruit Tree sale in Melbourne, Florida.

Llewellyn's New Worlds of Mind and Spirit

Krista Trempe, Editor, P.O. Box 64383, St. Paul, MN 55417   Phone: 612-291-1970, Fax: 612-291-1908

Profile: A new age magalog. Published by Llewellyn Worldwide. Issued 6 times a year. Circ: 60,000. Trim size: 7.5x10. Glossy color cover; spot color; saddle stitched. 144 pages. Subscription cost: $10. Sample copy cost: Free. Writer's guidelines available with SASE.

Focus and Tips: *Llewellyn's New Worlds of Mind and Spirit* features the latest information in the fields of new age human potential. It seeks practical articles that take readers beyond superficiality to a serious but popular presentation of subject pertinent to the new age and magickal communities. Articles should be lively, personal, experiential, informative, develop practical benefits, and play up the wonder of the subject matter. *New Worlds* also includes Llewellyn book excerpts, book reviews, a reader's forum, news and events, and current advertised products and services.

Editorial Interests

New age, magic, astrology, dreams, folklore, healing, holistic and natural health, meditation, metaphysics, mysticism, mythology, occult, parapsychology, psychic phenomenon, and self-help.

• *Nonfiction:* Practical, how-to articles, personal experiences, informative pieces, 500–1,500 words.

• *Illustrations:* High contrast B/W photos and illustrations to accompany articles. Supply captions.

Submission Policy: Query with outline. Include SASE. Accepts photocopies, computer printouts, Macintosh or IBM-compatible disks, and faxes. Reports in 1–3 months.

Terms and Payment: All rights or one-time rights. No payment. Offers advertising space in lieu of payment. Ads appear in the same issue as article. Authors receive 3 copies of the issue.

Advertising: Rates: B/W full-page, $850; 4-color, $1,020. Contact Nancy Trudelle, 612-291-1970. List rental available. Contact Jami Marketing.

Macrobiotics Today

Bob Ligon, Editor, 4374 Hilldale Road, San Diego, CA 92116   Phone/Fax: 619-282-9003

Profile: A magazine devoted to macrobiotics. Published by the George Ohsawa Macrobiotic Foundation. Established in 1960. Issued bimonthly. Circ: 5,000. Trim size: 8.5x11. Self cover; B/W; saddle stitched. 40 pages. Subscription cost: $15. Sample copy cost: $3.25. No writer's guidelines.

Focus and Tips: *Macrobiotics Today* publishes reports, interviews, and feature articles on macrobiotic lifestyle principles and practices. Readers are members of the George Ohsawa Macrobiotic Foundation and others interested in this field.

Editorial Interests

Macrobiotics, holistic and natural health, philosophy, and spirituality.

• *Nonfiction:* Features, interviews, profiles, essays, personal experiences, opinion pieces, news items, 1,000–2,500 words. Accepts reviews and filler.

Submission Policy: Send complete manuscript with cover letter. Include SASE. Accepts Macintosh, PC Word, and Windows disks. Reports in 1–2 months. If accepted, expect publication in 4 months.

Terms and Payment: All rights. No payment. Authors receive 3–5 copies of the issue.

Advertising: Accepts advertising. List rental available: $75/M. Contact Bob Ligon, 619-282-9003.

Magic Realism

C. Darren Butler, Editor-in-Chief, P.O. Box 620, Orem, UT 84059-0620

Profile: A literary magazine of poetry and prose. Published by Pyx Press. Issued 2 times a year. Circ: 800. Trim size: 5.5x8.5. Heavy bond color cover; B/W; stapled. 80 pages. Subscription cost: $14.95/3 issues. Sample copy cost: $4.95. Writer's guidelines available with SASE.

Focus and Tips: *Magic Realism* accepts a wide range of material including magic realism, exaggerated realism, and literary fantasy. This genre of work allows the human imagination to define reality. Magic realism subverts reality by shaping it into a human mold; bringing it closer to the imagination and to the subconscious. The best magic realism offers options for thinking, renews one's vision, and teaches about the human experience. Prefers work where the fabric of reality is affected, rather than simply tacking on fantastic elements. Avoid stories about wizardry, witches, occult, sword-and-sorcery, or sleight-of-hand magicians. This is not a market for moralistic, religious, or lesson-teaching stories, or work that talks down to readers.

Editorial Interests

Magic realism, literary fantasy, genre fantasy/dark fantasy, folklore, fables, and myths.

• *Fiction:* Stories, drama, serialized stories, and genre fiction, up to 8,000 words. Poetry, prefers 3–30 lines, but open to all lengths. Considers all styles.

• *Nonfiction:* Thematic essays, biographical or critical essays, translations, regular column, and book reviews, up to 8,000 words. Accepts reprints.

• *Illustrations:* Occasionally use illustrations as cover art. To be considered, submit a photocopied portfolio.

Submission Policy: Send complete manuscript with cover letter and short biography for pieces under 8,000 words. For longer pieces, query first with sample chapters. Include SASE. Accepts photocopies and computer printouts. Responds to queries in 1 month, to manuscripts in 3–6 months. If accepted, expect publication in 15 months.

Terms and Payment: First North American serial rights or one-time rights and translation rights. Pays on publication. Prose, $2 per published page. Poetry and artwork, $3 per published page. Authors receive 1–3 copies of the issue.

A   Butler, P.O. Box 620, Orem, UT 84059-0620.

Ma
Karen   17 Phone: 916-757-6033, Fax: 916-757-6041

Profile: d healing arts. Published by Noah Publishing. Issued
bimonthl\   . cover; 4-color 40 lb. inside; saddle stitched. 125+ pages.
Subscriptio.   able with SASE.
Focus and T   ess the needs of massage therapists and allied health
professional st   ts include investigative, technique-oriented, how-to
pieces and in-de   .ywork professionals. Articles dealing with technique
should be very so\   probably do better submitting profiles. Anything not related to
bodywork, preferal
Editorial Interests
Massage, bodywork, h   .tural health, and metaphysics.
• *Fiction:* Stories about i   .aywork, 1,000–2,000 words. Short-short stories, 500–1,500 words.
• *Nonfiction:* Features and   .es on bodywork and massage-related pieces in the areas of business, politics, law, health care,
insurance, intercultural exchange, travel, and humor, 2,000+ words. Interviews with and profiles of massage therapists,
1,000–2,000 words. Massage-related essays, personal experiences, and opinion pieces, 1,000–1,500 words. News items
250–1,000 words. Filler—newsbriefs, press releases, announcements.
• *Illustrations:* B/W photos, color slides, or professional illustrations.
Submission Policy: Query with outline and writing samples or send complete manuscript with cover letter and bibliography. Include SASE. Accepts photocopies, computer printouts, Microsoft Word disks, and faxes. Reports in 2 months. If
accepted, expect publication within 2–12 months.
Terms and Payment: First North American serial rights. Pays 30 days after publication. $25–$200 per piece. Authors receive 2
copies of the issue.
Advertising: Rates: B/W full-page, $900, 4-color full-page, $1,450. Contact Corey Gerhard, 916-757-6033. Active subscriber
list rental available. Contact Linda R. Gleen, 916-757-6033
Other Interests: Sponsors the Hi-Touch Tour, massage-related exhibits and product demonstrations.

Maui'arna Magazine

Suzi Osborn, Publisher, 52 Central Avenue, Wailuku, Maui, HI 96793   Phone: 808-244-7400, Fax: 808-242-5900

Profile: A regional publication for the Hawaiian Islands. Published by Alaya Unlimited. Issued monthly. Circ: 6,000. Trim
size: 7.75x11. Self cover; spot color; saddle stitched. 24–32 pages. Subscription cost: $15. Sample copy cost: free. No writer's
guidelines.
Focus and Tips: *Maui'arna Magazine* is a networking magazine designed to serve as a communications link for the business,
residents, and visitors to the Hawaiian Islands. Its focus is on environmental awareness, Hemp education, health consciousness, and human potential development. Readers are a vast cross-section of the Island population, mainstream and metaphysical. Articles should be fun to read and teach the reader something new or a new way.
Editorial Interests
Hawaiian Island regional interests, Hemp education, astrology, bodywork, cultural and ethnic issues, dreams, the environment, folklore, healing and health, holistic and natural health, inspiration, lifestyle, meditation, metaphysics, mysticism, new
age, nutrition, occult, parapsychology, psychic phenomenon, rebirthing, recovery, relationships, self-help, spirituality and
yoga.
• *Poetry:* Unlimited word length.
• *Nonfiction:* Articles, 450–500 words. Opinion pieces and news items on Hemp education. Book reviews, 300–500 words.
Submission Policy: Send complete manuscript with cover letter. Include SASE. Accepts photocopies, computer printouts,
and Macintosh MS Word or PageMaker disks. Reports in 1 month. If accepted, expect publication within 2–3 months.
Terms and Payment: One-time rights. No payment. Authors receive up to 25 copies of the issue.
Advertising: Rates: B/W full-page, $450. Contact Suzi Osborn, 808-244-7400.
Other Interests: Offers seminars and promotes various speakers. Contact Suzi Osborn.

Men As We Are

Jonathan Running Wind, Editor-in-Chief, P.O. Box 150615, Brooklyn, NY 11215-0007   Phone/Fax: 718-499-2829

Profile: A magazine exploring the male experience. Issued quarterly. Circ: 1,200. Trim size: 8.5x11. Self cover; B/W inside;
saddle stitched. 32–48 pages. Subscription cost: $12. Sample copy cost: $3.75. Writer's guidelines available with SASE.
Focus and Tips: *Men As We Are* offers an honest, vulnerable portrayal of the masculine experience in all its forms. It is both a

celebration and lament of who men are today. Welcomes perspectives from all races, ethnic groups, and sexual orientations. Readers include men and women who are examining and transforming traditional gender roles and who want to read high-quality literary writing. Encourages personal, radically honest pieces. Avoid how-to's, ungrounded speculation, and "new age crystal phoo-phoo."

Editorial Interests
Men's issues, parenting, cultural and ethnic concerns, ecosystems, feminism, gay and lesbian issues, healing, mysticism, philosophy, politics, psychology, recovery, relationships, seniors, social and world issues, spirituality, and women's issues.
• *Fiction:* Short stories, 500–5,000 words. Short-short stories, 50–500 words. Drama, 2,000 words. Book excerpts, 5,000 words. Poetry, no length restrictions.
• *Nonfiction:* Special interest in essays, 500–6,000 words. Features, articles, interviews and profiles, and personal experiences, 500–5,000 words. Opinion pieces, 500–1,000 words. Departments: Men in the Mass Media, 250–1,000 words; Man Is a Giddy Thing, 250–500 words; News of Men From All Over, 500–1,500 words; Fathering, 500–1,500 words; and Homeless, 500–1,500 words.
• *Illustrations:* Photos, illustrations, artwork, cartoons, and comic strips.

Submission Policy: Send complete manuscript with cover letter and bibliography. Include SASE. Accepts photocopies, computer printouts, and 3.5" MS-Word, WordPerfect, or ASCII disks. Simultaneous submissions okay. Reports in 3–6 months. If accepted, expect publication within 9 months.
Terms and Payment: First North American serial rights or one-time rights. Retains non-exclusive anthology rights. Pays on publication. $5 minimum per piece. Authors receive 3 copies of the issue.
Advertising: Rates per page: B/W, $350. One-time list rental available; rates negotiable. Contact Jonathan Running Wind, 718-499-2829.

Mentor
Dick Gilkeson, Editor, P.O. Box 10863, Portland, OR 97231   Phone: 503-287-8737, Fax: 503-621-3612

Profile: A quarterly journal about men and their journey of discovery. Issued quarterly. Circ: 7,000. Trim size: 8.5x11. Self cover; B/W; stapled. 32–40 pages. Subscription cost: $10. Sample copy cost: Free. Writer's guidelines available with SASE.
Focus and Tips: *Mentor* explores the male experience and encourages communications from the heart about life. Read predominantly by middle-aged men. Prefers personal experience pieces about issues related to being a man in the '90s. Avoid lecturing, third-person pieces, and articles that put down any category of human beings.
Editorial Interests
Men's issues.
• *Poetry:* No length restrictions.
• *Nonfiction:* Features, articles, interviews and profiles, personal experiences, and opinion pieces, 900–1,200 words. Reviews, 900 words. News items, no length restrictions. Gay Spirit column, 900–1,200 words.
Submission Policy: Send complete manuscript with cover letter. Include SASE. Accepts photocopies, computer printouts, and disks. Simultaneous submissions okay. Reports in up to 3 months. If accepted, expect publication in 8 weeks.
Terms and Payment: One-time rights. No payment. Authors receive copies of the issue.
Advertising: Rates per page: B/W, $160. Contact Doyle Banks, 503-797-3814.

Midwifery Today
Jan Tritten, Editor, 390 High Street, Eugene, OR 97401   Phone: 503-344-7438, Fax: 503-344-1422

Profile: A publication for birth practitioners. Issued quarterly. Circ: 2,900. Trim size: 8.5x11. Glossy cover; 50 lb. paper; B/W inside; saddle stitched. 56 pages. Subscription cost: $30. Sample copy cost: $6. Writer's guidelines available with SASE.
Focus and Tips: Written for birth practitioners, childbirth educators, and parents, *Midwifery Today* aims to empower midwives and birthing women. It emphasizes safe natural childbirth, networking, education, and the physiology of birth. Authors should balance between scientific or technical material and "softer" philosophical articles, poetry, and art. Not interested in interventive approaches to birth and pregnancy or in highly conservative attitudes about women and birth.
Editorial Interests
Pregnancy and birth, midwifery, childbirth education, parenting, holistic and natural health, healing and health, nutrition, and women's issues.
• *Nonfiction:* Features, articles, interviews and profiles, essays, opinion pieces, personal experiences, and news items, 1,000–3,000 words.
Submission Policy: Query with outline or send complete manuscript with cover letter. Include SASE. Accepts photocopies, computer printouts, Macintosh Microsoft Word 4.0 disks, and faxes. No simultaneous submissions. Reports in 1 month. If accepted, expect publication within 6–12 months.
Terms and Payment: All rights. No payment. Offers free, one-year subscription for full-length articles. Authors receive 1 copy of the issue.

Advertising: Accepts advertising. Contact Nicole VanDeVeere. List rental available: $.10 per name. Contact Teresa Sheppard, 503-344-7438.
Other Interests: Sponsors three conferences: East Coast, West Coast, and Pacific Rim. All offer networking opportunities for midwives and educators. For more information, contact Karen Bray, P.O. Box 2672, Eugene, OR 97402, 503-344-7438.

The Mirror
Rosamund Cunnington, Editor, 56 Woodycrest Ave., Toronto, ON, M4J 3A7 Canada   Phone: 416-465-3789, Fax: 905-842-8672

Profile: A journal of psychology and religion. Published by Pariah Press. Issued quarterly. Circ: 500. Trim size: 7x10. Heavy bond cover; B/W; perfect bound. 100 pages. Subscription cost: $50 (Canadian). Sample copy cost: $12.75 (Canadian). No writer's guidelines.
Focus and Tips: *The Mirror* is a psychological quarterly interested in a religious perspective on in-depth psychology. Readers are those who seek religious meaning in their daily experience. It is interested in works that express original thought based on personal experience and in issues of moral authority. Personal viewpoints should be born of reflection and not just an opinion. Avoid learned or didactic viewpoints.
Editorial Interests
Psychology, Christianity, bodywork, dreams, healing, mysticism, and spirituality.
• *Nonfiction:* Articles and personal experiences, 500–800 words.
Submission Policy: Query with outline or send complete manuscript with cover letter. Include SASE. Accepts photocopies, computer printouts, and faxes. No simultaneous submissions. Reports in 2–3 weeks. If accepted, expect publication in 2 months.
Terms and Payment: All rights. No payment. Authors receive 1 copy of the issue.
Other Interests: Sponsors the "Who Am I to Talk?" conference, six exploratory discussions on psychological self-discovery and Christian tradition, at Christ Church in Deer Park, Toronto, Ontario. Fee: $100. For more information, contact Rosamund Cunnington, 416-465-3789.

Modern Shaman Magazine
John Stehman, Editor, 1316 North Willow, Ellensburg, WA 98926   Phone: 509-925-1339

Profile: A publication exploring shamanistic practices. Published by Void Press. Issued quarterly. Circ: N/A. Trim size: 8.5x11. Color cover; photocopies; 20 lb. paper; saddle stitched. 30–34 pages. Subscription cost: $20. Sample copy cost: $5. No writer's guidelines.
Focus and Tips: *Modern Shaman Magazine* focuses on experiential shamanism from the point of view of those who practice it. The editor is eager to work with contributors as individuals and let the readers respond to the writing as well as the content of a piece. "Innocence, forthrightness, and lack of intellectual snobbery are important." Open to all writing that "comes from the heart."
Editorial Interests
Shamanism, spirits, Earth energies, Fengshui, totem magic, and Carlos Castaneda. Open to the following as pertaining to shamanism: Cultural and ethnic issues, dreams, the environment, feminism, folklore, gay and lesbian concerns, healing, inspiration, magic, meditation, men's issues, metaphysics, mysticism, mythology, natural health, new age, nutrition, occult, parapsychology, philosophy, politics, prayer, psychic phenomenon, psychology, recovery, relationships, religion, self-help, social and world issues, spirituality, and women's issues.
• *Fiction:* Short stories and chapbook excerpts, up to 2,000 words. Poetry, no length restrictions.
• *Nonfiction:* Especially interested in personal experiences, up to 2,000 words. Articles, interviews, profiles, essays, opinion pieces, news items, and book and tape reviews, up to 2,000 words. Filler, 15, 25, or 50 words. Departments include Q&A, reader's questions to spiritual guides; Fengshui; Gemstone Elixer. Accepts jokes.
• *Illustrations:* Accepts cartoons and B/W line art.
Submission Policy: Send complete manuscript with cover letter, author biography, and background information. Include SASE. Accepts photocopies and computer printouts. Simultaneous submissions okay. Reports in 3–4 weeks. If accepted, expect publication in 6 months.
Terms and Payment: Authors retain rights. No payment. Authors receive 1 copy of the issue.
Advertising: Accepts advertising. Contact John Stehman, 509-925-1339.
Other Interests: Sponsors a thematic photography contest. Also offers workshops and individual instruction on shamic initiation path.

The Monthly Aspectarian: Chicago's New Age Magazine
Guy Spiro, Publisher/Editor, P.O. Box 1342, Morton Grove, IL 60053   Phone: 708-966-1110, Fax: 708-966-6535

Profile: A regional new age publication. Published by TMA Communications, Inc. Issued monthly. Circ: 20,000. Trim size:

8x10. Color cover; B/W newsprint inside; stapled. 112 pages. Subscription cost: $36. Sample copy cost: $2. No guidelines.

Focus and Tips: *The Monthly Aspectarian* is dedicated to awakening consciousness. To that end, it seeks to publish as broad a range of subject matter and level of understanding as possible, primarily new age/metaphysical material. Avoid thinly disguised self-promotional pieces, i.e., "I do this, I do that, it's really great and you ought to try me." No negative reviews or articles attacking people or groups even if deserving.

Editorial Interests

New age, metaphysics, astrology, bodywork, channeling, crystals, cultural and ethnic issues, dreams, ecosystems, the environment, extraterrestrials, folklore, healing and health, holistic health, inspiration, lifestyle, magic, meditation, mysticism, mythology, nutrition, occult, parapsychology, parenting, philosophy, politics, prayer, psychic phenomenon, psychology, rebirthing, recovery, self-help, social and world issues, spirituality, witches, and yoga.

• *Fiction:* Short stories, short-short stories, drama, and book excerpts, up to 5,000 words. Occasionally publishes poetry.

• *Nonfiction:* Features, articles, interviews, profiles, essays, personal experiences, opinion pieces, and news items, up to 5,000 words. Accepts reviews and filler.

Submission Policy: Send complete manuscript with cover letter. Include SASE. Accepts photocopies, computer printouts, faxes, and IBM Microsoft Word for Windows, WordPerfect, or PageMaker disks. Reports in up to 7 months. If accepted, expect publication in up to 7 months.

Terms and Payment: Rights vary. Offers advertising space in lieu of payment. Authors receive copies of the issue.

Advertising: Rates: B/W full-page, $400; 4-color full-page, $500. Contact Guy Spiro, 708-966-1110.

Mother Jones

Cathy Liu, Assistant, 731 Market Street, Suite 600, San Francisco, CA 94103   Phone: 415-357-0509

Profile: A national progressive political magazine. Published by the nonprofit Foundation for National Progress. Established in 1976. Issued bimonthly. Circ: 120,000. Trim size: 8.5x11. Glossy color cover; 4-color; saddle stitched. 84 pages. Subscription cost: $18. Sample copy cost: $5. Writers guidelines available with SASE.

Focus and Tips: *Mother Jones* publishes investigative journalism on political corruption, government accountability, popular culture, and current events and social issues. All material is written from a progressive political perspective. Writers are encouraged to check past issues to see what has already been covered. "If you choose to cover an old issue, provide a new angle."

Editorial Interests

Politics, social issues, cultural and ethnic concerns, the environment, feminism, gay and lesbian issues, health, children's and teen issues, lifestyle, men's issues, nutrition, philosophy, religion, and women's issues.

• *Nonfiction:* Investigative features and articles, 3,000–4,000 words. Short pieces, 200–1,000 words. Interviews and profiles, 1,000–2,000 words. Essays and opinion pieces, 1,000–2,000 words. News, 3,000–4,000 words.

Submission Policy: Query with outline and resume or send complete manuscript with cover letter, bibliography, clips, and author biography. Include SASE. Accepts photocopies and computer printouts. Simultaneous submissions okay if noted. Reports in 4–6 weeks. Publication time varies.

Terms and Payment: First North American serial rights. Pays on acceptance. $.80 per word. Authors receive 2 copies of the issue.

Advertising: Accepts advertising. Contact Diane Raimondo, 415-357-0509. List rental available. Contact Suzanne McCloskey, 415-357-0509.

Other Interests: Sponsors the MoJo Awards for Young Activists writing contest, for social/political activists under 30 years of age. 500 words or less. Deadline is May 1, 1995. Contact Cathy Liu, 415-357-0509. Also sponsors various conferences for promoting political and social change and responsibility. Contact the Foundation for National Progress.

Mothers Resource Guide

Karla Harris, Editor, 800 17th Avenue, P.O. Box 38, South Milwaukee, WI 53172   Phone/Fax: 414-762-8303

Profile: An alternative parenting magazine. Published by Stork Deliveries, Inc. Issued quarterly. Circ: 30,000. Trim size: 8x10. Color cover; B/W inside; 50 lb. paper; saddle stitched. 40–56 pages. Subscription cost: $6.50. Sample copy cost: $2. Writer's guidelines available with SASE.

Focus and Tips: *Mothers Resource Guide* is dedicated to increasing communication and networking within the mothering community. It provides information, support, and answers for mothers looking for alternative and natural parenting methods. Writers are advised to be brief, and then cut some words. Preference given to short book reviews and how-to pieces on specific issues relating to motherhood. "No fluff, no fiction."

Editorial Interests

Natural mothering, parenting, women's issues, the environment, holistic and natural health, nutrition, relationships, self-help, and social and world issues.

• *Nonfiction:* Practical, informational material. Features, 2,000 words. How-to articles, interviews, and profiles, 1,000 words.

Short book reviews, 300–600 words. Filler, 100–300 words. Columns include Activities, Economizing, and Homebased Business, 1,000 words.

Submission Policy: Query with outline or send complete manuscript with cover letter and bibliography. Include SASE. Accepts photocopies, computer printouts, faxes, and WordPerfect or Word for Windows disks. Simultaneous submissions okay. Responds to queries in 2 months, to manuscripts in 4 months. If accepted, expect publication in 6 months.

Terms and Payment: One-time rights. Pays on publication. $.03 per word. Authors receive 3–10 copies of the issue.

Advertising: Rates: B/W full-page, $700; 4-color full-page, $995. Contact Karla Harris, 414-762-8303.

Mountain Luminary

Anne Thiel, Editor, P.O. Box 1187, Mountain View, AR 72560   Phone/Fax: 501-585-2260

Profile: A new age magazine. Issued quarterly. Circ: N/A. Trim size: 7x8.5. Bond cover; B/W; stapled. 16 pages. Subscription cost: $8. Sample copy cost: $2.25. Writer's guidelines available with SASE.

Focus and Tips: *Mountain Luminary* is dedicated to bringing information to people about the New Age—how to grow within it and work with resultant changes in spirituality, relationships, and environment. Readers are new agers including teachers and professionals. Authors should use technical knowledge in a manner that is understandable to a cross-section of people with diverse backgrounds. The editors reserve the right to edit or reject material not consistent with the magazine's objectives.

Editorial Interests

New age, astrology, crystals, cultural and ethnic concerns, dreams, ecosystems, the environment, extraterrestrials, feminism, folklore, healing and health, holistic and natural health, inspiration, juvenile and teen issues, lifestyle, meditation, men's issues, metaphysics, mysticism, nutrition, prayer, psychic phenomenon, self-help, spirituality, and women's issues.

• *Poetry:* Short to medium length pieces.

• *Nonfiction:* Features, articles, interviews, profiles, and essays, up to 8 double-spaced, typed pages. News items, up to 150 words. Accepts quotations as filler.

Submission Policy: Send complete manuscript with cover letter, bibliography, and resume. Include SASE. Accepts computer printouts and ASCII or Macintosh QuarkXpress 3.5" disks. Simultaneous submissions okay. Reports in 1 month. If accepted, expect publication within 1–6 months.

Terms and Payment: Offers advertising space in lieu of payment. Authors receive 2 copies of the issue; additional copies available at discounted prices.

Advertising: Rates: B/W full-page, $200; half-page, $100; quarter-page, $50; business card, $25. Contact Anne Thiel, 501-585-2260.

Mountain Record

Bonnie Treace, Editor, P.O. Box 156, Mount Tremper, NY 12457   Phone: 914-688-7993, Fax: 914-688-7995

Profile: A thematic Buddhist journal. Published by Dharma Communications, Inc., a nonprofit organization. Issued quarterly. Circ: 4,000. Trim size: 7x8.5. Heavy bond cover; B/W; perfect bound. 120 pages. Subscription cost: $18. Sample copy cost: Free. No writer's guidelines.

Focus and Tips: *Mountain Record* explores Buddhism in American and other world religions, reflecting and promoting the new possibilities suggested by Zen Buddhism in such areas as science, healing, business, social action, and ecology. Audience is students of the Zen Monastary at Mount Tremper and other supporters of Buddhism. Issues are thematic—all material must be relative and true in style. Past themes include Care Taking and The Mind.

Editorial Interests

Buddhism, Zen arts, social action, the environment, and the media.

• *Nonfiction:* Features, articles, interviews, profiles, essays, and personal experiences, 1,000–3,000 words. Reviews, 250–500 words. Departments include Zen Arts, Social Action, and Media Review, 1,000–1,500 words.

Submission Policy: Query with resume or send complete manuscript with cover letter and author biography. Include SASE. Accepts photocopies, computer printouts, Macintosh disks, and faxes. Simultaneous submissions okay. Reports in 2 months. If accepted, expect publication in 3–6 months.

Terms and Payment: Authors retain rights. Rarely offers payment. Authors receive 2 or more copies of the issue.

Advertising: Rates: B/W full-page, $228; eighth-page, $ 49.50. Contact Neville Price, 914-688-7993.

Other Interests: Sponsors ongoing retreats and workshops presented by established artists and masters on topics such as poetry, Zen arts, and martial arts. For more information, contact Dharma Communications, 914-688-7993.

The Muscle News

Robert Bazemore, President, P.O. Box 30827, Savannah, GA 31410   Phone: 912-351-7510

Profile: An educational publication for bodywork professionals. Published by RB Enterprises. Issued bimonthly. Circ: 200+. Trim size: 8.5x11. B/W; 60 lb. paper; folded. 8 pages. Subscription cost: $25. Sample copy cost: Free. No writer's guidelines.

Focus and Tips: *The Muscle News* is dedicated solely to soft tissue manipulation, nutrition and related concerns. Subscribers include massage therapists, chiropractors, M.D.s, physical therapists, nutritionists, and lay people interested in bodywork. It provides continuing education for professionals and easy reading for others. Distributed in the U.S., Canada, Brazil, Germany, Switzerland, and Bermuda. It strives for accuracy and reports medical studies, factual case histories, and information based on such studies and histories. Avoid opinion, slang, unconstructive criticism of any healthcare field, and racist or slanderous remarks.

Editorial Interests

Massage profession, bodywork, nutrition, health and healing, and holistic and natural health.

• *Nonfiction:* Features on bodywork techniques, 1,500–2,000 words. Nutrition articles, 1,000 words. Essays on Myofascial Disease processes, no length restriction. News on medical studies, 500 words. Q & A column, 150–300 words.

Submission Policy: Send complete manuscript with cover letter. Include SASE. Accepts laser printouts and WordPerfect 5.1 disks. No simultaneous submissions. Reports in 1 month. If accepted, expect publication in 3 months.

Terms and Payment: One-time rights. No payment. Authors receive 3 copies of the issue.

Advertising: Rates: B/W full-page, $225; half-page, $100. Contact Robert Bazemore, 912-351-7510.

NAPRA Trade Journal

Matthew Gilbert, Managing Editor, Six Eastsound Square, Eastsound, WA 98245   Phone: 206-376-2702, Fax: 206-376-2704

Profile: A thematic trade magazine for new age retailers. Published by the New Age Publishing and Retailing Alliance. Issued bimonthly. Circ: 10,000–12,000. Trim size: 8.5x11. Glossy color cover; spot color inside; recycled paper; saddle stitched or perfect bound. 100 pages. Subscription cost: $45. Sample copy cost: $5. No writer's guidelines. Theme list available with SASE.

Focus and Tips: *NAPRA Trade Journal* is the official publication of the NAPRA organization, whose members are involved in the creation, distribution, and sale of books and other products that support "positive individual and social change." Most material is conceived and written in-house.

Editorial Interests

Material of interests to new age retailers, distributors, and sellers.

Submission Policy: Send for theme list as a first step. Rarely uses freelance material. Query first with SASE. Reports on queries as soon as possible.

Terms and Payment: Rights negotiable. Pays on publication. Rates vary. Authors receive copies of the issue.

Advertising: Rates: B/W full-page, $1,020; 4-color full-page, $1,440. Contact Ian Bage, 800-669-6348. List rental available: $750 for list of 7,500 new age bookstores. Contact Marilyn McGuire, 206-376-2702.

Other Interests: Sponsors many events in conjunction with the annual Labor Day ABA Convention, including workshops, author's breakfasts, and exhibit booths. For more information, contact Carole Scarfuto, 206-376-2702.

The National Spiritualist–Summit

Rev. Sandra Pfortmiller, Editor, 3521 West Topeka Drive, Glendale, AZ 85308   Phone: 602-581-6686

Profile: A magazine of Spiritualism. Published by The National Spiritualist Association of Churches. Established in 1919. Issued monthly. Circ: 1,800. Trim size: 8.5x11. B/W; saddle stitched. 36 pages. Subscription cost: $12. Sample copy cost: $1.50.

Focus and Tips: *The National Spiritualist–Summit* is the official publication of The National Spiritualist Association of Churches. Its sole purpose is to promote Spiritualism for Spiritualist readers. Articles should be uplifting, educational, or inspirational. Avoid new age material, such as astrology or UFOs, and no negative articles.

Editorial Interests

Spiritualism, healing, inspiration, meditation, prayer, and religion.

• *Nonfiction:* Features and articles. No length restrictions.

Submission Policy: Send complete manuscript with cover letter. Include SASE. Accepts photocopies, computer printouts, and Macintosh or IBM disks. Simultaneous submissions okay. Reports in 3–4 months. If accepted, expect publication in 6 months.

Terms and Payment: First North American serial rights or one-time rights. No payment. Authors receive 3 copies of the issue.

Natural Foods Merchandiser

Frank Lampe, Editor, 1301 Spruce, Boulder, CO 80302   Phone: 303-939-8440, Fax: 303-938-1621

Profile: A trade publication for natural foods retailers. Published by New Hope Communications, Inc. Issued monthly. Circ: 16,000. Trim size: 11x14.5. Glossy paper; 4-color; saddle stitched. 80 pages. Subscription cost: $48. Sample copy cost: $8. No writer's guidelines.

Focus and Tips: *Natural Foods Merchandiser* focuses specifically on the natural foods industry. It serves retailers, manufacturers, and distributors of natural foods and related products such as personal care, sports, nutrition, and organic fair. Writers should be familiar with the natural foods trade.

Editorial Interests

Natural foods and natural product retailing, ecosystems, health, nutrition, and self-help.

• *Nonfiction:* Features, articles, interviews, and profiles, 500–600 words.

Submission Policy: Query with outline and 2–3 writing samples, or send complete manuscript with cover letter. Include SASE. Accepts photocopies, computer printouts, Macintosh Microsoft Word disks, and faxes. No simultaneous submissions. Reports if interested in 2–3 weeks. If accepted, expect publication in 10 weeks.

Terms and Payment: Pays on publication. $.15 per word. Authors receive 2 or more copies of the issue.

Advertising: Accepts advertising. Contact Janet Allsup, 303-939-8440. List rental available. Contact Gin Adlof, Circulation Department, 303-939-8440.

Other Interests: Holds two annual trade shows: Natural Products Expo–West, held in the Spring in Anaheim, CA; and Natural Products Expo–East, in the Fall in Baltimore, MD. For more information, contact Pam Breen, 303-939-8440.

Natural Health

Mark Bittman, Editor, 17 Station Street, Brookline Village, MA 02147   Phone: 617-232-1000, Fax: 617-232-1572

Profile: A national magazine of natural health and living. Published by Natural Health Limited Partnership. Issued bimonthly. Circ: 180,000. Trim size: 8.5x11. Glossy color cover; 4-color; saddle stitched. 160 pages. Subscription cost: $24. Sample copy cost: $4. Writer's guidelines available with SASE.

Focus and Tips: Formerly *East West Natural Health*, *Natural Health* provides practical information, new discoveries, and current trends about natural health and living.

Editorial Interests

Natural health, holistic health, healing, bodywork, the environment, meditation, men's issues, nutrition, psychology, recovery, relationships, self-help, spirituality, women's issues, and yoga.

• *Fiction:* Book excerpts.

• *Nonfiction:* Health features and personal experiences, 2,500–3,500 words. Accepts book reviews. Departments include Health Beat, Whole Foods, Cooking Lesson, My Story, Mind/Body, Living and Dying, Home Remedies, Natural Pharmacy, Health Pet, Products, and Reflections, 1,000–1,500 words.

Submission Policy: Query with outline and writing samples or send complete manuscript with cover letter, resume and clips. Include SASE. Accepts photocopies, computer printouts, and faxes. Simultaneous submissions okay. Reports in 3–4 weeks. If accepted, expect publication in 3 months.

Terms and Payment: First North American serial rights. Pays on acceptance, Features, $1,000–$2,000. Departments, $350–$750. Authors receive 1 copy of the issue.

Advertising: Rates: B/W full-page, $4,100; 4-color full-page, $5,350; 2-color full-page, $4,950. Contact Ann D'Alesandro, Advertising Director, 617-232-1000. List rental available. Contact Adrienne Kimball, Circulation Director, 617-232-1000.

The Neighborhood Works

Patti Wolter, Editor, 2125 West North Avenue, Chicago, IL 60647   Phone: 312-278-4800, Fax: 312-278-3840

Profile: A publication of community-building ideas. Published by the nonprofit Center for Neighborhood Technology. Issued bimonthly. Circ: 2,000. Trim size: 8.5x11. Two-color self cover; 2-color inside; saddle stitched. 32 pages. Subscription cost: $30. Sample copy cost: $3. Writer's guidelines available with SASE.

Focus and Tips: *The Neighborhood Works* covers community organizing, primarily in urban areas, around issues of energy, the environment, economic development, housing, transit, and community development. Readers are community-development professionals, activists, academics, and other media and government officials. Review a sample copy for style and scope. It is not interested in fiction, first-person pieces, stories of neighborhood crime-watch groups, or coverage of social service work.

Editorial Interests

Community organizing, economic development, community development, affordable housing, transportation, social justice, the environment, politics, social and world issues, and women's issues.

• *Nonfiction:* Features, 1,400–2,000 words. Articles, 900–3,000 words. Interviews and profiles, 1,400–1,800 words. Essays and opinion pieces, 900 words. News items, 200–1,400 words. Book reviews, 900–1,200 words. Columns: Alternative Visions for Cities and Neighborhoods, 900 words.

Submission Policy: Query with outline, writing samples, and resume. Include SASE. Accepts photocopies, computer printouts, and WordPerfect 5.1 disks. Simultaneous submissions okay. Reports in 2–4 months. If accepted, expect publication in 2 months.

Terms and Payment: All rights. Pays on publication. $200–$500 per piece. Authors receive 5 copies of the issue.

Advertising: Accepts advertising. Contact Carl Vogel, 312-278-4800, ext. 114. List rental available. Contact Bridget Torres, 312-278-4800, ext. 140.

The Networker

Robin Dunn, Publisher, 20 Battery Park Avenue, Suite 612, Asheville, NC 28801   Phone: 704-254-6852

Profile: An alternative newspaper for the North Carolina mountain area. Published by Delphi Communications. Issued monthly. Circ: 5,000. Trim size: 7x12. Newsprint; folded. 16 pages. Subscription cost: $16. Sample copy cost: free.

Focus and Tips: *The Networker* serves as a communication vehicle to improve the quality of life for those in the western North Carolina mountain region. It intends to network information about our common essence, holistic healing practices, lifestyles, education, and earth-friendly technologies, as well as our ability to co-create joyful and peaceful life experiences. Readers are college-educated professionals between 30–60 years of age, with interests in health, fitness, and planetary awakening. It seeks clearly written, meaningful articles.

Editorial Interests

New age, astrology, cooking, earth changes, healing and health, channeling, intuitive counseling, Native American and ethnic philosophy, home schooling, new technology, the environment, bodywork, meditation, mythology, parapsychology, parenting, rebirthing, recovery, religion, self-help, social issues, spirituality, and yoga.

• *Fiction:* Short-short stories, up to 500 words.

• *Nonfiction:* Features, articles, interviews, profiles, personal experiences, news, and reviews, up to 500 words.

Submission Policy: Query with writing samples and resume. Include SASE. Accepts photocopies, computer printouts, and computer disks. Responds to queries in 1 month, to manuscripts in 2 months. If accepted, expect publication in 1 month.

Terms and Payment: One-time rights. No payment.

Advertising: Rates: B/W one-time full-page, $550; one-time half-page, $285; one-time quarter page, $140. Contact Lori Theodore, 704-254-6852.

Networker Magazine

Diane Cooper, Editor, P.O. Box 2053, Jupiter, FL 33468-2053   Phone/Fax: 407-743-6305

Profile: A regional new age magazine. Issued bimonthly. Circ: 10,000. Trim size: 8.5x11. Two-color cover; newsprint; glued. 40 pages. Subscription cost: $12. Sample copy cost: $1. No writer's guidelines.

Focus and Tips: *Networker Magazine* is "dedicated to the preservation of the planet and is in direct service to creation." It covers new age and holistic health concerns, up-and-coming health and personal development technologies and research, the environment, and issues specific to the Jupiter, Florida area. Not interested in advertorials or academic language.

Editorial Interests

New age, holistic health, the environment, self-help, astrology, bodywork, channeling, crystals, cultural and ethnic concerns, dreams, extraterrestrials, feminism, folklore, healing, inspiration, lifestyle, meditation, men's issues, metaphysics, mysticism, mythology nutrition, parapsychology, parenting, philosophy, prayer, psychic phenomenon, psychology, rebirthing, recovery, regional issues, relationships, religion, seniors, social and world issues, spirituality, women's issues, and yoga.

• *Nonfiction:* Features, articles, interviews, profiles, and essays, 1,000–3,000 words. Personal experiences and news items, 1,000 words. Opinion pieces, 1,500 words. Reviews, 300 words.

Submission Policy: Query with writing samples, or send complete manuscript with cover letter and author biography. Include SASE. Accepts photocopies, computer printouts, and faxes. Simultaneous submissions okay if to a publication outside the Florida region. Reports in 2–6 weeks. If accepted, expect publication in 3–6 months.

Terms and Payment: Authors retain rights. No payment. Authors receive 1 copy of the issue.

Advertising: Rates: B/W full-page, $330. Contact Diane Cooper, 407-743-6305.

Other Interests: Offers a Course in Mastery, a meditation and women's retreat. Held twice yearly in different locations. For more information, contact Diane Cooper, 407-743-6305.

New Age Journal

Peggy Taylor, Editor, 42 Pleasant Street, Watertown, MA 02102   Phone: 617-926-0200, Fax: 617-926-5021

Profile: A leading national new age magazine. Established in 1974. Issued bimonthly. Circ: 185,000. Trim size: 8.5x11. Glossy color cover; 4-color; perfect bound. 160 pages. Subscription cost: $24. Sample copy cost: $3.95. Writer's guidelines available with SASE.

Focus and Tips: *New Age Journal* is a general-interest lifestyle magazine with a focus on issues that illustrate an alternative or holistic philosophy. It addresses a variety of issues in a variety of forms, but all share an underlying worldview. This magazine popularized the new age field by providing leading-edge reporting on holistic health, the body-mind connection, and ecological and holistic living. Accepts high-quality journalism prepared in accordance with understood trade standards. Pieces should be well-executed, with good ideas.

Editorial Interests

New age, bodywork, cultural and ethnic issues, dreams, ecosystems, elders, the environment, feminism, folklore, gay and lesbian issues, healing, health, holistic health, inspirational, juvenile and teen issues, lifestyle, meditation, men's issues, mysti-

cism, mythology, natural health, nutrition, parenting, philosophy, politics, prayer, psychic phenomenon, psychology, recovery, relationships, religion, self-help, social and world issues, spirituality, witches, women's issues, and yoga.
• *Nonfiction:* Features, essays, and personal experiences, 2,500 words. Articles, 4,500 words. Opinion pieces, 500–700 words. News items, 700 words. Reviews, 250–1,500 words.
Submission Policy: Query with outline, or send complete manuscript with cover letter, resume, and author biography. Include SASE. Accepts photocopies, computer printouts, and faxes. Send SASE to accompany fax submissions. Simultaneous submissions okay. Reports in 3 months. If accepted, expect publication in 2 months.
Terms and Payment: First North American serial rights. Pays on or before publication. $150–$2,500 per piece. Authors receive 2 copies of the issue.
Advertising: Media kit available. Offers numerous advertising options. General display rates: B/W full-page, $4,475; 2-color full-page, $4,775; 4-color full-page, $6,150. Mail-order Marketplace: B/W half-page, $1,995; spot color; $2,195. Connection Sections: ninth-page, $695; twelfth-page, $475. Connections Sections include Learning, Travel, and Readers' & A/V. Contact Cathi Mcgrath, Advertising Department, 617-926-0200.

New Age Marketing Opportunities Newsletter

Gerry White, Editor, P.O. Box 2578, Sedona, AZ 86339   Phone: 602-282-9574, Fax: 602-282-9730

Profile: An industry newsletter. Published by First Editions. Issued bimonthly. Circ: 500. Trim size: 8.5x11. Recycled paper; folded. 4 pages. Subscription cost: $20. Sample copy cost: Free.
Focus and Tips: *New Age Marketing Opportunities Newsletter* covers all aspects of product or service marketing in the new age arena. It has also published the New Age Market Background and Trends Special Report, an 80-page report detailing the background, financial news, statistics, and trends of the market. It seeks to define the market and its consumers, and how they fit into the mainstream market by covering the commercial aspect of the new age industry.
Editorial Interests
Timely marketing of new age products, marketing education and tips.
• *Nonfiction:* Paragraph-length news releases and marketing tips and techniques.
Submission Policy: Send material with cover letter. Include SASE.
Terms and Payment: No payment.

The New Age Reporter

Valli Aman, Executive Producer, P.O. Box 931555, Los Angeles, CA 90093   Phone: 213-969-0247

Profile: A newsletter covering the television program,"Visions." Published by Visions Production Company. Issued 4 times a year. Circ: 2,000. Photocopied; folded. 4–8 pages. Subscription cost: Free. Sample copy cost: Free. No writer's guidelines.
Focus and Tips: *The New Age Reporter* is mailed primarily to viewers of the television program, "Visions." It is in the process of expanding its editorial focus, however, and will be seeking more freelance writing. Articles should be concise, wise, and inspiring. Prefers non-denominational, human potential pieces.
Editorial Interests
New age, human potential, astrology, channeling, crystals, dreams, ecosystems, the environment, extraterrestrials, healing, holistic health, inspiration, meditation, metaphysics, natural health, parapsychology, philosophy, psychic phenomenon, rebirthing, and spirituality.
• *Poetry:* Will accept poetry beginning in the fall of 1993.
• *Nonfiction:* Letters and uplifting articles on human potential, 200–500 words. Special interest in UFOs and health and healing, both with data.
Submission Policy: Query first. Include SASE. Accepts photocopies and computer printouts. Simultaneous submissions okay. Reports in 2 months. If accepted, expect publication in 2–6 months.
Terms and Payment: No payment. May offer payment in the future. Authors receive up to 10 copies of the issue.
Advertising: Rates: B/W full-page, $200; half-page, $150.
Other Interests: Visions Publishing Company will coordinate conferences, workshops, seminars, and retreats upon request and acceptance of project.

New Editions Health World

Dr. Kumar Pati, Publisher, 1675 Rollins Road, Suite B-3, Burlingame, CA 94010   Phone: 415-697-4400, Fax: 415-697-7937

Profile: A national magazine of health-related issues. Published by New Editions. Issued bimonthly. Circ: 60,000. Trim size: 8.5x11. 48 pages. Glossy color cover; 4-color inside; saddle stitched. Subscription cost: $12. Sample copy cost: $3. Writer's guidelines available with SASE.
Focus and Tips: *New Editions Health World* is a leading national health publication for consumers and professionals. It seeks well-documented, research-based articles on health and fitness. No advertorials.

Editorial Interests
Health, fitness, nutrition, and natural health.
• *Nonfiction:* Research-based features, articles, interviews, profiles, essays, and opinion pieces, 1,000–3,000 words.
Submission Policy: Query first with outline, writing samples, and resume. No unsolicited manuscripts. Include SASE.
Accepts photocopies and computer printouts. Reports in 6 weeks. If accepted, expect publication in 3–6 months.
Terms and Payment: One-time rights. Pays on publication. Rates negotiable. Authors receive 10 copies of the issue.
Advertising: Accepts B/W and 4-color advertisements. Contact Kumar Pati, 415-697-4400. List rental available. Contact
NAM, Box 970, Santa Cruz, NM 87567, 505-753-5086.

New Frontier Magazine
Swami Virato, Executive Editor, 101 Cuthbert Street, Philadelphia, PA 19106   Phone: 215-627-5683, Fax: 215-440-9945

Profile: A general market magazine on the transformation of consciousness. Issued bimonthly. Circ: 60,000. Trim size: 8.5x11.
Glossy color cover; B/W inside; saddle stitched. 72 pages. Subscription cost: $18. Sample copy cost: $2. Writer's guidelines
available with SASE.
Focus and Tips: *New Frontier* explores and presents the dimensions of expanded consciousness. It seeks well-written material
that "comes from the heart" and is presented within a context of awareness for a holistic, new age audience. Prefers a crisp,
gentle, uplifting writing style that is of the new age spirit. Avoid negativity, violence, and articles about traditional religion.
Editorial Interests
Spirituality, holism (as applied to health, science, ecology, and lifestyles), transpersonal psychology, metaphysics, social and
planetary harmony and responsibility, environmental awareness, love, natural living, the transcendental, paranormal,
enlightenment, new science, sexuality, and other new age concerns.
• *Nonfiction:* Features and interviews, 3,000–4,000 words. Articles, 1,500–2,000 words. News Briefs and filler, 100–500 words.
Reviews, 500 words. Columns include Health Today, Beyond Science, Natural Living, Beyond Psychology, Contemplating
Yoga, Humor, and Astrology.
Submission Policy: Query first with outline, resume, writing samples, and clips. Include SASE. Allow 3–6 month lead time
for features and interviews. Accepts photocopies, computer printouts, and Word 5.0 for Windows disks. Simultaneous sub-
missions okay. Reports in 2–4 months. If accepted, expect publication within 2 months.
Terms and Payment: First North American serial rights or one-time rights. Pays on publication. $.05–$.10 per word or
$25–$200 per piece. Authors receive 2 copies of the issue.
Advertising: Rates per page: B/W, $1,000; 4-color, $1,600. Contact Sw. Virato, 215-627-5683. List rental available; $70/M, 5M
minimum. Contact Nam Lists.

New Letters
James McKinley, Editor, 5100 Rockhill Road, Kansas City, MO 64110   Phone: 816-235-1168

Profile: A literary journal. Published by the University of Missouri–Kansas City. Issued quarterly. Circ: 3,000. Trim size: 6x9.
Glossy cover; B/W; perfect bound. 125–200 pages. Subscription cost: $17. Sample copy cost: $5. Writer's guidelines available
with SASE.
Focus and Tips: *New Letters* is an international magazine publishing poetry, essays, art, and quality literature for the serious
reader. The best way to assess its needs is to read the magazine.
Editorial Interests
Open to all subjects and writing with literary quality.
• *Fiction:* Short stories, 5,000 words. Poetry, no length restrictions.
• *Nonfiction:* Features, articles, interviews, profiles, essays, and personal experiences, 5,000 words.
Submission Policy: Send complete manuscript with cover letter and author biography. Include SASE. Accepts photocopies
and computer printouts. No simultaneous submissions. Reports in 3 months. If accepted, expect publication in 1 year.
Terms and Payment: First North American serial rights. Pays on publication. Prose, $50 per piece. Poems, $10 each. Authors
receive 2 copies of the issue.
Advertising: Rates: B/W full-page, $150; half-page, $90. Contact Robert Stewart, 816-235-1120.
Other Interests: Sponsors The New Letters Literary Award for fiction, poetry, and creative nonfiction. Prizes: Fiction, $750;
poetry, $750; creative nonfiction, $500. Deadline is May 15 of each year. Write for guidelines or contact Glenda McCrary, 816-
235-1120, for more information.

New Lifestyles Newspaper
Dennis O'Connor, Publisher, 2314 Iowa Avenue, Cincinnati, OH 45206   Phone: 513-281-5544, Fax: 513-751-6463

Profile: A regional publication of alternative lifestyles. Published by Tri-State Entertainment Corporation. Established in
1981. Issued bimonthly. Circ: 10,000. Trim size: Tabloid. Newsprint; folded. 20–24 pages. Subscription cost: $10. Sample copy

cost: SASE with $.52 postage. No writer's guidelines.

Focus and Tips: *New Lifestyles Newspaper* caters to "new edge" thinking, covering alternative living, thinking, and being. Each issue concentrates on a selected environmental or ecological topic, as well as spirituality and noteworthy people. "Before sending material to us, check the field—are you offering something new or a new angle? Keep abreast of changes in your subject matter." Avoid trite material.

Editorial Interests

Astrology, bodywork, channeling, crystals, cultural and ethnic issues, dreams, ecosystems, the environment, extraterrestrials, feminism, folklore, gay and lesbian concerns, healing, health, holistic health, inspiration, lifestyle, magic, meditation, men's issues, metaphysics, mysticism, mythology, natural health, new age, nutrition, parapsychology, prayer, psychic phenomenon, psychology, rebirthing, recovery, regional issues, relationships, self-help, social and world issues, spirituality, witches, women's issues, and yoga.

• *Nonfiction:* Features and articles, 150–600 words. Q&A interviews, 100 words. Essays and opinion pieces, 300 words. Personal experiences, 200 words. Book reviews, 60–100 words. Departments include Calendar, regional alternative events.

Submission Policy: Send complete manuscript with cover letter. Include SASE. Accepts photocopies, computer printouts, and Macintosh 3.5" disks. Simultaneous submissions okay. Reports in 2 months. If accepted, expect publication in 6 months.

Terms and Payment: All rights. Pays on publication. Rates vary. Authors receive 2 copies of the issue.

Advertising: Rates: B/W full-page, $400. Accepts spot color ads. Contact Bob Firestone, 513-281-5544.

Other Interests: Sponsors Network Nights, networking program for services in Greater Cincinnati. For more information, Dennis O'Connor, 513-281-5544.

New Mexico Light

Jane Bartholomew, Editor, P.O. Box 90611, Albuquerque, NM 87199-0611   Phone/Fax: 505-897-4858

Profile: A regional new age newsmagazine. Established in 1992. Issued monthly. Circ: 27,000. Trim size: Tabloid. Newsprint; spot color; folded. 32 pages. Subscription cost: $6 for 6 issues. Sample copy cost: Free. Writer's guidelines available with SASE.

Focus and Tips: *New Mexico Light* is an alternative free newspaper reaching readers throughout New Mexico. It fosters education, increased awareness, awakening, and co-creation of wellness and human potential. Seeks uplifting, inspirational, informative pieces. "Write what you would want to read—something the reader's heart can respond to." Avoid political op/ed pieces or anything with a negative tone. Is launching a section of book and movie reviews.

Editorial Interests

New age, regional issues, astrology, bodywork, crystals and healing stones, cultural and ethnic concerns, dreams, ecosystems, the environment, extraterrestrials, feminism, folklore, healing, health, holistic and natural health, inspirational, juvenile and teen issues, lifestyle, magic, meditation, men's issues, metaphysics, mysticism, mythology, nutrition, parapsychology, parenting, philosophy, universal prayer, psychic phenomenon, psychology, rebirthing, recovery, relationships, self-help, spirituality, women's issues, and yoga.

• *Fiction:* Short stories and drama, 500–800 words. Poetry, no length restrictions.

• *Nonfiction:* Features articles, interviews, profiles, essays, and personal experiences, 800–1,200 words. Book and movie reviews for upcoming section, 800–1,200 words. With the purchase of a quarter-page or eighth-page advertisement, receive space for an advertorial in the LimeLight column.

Submission Policy: Query with outline or send complete manuscript with cover letter. Does not respond to submissions. Accepts photocopies, computer printouts, and IBM-compatible disks. Simultaneous submissions okay.

Terms and Payment: Authors retain rights. No payment. Authors receive 2 copies of the issue.

Advertising: Rates: B/W full-page, $624; quarter-page, $156; business-card, $29. Contact Jane Bartholomew, 505-897-4858.

New Moon: The Magazine for Girls and Their Dreams

Nancy Gruver, Editor, P.O. Box 3620, Duluth, MN 55803-3620   Phone: 218-728-5507, Fax: 218-728-1812

Profile: A international magazine for middle-grade girls. Published by New Moon Publishing. Established in 1992. Issued bimonthly. Circ: 18,000. Trim size: 7x9. Glossy color cover; 2-color; saddle stitched. 48 pages. Subscription cost: $25. Sample copy cost: $6. Writer's guidelines available with SASE.

Focus and Tips: *New Moon* seeks to offer strategies for the transformation from girlhood to womanhood. Each issue focuses on girls from a different country and culture. Edited by and for girls ages 8–14 years, *New Moon* was created for every girl who wants her voice heard and her dreams taken seriously. Avoid sexism and anything that enforces old stereotypes of girls and women. Portray girls and women as powerful, active, and in charge of their own lives. Its companion publication, *New Moon Parenting*, is written for parents and others involved with girls.

Editorial Interests

Girl's issues and accomplishments, women's issues, feminism, cultural and ethnic issues, ecosystems, the environment, folklore, lifestyle, and relationships.

• *Fiction:* Short stories, 300–600 words. Poetry, 30–100 words.

• *Nonfiction:* Features, articles, essays, and personal experiences, 600 words. Interviews and profiles, 1,000 words. Opinion pieces and news, 100–300 words. Departments include Herstory, Profiles, How Aggravating, Ask a Girl, The Puzzle, Check It Out!, Global Village, and Dream a Dream.

Submission Policy: Send complete manuscript with cover letter. Include SASE. Accepts photocopies, computer printouts, and 3.5" disks. Simultaneous submissions okay if noted. Reporting time varies. Publication time varies.

Terms and Payment: First North American serial rights. Pays on publication. $.04–$.08 per word. Authors receive 2 copies of the issue.

New Moon Parenting: For Adults Who Care About Girls

Nancy Gruver, Editor, P.O. Box 3620, Duluth, MN 55803-3620   Phone: 218-728-5507, Fax: 218-728-1812

Profile: A parenting newsletter. Published by New Moon Publishing. Issued bimonthly. Circ: 2,000. Trim size: 8.5x11. Self cover; B/W; stapled. 15 pages. Subscription cost: $25. Sample copy cost: $4.95. Writer's guidelines available with SASE.

Focus and Tips: *New Moon Parenting* is written by and for adults—parents, teachers, counselors, coaches, and others—who are working to raise healthy, confident girls. Created by parents to provide support, ideas, and resources to help girls as they become women. Its companion publication, *New Moon*, is written for girls ages 8–14 years. Both publications "celebrate girls and support their efforts to hang onto their voices, strengths, and dreams" as they mature. "Work for clarity and ease of understanding." Avoid academic style and sexist language. Send for detailed writer's guidelines.

Editorial Interests
Parenting, women's issues, feminism, cultural and ethnic issues, ecosystems, the environment, folklore, children's and teen concerns, lifestyle, and psychology.

• *Fiction:* Short stories, 400–1,000 words.

• *Nonfiction:* Features, articles, essays, personal experiences, and reviews, 400–1,000 words.

Submission Policy: Send complete manuscript with cover letter and author biography. Include SASE. Accepts photocopies, computer printouts, and 3.5" disks. Simultaneous submissions okay if noted. Reporting time varies. Publication time varies.

Terms and Payment: First North American serial rights. Pays on publication. $.04–$.08 per word. Authors receive 2 copies of the issue.

Advertising: Rates: B/W full-page, $500; half-page, $325; column-inch; $30. Contact Joe Kelly, 218-728-5507.

New Moon Rising

Scot Rhoads, Editor, 8818 Troy Street, Spring Valley, CA 91977   Phone: 619-466-8064

Profile: A magazine addressing magick, witchcraft, and related fields. Published by Mystic Moon. Issued 6 times a year. Circ: 2,200. Trim size: 8.5x11. Glossy cover; B/W; saddle stitched. 36 pages. Subscription cost: $14. Sample copy cost: $3.50. Writer's guidelines available with SASE.

Focus and Tips: *New Moon Rising* offers practical information on Wicca, seen as a wide variety of nature religions based primarily on the symbols of pre-Christian European nature religions, and magick, understood as a secular system of symbols and practices designed to nonphysically affect the self and the environment. Articles should have some kind of immediate application in people's lives, such as a piece on ritual that includes examples. No negative, abusive writing.

Editorial Interests
Wicca, magick, occult, astrology, channeling, crystals, culture and ethnic issues, dreams, ecosystems, extraterrestrials, feminism, folklore, gay and lesbian issues, healing, inspiration, meditation, men's and women's issues, metaphysics, mysticism, mythology, philosophy, psychic phenomenon, social and world issues, and spirituality.

• *Poetry:* Considers poems with connection to Wicca or magick.

• *Nonfiction:* Articles, no length restrictions.

Submission Policy: Query or send complete manuscript with cover letter. Include SASE. Accepts photocopies, computer printouts, and IBM-compatible disks. Simultaneous submissions okay. Reports in 1 month. If accepted, expect publication in 5 months.

Terms and Payment: One-time rights. No payment. Authors receive up to 6 copies of the issue.

Advertising: Rates: B/W full-page, $85. List rental available; $50/M for subscribers, $60/M for advertisers. Contact Scot Rhoads, 619-466-8064.

New Pages

Casey Hill, Publisher, P.O Box 438, Grand Blanc, MI 48439   Phone: 810-743-8055

Profile: A review journal on alternative media. Issued 3 times a year. Circ: 5,000. Trim size: 8.5x11. Color cover; B/W inside; saddle stitched. 50+ pages. Subscription cost: $12. Sample copy cost: $5. No writer's guidelines.

Focus and Tips: *New Pages* is a review journal of alternatives in print and media sent to librarians and book sellers. It is not interested in reviews of mainstream writing or bestsellers, but "real" alternative books—small press fiction and poetry, wom-

en's interests, environmental topics, and metaphysical material. It does not publish fiction or poetry.
Editorial Interests
Cultural and ethnic issues, ecosystems, the environment, feminism, gay and lesbian issues, health, men's issues, natural health, new age, parenting, politics, psychology, relationships, social and world issues, and women's issues.
• *Nonfiction:* Articles on cultural issues, publishing, and the media. Book reviews, 100–300 words.
Submission Policy: Query first with writing samples. Include SASE. Accepts photocopies, computer printouts, and IBM or Macintosh disks. No simultaneous submissions. Reports in 1–2 weeks. If accepted, expect publication in 3–6 months.
Terms and Payment: All rights. Pays on publication. Rates vary. Authors receive 1 copy of the issue.
Advertising: Accepts advertising. List rental available. Contact Casey Hill, 810-743-8055.

The New Press Literary Quarterly

Bob Abramson, Publisher, 53-35 Hollis Court Boulevard, Flushing, NY 11365   Phone: 718-229-6782

Profile: A literary journal. Published by The New Press Literary Quarterly and Literary Society, Inc. Established in 1984. Issued quarterly. Circ: 1,600. Trim size: 8.5x11. Glossy cover, B/W; stapled. 40 pages. Subscription cost: $15. Sample copy cost: $4. Writer's guidelines available with SASE.
Focus and Tips: *The New Press* seeks literary material with poetic voice and vision. Aimed at an educated audience with literate tastes. Essays should be informative and revelatory; short stories, imaginative. Avoid anger, hostility, complaints, violence, and hatred.
Editorial Interests
Literary, cultural and ethnic issues, environment, inspiration, lifestyle, philosophy, politics, psychology, relationships, social and world issues, spirituality, writers and writing, and humor.
• *Fiction:* Short stories, 6,000 words. Short-short stories, 1,500 words. Poetry, up to 200 lines.
• *Nonfiction:* Features, articles, interviews and profiles, essays, personal experiences, and opinion pieces, 3,000 words.
Submission Policy: Send complete manuscript with cover letter. Include SASE. Accepts photocopies and computer printouts. Simultaneous submissions okay. Reports in 1–2 months. If accepted, expect publication in 1 year.
Terms and Payment: One-time rights. Pays on publication. $15 per piece. Authors receive 3 copies of the issue.
Advertising: Rates per page: B/W, $100. Contact Bob Abramson, 718-229-6782.
Other Interests: Sponsors two contests: Quarterly Essay Contest and Quarterly Short Story Contest. Topics include writers, social and political commentary, and personal journalism. $100 award if published, $5 entry fee. Also sponsors numerous poetry readings and writers groups throughout the New York metropolitan area. Contact Bob Abramson, 718-229-6782.

New Texas Magazine

Marybeth Gradziel, Editor-at-Large, 1512 1/2 South Congress, Austin, TX 78704   Phone: 512-462-1990, Fax: 512-448-3927

Profile: A regional alternative lifestyle newsmagazine. Established in 1979. Issued bimonthly. Circ: 60,000. Trim size: Tabloid. Newsprint; folded. 40+ pages. Subscription cost: $10. Sample copy cost: $2. No writer's guidelines.
Focus and Tips: *New Texas Magazine* is a resource for positive lifestyles, personal growth, and enhanced quality of life for Texas. Its articles and features present a blend of the new and the old, the traditional and non-traditional. Reaches readers that are diverse, affluent, sensible, holistic, highly educated, and very selective. Write from the heart and keep it short, interesting, and easy to read.
Editorial Interests
Topics of interest to Texas area, new age, bodywork, cultural and ethnic issues, ecosystems, the environment, feminism, healing and health, holistic and natural health, lifestyle, meditation, men's issues, mythology, nutrition, parapsychology, parenting, philosophy, politics, prayer, psychology, rebirthing, recovery, relationships, self-help, social and world issues, spirituality, women's issues, and yoga.
• *Poetry:* Short, upbeat poems.
• *Nonfiction:* Features, articles, interviews, and profiles, 2,000 words. Essays, news, and reviews, 500–1,000 words.
Departments include Men's Journal, Women's Journal, Earth Matters, and Connections.
Submission Policy: Query with outline, writing samples, and resume, or send complete manuscript with clips. Include SASE. Accepts computer printouts and Macintosh disks with hard copy. No simultaneous submissions. Reporting time varies.
Terms and Payment: All rights. Pays on publication. Rates vary. Authors receive copies of the issue.
Advertising: Display rates: B/W full page, $600; half-page, $425; quarter-page, $280. Resource directory rates: $65–$200. Contact Marybeth Gradziel, 512-462-1990.
Other Interests: Sponsors several workshops and seminars throughout the year. Contact editor for more information.

New Thought Journal

Ed Wincentsen, Editor, P.O. Box 700754, Tulsa, OK 74170   Fax: 918-492-6237

Profile: A new age journal. Published by Momentary Pleasures Press. Issued quarterly. Circ: 600. Trim size: 8.5x11. Heavy bond cover; B/W; saddle stitched. 20 pages. Subscription cost: $15. Sample copy cost: $3. Writer's guidelines available with SASE.

Focus and Tips: *New Thought Journal* explores philosophy and religion with a goal of creating a dialogue between people of different views who are on a path toward truth. Seeks to inspire and uplift and not be dogmatic. Reviewing a sample copy is a must.

Editorial Interests

New age, healing, health, inspiration, meditation, metaphysics, mysticism, philosophy, politics, prayer, psychology, recovery, non-dogmatic religion, self-help, social and world issues, and spirituality.

• *Fiction:* Short stories, up to 1,500 words. Poetry, up to 5 poems per submission. Accepts book excerpts.

• *Nonfiction:* Features, articles, interviews, profiles, essays, personal experiences, opinion pieces, and news, up to 1,500 words. Reviews, 1,200 words. Accepts some filler.

Submission Policy: Query with outline, 2 sample chapters, writing samples, and resume. Also accepts complete manuscript with cover letter. Include SASE and brief author biography. Accepts photocopies and computer printouts. Simultaneous submissions okay if noted. Reports in 1 month. If accepted, expect publication in 3–6 months.

Terms and Payment: One-time rights. No payment. Authors receive copies of the issue.

Advertising: Accepts advertising. Contact Ed Wincentsen, P.O. Box 700754, Tulsa, OK 74170.

The New Times

Krysta Gibson, Publisher, P.O. Box 51186, Seattle, WA 98115-1186   Phone: 206-524-9071, Fax: 206-524-0052

Profile: A monthly newspaper of alternative spirituality. Issued monthly. Circ: 40,000. Trim size: 13x23.5. Newsprint; folded. 24 pages. Subscription cost: $13. Sample copy cost: $2. Writer's guidelines available with SASE.

Focus and Tips: *The New Times* publishes material that in some way inspires, informs, or encourages readers to create a more spiritually aware, happier, and healthier world. Writers are advised to "be original, write from the heart, follow our guidelines, and be clear and concise." Intelligently written articles that analyze or disagree with issues are welcomed. Articles that attack, demean, or otherwise negate other people, organizations, philosophies, or systems are not accepted.

Editorial Interests

New age, astrology, bodywork, channeling, crystals, cultural and ethnic issues, dreams, ecosystems, environment, extraterrestrials, feminism, healing, holistic and natural health, inspiration, children's and teen issues, meditation, men's and women's issues, metaphysics, mysticism, nutrition, parapsychology, parenting, philosophy, prayer, psychic phenomenon, psychology, rebirthing, recovery, relationships, self-help, seniors, social issues, spirituality, and yoga.

• *Nonfiction:* Articles, essays, and personal experiences, up to 1,800 words. Interviews, up to 2,000 words. News items, up to 1,000 words. Opinion pieces, up to 1,500 words.

Submission Policy: Send complete manuscript with cover letter. Include SASE. Accepts photocopies, computer printouts, and faxes (206-524-0052). Faxes must be followed by SASE for response. No simultaneous submissions. Reports in 1 month. If accepted, expect publication within 1–3 months.

Terms and Payment: First North American serial rights. No payment. Offers a free one-year subscription. Authors receive 1–10 copies of the issue upon request.

Advertising: Rates: B/W full-page, $1,277.10; $11 per column inch. Contact Rhonda Dickison, 206-524-9071. List rental available; one-time use only. Krysta Gibson, 206-524-9071.

New Visions

Edwin Treitler, Editor, 10 Taconic Street, Pittsfield, MA 01201   Phone: 413-443-4817, Fax: 413-443-8002

Profile: A regional holistic guide and new age advertising forum. Issued quarterly. Distributed free of charge. Trim size: 11x13. Newsprint; folded. 44 pages. Subscription cost: $4. Sample copy cost: Free. No writer's guidelines.

Focus and Tips: An independent quarterly publication dedicated to holistic health and the balance of mind, body, and spirit. *New Visions* is a free regional paper supported by advertisers in Western New England and New York State. It is open to new ideas, especially those related to social issues. Not interested in "flaky new age visions" but concrete solutions and scientifically researched claims. Writers should avoid articles about channeling and unfocused pieces.

Editorial Interests

Holistic health, alternative medicine, spirituality, metaphysics, sacred sites, ecology, art, recovery, parenting, social and women's issues.

• *Nonfiction:* Accepts features, articles, interviews and profiles, essays, personal experiences, opinion pieces, and news, 500–600 words.

Submission Policy: Query first with an outline. Include SASE. Accepts photocopies, computer printouts, and Macintosh computer disks. No simultaneous submissions. Reports in 1 month. If accepted, expect publication within 3 months.

Terms and Payment: One-time rights. Pays 30 days after publication. $50 maximum per piece. Authors receive 1 copy of the issue; additional copies available with SASE.

Advertising: Rates: Full-page B/W ad, $500. Contact Ed Treitler, 413-443-4817.

Next Phase

Kim Means, Editor, 33 Court Street, New Haven, CT 06511   Phone: 203-772-1697, Fax: 203-787-1461

Profile: An independent journal of environmental and social awareness. Published by Phantom Press. Issued 3 times a year. Circ: 1,500. Trim size: 8.5x11. Glossy cover; B/W; recycled paper; saddle stitched. 32–40 pages. Subscription cost: $8. Sample copy cost: $3. Writer's guidelines available with SASE.

Focus and Tips: *Next Phase* publishes environmentally and socially conscious fiction, poetry, reviews, and interviews. Most readers are writers and intellectuals interested in inspirational fiction. Avoid trite themes.

Editorial Interests

Fiction, science fiction and fantasy, ecosystems, the environment, inspiration, metaphysics, new age, and social and world issues.

• *Fiction:* Short stories, genre fiction, and book excerpts, up to 4,000 words. Poetry, no length restrictions.

• *Nonfiction:* Features and articles, up to 3,000 words. Interviews with or profiles of well-known writers, artists, or intellectuals, up to 3,000 words. Reviews of small press books or anthologies.

Submission Policy: Query with writing samples or send complete manuscript with cover letter. Include SASE. Accepts photocopies, computer printouts, MS Word for Mac or Macintosh-compatible ASCII disks, and faxes. Simultaneous submissions okay. Reports in 1 month. If accepted, expect publication within 6–12 months.

Terms and Payment: One-time rights. No payment. Authors receive 3 copies of the issue.

Advertising: Rates: B/W full-page, $100; half-page, $65; quarter-page, $40. List rental available; $15. Contact Kim Means, 203-772-1697.

Other Interests: Sponsors the Phantom Press Fiction Contest. Information available from editor with SASE.

Nexus: Colorado's Holistic Journal

Margo Faulk, General Manager, 1680 Sixth Street, Suite 6, Boulder, CO 80302   Phone: 303-442-6662

Profile: A regional publication of holistic living. Issued bimonthly. Circ: 50,000. Trim size: Tabloid. 60 pages. Subscription cost: $12. Sample copy cost: $3. No writer's guidelines.

Focus and Tips: *Nexus* publishes investigative articles on holistic health, psychology, spirituality, and alternative education for Colorado-area readers.

Editorial Interests

Holistic health, bodywork, psychology, spirituality, ecology, the environment, alternative education, nutrition, healing, metaphysics, and self-help.

• *Nonfiction:* Investigative and narrative features and interviews, 500–2,000 words. Book and music reviews, 300–1,000 words. Departments include Natural Cook and Research Update, a medical journal, 300–1,000 words.

• *Illustrations:* Cover art: 4-color slides depicting people. Inside: B/W photos, line drawings, and brush drawings of people.

Submission Policy: Query with outline, resume, writing samples, and clips, or send complete manuscript with cover letter and resume. Include SASE. Accepts photocopies and computer printouts. No simultaneous submissions. Reports in 2 months.

Terms and Payment: First North American serial rights. Pays on publication. $.10 per word. Authors receive 2 copies of the issue.

Advertising: Rates: B/W full-page, $1,185. List rental available; 2,700 names, $95/1,000 names, $.11 per name thereafter. Contact Margo Faulk, 303-442-6662.

Night Roses

Allen T. Billy, Editor/Publisher, P.O. Box 393, Prospect Heights, IL 60070   Phone: 708-392-2435

Profile: A small press review of poetry and arts. Issued twice a year. Circ: 250–350. Trim size: varies. Bond cover; B/W; strip or saddle stitched. 40 pages. Subscription cost: $10. Sample copy cost: $4. No writer's guidelines.

Focus and Tips: *Night Roses* publishes poetry, and, at present, is open to genre fiction for its new sister publication, *Primitive Bikini*. Twenty-five percent of its authors are high school students. Both liberal and conservative views are respected, but requests that "raw" language be used only as a last resort. Most readers are women or teenagers. Distribution is primarily in New England and the Midwest.

Editorial Interests

Poetry, genre fiction, astrology, crystals, dreams, the environment, extraterrestrials, feminism, folklore, gay and lesbian issues, inspiration, teen concerns, lifestyle, magic, meditation, men's issues, mysticism, mythology, new age, occult, parapsychology, parenting, philosophy, prayer, psychic phenomenon, psychology, relationships, self-help, seniors, spirituality, witches, and women's issues.

• *Fiction:* Poetry, no length restrictions. Romance, fantasy, and science fiction, 3–5 double-spaced, typed pages.

Submission Policy: Prefers a query first with outline. Will accept complete manuscripts with cover letter and clips. Author's name and address must appear on each page submitted. Include SASE. Accepts photocopies. Simultaneous submissions okay if noted. Responds to queries in 2 weeks, to manuscripts in 4–12 weeks. If accepted, expect publication in 20 months.

Terms and Payment: First North American serial rights or one-time rights. No payment. Authors receive copies of the issue.

North Dakota Quarterly

Robert Lewis, Editor, P.O. Box 7029, Grand Forks, ND 58202   Phone: 701-777-3321, Fax: 701-777-3650

Profile: A university journal. Published by the University of North Dakota. Issued quarterly. Circ: 800. Trim size: 6x9. Glossy color cover; B/W inside; perfect bound. 250 pages. Subscription cost: $20 individual; $23 institution. Sample copy cost: $5. No writer's guidelines.

Focus and Tips: *North Dakota Quarterly* is a literary journal offering prose and poetry on the humanities, arts, and social sciences. Writing must be of high quality. "Look at the journal to get a feel for our interests."

Editorial Interests

Literary material, cultural and ethnic issues, the environment, feminism, folklore, metaphysics, mythology, philosophy, politics, Native American studies, social and world issues, and spirituality.

• *Fiction:* Short stories, 2,500 words. Poetry, no length restrictions.

• *Nonfiction:* Features and articles, 2,000–10,000 words. Interviews and profiles, 2,500 words. Essays, personal experiences, and opinion pieces, 1,500–10,000 words. Reviews, 750–1,000 words. Departments include Sea Changes: Books that Mattered, reflective essays on the effects of a novel.

Submission Policy: Query with resume or send complete manuscript with cover letter. Include SASE. Accepts photocopies, laser-quality printouts, and IBM WordPerfect disks. Simultaneous submissions okay for prose. No simultaneous poetry submissions. Responds to queries in 1 month, to manuscripts in 6 weeks. If accepted, expect publication in 1 year.

Terms and Payment: First North American serial rights. No payment. Authors receive 5 copies of the issue.

Advertising: Rates: B/W full-page, $125; half-page, $75. List rental available. Contact Robert Lewis, 701-777-3321.

Other Interests: Sponsors an annual writing conference in March at the University of North Dakota. Conference features guest speakers, readings, panel discussions, and social events. For more information, contact Robert King, 701-777-3321.

NorthEast Arts

Mr. Leigh Donaldson, Publisher, John F. Kennedy Station, P.O. Box 6061, Boston, MA 02114

Profile: A literary arts journal. Published by the Boston Arts Organization, Inc., a non-profit organization. Issued 2 times a year. Circ: 1,000. Trim size: 6x9. Glossy cover; B/W; saddle stitched. 24–36 pages. Subscription cost: $10. Sample copy cost: $4.50. Writer's guidelines available with SASE.

Focus and Tips: *NorthEast Arts* is interested in a variety of material and perspectives, especially work that somehow focuses on inventive efforts. Strongly discourages work that reflects a lack of moral, social, and political consciousness. Submissions from "so-called" minorities are encouraged.

Editorial Interests

Literary material, cultural and ethnic issues, folklore, gay and lesbian issues, and lifestyle.

• *Fiction:* Short stories, 750–1,500 words. Poetry, under 30 lines.

• *Nonfiction:* Features, 750–1,500 words.

• *Illustrations:* B/W camera-ready art and halftone/screened photos either 5x8 or 5x4.5. Should be general and creatively artistic enough to stand on their own.

Submission Policy: Send complete manuscript with brief author biography. Include SASE. Reports in 3 months.

Terms and Payment: No payment. Authors receive 2 copies of the issue.

Advertising: Space and classified advertising rates available upon request.

The Northeast Recovery Networker

Lois Grasso, Editor, 504 Main Street, Farmington, CT 06032   Phone: 203-678-8686, Fax: 203-677-8112

Profile: A regional newsmagazine of recovery-related issues. Issued monthly. Circ: 35,000. Trim size: 11x17. Newsprint; spot color; folded. 16–20 pages. Subscription cost: $20. Sample copy cost: Free. Writer's guidelines available with SASE.

Focus and Tips: *The Northeast Recovery Networker* is dedicated to promoting personal growth, healing, and recovery from the effects of trauma and addiction. Its primary purpose is to support and encourage families and individuals in the healing process. Not affiliated with any group, organization, or 12-Step Fellowship. Submissions should offer one or more of the following elements: education, inspiration, or information valid to readers. Semantics are fairly conservative, therapeutic, and 12-Step oriented. Avoid controversial opinion; lecturing; pep talks; lofty, philosophical theory; and flamboyant, fanatic Eastern-style lingo.

Editorial Interests

Recovery, eating disorders, AIDS, sexual abuse survival, codependency, adult child/inner child, bodywork, dreams, healing, holistic and natural health, health care, inspiration, meditation, men's and women's issues, nutrition, parenting, prayer, psychology, rebirthing, relationships, self-help, social and world issues, spirituality, and yoga.

• *Fiction:* Short stories, 500–1,500 words. Book excerpts, 750–1,000 words. Poetry, 100–300 words.

• *Nonfiction:* Features, interviews, and profiles, 1,000–2,000 words. Articles, 750–1,500 words. Essays and personal experiences, 500–1,000 words. Opinion pieces, up to 500 words. News items, 300–750 words. Reviews, 500–750 words. Filler, 300–600 words. Departments include What's News, briefs on topic-related happenings or upcoming events, 300–500 words.

Submission Policy: Query with outline, writing samples, resume, and statement of objective; or send complete manuscript with cover letter. Include SASE. Accepts photocopies, 3.5" disks, and faxes. Reports in 1–3 months. If accepted, expect publication within 2–3 months.

Terms and Payment: First North American serial rights. Payment is negotiated on individual basis. Authors receive up to 10 copies of the issue.

Advertising: Rates: B/W full-page, $1,075; 4-color full-page, $1,600; spot color full-page, $1,275. List rental available; $95/M. Up to 2-time use; advanced payment required. Contact Lois Grasso, 203-678-8686.

Ocean Gypsy

Marie Hart-Gurrere, Publisher, P.O. Box 828, Nyack, NY 10960

Profile: A special-interest publication on mermaids. Issued bimonthly. Circ: 200+. Trim size: 8.5x11. 20 lb. paper; B/W; stapled. 20 pages. Subscription cost: $16. Sample copy cost: $3. No writer's guidelines.

Focus and Tips: *Ocean Gypsy* is a magazine for mermaid collectors and fantasy lovers. "Use your imagination and write about yourself. Our readers like to know about fellow mermaid collectors." All material must deal with mermaids; no general ocean-related pieces. Avoid psychological or prejudice viewpoints.

Editorial Interests

Mermaids. Considers folklore, inspiration, magic, meditation, mythology, spirituality, and women's issues as related to mermaids.

• *Fiction:* Mermaid tales, short stories, fairy tales, drama, and poetry. Considers serialized pieces. No length restrictions.

• *Nonfiction:* Articles profiling the writer and his or her collections. Travel pieces on places to swim or "inspirational spots for meditation or mermaid watching." Articles on events and places to visit such as shops, antique shows, flea markets, fairs, etc. Reviews of new or old books on mermaids. No length restrictions.

Submission Policy: Query first with outline and writing samples, or send complete manuscript with cover letter. Include SASE. Accepts photocopies and computer printouts. Simultaneous submissions okay. Responds to queries in 1 month, to manuscripts in 1–2 months. If accepted, expect publication in 6–8 months.

Terms and Payment: One-time rights. No payment. Authors receive copies of the issue upon request.

Advertising: Rates: B/W full-page, $79. Contact Marie Hart-Gurrere.

Odyssey

Gail Rossi, Publisher, R.R. 2, Box 466, Casco, ME 04015   Phone: 207-655-3103

Profile: A holistic newspaper serving Maine and New Hampshire. Established in 1990. Issued monthly. Circ: 10,000. Trim size: Tabloid. Newsprint; folded. 16–20 pages. Subscription cost: $10. Sample copy cost: Free. No writer's guidelines.

Focus and Tips: *Odyssey* is a tool for expressing professional or personal information and experiences that help move all toward personal and planetary well being. It is open to a diversity of thought. Distributed free at over 125 locations throughout Maine and eastern New Hampshire. Prefers thought-provoking, enlightening, positive articles that are focused and relevant to the Maine/New Hampshire region. Lengthy, rambling articles are discouraged.

Editorial Interests

New age, astrology, bodywork, channeling, crystals, dreams, environment, extraterrestrials, healing, health, holistic and natural health, magic, meditation, metaphysics, mysticism, mythology, nutrition, occult, parapsychology, prayer, psychic phenomenon, psychology, rebirthing, recovery, religion, spirituality, witches, and yoga.

• *Nonfiction:* Features, articles, and personal experiences, 700–1,200 words.

Submission Policy: Send complete manuscript with cover letter. Include SASE. Accepts photocopies, computer printouts, and Macintosh MS Word or WordPerfect disks. No simultaneous submissions. Reports in 1 month. If accepted, expect publication in 2 months.

Terms and Payment: One-time rights. Payment negotiable.

Advertising: Rates per page: B/W, $300. Contact Gail Rossi, 207-655-3103.

Other Interests: Sponsors Alternative Path, a holistic fair offered periodically. For more information, contact Gail Rossi, 207-655-3103.

Of A Like Mind

Lynnie Levy, Editor, P.O. Box 6677, Madison, WI 53716   Phone: 608-244-0072

Profile: A newspaper of feminist spirituality and goddess worship. Published by the Reformed Congregation of the Goddess, Inc. Issued quarterly. Circ: 35,000. Trim size: 11x17. Newsprint; folded. 24 pages. Subscription cost: $15–$35. Sample copy cost: $4. Writer's guidelines available with SASE.

Focus and Tips: *Of A Like Mind* publishes spiritually positive writings and artwork for, by, and about spiritual women. It serves as a network dedicated to bringing together women following positive paths, and offers a forum for sharing knowledge, dreams, and visions. Its focus is on goddess religions, paganism, and earth connections from a women-centered perspective. Especially interested in articles that are thought provoking and that will stimulate dialogue on issues from a spiritual and feminist perspective. "Read the paper, understand our audience, ask what we need, be persistent, and don't start letters with 'Dear Sirs'."

Editorial Interests

Paganism, Wicca, wellness, astrology, herbs, crystals, witchcraft, tarot, chants, ritual, psychic development, I-Ching, herstories, goddesses, numerology, palmistry, crone power, women's spirituality, and natural living.

• *Nonfiction:* Features, articles, interviews, profiles, essays, personal experiences, and opinion pieces, 1,500 words. Reviews, 500–1,500 words.

• *Illustrations:* B/W artwork no larger than 8.5x11.

Submission Policy: Query with outline or send complete manuscript with cover letter and short biography. Include SASE. Accepts photocopies, computer printouts, and Macintosh Works, Word, or PageMaker disks. Simultaneous submissions okay if to a non-competing market. Responds to queries in 1 month, to manuscripts in 3 months. If accepted, expect publication in 3 months.

Terms and Payment: One-time rights. No payment. Authors receive 2 copies of the issue.

Advertising: Rates: B/W full-page, $560. Contact Lynnie Levy, 608-244-0072. List rental available: $50/M. Contact Jade, 608-244-0072.

Other Interests: Sponsors several conferences: Midwest Women's Writers Conference; Lesbian Sex Camp; and Sharing Spirit/Sharing Skills, a psychic skills conference. Contact Jade, 608-244-0072.

Off Our Backs

April Jackson, Office Coordinator, 2423 18th Street, 2nd Floor, Washington, DC 20009   Phone: 202-234-8072

Profile: A feminist/lesbian newspaper. Issued 11 times a year. Circ: 50,000. Trim size: 11.5x14.5. Newsprint; folded. 28 pages. Subscription cost: $21. Sample copy cost: $3. Writer's guidelines available with SASE.

Focus and Tips: *Off Our Backs* is a newsjournal by, for, and about women. It addresses a feminist, politically active audience. Be aware of audience when writing—"offensive is not the same as provocative."

Editorial Interests

Feminism, gay and lesbian issues, cultural and ethnic issues, philosophy, politics, relationships, social and world issues, and women's issues.

• *Nonfiction:* No specific requirement beyond writing that is somehow feminist.

Submission Policy: Send complete manuscript. Include SASE. Accepts photocopies, computer printouts, and ASCII disks. No simultaneous submissions. Reports in 2–4 weeks. If accepted, expect publication in 3–4 weeks.

Terms and Payment: No payment. Authors receive 2 copies of the issue; more upon request.

Advertising: Rates: B/W full-page, $400; half-page, $210; quarter page, $120. Camera-ready copy is required. Classified ads: $.40 per word.

Omega New Age Directory

John Rodgers, Editor, 6418 South 39th Avenue, Phoenix, AZ 85041   Phone: 602-237-3213

Profile: A new age newsmagazine. Published by the New Age Community Church. Issued monthly. Circ: 20,000. Trim size: Tabloid. Newsprint; spot color; folded. 20 pages. Subscription cost: $5 in Arizona; $15 out of State. Sample copy cost: $1.50. No writer's guidelines.

Focus and Tips: *Omega New Age Directory* reports on global new age and interreligious news, personalities, and events. Readers are open-minded, iconoclastic, and of all ages. It looks for short, pithy articles written from unique, interesting viewpoints. "We want new ideas. Avoid old assumptions and the over-use of sectarian religious authorities. Don't preach."

Editorial Interests

New age, philosophy, comparative religion, astrology, channeling, crystals, dreams, the environment, extraterrestrials, healing, health, holistic health, lifestyle, magic, meditation, metaphysics, mysticism, occult, parapsychology, politics, psychic phenomenon, social and world issues, spirituality, and yoga.

• *Nonfiction:* Personal experiences and dissertation-style features and essays on new insights or unusual theories. 200–700

words.
Submission Policy: Send complete manuscript with cover letter. Include SASE. Accepts photocopies and computer print-outs. No simultaneous submissions. Reports in 2–3 months. If accepted, expect publication in 2–3 months.
Terms and Payment: All rights. No payment. Authors receive copies of the issue upon request.
Advertising: Rates: B/W full-page, $440; business-card, $29. Contact John Rodgers, 602-237-3213.

Omni Magazine

Keith Ferrell, Editor, 324 West Wendover Avenue, Suite 205, Greensboro, NC 27408   Phone: 910-275-9809

Profile: A national magazine of future technology. Published by General Media International. Issued monthly. Circ: 700,000+. Trim size: 8.5x11. Glossy paper; full-color; saddle stitched. 100+ pages. Writer's guidelines available with SASE.
Focus and Tips: *Omni Magazine* publishes articles on speculative science and technological innovations. It is also open to futuristic and science fiction.
Editorial Interests
Science fiction, future technology, science, bodywork, dreams, ecosystems, the environment, extraterrestrials, health, lifestyle, meditation, natural health, new age, nutrition, occult, parapsychology, philosophy, politics, psychic phenomenon, psychology, and social and world issues.
• *Nonfiction:* Features, 2,500–4,000 words. Continuum department, 200 words. Columns, 750 words. Accepts interviews and profiles.
Submission Policy: Query first with outline and writing samples. Include SASE. Accepts computer printouts and MS-DOS disks. No simultaneous submissions. Reports in 6–8 weeks. If accepted, expect publication in up to 1 year.
Terms and Payment: First North American serial rights. Pays on acceptance. Rates vary. Authors receive 1 copy of the issue.
Advertising: Accepts advertising. Contact Corey Friedman, 212-496-6100. List rental available. Contact Bea Hanks, 212-496-6100.

On Course

Jon Mundy, Editor, 459 Carol Drive, Monroe, NY 10950   Phone: 914-783-0383, Fax: 914-774-7747

Profile: A magazine based on *A Course in Miracles*. Published by Interfaith Fellowship. Issued biweekly. Circ: 3,000. Trim size: 5.5x8.5. Color cover; B/W; saddle stitched. 48 pages. Subscription cost: $49. Sample copy cost: Free. No writer's guidelines.
Focus and Tips: *On Course* is an interfaith publication exploring all world religions from a view based on the book *A Course in Miracles*. Most material is written in-house or by subscribers.
Editorial Interests
A Course in Miracles, inspiration, mysticism, philosophy, prayer, psychology, self-help, and spirituality.
• *Poetry:* Inspirational poetry.
• *Nonfiction:* Short inspirational essays, up to 500 words.
Submission Policy: Query or send complete manuscript. Include SASE. Accepts photocopies, computer printouts, and IBM-compatible disks with hard copy. Simultaneous submissions okay. Reports in 2–3 weeks. If accepted, expect publication in 2–3 months.
Terms and Payment: One-time rights. No payment. Authors receive copies of the issue.
Advertising: Rates: B/W full-page, $70; half-page, $40. List rental available: $.10 per name. Contact Jon Mundy, 914-783-0383.
Other Interests: Interfaith Fellowship offers a variety of conferences, workshops, seminars, and retreat programs. Send an SASE for more information.

On The Issues: The Progressive Woman's Quarterly

Ronni Sandroff, Editor, 97-77 Queens Boulevard, Flushing, NY 11374   Phone: 718-275-6020, Fax: 718-997-1206

Profile: A feminist humanist magazine. Published by CHOICES Women's Medical Center, Inc. Issued quarterly. Circ: 21,700. Trim size: 8.5x11. Glossy color cover; 50 lb. coated paper; 4-color; saddle stitched. 64 pages. Subscription cost: $14.95. Sample copy cost: $4. Writer's guidelines available with SASE.
Focus and Tips: *On The Issues* is aimed at "thinking feminists," women and men interested in progressive social change. It represents a range of feminist viewpoints. Writers are advised to read the magazine. Looking for "fresh ideas about feminism today." Avoid polemics and go beyond the obvious.
Editorial Interests
Feminism, women's issues, social movements, health, philosophy, politics, psychology, and relationships.
• *Nonfiction:* Features, investigative articles, international and minority stories, interviews, and profiles, 1,500–3,000 words. Provocative point-of-view pieces and essays, 750–1,500 words. News items, 250–500 words. Art, book, and music reviews, 150–750 words. Talking Feminist column, 1,000–1,500 words.
Submission Policy: Query with outline and writing samples or send complete manuscript with cover letter and clips.

Include SASE. Accepts photocopies, computer printouts, WordPerfect disks, and faxes. Simultaneous submissions okay if noted. Reports in 4–6 weeks. If accepted, expect publication in 3–6 months.

Terms and Payment: One-time rights. Pays on acceptance. $50–$500 per piece. Authors receive 2 copies of the issue.

Advertising: Rates: B/W full page, $600; 4-color full-page, $900. Contact Carolyn Handel, 212-410-2047. List rental available: $90/M. Contact Karen Aisenberg, 718-275-6020.

Open Hands

Mary Jo Osterman, Editor, 3801 North Keeler Avenue, Chicago, IL 60641   Phone: 312-736-5526, Fax: 312-736-5475

Profile: A thematic magazine for those involved in gay and lesbian Christian ministry. Published by the Reconciling Congregation Program, Inc. Issued quarterly. Circ: 2,000. Trim size: 8.5x11. Self cover; 2-color; saddle stitched. 32 pages. Subscription cost: $16. Sample copy cost: $5. Writer's guidelines available with SASE.

Focus and Tips: *Open Hands* is a resource for congregations and individuals seeking to be in ministry with lesbian, bisexual, and gay persons. Each issue focuses on a specific area of concern. Write for a liberal Protestant audience that is mixed in orientation, all working on or supporting welcoming congregations. Very little interest in "coming out" stories.

Editorial Interests

Gay and lesbian concerns, progressive Christianity, inspiration, prayer, spirituality, homophobia, heterosexism, and Biblical analysis.

• *Fiction:* Short stories, 1,600 words. Short story sermons, 800–1,600 words. Poetry, up to 45 lines.

• *Nonfiction:* Features, 2,500 words. Articles, interviews and profiles, 800–1,600 words. Personal experiences, and opinion pieces, 800 words. Reviews and filler, 100–250 words. Inspirational column, 500–1,000 words.

Submission Policy: Prefers a query with outline and resume. Accepts complete manuscript with cover letter. Include SASE. Accepts photocopies, computer printouts, and IBM-compatible disks (request list of acceptable programs). Simultaneous submissions okay. Responds to queries in 1–2 months, to manuscripts in 2–3 months.

Terms and Payment: One-time rights. No payment. Authors receive 1–3 copies of the issue.

Advertising: Accepts advertising. Contact Mark Bowman, 312-736-3526, for rate sheet.

The Oregon PeaceWorker

Peter Bergel, Editor, 333 State Street, Salem, OR 97301   Phone: 503-371-8002, Fax: 503-585-2767

Profile: A regional newsmagazine on social justice issues. Published by Oregon PeaceWorks. Issued 10 times a year. Circ: 11,000. Trim size: Tabloid. Newsprint; folded. 16 pages. Subscription cost: $15. Sample copy cost: Free. Writer's guidelines available with SASE.

Focus and Tips: *The Oregon PeaceWorker* offers news and views of the peace, justice, and environmental communities in Oregon. It prefers a journalistic writing style; avoid injecting strong biases into the story. Authors are advised to contact the publication before submitting to check on special themes and interests.

Editorial Interests

Peace work, social justice, the environment, ecosystems, feminism, gay and lesbian issues, inspiration, politics, and social and world issues.

• *Nonfiction:* Features, 750–1,200 words. Articles, interviews, and profiles, 300–1,000 words. Essays, 500–1,000 words. Opinion pieces, 250–750 words. Accepts news items and reviews.

Submission Policy: Query with outline and writing samples. Include SASE. Accepts photocopies, computer printouts, ASCII or Microsoft Word disks, and faxes. Simultaneous submissions okay. Reports in 1–2 months.

Terms and Payment: One-time rights. No payment. Authors receive copies of the issue upon request.

Advertising: Rates: B/W full-page, $500; 2-color, $650. Contact Peter Bergel, 503-371-8002.

Other Interests: Sponsors several Oregon-area conferences. For more information, contact Susan Gordon, 503-371-8002.

Organica Quarterly

Susan Hussey, Editor-in-Chief, 4419 North Manhattan Avenue, Tampa, FL 33614   Phone: 813-876-4879

Profile: An environmental newsmagazine. Underwritten by Aubrey Organics, Inc. for commercial considerations. Issued quarterly. Circ: 200,000. Trim size: Tabloid. Newsprint; spot color; folded. 28 pages. Subscription cost: $10. Sample copy cost: $1. No writers guidelines.

Focus and Tips: *Organica Quarterly* publishes writings on social and ecological issues, sciences, and the arts as it promotes Aubrey Organics products. It is distributed free in many book stores and healthfood stores. Avoid new age-oriented articles.

Editorial Interests

The environment, ecosystems, holistic health, cultural and ethnic issues, feminism, folklore, gay and lesbian concerns, health, meditation, men's issues, metaphysics, natural health, nutrition, philosophy, politics, psychology, social and world issues, and women's issues.

• *Nonfiction:* Features, articles, interviews, profiles, essays, and opinion pieces, 1,500–3,000 words. Reviews, 300–500 words.
Submission Policy: Query with outline and writing samples. Include SASE. Accepts photocopies, computer printouts, and Macintosh MacWrite Pro I and II disks. Simultaneous submissions okay. Reports in 3–6 months. If accepted, expect publication in 3–12 months.
Terms and Payment: First North American serial rights. Pays on publication. Per piece rates vary. Authors receive 2–3 copies of the issue.

The Other Paper

Paul Prensky, P.O. Box 11376, Eugene, OR 97440   InterNet: news–staff@efn.org

Profile: A regional, progressive newspaper. Issued monthly. Circ: 4,000. Trim size: 10x15. Newsprint; folded. 16 pages. Subscription cost: $15. Sample copy cost: Free. Writer's guidelines available with SASE.
Focus and Tips: *The Other Paper* seeks to publish news, art, commentary, analysis, and creative writing from a variety of progressive perspectives, with the aim of improving the progressive community in Eugene, Oregon. It prefers articles on regional Oregon issues such as local organizations, media, and government, but is interested in all progressive viewpoints.
Editorial Interests
Regional issues, cultural and ethnic issues, ecosystems, the environment, feminism, gay and lesbian concerns, men's issues, new age, philosophy, politics, social and world issues, and women's issues.
• *Fiction:* Short-short stories, up to 1,000 words. Poetry, no length restrictions. Submit material to Arts & Letters Editor.
• *Nonfiction:* Articles, interviews, profiles, essays, opinion pieces, and news items, 500 words. Letters to the Editor, 200 words. Accepts filler.
• *Illustrations:* Drawings and artwork.
Submission Policy: Query first with outline and resume. Include SASE. Accepts photocopies, computer printouts, and IBM or Macintosh WordPerfect or Word disks. No simultaneous submissions. Reports in 1 month. If accepted, expect publication in 2–3 months.
Terms and Payment: One-time rights. No payment. Authors receive 1 copy of the issue.
Advertising: Rates: B/W full-page, $320. Contact Wanda Ballentine, 503-688-3549.

Otisian Directory

Jeff Stevens, Editor, P.O. Box 783, Cambridge, MA 02139-0783

Profile: A review journal. Published by IGHF. Issued quarterly. Circ: 250. Trim size: 8.5x11. Perfect bound. 30 pages. Subscription cost: $8. Sample copy cost: $3. Writer's guidelines available with SASE.
Focus and Tips: *Otisian Directory* offers alternative reviews, humor and select poetry and prose on anything outside the mainstream. "Write what you want—don't listen to pushy editors."
Editorial Interests
Alternative reviews, Otisianism, mysticism, mythology, occult, philosophy, social and world issues, and spirituality.
• *Fiction:* Short stories, drama, and book excerpts, 2,500 words. Short-short stories, 1,500 words. Genre fiction, 3,000 words. Poetry, 1,000 words.
• *Nonfiction:* Features, articles, essays, and news, 3,000 words. Interviews, profiles, and opinion pieces, 2,000 words. Personal experiences, 1,000 words. Reviews, 2,500 words. Filler, 1,000 words. Departments and columns, 2,000 words.
Submission Policy: Query with writing samples and resume or send complete manuscript with cover letter and biography, resume, or clips. Include SASE. Accepts photocopies, computer printouts, Macintosh or IBM disks, and faxes. Simultaneous submissions okay. Responds to queries in 2 weeks, to manuscripts in 2 months. If accepted, expect publication in 9 months.
Terms and Payment: One-time rights. No payment for unsolicited material. Authors receive 1 copy of the issue.
Advertising: Rates: B/W full-page, $25; 4-color full-page, $100. Contact Jeff Stevens.

Outpost Exchange

Malcolm Woods, Editor, 102 East Capital Drive, Milwaukee, WI 52312   Phone: 414-964-7789

Profile: A regional health publication. Published by Outpost Natural Foods. Issued monthly. Circ: 28,000. Trim size: 8.5x10. Newsprint; stapled. 40 pages. Subscription cost: $12. Sample copy cost: Free. Writer's guidelines available with SASE.
Focus and Tips: *Outpost Exchange* is Milwaukee's food and wellness magazine that covers area attractions and events. Reading a sample copy before submitting is a must. Avoid academic language.
Editorial Interests
Regional issues, bodywork, cultural and ethnic concerns, dreams, ecosystems, the environment, feminism, gay and lesbian issues, healing, health, holistic health, lifestyle, meditation, natural health, new age, nutrition, parapsychology, parenting, philosophy, politics, psychology, self-help, social and world issues, spirituality, women's issues, and yoga.
• *Nonfiction:* Features, 800–1,200 words. Articles, interviews, profiles, essays, and personal experiences, 400–800 words.

Opinion pieces, 200–500 words. News, 400 words. Accepts restaurant and book reviews.
Submission Policy: Query with outline, writing samples, and resume. No unsolicited manuscripts. Include SASE. Accepts photocopies, laser-quality printouts, and Macintosh Microsoft Word disks. Simultaneous submissions okay. Reports in 2 months. If accepted, expect publication in 2 months.
Terms and Payment: Authors retain rights. No payment. Contributor's receive a 15% discount at Outpost Natural Foods in Milwaukee. Authors receive 2 copies of the issue.
Advertising: Accepts advertising. Contact Malcolm Woods, 414-964-7789.

Pacific Coast Journal

John S. F. Graham, Editor, P.O. Box 355, Campbell, CA 95009-0355

Profile: A literary journal. Published by French Bread Publications. Issued quarterly. Circ: 200. Trim size: 5.5x8.5. Bond cover; B/W; saddle stitched. 54–64 pages. Subscription cost: $10. Sample copy cost: $2.50. Writer's guidelines available with SASE.
Focus and Tips: *Pacific Coast Journal* is a general-interest literary magazine with a focus on meta-writing and linguistics. Advises writers to "know who your characters are, not necessarily what they say."
Editorial Interests
Literary, cultural and ethnic issues, education, and linguistics.
• *Fiction:* Short stories, 4,000 words. Short-short stories, 1,500 words. Non-serialized book excerpts, 4,000 words. One-act plays and poetry, no length restrictions.
• *Nonfiction:* Interviews with and profiles of fiction or poetry authors, 4,000 words. Personal and literary essays, 4,000 words. Opinion pieces on literature and grammar, 2,000 words. Book reviews, 1,500 words. Accepts recipes and computer programs.
• *Illustrations:* B/W photos, no larger than 5x7.
Submission Policy: Send complete manuscript with cover letter. Include SASE and SASP. Accepts photocopies, computer printouts, and Macintosh or IBM 3.5" or IBM 5.25" disks. Simultaneous submissions okay if noted. Reports in 2–4 months. If accepted, expect publication in 6–9 months.
Terms and Payment: One-time rights. No payment. Authors receive 1 copy of the issue.
Advertising: Rates: B/W full-page, $35; half-page, $25; quarter-page, $15. Contact John S. F. Graham.
Other Interests: Sponsors the French Bread Awards for poetry, short fiction, and essays. First prize, $50; second prize, $25. Deadline is August 1. Contact John S. F. Graham.

Pan-American Indian Association News

Chief Piercing Eyes-Penn, Editor, P.O. Box 244, Nocatee, FL 33864   Phone: 813-494-6930

Profile: A membership newspaper. Published by the Pan-American Indian Association, Inc. Issued quarterly. Circ: 5,000. Trim size: 11x17. Newsprint; folded. 16 pages. Subscription cost: $8 for 5 issues. Sample copy cost: Free. Writer's guidelines available with SASE.
Focus and Tips: *Pan-American Indian Association News* is the official publication of the Pan-American Indian Association, a nonprofit educational, religious, and cultural corporation. Readers are those wishing to discover and/or study their ethnic tribal heritage, with emphasis on Native Americans. "Camera-ready copy will put contributors on top of the list of consideration." No "hate" pieces.
Editorial Interests
Native Americans, genealogy, cultural and ethnic issues, the environment, folklore, holistic health, lifestyle, mysticism, mythology, natural health, politics, tribal religion, spirituality, and women's issues.
• *Poetry:* Up to 300 words.
• *Nonfiction:* Features, articles, interviews, profiles, essays, personal experience, opinion pieces, news, and reviews, 800 words.
• *Illustrations:* B/W photos; cartoons.
Submission Policy: Send complete manuscript with resume. Prefers camera-ready copy. Include SASE. Accepts photocopies and computer printouts. Simultaneous submissions okay. Reports in 1 week. If accepted, expect publication in 3 months.
Terms and Payment: Authors retain rights. No payment. Authors receive copies of the issue.
Advertising: Rates: B/W full-page, $100. Contact Trudi Rosebud, 813-494-6930.

Panegyria

Pete Pathfinder, Editor, P.O. Box 409, Index, WA 98256   Phone: 206-793-1945, Fax: 206-793-3537

Profile: A Neopagan Wiccan publication. Published by Aquarian Tabernacle Church. Issued 8 times a year. Circ: 800–900. Trim size: 8.5x11. Stapled. 10–20 pages. Subscription cost: $12. Sample copy cost: Free with 2 oz. postage. Writers guidelines available with SASE.
Focus and Tips: *Panegyria* is aimed broadly at the Neopagan and Wiccan community. It is interested in material with specific

applicability to Wiccan and Neopagan fields, rather than broader new age issues. Avoid "folksy, Mother-Earth, newsy material." Use a professional writing style that is not too wordy or self-important. Identify any "sacred cows" prior to submitting. A favorite topic is Professionalization of the Neopagan and Wiccan Clergy.

Editorial Interests

Wiccan and Neopagan beliefs, astrology, cultural and ethnic issues, dreams, ecosystems, the environment, feminism, folklore, gay and lesbian issues, healing, holistic health, inspiration, lifestyle, magic, men's issues, meditation, mysticism, mythology, natural health, occult, parenting, philosophy, politics, prayer, psychic phenomenon, psychology, rebirthing, relationships, spirituality, witches, and women's issues.

• *Fiction:* Short stories, 1,500 words.

• *Nonfiction:* Features and articles, 2,000–2,500 words. Interviews and profiles, 2,000 words. Essays, 200 words. Personal experiences, opinion pieces, and news, 1,500 words.

Submission Policy: Send complete manuscripts with cover letter and author biography. Include SASE. Accepts photocopies, computer printouts, faxes, and CPM, DOS, or Macintosh disks, preferably ASCII 7.6. Use E-mail address for submissions under 15 pages, aquat abch@aol.com. Simultaneous submissions okay if noted. Reports in 45 days. Publication times varies.

Terms and Payment: No payment. Authors receive 2 copies of the issue.

Advertising: Rates: Business-card, $10. Contact Pete Pathfinder, 206-793-1945.

Parabola

Ellen Draper and Virginia Baron, Co-Editors, 656 Broadway, New York, NY 10012   Phone 212-505-9037

Profile: A thematic journal that explores mythology. Published by the Society for the Study of Myth and Tradition, Inc., a nonprofit organization. Issued quarterly. Circ: 40,000. Trim size: 6.5x10. Glossy color cover; B/W inside; perfect bound. 128 pages. Subscription cost: $20. Sample copy cost: $6. Writer's guidelines and theme list available with SASE.

Focus and Tips: *Parabola* is devoted to the study of the quest for meaning as expressed in the myths, symbols, legends, sacred art, folklore, and rituals of the world's religions. Articles must relate to issue theme. Past themes include Relationships, Creation, Solitude and Community, Sacred Space, Death, The Sense of Humor, and Healing. Avoid academic jargon, "pop" mysticism, and self-help.

Editorial Interests

Mythology, folklore, and all religions.

• *Nonfiction:* Theme-related articles and essays, 2,000–4,000 words. Retellings of traditional stories, 500–1,500 words. Reviews, 750 words.

Submission Policy: Send for theme list before submitting. Query with outline or send complete manuscript with cover letter. Include SASE. Accepts photocopies and computer printouts. Responds to queries in 1 month, to manuscripts in 3 months. If accepted, expect publication in 3 months.

Terms and Payment: One-time rights. Pays on publication. Rates vary. Authors receive 2 copies of the issue.

Advertising: Rates per page: B/W, $815. List rental available. Subject to approval. Contact Beth Leonard, 212-505-6200.

Pathfinder

Patsy Nelson, Editor, 3228 Laclede Station Road, Suite A, St. Louis, MO 63143   Phone: 314-645-2292, Fax: 314-645-4727

Profile: A new age magazine. Issued bimonthly. Circ: 30,000. Trim size: 11.5x14. Newsprint; folded. 20–24 pages. Subscription cost: $10. Sample copy cost: Free. No writer's guidelines.

Focus and Tips: *Pathfinder* provides a network of resources for holistic health, spiritual growth, higher consciousness, and reverence for the Earth. Material should be educational and not self-serving.

Editorial Interests

New age, astrology, bodywork, channeling, crystals, cultural and ethnic issues, dreams, ecosystems, the environment, extraterrestrials, feminism, folklore, gay and lesbian issues, healing and health, holistic health, inspiration, juvenile and teen issues, lifestyle, magic, meditation, men's issues, metaphysics, mysticism, mythology, natural health, nutrition, occult, parapsychology, parenting, philosophy, politics, prayer, psychic phenomenon, psychology, rebirthing, recovery, relationships, self-help, seniors, social and world issues, spirituality, witches, women's issues, and yoga.

• *Nonfiction:* Features and articles with educational value, 3 typed, double-spaced manuscript pages.

• *Illustrations:* Photographs and artwork.

Submission Policy: Send complete manuscript with 1–2 line biography and photo. Include SASE. Accepts computer printouts. No simultaneous submissions. Reporting time varies. If accepted, expect publication in 4 months.

Terms and Payment: Authors retain rights. No payment. Authors receive copies of the issue.

Advertising: Rates: B/W full-page, $650; half-page, $375; quarter-page, $200. Contact Mike Elliff, 314-645-2292.

PDXS

Jim Redden, Editor, 2305 NW Kearny, Portland, OR 97210   Phone: 503-224-7316

Profile: An alternative paper of culture and rock 'n' roll. Established in 1990. Issued biweekly. Circ: 12,000. Trim size: Tabloid. Newsprint; folded. 20–24 pages. Subscription cost: Free. Sample copy cost: Free. No writer's guidelines.
Focus and Tips: *PDXS* reaches the 18- to 24-year-old market interested in alternative culture, politics, and music. It is most open to cutting edge topics and writing, anything out of the mainstream. Regional focus is on the Portland, Oregon area.
Editorial Interests
Alternative culture, politics, rock 'n' roll, the environment, extraterrestrials, feminism, gay and lesbian concerns, teen issues, lifestyle, men's issues, occult, regional news, and social and world issues.
• *Nonfiction:* Bizarre and unusual features, articles, interviews, and profiles, 2,000–2,500 words. Essays, 1,000–1,500 words. Documented opinion pieces, 1,000 words. News items, 2,500 words. Music and movie reviews, 300–400 words.
Submission Policy: Query first with outline. Include SASE. Accepts photocopies, computer printouts, and Macintosh disks. Simultaneous submissions okay if noted. Reports in 1 week. If accepted, expect publication within 1 month.
Terms and Payment: Rights vary. Pays on publication. $35–$65 per piece. Authors receive 2 copies of the issue.
Advertising: Rates: B/W full-page, $550; one-sixth-page, $65. Contact Bill Reddenisame, 503-224-7316.

The Peace Newsletter
Bill Mazza, 924 Burnet Avenue, Syracuse, NY 13203   Phone: 315-472-5478

Profile: A regional social justice newsletter. Published by The Syracuse Peace Council. Issued monthly. Circ: 4,500. Trim size: 8.5x11. Newsprint; folded. 24 pages. Subscription cost: $12. Sample copy cost: $1. No writer's guidelines.
Focus and Tips: *The Peace Newsletter* is dedicated to the activities of The Syracuse Peace Council, a grassroots, political action organization. It provides a forum for discussion of issues of concern to the peace movement. Direct articles to contemporary social justice issues relevant to a Central New York readership. Avoid gendered and heterosexist language.
Editorial Interests
Social justice, peace work, criminal justice, indigenous rights, cultural and ethnic issues, the environment, feminism, gay and lesbian concerns, politics, and women's issues.
• *Fiction:* Short-short stories and genre fiction, 700–900 words.
• *Nonfiction:* Features, articles, interviews, profiles, essays, personal experiences, opinion pieces, news items, and reviews, 700–1,800 words.
Submission Policy: Send complete manuscript with cover letter. Include SASE. Accepts photocopies, computer printouts, IBM-compatible disks, and faxes. If accepted, expect publication in 1 month.
Terms and Payment: Rights vary. No payment. Authors receive 1–5 copies of the issue, more upon request.
Advertising: Rates: B/W full-page, $150. Contact Joe Carpenter, 315-472-5478.

Peacework
Pat Farren, Editor, American Friends Service Committee, 2161 Mass. Ave., Cambridge, MA 02140
Phone: 617-661-6130, Fax: 617-354-2832

Profile: A grassroots peace and social justice newsletter. Published by the New England Regional Office of the American Friends Service Committee. Issued monthly. Circ: 2,000. Trim size: 8.5x11. Self cover; B/W; stapled. 16 pages.
Focus and Tips: Founded in 1972, *Peacework* presents current events and analysis of global thought and local action toward nonviolent social change. Readers are socially concerned activists who think globally and act locally. Encourages concise, tightly written material aimed at activist readers. Query first; freelance space is very limited.
Editorial Interests
Nonviolent social action, anti-racism, feminism, gay and lesbian issues, politics, and women's issues.
• *Nonfiction:* Accepts features, articles, interviews, profiles, essays, personal experiences, and opinion pieces, all 500-1,000 words. Reviews, 300 words.
Submission Policy: Send for writer's guidelines and sample before submitting. Query first; no unsolicited manuscripts. Include SASE. Accepts computer printouts and fax submissions. No simultaneous submissions. Reports in 1 month.
Terms and Payment: One-time rights. No payment. Authors receive 5 copies of the issue.

Perceptions
Gwenn Wycoff, Managing Director, 11664 National Boulevard, Suite 314, Los Angeles, CA 90064
Phone: 310-398-1705, Fax: 310-398-6370

Profile: A magazine exploring government, health, and metaphysics. Published by Gypsy Spirit. Issued quarterly. Circ: 10,000. Trim size: 8.5x11. Glossy color cover; B/W 50 lb. inside; saddle stitched. 60 pages. Subscription cost: $15. Sample copy cost: $3.50. Writer's guidelines and a list of requested articles available with SASE.
Focus and Tips: *Perceptions* seeks to expand options by providing non-mainstream media information in the areas of government, health, and metaphysics. Its provocative, enlightening, sometimes shocking articles give depth and insight into under-

lying motives and agendas. Articles are designed to empower individuals and to promote freedom through historical facts.
Editorial Interests
Politics, healing, astrology, bodywork, channeling, crystals, environment, extraterrestrials, health, holistic health, metaphysics, mysticism, nutrition, psychic phenomenon, rebirthing, recovery, and self-help.
• *Nonfiction:* Features and articles, 2,000–2,500 words. Essays, can be esoteric, 2,000–2,500 words. Personal experiences of UFOs and astral projection, 2,000–2,500. Opinion pieces, 1,000 words. Short news items, 30–500 words. Book reviews, 500 words. Short quotes as filler. Departments include Government, historical insights into today's issues; Health, pieces that promote independence; and Metaphysics, empowerment pieces with realistic, grounded information.
• *Illustrations:* Photographs, slides, negatives, and graphics to accompany articles.
Submission Policy: Send for list of Requested articles before submitting. Send 2 copies of complete manuscript with cover letter. Include SASE. Allow 7 week lead time. Accepts IBM, Macintosh, or Apple IIe disks with hard copy.
Terms and Payment: All rights. Authors must sign a Work for Hire Contract. Author retains reprint rights. Pays $5 per piece. Authors receive 3 copies of the issue.
Advertising: Rates: B/W full-page, $600; half-page, $325; quarter-page, $189. Add $250 per color.

Personal & Family History Newsletter

Margaret L. Ingram, Owner, 201 First Avenue West, Suite 114, Albany, OR 97321   Phone: 503-928-4798

Profile: A newsletter on autobiographical writing. Published by Memories Plus. Issued monthly. Circ: N/A. Trim size: 8.5x11. Photocopied; stapled. 4 pages. Subscription cost: $5. Sample copy cost: $1. Writer's guidelines available with SASE.
Focus and Tips: *Personal & Family History Newsletter* aims to provide information, instruction, and encouragement for those interested in writing personal and family biographies. Articles must relate to writing autobiographies or biographies or convey a personal experience, preferably of childhood. Avoid politics, religion, and pornography.
Editorial Interests
Autobiography, biography, personal history, and seniors.
• *Nonfiction:* Articles and personal experiences, 500 words.
Submission Policy: Send complete manuscript with cover letter. Include SASE. Accepts photocopies and computer printouts. No simultaneous submissions. Reports in 1 month. If accepted, expect publication in 2 weeks.
Terms and Payment: One-time rights. No payment. Authors receive 1–5 copies of the issue.
Advertising: Rates: B/W full-page, $40; business-card, $5. Contact Margaret Ingram.
Other Interests: Will organize and direct workshops on Gathering Family Memories, 2–6 hour workshop on autobiographical writing. For more information, Margaret Ingram, P.O. Box 1339, Albany, OR 97321.

The Personal Magnetism Home Study Course on All Human Powers

Gil Magno, Director, 2870 Pine Tree Drive, No. F2, Miami Beach, FL 33140   Phone: 305-538-8427

Profile: A self-improvement course. Published by Magnoart Culture Institute. Issued monthly. Circ: 500. Trim size: 8.5x11. Photocopied; stapled. 10–24 pages. Subscription cost: $120. Sample copy cost: $5. No writer's guidelines.
Focus and Tips: *The Personal Magnetism Home Study Course* is a newly development study program that focuses on the revision and expansion of the works of Webster Edgerly on personal magnetism, self-improvement, and success principles. Not interested in "superficial concepts of metaphysics and magic."
Editorial Interests
Self-improvement, healing, health, holistic health, inspiration, magic, metaphysics, mysticism, natural health, new age, occult, psychic phenomenon, relationships, and witches.
• *Nonfiction:* Study course lessons that explore the works of Webster Edgerly. No length restrictions.
Submission Policy: Send complete manuscript with cover letter. Include SASE. Accepts photocopies and computer printouts. Simultaneous submissions okay. Reports in 1 month. Publication time varies.
Terms and Payment: No payment. Authors receive copies of the issue.
Advertising: List rental available. Contact Gil Magno, 305-538-8427.

The Phoenix

Rosanne Bane, Editor, 3307 14th Avenue South, Minneapolis, MN 55407   Phone: 612-722-1149

Profile: A self-help recovery publication. Issued monthly. Circ: 41,000. Trim size: Tabloid. Newsprint; folded. 24 pages. Subscription cost: $15. Sample copy cost: Free with 7x9 SASE and 4 first-class stamps. Writer's guidelines and editorial calendar available with SASE.
Focus and Tips: *The Phoenix* is for people actively working toward physical, mental, emotional, and spiritual well being. Through articles and advertising, it provides a broad spectrum of recovery, renewal, and growth information to assist readers on their journey toward peace and serenity. "Obtain editorial calendar and guidelines and study sample copies. Really know

who we are and what we look for." Most readers are members of 12-step programs and are beyond the first step. Not interested in articles about recovery from surgery or diseases—"that's not what we mean by recovery!"

Editorial Interests
Recovery, self-help, bodywork, cultural and ethnic issues, dreams, the environment, feminism, gay and lesbian issues, healing, health, holistic health, inspiration, lifestyle, meditation, men's issues, metaphysics, natural health, nutrition, parenting, philosophy, politics, prayers, psychology, relationships, religion, spirituality, and women's issues.
• *Nonfiction:* Articles, interviews, profiles, essays, personal experiences, opinion pieces, and news items, 800–1,000 words. Columns include Bodywise, Family Skills, and Twelve Step.
Submission Policy: Prefers a query with outline and author qualifications. Accepts complete manuscript with cover letter. Include SASE. Accepts photocopies, computer printouts, and computer disks with hard copy. Simultaneous submissions okay. Reports in 2–4 months. Publication time varies.
Terms and Payment: First North American serial rights or second rights. Pays on publication. $.03–$.05 per word or offers an extended byline of 3–5 sentences at the end of the article. Authors receive 1 copy of the issue.
Advertising: Accepts B/W and 4-color advertising. Contact Susan Kramer, 612-291-2691. List rental possible. Contact Fran Jackson, 612-291-2691.

Plain Brown Wrapper

Richard Freeman, Editor, 130 West Limestone, Yellow Springs, OH 45387   Phone: 513-767-7416

Profile: A computer-generated, electronic magazine. Issued quarterly. 700 pages in electronic format. Sample copy cost: $2. No writer's guidelines.
Focus and Tips: *Plain Brown Wrapper* is accessible on electronic bulletin board throughout the country. Any good fiction or quality articles are likely to be published—those submitted on a disk stand the best chance of acceptance.
Editorial Interests
Cultural and ethnic issues, dreams, ecosystems, the environment, feminism, folklore, gay and lesbian concerns, mythology, philosophy, politics, relationships, social and world issues, spirituality, and women's issues.
• *Fiction:* Short stories and one-act plays, 5–10 manuscript pages. Book excerpts and poetry, no length restrictions.
• *Nonfiction:* Features, articles, interviews, profiles, essays, personal experiences, opinion pieces, and news items, 5–10 manuscript pages.
Submission Policy: Send complete manuscript. Include SASE. Prefers Macintosh disk submissions. Accepts photocopies and computer printouts. Simultaneous submissions okay. Responds to queries in 1 week, to manuscripts in 1–3 weeks. If accepted, expect publication in 3–6 months.
Terms and Payment: Authors retain rights. No payment. Authors receive 1 copy of the issue.

Plainsong

Frank Steele, Editor, Western Kentucky University, P.O. Box 8245, Bowling Green, KY 42101   Phone: 502-745-5708

Profile: An international poetry journal. Issued irregularly. Circ: 500. Trim size: 6x9. Heavy bond cover; B/W inside; perfect bound. 48–56 pages. Subscription cost: $7. Sample copy cost: $3.50. Writer's guidelines available with SASE.
Focus and Tips: *Plainsong* selects poems that speak of a sense of place, especially the mystery of how places create people and how people interact with places. Also interested in poems about generations and family relationships, Its slant is more liberal than conservative anti-nuclear, ecological, optimistic about the chance that there will be a future. Prefers free verse to traditional forms. Poems that "could be mistaken for, simply, the human voice speaking" get attention. Avoid light verse and superficial ironies.
Editorial Interests
Poetry, astrology, dreams, the environment, feminism, folklore, magic, meditation, men's issues, metaphysics, mysticism, mythology, new age, occult, politics, regional issues, self-help, seniors, and women's issues.
• *Poetry:* Short poems that come from a sense of place, up to 25 lines. Accepts translations.
Submission Policy: Send complete manuscript with cover letter and resume. Include SASE. Accepts computer printouts. No simultaneous submissions. Reports in 6–8 weeks.
Terms and Payment: First North American serial rights. No payment. Authors receive 5 copies of the issue.

Planetary Connections

Michael Lightweaver, Publisher, Seven Green Oaks Road, Asheville, NC 28804   Phone: 704-259-9774, Fax: 704-254-1181

Profile: A new consciousness newspaper. Published by Conscious Communications Network. Issued bimonthly. Circ: 20,000. Trim size: Tabloid. Newsprint; folded. 20+ pages. Subscription cost: $37 for 12 issues. Sample copy cost: $2. Writer's guidelines available with SASE.
Focus and Tips: *Planetary Connections* is dedicated to networking people interested in new consciousness around the world

and encouraging cooperation and communication in working toward the goal of planetary transformation. It reports solution-oriented news of people and events that indicate the movement toward a new consciousness. Currently, it is looking for reporters and correspondents to cover regional news. Material should have broad appeal and be newsworthy, non-promotional, of interest to readers, well-written, specific, and to the point. Does not accept magazine-style how-to, self-help, inspirational articles, or opinion.

Editorial Interests

New age, astrology, cultural and ethnic issues, ecosystems, the environment, extraterrestrials, healing and health, holistic and natural health, lifestyle, metaphysics, nutrition, parapsychology, parenting, politics, prayer, psychic phenomenon, recovery, relationships, self-help, social and world issues, and spirituality.

• *Nonfiction:* Feature news articles, 300–800 words. Brief news, 50–250 words. Letters, 75–150 words. Articles, 125–300 words.

Submission Policy: Query first for news pieces. Include SASE. Accepts photocopies, computer printouts, and faxes. Simultaneous submissions okay. Reports in 1 month. If accepted, expect publication in 2–6 months.

Terms and Payment: All rights. No payment. Authors receive copies of the issue.

Advertising: Rates: B/W full-page, $500. Contact Chris Tunstall, 704-687-6794.

The Portable Wall

Daniel Struckman, Publisher, 215 Burlington, Billings, MT 59101   Phone: 406-256-3588

Profile: A regional journal of eclectic writings. Published by Basement Press. Issued irregularly. Circ: 400. Trim size: 6x9.5. Heavy bond cover; B/W; 80 lb. paper; saddle stitched. 56 pages. Subscription cost: $18 for 4 issues. Sample copy cost: $6.50. No writer's guidelines.

Focus and Tips: *The Portable Wall* prints "whatever truths and lies we want to share with our intelligent friends. We try to keep our editorial microscopes focused wide." Encourages writers to "use your own voice" and "write about things you care about." Welcomes fiction that employs regional dialects. Most readers are Montana-area residents.

Editorial Interests

Open to all topics especially physical fitness, Native American tribes, juggling, and caves.

• *Fiction:* Short, concise stories and drama, up to 3,000 words. Accepts poetry.

• *Nonfiction:* Features, articles, interviews, and profiles, up to 3,000 words. Essays and personal experiences, up to 1,000 words. Short reviews. Fryberger's Cosmos column, 2,000 words.

Submission Policy: Send complete manuscript with cover letter. Include SASE. Accepts photocopies, computer printouts, and 3.5" Macintosh disks. No simultaneous submissions. Responds to queries in 1 month, to manuscripts in 3 months. If accepted, expect publication in up to 2 years.

Terms and Payment: One-time rights. Pays on publication for prose. Rates vary. No payment for poetry. Authors receive 3 copies of the issue plus a 4-issue subscription.

Potato Eyes

Carolyn Page, Editor, P.O. Box 76, Troy, ME 04987   Phone: 207-948-3427

Profile: A literary arts journal. Published by Nightshade Press. Issued twice a year. Circ: 800+. Trim size: 5.5x8.5. Heavy bond cover; B/W inside; perfect bound. 102 pages. Subscription cost: $11. Sample copy cost: $5. Writer's guidelines available with SASE.

Focus and Tips: *Potato Eyes* purposes to showcase talent regardless of the writer's connections, associations, education, or famous mentors. It is particularly interested in the work of women and minorities. Themes tend to be more rural than urban. Authors should read a sample copy for style. Avoid pieces with barroom settings, excessive violence, or "cute" kids. In addition to the journal, Nightshade Press has published three poetry collections that focus on healing.

Editorial Interests

Literary, poetry, dreams, folklore, gay and lesbian issues, healing, lifestyle, men's issues, and rural settings.

• *Fiction:* Short stories, 2,000–3,000 words. Poetry, no Hallmarkian or religious poems or haiku.

• *Nonfiction:* Essays, 400–800 words.

Submission Policy: Send complete manuscript with cover letter. Include SASE. Accepts photocopies and computer printouts. Simultaneous submissions okay for fiction. No simultaneous poetry submissions. Reports in 2–3 months. If accepted, expect publication in 1 year.

Terms and Payment: First North American serial rights. No payment. Authors receive copies of the issue.

Other Interests: Sponsors the William & Kingman Page Chapbook Award, an annual open competition for publication of a 36-page chapbook. Winner receives 50 copies of the chapbook, in lieu of royalties, and $500. Deadline is November 1. Requires a $10 entry fee. For more information, write to Chapbook, Potato Eyes Foundation, P.O. Box 76, Troy, ME 04987.

Priority Parenting

Tamra B. Orr, Editor, 830 South Union Street, Warsaw, IN 46580   Phone: 219-268-1415

Profile: A parenting newsletter. Issued bimonthly. Circ: 150. Trim size: 6.5x9. Photocopied; 20 lb. paper; stapled. 20 pages. Subscription cost: $10. Sample copy cost: Free. Writer's guidelines available with SASE.

Focus and Tips: *Priority Parenting* is for "parents who follow their natural instincts and not culture's dictates in their child-rearing." It explores a variety of alternative parenting options; mainstream parenting material would not be appropriate here. No third-person researched pieces, prefers instead first-person opinions or experiences. Writers should send for guidelines before submitting.

Editorial Interests

Parenting, cultural and ethnic issues, environment, health, holistic health, juvenile and teen issues, natural health, nutrition, self-help, social and world issues, and women's issues.

• *Nonfiction:* Topical articles, 700–1,200 words. Personal experiences of alternative parenting choices. Welcomes opinion pieces.

Submission Policy: Send complete manuscript with cover letter. Include SASE. Accepts photocopies and computer print-outs. Simultaneous submissions okay. Reports in 2 weeks. If accepted, expect publication in 1–3 months.

Terms and Payment: One-time rights. No payment. Authors receive 2–5 copies of the issue.

Advertising: Rates: Business card ads, $10; classifieds, $.25 per word. Contact Tamra Orr, 219-268-1415.

The Psychic Reader

Jodi MacMillan, Editor, 2210 Harold Way, Berkeley, CA 94704   Phone: 510-644-1600, Fax: 510-644-1686

Profile: A newspaper of psychic phenomenon. Published by Deja Vu Publishing Co. Issued monthly. Circ: 210,000. Trim size: 11.5x15. Newsprint; folded. 32 pages. Subscription cost: $11.50. Sample copy cost: Free. Writer's guidelines available with SASE.

Focus and Tips: *The Psychic Reader* is designed to appeal to people interested in psychic development and spiritual growth, self-healing, and planetary changes. Regional focus is on Northern California.

Editorial Interests

Psychic phenomenon, astrology, bodywork, channeling, crystals, cultural and ethnic issues, dreams, ecosystems, the environment, extraterrestrials, healing, health, holistic health, juvenile and teen issues, meditation, men's issues, mythology, natural health, new age, nutrition, occult, parapsychology, parenting, relationships, social and world issues, spirituality, witches, women's issues, and yoga.

• *Fiction:* Short stories and book excerpts, 1,000–1,500 words.

• *Nonfiction:* Features, articles, interviews, and profiles, 1,000–1,500 words. Opinion pieces and news, 500 words. Reviews, 700 words. Columns include Wellness in the Body, Moon Guide, Herbs, Psychic Solutions, UFO Report, and Healing and the Evolving Spirit, 750 words.

• *Illustrations:* Photos and artwork to accompany articles.

Submission Policy: Query with outline, 1 sample chapter, and writing samples, or send complete manuscript with bibliography and artwork. Include SASE. Accepts computer printouts, faxes, and Microsoft Word 4.0 disks. Reports in 1 month. If accepted, expect publication in 1 month.

Terms and Payment: One-time rights. No payment. Authors receive 3 copies of the issue.

Advertising: Accepts advertising. Contact Pat King, 510-644-1600. List rental available. Contact Leslie Medina, 510-644-1600.

Other Interests: Affiliated with the Berkeley Psychic Institute, a not-for-profit organization: contact Susan Hall Bostwize, 510-644-1600. Sponsors Intuitive Leadership Seminars and Women's Intuitive Retreats and Workshops: contact Carolyn Gregory, 510-644-1600. Also offers Deja Vu Tours worldwide: contact Joan Huddleston, 510-644-1600.

Qi: The Journal of Traditional Eastern Health & Fitness

Lily Chiu, President, P.O. Box 221343, Chantilly, VA 22021   Phone: 703-378-3859, Fax: 703-378-0663

Profile: A magazine of Asian health and fitness. Published by Insight Graphics, Inc. Issued quarterly. Circ: 15,000. Trim size: 8.5x11. Glossy color cover; spot color; saddle stitched. 48+ pages. Subscription cost: $18.95. Sample copy cost: $4. Writer's guidelines available with SASE.

Focus and Tips: *Qi* publishes a variety of articles dealing with the multi-faceted topic of Qi, including traditional Chinese healing, internal martial arts, and Eastern philosophies. Not interested in articles that are purely self-promotional.

Editorial Interests

Chinese medicine, internal martial arts, acupuncture, herbs, qigong, bodywork, healing, holistic and natural health, meditation, Eastern philosophy, shiatsu, and yoga.

• *Nonfiction:* Features, interviews, and profiles, 4,000–6,000 words. Articles, 750–1,500 words. New items, 100–750 words.

Submission Policy: Send complete manuscript with cover letter. Include SASE. Accepts photocopies, computer printouts, IBM or Macintosh disks, and faxes. Simultaneous submissions okay. Reports in 1 month.

Terms and Payment: One-time rights. Pays on publication for features only. $100 per feature. Authors receive copies of the issue upon request.

Advertising: Rates: B/W full-page, $800; 4-color full page, $1,100. Contact Lily Chiu, 703-378-3859.

The Quest

William Metzger, Editor, 1926 North Main Street, Wheaton, IL 60189-0270   Phone: 708-668-1571, Fax: 708-668-4976

Profile: A magazine of philosophy, religion, science, and the arts. Published by the Theosophical Society in America. Issued quarterly. Circ: 25,000. Trim size: 8x10. Glossy color cover; 4-color; saddle stitched. 96 pages. Subscription cost: $13.97. Sample copy cost: $4.50. Writer's guidelines available with SASE.

Focus and Tips: The unifying theme of *The Quest* is the concept of wholeness, that all of life is interrelated. It embraces the idea of the Ageless Wisdom found in all traditions and is more interested in religious and mystical thought and experience than in the history of religious institution and doctrine. While it seeks to explore esoteric themes, articles should be accessible, striking "a good balance of the philosophical and the practical." Authors are advised to familiarize themselves with the magazine and avoid fundamentalisms and new age topics like channeling and crystals.

Editorial Interests

Philosophy, Eastern and Western religions, meditation, metaphysics, mysticism, mythology, occult, parapsychology, prayer, psychology, spirituality, and perenial new age philosophy.

• *Nonfiction:* Articles, interviews and profiles, essays, and personal experiences grounded in traditions, 2,000–3,000 words. Book reviews, 1,000–2,000 words. Departments include Explorations, Thinking Aloud, Transitions, and Personal Glimpses, 1,000–2,000 words.

• *Illustrations:* Accepts photos and artwork.

Submission Policy: Query with outline or send complete manuscript with cover letter and brief author biography. Include SASE. Accepts photocopies, computer printouts, MS-DOS WordPerfect disks, and faxes. Simultaneous submissions okay. Reports in 1–2 months. If accepted, expect publication in 6–9 months.

Terms and Payment: First North American serial rights. Pays on publication. $75–$400 per piece. Authors receive 5 copies of the issue.

Advertising: Rates per page: B/W, $500. Contact Ray Grasse, 708-668-1571.

Other Interests: Sponsors several programs—lectures, workshops, and retreats. For dates and information, contact Ruthann Fowler, Public Programs, Theosophical Society in America, P.O. Box 270, Wheaton, IL 60189, 708-668-1571.

Rainbow City Express

Helen Harvey, Editor/Publisher, P.O. Box 8447, Berkeley, CA 94707-8447

Profile: An independently produced new age publication. Issued twice a year. Circ: 1,000. Trim size: 8.5x11. Photocopied; stapled. 60–80 pages. Subscription cost: N/A. Sample copy cost: $7. Writer's guidelines available with SASE and 2 first-class stamps.

Focus and Tips: *Rainbow City Express* is devoted to the process of spiritual unfolding and creative self-expression. Readers are an eclectic, educated, psychologically sophisticated and aesthetically evolved audience. "We resonate to truth and 'clean' energy; study a recent sample and guidelines and you will recognize what we are after." Avoid divisive, separatist material and anything that smacks of victimization or scapegoating.

Editorial Interests

New age, spirituality, goddess worship, the environment, healing, recovery, transformation, self-expression, creativity, meditation, dreams, mythology, psychic phenomenon, and natural health.

• *Fiction:* Short stories and poetry. Currently overstocked.

• *Nonfiction:* Articles and personal experiences, 3–5 manuscript pages. Accepts book reviews. Departments include Healing Forum.

• *Illustrations:* B/W prints and line drawings.

Submission Policy: Send complete manuscript with cover letter. Include SASE. Accepts photocopies and computer printouts. No simultaneous submissions. Reports in 1–3 months.

Terms and Payment: One-time rights and reprint rights. Occasionally pays an honoraria. Authors receive 1 copy of the issue.

Rainbow Network

Geoff Turtley, Publisher, P.O. Box 47553, Ponsonby, Auckland, New Zealand 1001   Phone: 64-9-376-4620, Fax: 64-9-376-4630

Profile: A new age magazine. Issued bimonthly. Circ: 12,000. Glossy color cover; 4-color; saddle stitched. 72–80 pages. Subscription cost: $18 New Zealand dollars; USA, $32 New Zealand dollars. Sample copy cost: Free. Writer's guidelines available with SASE/IRCs.

Focus and Tips: *Rainbow Network* is designed to inform and provide a focus for a wide range of people interested in health, healing, and personal growth. Prefers conceptual articles covering body-mind-spirit, new ideas and phenomenon, as well as environmental and topical issues. Also open to travel articles on spiritual places. Avoid any form of advertorial. Available primarily in New Zealand, it is also distributed worldwide.

Editorial Interests
New age, astrology, bodywork, channeling, crystals, cultural and ethnic issues, dreams, ecosystems, the environment, extraterrestrials, folklore, healing, health, holistic health, inspiration, juvenile and teen issues, lifestyle, meditation, men's issues, metaphysics, mysticism, mythology, natural health, nutrition, parapsychology, psychic phenomenon, rebirthing, recovery, self-help, spirituality, women's issues, and yoga.
• *Nonfiction:* Features, 1,500–2,500 picas. Articles, 800–2,000 picas. Interviews and profiles, 500–1,500 picas. Personal experiences, 800 words. News items, 150 words.
Submission Policy: Query or send complete manuscript. Include SASE/IRCs. Accepts computer printouts and Macintosh Word or QuarkXPress disks. Reports in 1 month. If accepted, expect publication in 2–3 months.
Terms and Payment: Australasian/Pacific rights. Pays on publication. Rates vary depending on quality. Authors receive 1 copy of the issue; more upon request.
Advertising: Rates: B/W full-page, $1,050; half-page, $625; quarter-page, $320; business card, $125. Contact Geoff Turtley.

Rays from the Rose Cross

Barbara Joiner, Editorial Assistant, 2222 Mission Avenue, Oceanside, CA 92054   Phone: 619-757-6600

Profile: A Christian esoteric magazine. Published by the Rosicrucian Fellowship. Issued bimonthly. Circ: 800–1,000. Trim size: 8.5x11. Glossy cover; B/W; staddle stitched. 30–60 pages. Subscription cost: $15. Sample copy cost: $3. Writer's guidelines available with SASE.
Focus and Tips: *Rays from the Rose Cross* is primarily based on the teachings of Max Heindel or on the Rosicrucian Cosmo Conception. Readers are members of the Rosicrucian Fellowship.
Editorial Interests
Rosicrucian Christianity, astrology, the environment, healing, health, meditation, philosophy, prayer, recovery, self-help, social and world issues, and spirituality.
• *Fiction:* Short stories, 1,500 words.
• *Nonfiction:* Features, articles, interviews, profiles, essays, and personal experiences, 1,500–5,000 words.
Submission Policy: Query first with outline. Include SASE. Accepts photocopies and computer printouts. Simultaneous submissions okay. Reports in 2 weeks. If accepted, expect publication in 6 months.
Terms and Payment: No payment. Authors receive 1 copy of the issue.
Other Interests: Often offers workshops or conferences on astrology, the Bible, or philosophy. For more information, contact Barbara Joiner, 619-757-6600.

Reclaiming

Editor, P.O. Box 14404, San Francisco, CA 94114

Profile: A newsletter of the Reclaiming collective, an organization working to unify spirit and politics. Issued quarterly. Circ: 350–400. Trim size: 6.25x8.5. Self cover; B/W; stapled. 39–40 pages. Subscription cost: up to $15. Sample copy cost: $2.
Focus and Tips: *Reclaiming* explores the connection between pagan spirituality and politics. In particular, its vision is rooted in the religion and magic of the Goddess. Its focus is on "teaching and making magic—the art of empowering ourselves and each other." Avoid personal charges or countercharges.
Editorial Interests
Magic, cultural and ethnic issues, dreams, ecosystems, the environment, extraterrestrials, feminism, folklore, gay and lesbian issues, juvenile and teen issues, men's issues, metaphysics, mysticism, mythology, occult, politics, psychic phenomenon, rebirthing, social and world issues, spirituality, witches, and women's issues.
• *Poetry:* Poems relating to publication's theme.
• *Nonfiction:* Articles and letters related to political, page, or spiritual issues and happenings.
• *Illustrations:* B/W graphics and line art.
Submission Policy: Query with writing samples. Include SASE. Accepts photocopies, computer printouts, and 3.5" WordPerfect or Microsoft Word disks. Reports in 3–4 weeks. If accepted, expected publication in up to 3 months.
Terms and Payment: No payment. Authors receive 1 copy of the issue; more upon request.

Recovery Times

Ann Taylor, Editor, 6600 Stage Road, Suite 126, Memphis, TN 38134   Phone/Fax: 901-377-7963 or 800-882-7775

Profile: A regional recovery-oriented magazine. Issued monthly. Circ: 28,000 Mid South; 24,000 Northeast. Trim size: Tabloid. Newsprint; spot color; folded. 24 pages. Subscription cost: $25. Sample copy cost: $2.50. Writer's guidelines available with SASE.
Focus and Tips: *Recovery Times* is published in two regional editions, the Mid South and Northeast, and seeks recovery-relat-

ed material on issues of interest to those areas. Both editions offer timely news and views about the many aspects of healthy, substance-free lifestyles for recovering individuals and others interested in physical, emotional, and spiritual well being. Address writing to a lay audience and use appropriate, non-technical language. Does not accept poetry or articles on recovering from surgery or diseases that are not addiction related.

Editorial Interests

Recovery, regional issues, addictions, AIDS and HIV issues as related to chemical dependency, bodywork, feminism, gay and lesbian issues, healing, health, holistic health, inspiration, meditation, men's issues, natural health, nutrition, parenting, prayer, psychology, relationships, self-help, spirituality, and women's issues.

• *Fiction:* Recovery-related short stories, 250–1,500 words.

• *Nonfiction:* Articles, personal experiences, opinion pieces, and news items, 250–1,500 words. Accepts book reviews.

Submission Policy: Send complete manuscript with cover letter. Include SASE. Accepts photocopies, computer printouts, and Macintosh Microsoft Word, MacWrite, or Pagemaker disks. Query for IBM disk submissions. No simultaneous submissions. Reporting and publication times vary.

Terms and Payment: One-time rights. *Recovery Times* requires credit for reprints. No payment. Authors receive up to 10 copies of the issue.

Advertising: Rates: B/W, up to $1,200; spot-color, add 10% surcharge. Discounts available for multiple insertions and for ads appearing in both editions. Contact Ann Taylor, 800-882-7775.

Other Interests: Sponsors an annual OcSober Fest™. For more information, contact Ann Taylor, 800-882-7775.

Red Clay

Kathleen Lee Mendel, Editor, P.O. Box 65656-566, Lubbock, TX 79464

Profile: A quarterly magazine of Native American lore. Published by Telstar. Issued quarterly. Circ: 50. Trim size: 8.5x11. 60 lb paper; spiral bound. 24–30 pages. Subscription cost: $20. Sample copy cost: $7. Writer's guidelines available with SASE.

Focus and Tips: *Red Clay* is devoted to exploring North or South Native American legends, lore, mythology, and spirituality. Send for a sample copy and guidelines before submitting work. Avoid material that portrays racial disharmony—keep to the magazine's theme.

Editorial Interests

Native American, channeling, crystals, folklore, healing, inspiration, meditation, metaphysics, mysticism, mythology, new age, religion, and spirituality.

• *Fiction:* Short stories, 1,000 words. Poetry, 20 lines.

• *Nonfiction:* Special interest in interviews, profiles, and essays in keeping with theme, 1,000 words. Accepts features, articles, personal experiences, news, and reviews, 1,000 words.

Submission Policy: Send complete manuscript with cover letter. Include SASE. Accepts photocopies, computer printouts, and ASCII disks. Simultaneous submissions okay. Responds to queries in 1 month, to manuscripts in 3 months. If accepted, expect publication within 3–6 months.

Terms and Payment: One-time rights. Pays on publication. $5 per piece. Authors receive 1 copy of the issue.

Other Interests: Sponsors the *Red Clay* Quarterly contest for poetry on Native American themes. Deadlines are the 15th of January, April, July, and October. Requires a $1 reading fee per poems. Include SASE for selection results. Awards are $15, $10, $5, and seven honorable mentions. For more information, contact Kathleen Lee Mendel.

The Red Queen

Susannah McBride, Editor, 603 West 13th Street, No. 1A-132, Austin, TX 78701

Profile: A publication of women's experiences and sexuality. Issued quarterly. Circ: N/A. Trim size: 8.5x11. B/W; saddle stitched. 28 pages. Subscription cost: $13. Sample copy cost: $3.50. Writer's guidelines available with SASE.

Focus and Tips: *The Red Queen* is a forum for women of all ages to discuss, explore, share, create, and view life and its experiences from a goddess perspective. It is interested in a variety of viewpoints and does not promote any "one true way" of women's spirituality. Avoid personal attacks and "witch wars."

Editorial Interests

Women's issues, feminism, astrology, ecosystems, the environment, folklore, healing, holistic health, magic, mythology, natural health, occult, parenting, philosophy, psychology, social and world issues, spirituality, and witches.

• *Fiction:* Short stories, 1,000–1,500 words. Short-short stories, 500 words. Poetry, no length restrictions.

• *Nonfiction:* Features, articles, and news items, 2,000–4,000 words. Interviews and profiles, 1,500–4,000 words. Essays and personal experiences, 1,500–3,000 words. Opinion pieces, 1,500–2,500 words. Reviews, 200–700 words.

Submission Policy: Send complete manuscript with cover letter and bibliography. Include SASE. Accepts photocopies, computer printouts, and 3.5" IBM or Macintosh disks. No simultaneous submissions. Responds to queries in 1 month, to manuscripts in 1–2 months. If accepted, expect publication in 13 weeks.

Terms and Payment: Full rights for one year, then retains reprint rights. No payment. Authors receive 1 copy of the issue.

Advertising: Rates: B/W full-page, $35. Contact Susannah McBride.

Reflections Directory

Patrick Mazza, Editorial Coordinator, P.O. Box 548, Portland, OR 97207   Phone: 503-241-3776, Fax: 503-241-3865

Profile: A regional magazine on health and personal development. Published by Portland Reflections. Issued quarterly. Circ: 45,000. Trim size: 8.5x11. Newsprint; stapled. 135 pages. Subscription cost: $15. Sample copy cost: $3. Writer's guidelines available with SASE.

Focus and Tips: Reaching readers in the northern California, Oregon, and Southwest Washington areas, *Reflections Directory* explores natural health, human potential, and ecological sustainability. It is especially interested in articles offering innovations, edges, and creative solutions. Looks for magazine-quality material and appreciates the use of journalistic techniques like quotes and sourcing. Avoid overly academic or promotional pieces. "Write for a general audience with an aim to share knowledge and help readers apply it to their lives." Request guidelines before submitting.

Editorial Interests

Regional issues, astrology, bodywork, channeling, crystals, cultural and ethnic issues, dreams, ecosystems, the environment, feminism, folklore, gay and lesbian issues, healing, health, holistic health, inspiration, juvenile and teen issues, lifestyle, meditation, men's issues, metaphysics, mysticism, mythology, natural health, new age, nutrition, parenting, philosophy, politics, prayer, psychic phenomenon, psychology, rebirthing, recovery, relationships, religion, self-help, seniors, social and world issues, spirituality, witches, women's issues, and yoga.

- *Fiction:* Short stories and genre fiction, 2,000 words. Poetry, 500 words.
- *Nonfiction:* Features, articles, interviews, profiles, essays, personal experiences, opinion pieces, and news, 1,250 words. Book reviews, 700 words.

Submission Policy: Query first with outline or send complete manuscript with cover letter. Include SASE. Accepts photocopies and computer printouts. Simultaneous submissions okay. Reporting time varies. Publication time varies.

Terms and Payment: Rights vary. Pays on occasion. Authors receive 1 copy of the issue upon request.

Advertising: Rates: B/W full-page, $780. Directory ads, $110. Contact Michelle Thompson, 503-241-3776.

Reiki News

William Rand, Editor, 29209 North Western Highway, No. 592, Southfield, MI 48034   Phone: 810-948-8112

Profile: A newsletter for Reiki healers. Published by Visions Publications. Issued quarterly. Circ: 40,000. Trim size: 8.5x11. 24 lb. recycled paper; stapled. 28 pages. Subscription cost: $5. Sample copy cost: Free. Writer's guidelines available with SASE.

Focus and Tips: *Reiki News* focuses on Reiki, a healing process involving the laying on of hands. Read by Reiki practitioners.

Editorial Interests

Reiki healing.

- *Nonfiction:* Articles, 1 manuscript page.

Submission Policy: Call first to determine interests. Then send complete manuscript with cover letter. Include SASE. Accepts photocopies, computer printouts, and faxes. Simultaneous submissions okay. Reports in 3–4 weeks.

Terms and Payment: No payment. Authors receive copies of the issue.

Other Interests: Affiliated with the Center for Reiki Training. For more information, call 810-948-8112.

RFD

Gabby Haze, Business Manager, P.O. Box 68, Liberty, TN 37095   Phone: 615-536-5176

Profile: A publication for gay men. Issued quarterly. Circ: 3,600. Trim size: 8.5x11. Glossy cover; stapled. 80 pages. Subscription cost: $18 for second-class; $25 for first-class. Sample copy cost: $5. Writer's guidelines available with SASE.

Focus and Tips: *RFD* is a country journal for gay men everywhere. Focus is on gay spirituality and alternative lifestyles. All material should cover gay men's issues that relate to alternative experiences in society. Reaches an international audience.

Editorial Interests

Gay men's issues, bodywork, cultural and ethnic issues, dreams, ecosystems, the environment, healing, health, holistic health, inspiration, lifestyle, meditation, men's issues, metaphysics, mysticism, natural health, new age, nutrition, occult, parenting, philosophy, politics, psychology, relationships, paganism, self-help, social and world issues, and spirituality.

- *Fiction:* Short stories, drama, and book excerpts, 1,500 words. Poetry, no length restrictions.
- *Nonfiction:* Features, articles, essays, and personal experiences, 5,000 words. Interviews, profiles, opinion pieces, news items, and book and music reviews 1,500 words. Accepts jokes and cartoons.

Submission Policy: Send complete manuscript with cover letter. Include SASE. Accepts photocopies, computer printouts, and IBM or Macintosh disks. Simultaneous submissions okay. Reports in 6 months. If accepted, expect publication in 9 months.

Terms and Payment: Authors retain rights. No payment. Authors receive 1 copy of the issue.

Advertising: Rates: B/W full-page, $600. Contact Gabby Haze, 615-536-5176.
Other Interests: Affiliated with the nonprofit Seattle Gay Community Services organization. Sponsors seminars and retreats at the Short Mountain Sanctuary, a gay men's commune in Tennessee. For more information, contact Gabby Haze, 615-536-5176.

Rosicrucian Digest

Robin Thompson, Editor, 1342 Naglee Avenue, San Jose, CA 95141   Phone: 408-287-9171

Profile: A publication for Rosicrucian followers. Published by the nonprofit Rosicrucian Order, AMORC. Issued quarterly. Circ: N/A. Saddled stitched. 32 pages. Subscription cost: $12. Sample copy cost: Free. Writer's guidelines available with SASE.
Focus and Tips: Distributed to an international audience, *Rosicrucian Digest* is geared toward Rosicrucian followers and others interested in philosophy, psychology, and metaphysical and mystical subjects. Interested in the latest developments in science, literature, the arts, and philosophy. Material should be uplifting and inspirational. "Don't grind your ax—closed-mind attitudes are not welcome. Stay away from proselytizing and political or religious viewpoints."
Editorial Interests
Bodywork, cultural and ethnic issues, dreams, ecosystems, the environment, folklore, healing, health, holistic health, inspiration, lifestyle, meditation, metaphysics, mysticism, mythology, nutrition, occult, parapsychology, parenting, philosophy, psychology, recovery, relationships, self-help, seniors, social and world issues, and spirituality.
• *Nonfiction:* Features, articles, and essays, 1,500 words. Personal experiences, 1,000 words. Contact editor before submitting interviews or profiles.
Submission Policy: Query first with outline and writing samples. Include SASE. Accepts photocopies and computer printouts. Simultaneous submissions okay if noted. Responds to queries in 1 month, to manuscripts in 6–8 weeks. If accepted, expect publication in 6–12 months.
Terms and Payment: One-time rights. Pays on acceptance. $.06 per word. Authors receive 2 copies of the issue.

SageWoman

Anne Niven, Editor, P.O. Box 641, Point Arena, CA 95468   Phone: 707-882-2052, Fax: 707-882-2793

Profile: A thematic magazine of women's spirituality. Issued twice a year. Circ: 10,000. Trim size: 8.5x11. Glossy color cover; B/W inside; 50 lb. paper; saddle stitched. 72 pages. Subscription cost: $18. Sample copy cost: $6. Writer's guidelines and theme list available with SASE.
Focus and Tips: Summed up in the statement "Celebrating the Goddess in every woman," *SageWoman* is dedicated to helping women explore their spiritual, emotional, and mundane lives in a way that respects all people, creatures, and the Earth. Each issue focuses on one theme. Readers are generally women who identify positively with the term "Goddess" and are comfortable with the classifications of Goddess worshippers, pagans, or Wiccans. While not a separatist magazine, *SageWoman* accepts writing from women only. It welcomes the work of women of all races, ages, sexual orientations and socio-economic backgrounds, and strongly encourages contributions from women of color. Interested writers are advised to study writer's guidelines.
Editorial Interests
Goddess worship, women's issues, feminism, astrology, bodywork, cultural and ethnic issues, dreams, ecosystems, the environment, folklore, gay and lesbian issues, healing, magic, mythology, new age, occult, parenting, spirituality, and witches.
• *Nonfiction:* Theme-related features, articles, interviews, profiles, essays, personal experiences, and opinion pieces, 500–5,000 words. Reviews and filler, 100–500 words.
Submission Policy: Query with outline and writing samples or send complete manuscript with cover letter. Include SASE. Accepts photocopies, computer printouts, faxes, and IBM 3.5" DS/DD disks. No simultaneous submissions. Reports in 1 month. If accepted, expect publication in 3–6 months.
Terms and Payment: First North American serial rights and reprint rights. Pays on publication. $.01–$.05 per word. Authors receive 1 copy of the issue.
Advertising: Rates: B/W full-page, $400. Contact Christina Alexander, 503-756-1358.

Samsara

R. David Fulcher, Editor, P.O. Box 367, College Park, MD 20741-0367

Profile: An independent literary magazine. Issued twice a year. Circ: 300. Trim size: 8.5x11. Self cover; B/W; stapled. 60 pages. Subscription cost: $5. Sample copy cost: $2.50. Writer's guidelines available with SASE.
Focus and Tips: *Samsara*'s sole interest is in fiction and poetry related to suffering, common to all living creatures. The editor hopes that "this constant under the fluctuating patterns of humanity can become the flexible backbone for a magazine whose stories are worlds apart in subject matter and approach." Contributors are invited to "follow the story's natural development without unnecessary restriction on content." Especially interested in stories incorporating dreams and myths.

Editorial Interests
Suffering, mythology, and dreams.
• *Fiction:* Short stories, 3,000 words. Poetry, no length restrictions.
Submission Policy: Send complete manuscript with cover letter. Include SASE. Accepts photocopies, computer printouts, and IBM ASCII disks. No simultaneous submissions. Reports in 2 months. If accepted, expect publication in 3 months.
Terms and Payment: First North American serial rights. No payment. Authors receive 1 copy of the issue.

The San Francisco Bay Guardian

Miriam Wolf, Features Editor, 520 Hampshire Street, San Francisco, CA 94110-1417   Phone: 415-255-3100, Fax: 415-255-8955

Profile: A regional alternative newspaper. Established in 1966. Issued biweekly. Circ: 130,000. Trim size: Tabloid. Newsprint; folded. 100 pages. Subscription cost: $32. Sample copy cost: Free. Writer's guidelines available with SASE.
Focus and Tips: *The San Francisco Bay Guardian* is the largest and oldest publication in the Bay area and one of the oldest alternative newspapers in the country. It focuses on progressive politics, news, arts, and articles of interest to the San Francisco community. Work must be of high quality. Local interest preferred.
Editorial Interests
Regional issues, cultural and ethnic issues, ecosystems, the environment, feminism, gay and lesbian concerns, health, holistic health, lifestyle, men's issues, natural health, parenting, politics, social and world issues, and women's issues.
• *Nonfiction:* Features, articles, interviews, profiles, essays, personal experiences, opinion pieces, news items, reviews, and filler. Word lengths vary.
Submission Policy: Query first with outline, 3 sample chapters, writing samples, and resume, or send complete manuscript with cover letter. Include SASE. Prefers submissions on computer disks. Accepts photocopies and computer printouts. No simultaneous submissions. Responds to queries in 3 months, longer to manuscripts. Publication time varies.
Terms and Payment: First North American serial rights. Pays on publication. $.10 per word. Does not offer contributor's copies.
Advertising: Rates: B/W full-page, $1,764. Contact Robin McLean, 415-255-7600.
Other Interests: Sponsors fiction and poetry contests. For more information, contact Fiction or Poetry Contest Editor, 415-255-3100.

Santa Fe Sun

Shawn Townsend, Editor, P.O. Box 23168, Santa Fe, NM 87502   Phone: 505-989-8381, Fax: 505-989-4767

Profile: A regional new age newspaper. Established in 1988. Issued monthly. Circ: 20,000. Trim size: Tabloid. Newsprint; folded. 24 pages. Subscription cost: $30. Sample copy cost: $3. No writer's guidelines.
Focus and Tips: *Santa Fe Sun* focuses on New Mexico residents, regional issues and arts, and indigenous peoples. Articles of regional interest stand the best chance. "Be concise and don't use flowery verbiage."
Editorial Interests
Regional issues, astrology, bodywork, channeling, crystals, cultural and ethnic issues, dreams, ecosystems, the environment, feminism, folklore, gay and lesbian issues, healing, health, holistic health, inspiration, juvenile and teen issues, lifestyle, magic, meditation, men's issues, metaphysics, mysticism, mythology, natural health, new age, nutrition, parapsychology, parenting, philosophy, prayer, psychic phenomenon, psychology, rebirthing, recovery, relationships, religion, self-help, seniors, social issues, spirituality, witches, women's issues, and yoga.
• *Nonfiction:* Features, 1,200–1,500 words. Articles, 800 words. Interviews and profiles, 800–1,000 words. Essays, 500–800 words. Opinion pieces, 350–500 words. News items, 250–500 words. Reviews, 600–800 words.
Submission Policy: Query first with outline, 1 sample chapter, and writing samples, or send complete manuscript with cover letter and author biography. Include SASE. Accepts photocopies, computer printouts, and Macintosh Microsoft Word disks. Simultaneous submissions okay if noted. Reports in 2 months. If accepted, expect publication in 2 months.
Terms and Payment: One-time rights. Pays on publication. Rates vary. Authors receive 1 copy of the issue.
Advertising: Rates: B/W full-page, $760. Contact Betty Townsend, 505-989-8381.

Science Journal and Newsletter

Shirley Smith, Editor, P.O. Box 520, Swannanoa, Waynesboro, VA 22980   Phone: 703-942-5161

Profile: A newsletter on the theories of creation. Published by the University of Science and Philosophy. Issued twice a year. Circ: 4,000. Trim size: 8.5x11. Photocopied. 24–36 pages. Subscription cost: $25.
Focus and Tips: *Science Journal and Newsletter* is a science-based journal that explores the spirituality, science, and philosophy of creation, especially concepts pertinent to Russel Cosmology. Avoid articles that are too technical.
Editorial Interests
Philosophy, ancient wisdom, alternative health, and concepts of creation.

• *Nonfiction:* Articles, 4–12 manuscripts pages.
Submission Policy: Send complete manuscript with cover letter. Include SASE. Accepts Macintosh computer disks.
Terms and Payment: All rights. No payment.

Science of Mind

Sandra Sarr, Editor, P.O. Box 75127, Los Angeles, CA 90075   Phone: 213-388-2181, Fax: 213-388-1926

Profile: A magazine of positive thinking. Published by the United Church of Religious Science. Issued monthly. Circ: 60,000. Trim size: 5.25x7.75. Glossy cover; 4-color; coated paper; perfect bound. 112 pages. Subscription cost: $18. Sample copy cost: $1.95. Writer's guidelines available with SASE.
Focus and Tips: *Science of Mind* offers a philosophy of spiritual and positive thinking that correlates the laws of science, opinions of philosophy, and revelations of religion applied to the needs and aspirations of humankind. It promotes New Thought and includes articles from first-rate published authorities. Seeks inspirational articles illustrating Science of Mind principles and requests inclusive, gender-neutral language. Avoid new age topics, magic, astrology, channeling, and the like.
Editorial Interests
Philosophy, spirituality, self-help, cultural and ethnic issues, healing, health, holistic health, inspiration, meditation, metaphysics, mysticism, mythology, prayer, recovery, relationships, religion, and social and world issues.
• *Poetry:* Prefers 8–12 lines. 25–30 lines maximum.
• *Nonfiction:* Features and articles, 1,800 words. Interviews and profiles, 3,000–3,500 words. Personal experiences dealing with Science of Mind principles, 1,000–2,000 words.
• *Illustrations:* 5x7 and 8x10 B/W prints and 35 mm transparencies.
Submission Policy: Query with outline and resume. Include SASE. Accepts photocopies, faxes, and Macintosh disks. Simultaneous submissions okay. Reports in 1–2 months. If accepted, expect publication in 5 months.
Terms and Payment: First North American serial rights. Pays on publication. Unsolicited pieces, $25 per magazine page. Interviews, $500–$700. Assigned articles are negotiated. Authors receive copies of the issue.
Advertising: Rates: B/W full-page, $1,850; 4-color full-page, $2,500. List rental available: $75/M with 5,000 minimum. Contact Kalpnaa Shah, 213-388-2181.
Other Interests: Sponsors Asilomax, a retreat featuring speaker, workshops, and social activities. Contact June Crockett, 714-374-0296.

Second Mile

William Pope, Editor, Box 425, Hatsport, NS B0P 1P0 Canada   Phone: 902-684-9129, Fax: 902-684-3685

Profile: A spiritually oriented magazine. Published by Lancelot Press LTD. Established in 1973. Issued bimonthly. Circ: 1,000. Trim size: 5.5x8. Stapled. 32 pages. Subscription cost: $12. Sample copy cost: Free with SASE/IRC. No writer's guidelines.
Focus and Tips: *Second Mile* takes a broad look at life from a spiritual point of view, focusing on the "Divine Force wherever it may be found." It has no denominational ties, but zeroes in on constructive, uplifting approaches to life. "Our readership is small, but influential. Therefore, work is seen by thoughtful, sensitive readers." Avoid topics or approaches with no constructive or spiritual viewpoint.
Editorial Interests
Astrology, bodywork, cultural and ethnic issues, dreams, ecosystems, the environment, folklore, healing, health, holistic health, inspiration, lifestyle, meditation, natural health, nutrition, parenting, philosophy, prayer, psychology, recovery, relationships, religion, self-help, seniors, social and world issues, spirituality, and yoga.
• *Nonfiction:* Features, 1,500–2,000 words. Articles, interviews, and profiles, 1,000–1,500 words. Essays, personal experiences, opinion pieces, and news items 1,000 words.
Submission Policy: Query first with outline or send complete manuscript with cover letter and author biography. Include SASE/IRCs. Accepts photocopies, computer printouts, and Macintosh disks. Simultaneous submissions okay if noted. Responds to queries in 1 month, to manuscripts in 1–2 months. If accepted, expect publication in 2 months.
Terms and Payment: Authors retain rights. No payment. Authors receive copies of the issue.

Sequoia: News of Religion and Society

Robert Forsberg, Editor, 942 Market Street, Room 303, San Francisco, CA 94102-4046   Phone: 415-434-0672, Fax: 415-434-3110

Profile: A regional ecumenical newspaper. Published by Sequoia Interreligious Newsmagazine, Inc. Established in 1983. Issued quarterly. Circ: 1,000. Trim size: Tabloid. Newsprint; folded. 12–16 pages. Subscription cost: $12. Sample copy cost: $1. No writer's guidelines.
Focus and Tips: *Sequoia* is geared toward Christian and other religions with a special emphasis on cooperative and ecumenical activities. It explores issues of peace and social justice for readers in the northern California area.

Editorial Interests
Religion, social justice, peace work, cultural and ethnic issues, dreams, ecosystems, the environment, feminism, gay and lesbian issues, healing, health, holistic health, inspiration, juvenile and teen issues, meditation, men's issues, mysticism, mythology, natural health, nutrition, parenting, philosophy, politics, prayer, psychology, recovery, regional issues, relationships, seniors, spirituality, and women's issues.
• *Fiction:* Short stories, 1,000 words. Poetry, 500 words.
• *Nonfiction:* Features, articles, interviews, profiles, essays, personal experiences, and opinion pieces, 1,200 words. News items, 700 words. Book reviews, 500 words.
Submission Policy: Call first to determine interests. Accepts a query with outline and writing samples or send complete manuscript with cover letter and author biography. Include SASE. Accepts photocopies, computer printouts, faxes, and DOS or Macintosh disks. Simultaneous submissions okay. Reports in 1 month. If accepted, expect publication in 3–4 months.
Terms and Payment: Authors retain rights. No payment. Authors receive 2–3 copies of the issue.
Advertising: Accepts advertising. Contact Robert Forsberg, 415-434-0672.

The Shaman Papers

Wade Greyfox, Editor, HC 89, Box 451, Willow, AK 99688-9705

Profile: A newsletter exploring shamanism. Issued quarterly. Circ: 100. Trim size: 8.5x11. Photocopies; folded. 8 pages. Subscription cost: $9. Sample copy cost: $3. No writer's guidelines.
Focus and Tips: *The Shaman Papers* seeks material written by shamans for people interested in shamanism and related topics. Avoid religious writing and Castenada-style pieces.
Editorial Interests
Shamanism, astrology, channeling, crystals, extraterrestrials, healing, health, holistic health, magic, meditation, metaphysics, mysticism, mythology, natural health, new age, nutrition, occult, parapsychology, psychic phenomenon, psychology, and spirituality.
• *Nonfiction:* Features, articles, interviews, profiles, essays, personal experiences, opinion, and news items, 100–600 words.
Submission Policy: Send complete manuscript with cover letter. Include SASE. Accepts photocopies and computer printouts. Simultaneous submissions okay. Reports in up to 6 months. If accepted, expect publication in 1–3 months.
Terms and Payment: One-time rights. No payment. Authors receive 1 copy of the issue, more upon request.

Shaman's Drum

Timothy White, Editor, P.O. Box 430, Willits, CA 95490   Phone: 707-459-0486

Profile: A journal on experiential shamanism. Published by Cross-Cultural Shamanism Network. Issued quarterly. Circ: 18,000. Trim size: 8.5x10.75. Glossy color cover; B/W inside; 4-color centerfold; saddle stitched. 72+ pages. Subscription cost: $15. Sample copy cost: $5. Writer's guidelines available with SASE.
Focus and Tips: The primary purpose of *Shaman's Drum* is to educate its well-informed audience about shamanism, ethnospirituality, and transpersonal healing. It seeks to expand, challenge, and refine the understanding of shamanism in practice. Focus is on experiential, cross-cultural shamanism, but prefers culture-specific articles that portray specific ethnic traditions or personal practices about which an author has firsthand knowledge. Looks for practical ways in which shamanism can help ensure survival of life on this planet. Avoid generalizing about shamanism or native cultures.
Editorial Interests
Shamanism, dreams, folklore, mysticism, and parapsychology.
• *Fiction:* Short stories and retellings of myths, 1,000–3,000 words. Occasionally publishes poetry.
• *Nonfiction:* Feature articles and pre-publication book excerpts with clear relationship to shamanism, 3,000–6,000 words. Well-focused interviews with practicing shamans and medicine persons, 2,000–5,000 words. First-person accounts of shamanic or medicineway experiences, 2,000–5,000 words. Earth Circles, shaman-related news, 1,000–2,000 words. Book, magazine, movie, record, and tape reviews, 500–1,500 words. Open Dialogue, guest editorial column, 1,000–2,000 words.
• *Illustrations:* B/W and color photos, transparencies, and illustrations. Cover art, prefers 120mm or 4x5 color transparencies.
Submission Policy: Query with outline or send complete manuscript with cover letter and bibliography. Include SASE. Accepts computer printouts and Macintosh Microsoft Word disks. No simultaneous submissions. Reports in 1–2 months. If accepted, expect publication in 3–5 months.
Terms and Payment: First North American serial rights. Pays on publication. At least $.05 per word. Illustrations. $30–$100. Authors receive 2–5 copies of the issue.
Advertising: Rates: B/W full-page, $1,125; 4-color full-page, $1,425. Contact Allegra McAbee.

Shambhala Sun

Molly DeShong, Managing Editor, 1585 Barrington Street, Suite 300, Halifax, NS B3J 1Z8 Canada
Phone: 902-422-8404, Fax: 902-423-2750

Profile: A magazine exploring spiritual traditions. Issued bimonthly. Circ: 15,000. Trim size: 8x11. Glossy color cover; spot color inside; 50 lb. book paper; saddle stitched. 96 pages. Subscription cost: $20. Sample copy cost: $3.95. Writer's guidelines available with SASE/IRCs.

Focus and Tips: *Shambhala Sun* is a leading publication in the mind-body-spirit field. Its focus is on contemplative teachings and writings from Buddhist and other spiritual traditions on all aspects of life. Readers are well-educated, health-conscious professionals who are involved in a specific contemplative tradition.

Editorial Interests

Buddhism and non-theistic traditions, Japan and the Himalayas, martial arts, meditative practices and forms, the environment, feminism, folklore, gay and lesbian concerns, healing, health, holistic health, inspiration, juvenile and teen issues, lifestyle, men's issues, metaphysics, mysticism, mythology, natural health, nutrition, parenting, philosophy, politics, psychology, recovery, relationships, self-help, seniors, social and world issues, spirituality, women's issues, and yoga.

• *Fiction:* Short stories and drama, 1,000 words. Short-short stories, 500 words. Book excerpts, 1,000–2,000 words. Poetry, 500 words.

• *Nonfiction:* Features, interviews, and profiles, 2,000–3,000 words. Opinion pieces, 500–1,000 words. News items, 500 words. Columns include Celebration and Traveling Spirit, 500 words.

Submission Policy: Query with 1–2 sample chapters, writing samples, and resume, or send complete manuscript with cover letter and clips. Include SASE/IRCs. Accepts photocopies, computer printouts, 3.5" computer disks, and faxes. Simultaneous submissions okay. Reports in 1 month. If accepted, expect publication in 1–6 months.

Terms and Payment: First North American serial rights or one-time rights. Pays on publication. Rates vary. Authors receive 1–2 copies of the issue.

Advertising: Rates: B/W full-page, $624; 4-color full-page, $849. Contact Alex Gault, 902-422-8404. List rental available; terms negotiable. Contact Molly DeShong, 902-422-8404.

Other Interests: Sponsors Shambhala/Vajradhata programs of meditation and the arts. Contact Howard Moore, 1084 Tower Road, Halifax, NS B3H 2Y5 Canada, 902-425-4275.

Sharing Spirit Newsletter

Judy Pearson, Owner, 2459 SE Tualatin Valley Highway, No. 108, Hillsboro, OR 97123-7919
Phone: 503-640-3208, Fax: 503-648-2261

Profile: A newsletter of uplifting spiritual messages. Published by J.P. Productions/Awe Book Publishing. Issued monthly. Circ: 300. Trim size: 5x8.5. Self cover; B/W; folded. 6–8 pages. Subscription cost: $12. Sample copy cost: $1.25. No writer's guidelines.

Focus and Tips: *Sharing Spirit Newsletter* is an uplifting publication meant to bring "a little, light spiritual message for all walks of life." Most interested in articles exploring the mind-body-spirit connection that "come from the heart and a sense of openness." Avoid purely factual or informational pieces. Readers range from metaphysical enthusiasts, healthcare professionals, chiropractors, naturopathic healers, and new age churches.

Editorial Interests

New age, holistic health, meditation, metaphysics, natural health, and spirituality.

• *Fiction:* Human-interest stories about lifestyle changes.

• *Nonfiction:* Features on lifestyle changes, 200–500 words. Personal experiences, 200 words. Book reviews.

Submission Policy: Send complete manuscript with cover letter. Include SASE. Accepts computer printouts, faxes, and computer disks. Simultaneous submissions okay. Responds to queries in 1 month, to manuscripts in 3 months. If accepted, expect publication in 2–3 months.

Terms and Payment: Pays on publication or acceptance. $35 per piece. Authors receive 10 copies of the issue.

Advertising: Rates: B/W full-page, $40. Contact Susan Pearson, 503-640-3208.

Other Interests: Sponsors a one-day conference entitled Using a Healthy Mind to Stay Well and Overcome Illness, which focuses on meditation, nutrition, and mind power. Date: June 15th. Cost: $75. Contact Judy Pearson, 503-640-3208.

SingleMOTHER

Andrea Engber, Editor, P.O. Box 68, Midland, NC 28107-0068   Phone: 704-888-2337, Fax: 704-888-1752

Profile: A national newspaper for single mothers. Published by the National Organization of Single Mothers, Inc., a nonprofit organization. Issued bimonthly. Circ: 4,000. Trim size: 8.5x11. Two-color; stapled. 12 pages. Subscription cost: $12.80. Sample copy cost: $2.47. Writer's guidelines available with SASE.

Focus and Tips: *SingleMOTHER* is committed to helping and empowering single parents and their families to meet the challenges of daily life with wisdom, dignity, courage, and a sense of humor. Of special interest are articles that shatter myths about single mothers and their children. Most readers are members of the National Organization of Single Mothers.

Editorial Interests

Parenting, feminism, children's and teen issues, self-help, and women's issues.

• *Fiction:* Rarely publishes fiction. Consider exceptional stories that focus specifically on single mothers, up to 700 words.
• *Nonfiction:* Features, articles, interviews, profiles, essays, and personal experiences, up to 700 words.
Submission Policy: Send complete manuscript with cover letter. Include SASE. Accepts photocopies, computer printouts, faxes, and 3.5" IBM or Macintosh disks. Simultaneous submissions okay. Reports in 2 months. If accepted, expect publication in 4 months.
Terms and Payment: First North American serial rights. No payment. Authors receive up to 5 copies of the issue upon request.
Advertising: Accepts advertising. Contact Angie Toole, 704-888-2337.

Single Mothers by Choice

Jane Mattes, Director, P.O. Box 1642, Gracie Square Station, New York, NY 10028   Phone: 212-988-0993

Profile: A special-interest newsletter. Issued quarterly. Circ: 2,500. Trim size: 8.5x11. B/W; stapled. 12–15 pages. Subscription cost: $20. Sample copy cost: $3. No writer's guidelines.
Focus and Tips: *Single Mothers by Choice* is the membership newsletter of the nonprofit organization of the same name, founded in 1981 for single women who are considering or have chosen motherhood. All material must be related to single motherhood.
Editorial Interests
Single motherhood, parenting, feminism, and women's issues.
• *Nonfiction:* Features, articles, essays, personal experiences, opinion pieces, news, and reviews, no length restrictions.
Submission Policy: Query first with outline or send complete manuscript with cover letter. Include SASE. Accepts photocopies and computer printouts. Responds to queries in 1 month, to manuscripts in 1–2 months. If accepted, expect publication in 1–3 months.
Terms and Payment: One-time rights. No payment. Authors receive 1 copy of the issue.
Advertising: Rates: B/W full-page, $200.

Sipapu

Noel Peattie, Editor, 23311 County Road 88, Winters, CA 95694   Phone: 916-662-3364

Profile: A newsletter of alternative press reviews. Issued twice a year. Circ: 450. Trim size: 8.5x11. 2-color; stapled. 24 pages. Subscription cost: $8. Sample copy cost: $4. No writer's guidelines.
Focus and Tips: *Sipapu* is aimed at librarians, collectors, and others interested in alternative presses, which includes small and "underground" presses, Third World, dissent, feminist, peace, and all forms of indescribable publishing in general. Writers should call or write to determine interests before sending material. Content must concern issues not readily available elsewhere. Focus on the printed word or printing. No "no ax-grinding, whining, or conspiracy theories." Not interested in religious material. Avoid extremism.
Editorial Interests
Libraries, publishing, small presses, cultural and ethnic issues, the environment, feminism, men's issues, social and world issues, and women's issues.
• *Nonfiction:* Features, articles, interviews, profiles, and essays, 3,000–5,000 words. Accepts poetry reviews.
Submission Policy: Call first to determine interests or query with outline. No unsolicited manuscripts. Include SASE. Accepts photocopies, computer printouts, and Macintosh 3.5" disks. Simultaneous submissions okay if noted. Reports in 2 weeks. If accepted, expect publication in several months.
Terms and Payment: Authors retain rights. Pays on publication. $.05 per word. Authors receive 2 copies of the issue.

The Skeptical Inquirer

Kendrick Frazier, Editor, CSICOP Inc., 3965 Rensch Road, Amherst, NY 14228   Phone: 716-636-1425, Fax: 716-636-1733

Profile: The official journal of the Committee for the Scientific Investigation of Claims of the Paranormal, an international organization. Issued quarterly. Circ: 40,000. Trim size: 5.5x9; Color glossy cover; B/W inside; saddle stitched. 112 pages. Subscription cost: $25. Sample copy cost: $6.25. Writer's guidelines available with SASE.
Focus and Tips: *The Skeptical Inquirer* examines paranormal, fringe-science, and pseudoscientific phenomena from a responsible, scientific point of view. It encourages scientific inquiry, critical thinking, and the use of reason in exploring important issues. Readers include scholars and researchers as well as lay readers of diverse backgrounds. Write clearly, interestingly, and simply. Maintain a professional tone, but avoid unnecessary technical terms. Submissions are judged on the basis of interest, clarity, significance, relevance, authority, and topicality.
Editorial Interests
Examinations of astrology, channeling, extraterrestrial sitings, folklore, healing, magic, new age claims, the occult, parapsychology, and psychic phenomenon.

• *Nonfiction:* Articles, 2,000–3,500 words. Essays (Forum), 1,000 words. News and Comment, 250–1,000 words. Book reviews, 600–1,200 words. Letters to the Editor, 250 words.
Submission Policy: Query first with outline. Include SASE. Accepts photocopies, computer printouts, and faxes. Simultaneous submissions okay.
Terms and Payment: No payment. Authors receive 2 copies of the issue.
Advertising: List rental available. $90/M. Contact Mary Rose Hays, 716-636-1425.
Other Interests: Sponsors a number of annual conferences and workshops throughout the United States. For more information, contact Barry Karr, 716-636-1425.

Skipping Stones
Arun N. Toke, Editor, P.O. Box 3939, Eugene, OR 97403   Phone: 503-342-4956

Profile: A multicultural children's magazine. Issued 5 times a year. Circ: 3,000. Trim size: 8.5x11. Bond cover; 50 lb. recycled paper; saddle stitched. 36 pages. Subscription cost: $18. Sample copy cost: $5. Writer's guidelines available with SASE.
Focus and Tips: *Skipping Stones* is a nonprofit, educational, and worldwide multicultural and ecological magazine for 7- to 14-year-old children. It promotes art and writings by youth and offers a forum for communication among children from different lands and backgrounds. Prefers material with multicultural or multiethnic themes, bilingual articles, and writings in other languages or using phrases from other languages. Involve the readers with interactive writing—make it interesting yet educational. Avoid "preachy" language and don't promote stereotypes.
Editorial Interests
Cultural and ethnic concerns, juvenile and teen issues, ecosystems, the environment, folklore, health, inspirational pieces, lifestyle, religion, self-help, and social and world issues.
• *Fiction:* Accepts fiction only on multicultural/multilingual themes.
• *Nonfiction:* Features, articles, interviews, and profiles, up to 1,000 words. Personal experiences, 750–1,000 words. Opinion pieces and reviews, 100–200 words. News items, up to 100 words. Columns: People & Passions (include 2 photos), up to 500 words, and Proverbs from Other Cultures, up to 200 words.
• *Illustrations:* Photos, artwork, and celebrations from a specific culture.
Submission Policy: Query with outline or send complete manuscript with cover letter. Include SASE. Accepts photocopies, computer printouts, and Macwrite, MS Word, RSG, and PageMaker disks. Responds to queries in 2–3 months, to manuscripts in 3 months. If accepted, expect publication within 4–6 months.
Terms and Payment: First North American serial rights. No payment. Authors receive 1–5 copies of the issue.
Other Interests: Sponsors the annual *Skipping Stones* Youth Honor Awards, multicultural and nature/ecology stories from young authors from 7–15 years. Deadline is May 21; $4 entry fee. Contact Arun Toke.

S.L.U.G.fest, Ltd.
Mike Nowak, Editor, P.O. Box 536, Leominster, MA 01453

Profile: A small magazine of fiction, poetry and essays. Issued quarterly. Circ: 7,500. Trim size: 9x12. Glossy cover; B/W; saddle stitched. 50–60 pages. Subscription cost: $20. Sample copy cost: $5. Writer's guidelines available with SASE.
Focus and Tips: *S.L.U.G. fest, Ltd.* is "a magazine of free expression." It is open to interesting, novel essays, poetry, art, fiction, philosophy, and ramblings.
Editorial Interests
Environment, feminism, lifestyle, men's issues, philosophy, politics, and relationships.
• *Fiction:* Short stories, up to 15,000 words. Short-short stories, up to 3,000 words. Poetry, no length restrictions.
• *Nonfiction:* Open to all types of essays, articles, opinion pieces, personal experiences, reviews, and news.
Submission Policy: Send complete manuscript with cover letter. Include SASE. Accepts photocopies. Simultaneous submissions okay. Reports in 1 month. If accepted, expect publication in 4 months.
Terms and Payment: Authors retain rights. No payment. Authors receive 1 copy of the issue.

Smart Drug News
Steven Fowkes, Editor, P.O. Box 4029, Menlo Park, CA 94026   Phone: 415-321-CERI, Fax: 415-323-3864

Profile: A newsletter on medicinal research. Published by Cognitive Enhancement Research Institute. Issued 10 times a year. Circ: 2,000. Trim size: 8.5x11. B/W; folded. 8–12 pages. Subscription cost: $44. Sample copy cost: $6. No writer's guidelines.
Focus and Tips: *Smart Drug News* is a lay-oriented newsletter about "smart drugs," medications, and cognitive science.
Editorial Interests
Drugs, bio-rhythms, science, the environment, healing and health, holistic health, lifestyle, nutrition, politics, psychology, self-help, and social and world issues.
• *Nonfiction:* Articles on new drugs, 1,000–5,000 words. Interviews with physicians, 1,000–5,000 words. Personal experiences,

200–1,000 words. Opinion pieces on the Federal Drug Administration, 1,000–2,000 words. Book reviews, 1,000–3,000 words.
Submission Policy: Query with outline. Include SASE. Accepts photocopies, computer printouts, faxes, and IBM ASCII disks. Simultaneous submissions okay. If accepted, expect publication in 1–2 months.
Terms and Payment: All rights unless otherwise negotiated. Pays on publication. Rates negotiable. Authors receive 2 copies of the issue.
Advertising: List rental available. Contact John Morgenthaler, 707-769-8078.

Snake River Reflections

William White, Editor, 1863 Bitterroot Drive, Twin Falls, ID 83301 Phone: 208-734-0746

Profile: A writer's newsletter. Issued 10 times a year. Circ: 200. Trim size: 8.5x11. Photocopied; stapled. 6–8 pages. Subscription cost: $6.50. Sample copy cost: Free with SAE and $.29 stamp. Writer's guidelines available with SASE.
Focus and Tips: *Snake River Reflections* offers articles, tips, news, and event coverage of interest to writers. It is also open to social commentary and poetry.
Editorial Interests
Writing, cultural and ethnic issues, ecosystems, the environment, feminism, folklore, lifestyle, men's issues, mythology, new age, philosophy, politics, relationships, religion, social and world issues, and women's issues.
• *Poetry:* Up to 30 lines. Should be directed toward contemporary social commentary.
• *Nonfiction:* Articles and social commentary, 1,500 words.
Submission Policy: Query with writing samples or send complete manuscript with cover letter. Include SASE. Accepts photocopies, computer printouts, and IBM 3.5" or 5.25" disks, preferably WordPerfect. No simultaneous submissions. Reports in 1 month. If accepted, expect publication in 2 weeks.
Terms and Payment: First North American serial rights. No payment. Authors receive 2 copies of the issue.
Other Interests: Sponsors writing contests.

Somatics

Eleanor Hanna, Editor, 1516 Grant Avenue, No. 220, Novato, CA 94947-3146 Phone: 707-664-2585, Fax: 415-897-9618

Profile: A journal of mind and art sciences. Published by the Novato Institute for Somatic Research. Established in 1976. Issued twice a year. Circ: 2,000–3,000. Trim size: 8.5x11. Saddle stitched. 64 pages. Subscription cost: $20. Sample copy cost: Free. No writer's guidelines.
Focus and Tips: *Somatics* presents articles concerned with the mind, body, and arts sciences. Professional and interested lay people comprise its readership, which is international. All articles must have a somatic angle.
Editorial Interests
Mind, body, or arts sciences, bodywork, cultural and ethnic issues, dreams, ecosystems, the environment, feminism, gay and lesbian issues, healing, health, holistic health, inspiration, lifestyle, meditation, mysticism, mythology, natural health, nutrition, philosophy, politics, prayer, psychology, recovery, relationships, religion, self-help, seniors, social and world issues, spirituality, women's issues, and yoga. All with a somatic connection.
• *Poetry:* Up to 500 words.
• *Nonfiction:* Features, articles, interviews with or profiles of individuals involved in somatic disciplines, essays, and personal experiences, 12 manuscript pages. Book reviews, 250 words.
Submission Policy: Query with outline or send complete manuscript with cover letter, and author biography. Include SASE. Accepts photocopies, computer printouts, and IBM ASCII or WordPerfect disks with hard copy. Simultaneous submissions okay if noted.
Terms and Payment: Rights vary. No payment. Authors receive 6 copies of the issue.

Somnial Times

Gloria Reiser, Editor, P.O. Box 561, Quincy, IL 62306-0561 Phone: 217-222-9082

Profile: A dream-related newsletter. Issued bimonthly. Circ: 100. Trim size: 8.5x11. Photocopied; stapled. 10 pages. Subscription cost: $9. Sample copy cost: $2. No writer's guidelines.
Focus and Tips: *Somnial Times* is the newsletter of the DREAMERS Special Interest Group of American Mensa. It is a reader-participation forum for all those interested in dream work, dream research, and related states.
Editorial Interests
Dreams.
• *Nonfiction:* Open to features, articles, interviews, profiles, essays, personal experiences, opinion pieces, news, reviews, and filler. No length restrictions.
Submission Policy: Send complete manuscript with cover letter. Include SASE. Accepts photocopies, computer printouts and IBM WordPerfect disks. Simultaneous submissions okay. Reports in 2–4 months. If accepted, expect publication in 2

months.
Terms and Payment: One-time rights. No payment. Authors receive 1–5 copies of the issue.
Advertising: Rates: B/W full-page, $50. Classified ads, $.30 per word. Contact Gloria Reiser, 217-222-9082.
Other Interests: Sister publications include *Tarot News* and *Intuitive Explorations*.

Spirit Magazine

Carol Woodruff Youssef, Editor, P.O. Box 21974, Columbia, SC 29221   Phone: 803-731-6657

Profile: A new age magazine. Issued bimonthly. Circ: 500. Trim size: 8.5x11. 65 lb. cover; 50 lb. inside; stapled. 32–40 pages. Subscription cost: $22. Sample copy cost: $3. Writer's guidelines available with SASE.
Focus and Tips: *Spirit* is dedicated to opening minds and hearts to a higher consciousness. Open to interesting, creative writing that comes from the heart.
Editorial Interests
Astrology, bodywork, channeling, crystals, dreams, environment, feminism, folklore, healing, holistic and natural health, meditation, mythology, nutrition, philosophy, politics, prayer, rebirthing, recovery, religion, relationships, self-help, social issues, yoga, and other topics associated with new age concepts.
• *Fiction:* Short stories, drama, and genre fiction, 500–2,000 words. Short-short stories, 500 words. Book excerpts, to 5,000 words. Poetry, any length.
• *Nonfiction:* Features, articles, interviews and profiles, essays, personal experiences, and opinion pieces, 500–2,000 words. Reviews and filler, 500–1,000 words. Departments include Divine Dreamer, Magic Healers, Spiritual Exercising, Soul's Playground (poetry), and the New Philosopher's Awakenings.
• *Illustrations:* Accepts artwork and cartoons.
Submission Policy: Send complete manuscript with cover letter. Include SASE. Accepts photocopies and computer printouts. No simultaneous submissions. Reports in 1 month. If accepted, manuscript will be published within 6 months.
Terms and Payment: No payment. Authors receive 3 copies of the issue.
Advertising: Rates per page: B/W, $275. Contact E.S. Reed, 803-731-6657.

Spirit of Change Magazine

Carol Bedrosian, Publisher/Editor, P.O. Box 493, Grafton, MA 01519   Phone: 508-839-2228, Fax: 508-839-1173

Profile: A regional publication of new consciousness and holistic living. Established in 1987. Issued quarterly. Circ: 45,000. Trim size: 10.5x13.5; Color cover; B/W newsprint inside; stapled. 64–72 pages. Subscription cost: $15. Sample copy cost: $5. No writer's guidelines.
Focus and Tips: Published quarterly, *Spirit of Change Magazine* reaches New England-area readers. Encourages articles that strive to present universal truth, but has very little interest in narrow or dogmatic viewpoints.
Editorial Interests
Personal growth, quality lifestyle, holistic health, spirituality, cultural awareness, and the environment.
• *Fiction:* Short stories, short-short stories, drama, genre fiction, and book excerpts, all 500–5,000 words.
• *Nonfiction:* Special interest in human interest pieces. Features, articles, interviews and profiles, essays, personal experiences, and opinion pieces, 500–5,000 words. News pieces, 100–1,200 words. Reviews, 100–600 words.
Submission Policy: Send complete manuscript for fiction pieces and feature articles. To be considered as a reviewer, send sample reviews. Accepts photocopies and computer printouts. No simultaneous submissions. Does not respond to unsolicited manuscripts unless accepted for publication. Writers can call to check status.
Terms and Payment: One-time rights. Pays on publication. $.05–$.10 per word. Authors receive 1–5 copies of the issue.
Advertising: Rates per page: B/W, $1,000; 4-color, $1,000 plus color separation cost. 20% discount for contract advertising prepaid for 4 issues in advance. 10% discount for one-year contract, paid quarterly. Contact Carol Bedrosian, 508-839-2228.
Other Interests: Sponsors the "Celebrating the Artist Within Annual Art Show," held during the second week of September. Contact Jeane Robinson, 508-435-5556, for more information.

Spirit of the Times

Carol Ann F., Editor, P.O. Box 12115, Denver, CO 80212-0115   Phone: 303-836-6099, Fax: 303-455-8802

Profile: A regional journal of recovery and healing. Issued every sixth Thursday. Circ: 14,000. Trim size: 10x16. Newsprint; folded. 12–16 pages. Subscription cost: $16/15 issues. Sample copy cost: $1. No writer's guidelines.
Focus and Tips: *Spirit of the Times* provides entertainment, information, and wisdom from people currently in recovery from an addiction or those interested in a healthier lifestyle. It reaches readers in the Colorado Rocky Mountain region. The editors state that they "neither endorse nor oppose any subject. Our purpose is to present the subject matter."
Editorial Interests
Recovery, relationships, self-help, spirituality, healing, bodywork, health, inspiration, lifestyle, men's and women's issues,

natural health, nutrition, philosophy, and psychology.
• *Nonfiction:* Features, 1,000–1,500 words. Articles, 500 words, Reviews, 250–500 words. Also accepts interviews and profiles, personal experiences, and news briefs.
Submission Policy: Send complete manuscript with cover letter. Include SASE. Accepts photocopies, computer printouts, and Macintosh Quark Xpress 3.0 disks. Simultaneous submissions okay if to a publication outside of the Colorado region. Reports in 3 months. If accepted, expect publication within 3–6 months.
Terms and Payment: One-time rights. Pays on publication. $25 per piece. Authors receive 5–10 copies of the issue.
Advertising: Rates per page: B/W, $1,033. Contact Michael Gipe, Advertising Manager at 303-836-6099.

Spring: A Journal of Archetype and Culture

Jay Livernois, Managing Editor, P.O. Box 583, Putnam, CT 06260   Phone: 203-974-3229, Fax: 203-974-3195

Profile: A journal of Jungian thought and psychology. Published by Spring Publications. Established in 1941. Issued 2 times a year. Circ: 3,000. Trim size: 6x9. Glossy cover; B/W inside; perfect bound. 160 pages. Subscription cost: $20. Sample copy cost: $15. No writer's guidelines.
Focus and Tips: *Spring* is the oldest Jungian journal in the world. All material discusses and explores the thought and impact of psychologist Carl Jung as founder of the archetypal and ecological psychology and his contributions to the the intellectual component of the men's movement. Be certain to read a recent journal before submitting material. Not interested in clinical psychological studies, psychological case studies that are not historically relevant, or academic writing.
Editorial Interests
Psychology, mythology, philosophy, polytheism, I Ching, divination, astrology, cultural and ethnic issues, gay and lesbian concerns, magic, men's and women's issues, mysticism, occult, recovery, and social and world issues.
• *Nonfiction:* Features, articles, interviews and profiles, essays, Jungian-related personal experiences, and opinion pieces, 200–2,000 words.
Submission Policy: Query with outline or send complete manuscript with cover letter. Include SASE. Accepts computer printouts and IBM-compatible disks. No simultaneous submissions. Responds to queries in 3 months, to manuscripts in 6 months. If accepted, expect publication within 6–12 months.
Terms and Payment: All rights. No payment. Authors receive 7 copies of the issue.
Advertising: Rates: Full-page B/W, $200; half-page B/W, $125. Contact Jay Livernois, 203-974-3229.
Other Interests: Will sponsor the Myth and Theater Festival, to be held in Avignon, France in August 1995. Theme will be magic. For information contact Enrique Pardo in Paris, 33-1-44.67.70.53.

Sproutletter

Michael Linden, Publisher/Editor, P.O. Box 62, Ashland, OR 97520   Phone: 503-488-2326, Fax: 503-488-4712

Profile: A newsletter covering sprouting, live foods, and indoor food gardening. Published by Sprouting Publications. Issued quarterly. Circ: 3,000. Trim size: 8.5x11. Photocopied; stapled. 12 pages. Subscription cost: $12. Sample copy cost: $3.50. Writer's guidelines available with SASE.
Focus and Tips: *Sproutletter* emphasizes growing foods indoors for health, economy, nutrition, and self-sufficiency. Covers sprouting, holistic health, and live foods, including the growing interest in edible fresh water algae. Looks for optimistic, interesting, and informative articles that are tightly written. Articles should offer in-depth coverage, thorough, accurate infor-mation, and enjoyable reading. Not interested in articles on general health and nutrition or ornamental plant growing.
Editorial Interests
Sprouting, indoor food gardening, vegetarianism, freshwater algae, healing, holistic and natural health, lifestyle, meditation, metaphysics, nutrition, and self-help.
• *Nonfiction:* Practical, how-to articles, technical pieces, and personal experiences, 500–2,400 words. Book reviews, news items, and recipes, 100–450 words. Filler, humor and newsbreaks, 50–150 words.
Submission Policy: Query with outline. Include SASE. Accepts photocopies, computer printouts, 3.5" ASCII disks, and faxes (503-488-4712). Responds to queries in 2 weeks, to manuscripts in 3 weeks. If accepted, expect publication in 6 months.
Terms and Payment: All rights. Pays on publication. Articles, $25–$75. Book reviews, news, and recipes, $5–$20. Filler, $2–$6. Authors receive 3 copies of the issue.
Advertising: Rates: B/W full-page, $160. Contact Michael Linden, 503-488-2326.

Star Wars Collection Trading Post

Laura Kyro, President, 6030 Magnolia, St. Louis, MO 63139   Phone: 314-645-6692

Profile: A fanzine for collectors. Published by Kyro, Inc. Issued quarterly. Circ: N/A. Trim size: 5.5x8. Stapled. 20 pages. Subscription cost: $12. Sample copy cost: $3. No writer's guidelines.
Focus and Tips: *Star Wars Collection Trading Post* provides fans of the *Star Wars* movies information on related collectibles and

a forum for the exchange of ideas. It is also open to science and space-oriented articles.
Editorial Interests
Star Wars topics, science and space, extraterrestrials, and lifestyle.
• *Nonfiction:* Features, articles, personal experiences, and opinion pieces, 1,000 words. Interviews and profiles, 1,000 words and up. Essays, 500 words. Accepts new items and contributions to its Letters department.
Submission Policy: Send complete manuscript with cover letter and resume. Include SASE. Accepts photocopies, computer printouts, and Macintosh disks. Simultaneous submissions okay. Responds to queries in 1 week, to manuscripts in 3 weeks. If accepted, expect publication in 2 months.
Terms and Payment: One-time rights. No payment. Authors receive 3–5 copies of the issue.
Advertising: Rates: Classified ads, $.15 per word. List rental available: $25 for one-time use. Contact Laura Kyro, 314-645-6692.

Stepping Up

Ellen Oestreicher, Editor/Publisher, 7021 Halstead Drive, Mound, MN 55364   Phone/Fax: 612-472-6329

Profile: A regional newsmagazine of personal and spiritual growth. Published by Presentation Images. Established in 1990. Issued monthly. Circ: 15,000. Trim size: Tabloid. Newsprint; folded. 16 pages. Subscription cost: $12. Sample copy cost: $1.50. Writer's guidelines available with SASE.
Focus and Tips: *Stepping Up* provides a network for people working on emotional, behavioral, and spiritual growth. It serves as a forum for readers in the Twin Cities to share aspirations, idealisms, interests, information, and values in order to increase personal growth and fulfillment. Audience includes people in recovery and those interested in holistic thinking, positive thinking, spiritual growth, and behavior changes.
Editorial Interests
Self-help, the environment, holistic health, metaphysics, spirituality, bodywork, cultural and ethnic issues, dreams, ecosystems, feminism, folklore, gay and lesbian issues, healing and health, inspiration, lifestyle, meditation, men's issues, mythology, new age, nutrition, philosophy, psychology, rebirthing, recovery, relationships, social and world issues, women's issues, and yoga.
• *Fiction:* Growth-oriented short stories, 500 words.
• *Nonfiction:* Growth-oriented features, articles, interviews, profiles, essays, personal experiences, opinion pieces, and news items, 500–1,000 words.
Submission Policy: Send complete manuscript with cover letter. Include SASE. Accepts photocopies, computer printouts, and disks, preferably IBM WordPerfect. Simultaneous submissions okay. Reporting time varies. If accepted, expect publication in 1–6 months.
Terms and Payment: One-time rights. No payment. Authors receive copies of the issue.
Advertising: Rates: B/W full-page, $795; half-page, $435; quarter-page, $220. List rental available. Contact Ellen Oestreicher, 612-472-6329.

Story Quarterly

Anne Brashler, Editor, P.O. Box 1416, Northbrook, IL 60065

Profile: A literary journal. Issued annually. Circ: 1,500. Glossy color cover; B/W; perfect bound. 82 pages. Subscription cost: $12. Sample copy cost: $5. Writer's guidelines available with SASE.
Focus and Tips: *Story Quarterly* is an independent magazine that publishes short story. Writers are encouraged to send their best work.
Editorial Interests
Literary short fiction.
• *Fiction:* Short stories, no restrictions on length, content, or style.
Submission Policy: Send complete manuscript. Include SASE. Accepts photocopies and computer printouts. Simultaneous submissions okay. Reports in 3 months. If accepted, expect publication in up to 1 year.
Terms and Payment: First North American serial rights. No payment. Authors receive 5 copies of the issue.

Struggle

Tim Hall, Editor, P.O. Box 13261, Detroit, MI 48213-0261   Phone: 313-441-1204

Profile: An anti-establishment, revolutionary literary journal. Issued quarterly. Circ: 500. Trim size: 5.5x8.5. Heavy bond cover; B/W inside; saddle stitched. 36 pages. Subscription cost: $10. Sample copy cost: $2.50. Writer's guidelines available with SASE.
Focus and Tips: *Struggle* is a magazine of creative literature representing the anger and rebellion of the working class and all oppressed peoples against the repressive rule and culture of capitalist rulers. Provides a forum for the literature and art of

working-class rebellion and anti-establishment political and cultural views. Seeks work with artistic power that rebels against some element of capitalism. Be concrete, lively, and base writing on real oppression. Make sharp, exposing use of concrete detail. Avoid spacey, abstract, convoluted notions. No racist, sexist, homophobic material.

Editorial Interests

Social justice, socialism, labor, anti-racism, internationalism, cultural and ethnic issues, the environment, feminism, gay and lesbian concerns, politics, world issues, and women's issues.

• *Fiction:* Short stories, short-short stories, and drama, up to 5,000 words. Poetry, no length restrictions.

• *Illustrations:* B/W line art and cartoons.

Submission Policy: Send complete manuscript with cover letter. Include SASE. Accepts photocopies, computer printouts, and IBM-compatible 5.25" disks. Simultaneous submissions okay. Reports in 1–3 months. If accepted, expect publication within 3–6 months.

Terms and Payment: Authors retain rights. No payment. Authors receive 2 copies of the issue.

Advertising: No advertising.

The Sun: A Magazine of Ideas

Sy Safransky, Editor, 107 North Roberson Street, Chapel Hill, NC 27516

Profile: A general-interest magazine of ideas and personal experiences. Issued monthly. Circ: 25,000. Trim size: 8.5x11. 40 pages. Subscription cost: $32. Sample copy cost: $3.50. Writer's guidelines available with SASE.

Focus and Tips: *The Sun* is an eclectic magazine open to discourse on a variety of ideas. It is open to essays, fiction, interviews, poetry, and photography that foster personal, illuminating, intimate exploration. Welcomes personal experiences of any form. Avoid material that is traditionally "inspirational."

Editorial Interests

Personal experiences, cultural and ethnic issues, philosophy, politics, and spirituality.

• *Fiction:* All types, up to 7,000 words. Poetry, no length restrictions.

• *Nonfiction:* Personal experiences, essays, and interviews, up to 7,000 words.

• *Illustrations:* Accepts photographs.

Submission Policy: Send complete manuscript with cover letter. Accepts reprints. Include SASE. Accepts photocopies and computer printouts. Simultaneous submissions okay. Reports in 5 months.

Terms and Payment: First North American serial rights. Pays on publication. Nonfiction, $100–$300. Fiction, $100. Poems, $25. Reprints, 50% of standard rate. Authors receive 2 copies of the issue plus a free 1-year subscription.

The Suspicious Humanist

Stephen Weiner, Editor, 549 B Street, No. 3, Ashland, OR 97520   Phone: 503-482-1855

Profile: A regional publication of eclectic writing. Issued 3–7 times a year. Circ: 500. Trim size: 8.5x11. Photocopied. Subscription cost: Sliding scale. Sample copy cost: $1. No writer's guidelines.

Focus and Tips: *The Suspicious Humanist* is a small, independent publication of eclectic, non-dogmatic prose and poetry with a regional West Coast focus. Primary interests include social commentary and philosophy.

Editorial Interests

Social issues, politics, philosophy, mental illness, ecosystems, the environment, health, children's and teen issues, psychology, regional issues, and Jewish and interfaith religions.

• *Fiction:* Short-short stories, 100–250 words. Poetry, no length restrictions.

• *Nonfiction:* Open to all forms: articles, memoirs, interviews, essays, personal experiences, opinion, news, reviews, and filler. No length restrictions.

Submission Policy: Query with writing samples or send complete manuscript with cover letter, bibliography, and clips. Include SASE. Accepts photocopies. Reports in at least 6 months. Publication time varies.

Terms and Payment: No payment. Authors receive 5 copies of the issue.

Sweet Fern: Soothing Verbs for a Positive World

Bob or Celeste Longacre, Editors, R.R. 1, Box 566, Walpole, NH 03608   Phone: 603-756-4152

Profile: A new age publication on holistic living. Issued quarterly. Circ: 5,000. Trim size: 8.5x11. Recycled paper, stapled. 24 pages. Subscription cost: $12. Sample copy cost: $3.50.

Focus and Tips: *Sweet Fern* offers practical information on wholeness, wellness, and positive living. No racist, sexist, or prejudiced articles.

Editorial Interests

Holistic health, Feng Shui, self-help, astrology, bodywork, channeling, crystals, cultural and ethnic issues, dreams, ecosystems, the environment, extraterrestrials, feminism, folklore, gay and lesbian issues, healing, health, inspiration, juvenile and

teen issues, lifestyle, magic, meditation, men's issues, metaphysics, mysticism, mythology, natural health, new age, nutrition, occult, parapsychology, parenting, philosophy, politics, prayer, psychic phenomenon, psychology, rebirthing, recovery, religion, seniors, social and world issues, spirituality, witches, women's issues, and yoga.
• *Nonfiction:* Practical, informative articles. Query for word length.
Submission Policy: Send complete manuscript with cover letter. Include SASE. Accepts computer printouts and PageMaker disks. Simultaneous submissions okay. Reports in 1–4 weeks.
Terms and Payment: First North American serial rights and microfilm rights. No payment. Offers ad exchange in lieu of payment.

Sword of Dyrnwyn

Vickie Von Temske, Editor, P.O. Box 674884, Marietta, GA 30067   Phone 404-516-8500

Profile: A metaphysical pagan newsletter. Published by Camelot Press, LTD. Issued 8 times a year. Circ: 3,200. Trim size: 8.5x11. 60 lb. paper. 12 pages. Subscription cost: $15.95. Sample copy cost: $3.50. Writer's guidelines available with SASE.
Focus and Tips: *Sword of Dyrnwyn* is an occult-based newsletter focusing on pagan beliefs. It is interested only in serious nonfiction articles.
Editorial Interests
Druidism, Wicca, astrology, channeling, crystals, ecosystems, the environment, feminism, folklore, healing, holistic health, magic, meditation, metaphysics, mysticism, mythology, natural health, new age, nutrition, occult, parapsychology, parenting, philosophy, psychic phenomenon, psychology, rebirthing, spirituality, witches, and women's issues.
• *Nonfiction:* Features, 250–350 words. Articles, 500–1,000 words. Interviews and profiles, 250 words. Essays, 350–600 words. Personal experiences, 200–400 words. Opinion and news pieces, 100–200 words. Reviews, 50–100 words.
Submission Policy: Query with outline or send complete manuscript with cover letter. Include SASE. Accepts photocopies, computer printouts, and computer disks. No simultaneous submissions. Responds to queries in 1 month, to manuscripts in 2 months. If accepted, expect publication in 6–12 months.
Terms and Payment: One-time rights. Payment is negotiable. Authors receive copies of the issue.
Advertising: Rates: B/W full-page, $125. List rental available: $85/M. Contact Vickie Von Temske, 404-516-8500.
Other Interests: Affiliated with the Church of Y Tylwyth Teg, Inc. Sponsors the Gathering of the Tribes, a yearly leadership conference for Wiccan, Pagan, and Earth religion leaders. Held in September. For more information, contact Lady Cerridwen, P.O. Box 674884, Marietta, GA 30067, 404-516-8500.

Symposium

Tiffany Baugher, Publisher/Editor, 1930 North Boulevard, Suite 5, Houston, TX 77098   Phone/Fax: 713-528-5631

Profile: A regional arts and alternative lifestyle magazine. Published by Modern Mythos Press. Issued bimonthly. Circ: 50,000. Trim size: 8.5x11. Two-color cover; B/W inside; saddle stitched. 24–48 pages. Subscription cost: $10. Sample copy cost: $2. Writer's guidelines available with SASE.
Focus and Tips: Distributed throughout metropolitan Houston, *Symposium* is dedicated to art, myth, medicine, and the science of self-knowledge. It seeks original, fresh writing that comes from the heart and is grounded in research and experience. Avoid being too "new age" in style or subject matter.
Editorial Interests
Arts, mythology, self-help, Jungian psychology, astrology, bodywork, cultural and ethnic issues, dreams, folklore, holistic and natural health, meditation, men's issues, mythology, new age, parenting, philosophy, politics, recovery, relationships, religion, social and world issues, spirituality, and women's issues.
• *Fiction:* Short stories, and genre fiction, 1,500–3,000 words. Drama, 1,500–2,500 words. Short-short stories, 750–1,500 words. Book excerpts, 2,000–3,000 words. Poetry, up to 750 words.
• *Nonfiction:* Features, 2,000–3,500 words. Articles, interviews, profiles, 1,500–2,500 words. Essays, personal experiences, and opinion pieces, 1,000–2,000 words. News items, 500–750 words. Reviews, 1,500–2,000 words. Filler, 500–1,000 words. Departments include Small Gems, unique shops and products, 750 words; Astrology, up to 2,000 words; Cupid and Psyche, relationships, 1,750 words, and Alternatives, holistic health, 1,750 words.
Submission Policy: Query with 3 sample chapters and resume or send complete manuscript with cover letter. Include SASE. Accepts photocopies, computer printouts, IBM-compatible disks, and faxes. Simultaneous submissions okay. Reports in 2 months. If accepted, expect publication in 3 months.
Terms and Payment: One-time rights. Pays on publication. $25–$75 per piece. Authors receive 10 copies of the issue.
Advertising: Rates: B/W full-page, $400; 2-color full-page, $600. Contact Ariel, 713-528-5631.

Synthesis

Jason Marcewicz, Editor, 219 Napfle Street, Philadelphia, PA 19111   Phone: 215-725-1686

Profile: A music magazine. Issued quarterly. Circ: N/A. Trim size: 8.5x11. 60 lb. coated paper; stapled. 16 pages. Subscription cost: $10. Sample copy cost: $2.50. No writer's guidelines.

Focus and Tips: *Synthesis* is a forum for electronic musicians and fans. It has a particular interest in trance and new age synthesized music.

Editorial Interests

Computer, keyboard, and synthesized music.

• *Nonfiction:* Features, articles, interviews, profiles, music reviews, and columns on trance music, new age music, contemporary instrumental, electric ambient music, and electric world music.

Submission Policy: Query with outline or send complete manuscript with cover letter. Include SASE. Accepts photocopies, computer printouts, and WordPerfect ASCII or IBM-compatible disks. Simultaneous submissions okay. Reporting and publication times vary.

Terms and Payment: Authors retain rights. No payment. Authors receive 1 copy of the issue; more upon request.

Advertising: Accepts advertising. Contact Jason Marcewicz, 215-725-1686.

T'ai Chi

Marvin Smalheiser, Editor, P.O. Box 26156, Los Angeles, CA 90026   Phone: 213-665-7773, Fax: 213-665-1627

Profile: A popular magazine for practitioners of T'ai Chi Ch'uan. Published by Wayfarer Publications. Issued bimonthly. Circ: 30,000. Trim size: 8.25x10.75. Glossy color cover; glossy paper; B/W; saddle stitched. 56 pages. Subscription cost: $20. Sample copy cost: $3.50. Writer's guidelines available with SASE.

Focus and Tips: Read by novices, serious students and masters, *T'ai Chi* offers informative and insightful articles on T'ai Chi Ch'uan, other internal martial arts, and related topics such as qigong, Chinese traditional medicine and healing practices, Chinese philosophy and culture, and news about teachers and their schools. It prefers articles that stress specific aspects of the art, such as style, self-defense techniques, principles and philosophy, training methods, and weapons. Present information clearly, fairly, and objectively. All material must have practical application to readers. General martial arts articles and promotional pieces are rejected.

Editorial Interests

T'ai Chi, qigong, traditional Chinese medicine, Chinese herbs, acupuncture, health and fitness, natural health, philosophy, meditation, self-improvement, and spiritual growth.

• *Nonfiction:* Features and articles, 1,500–3,000 words. Essays and personal experiences, 600–1,500 words.

• *Photos:* One or more 4x6, 5x7, or 8x10 B/W glossy prints to accompany article. Model releases are required.

Submission Policy: Query first with outline. Include SASE. Accepts computer printouts. No simultaneous submissions. Reports in 3–4 weeks. If accepted, expect publication within 3–5 months.

Terms and Payment: First North American serial rights and one-time rights. Pays on publication. $35–$350 per piece including photos. Authors receive copies of the issue.

Advertising: Accepts advertising. Contact Marvin Smalheiser, 213-665-7773.

Take Note! Music Magazine

Ms. P. J. Grimes, Publisher/Editor, P.O. Box 230542, Encinitas, CA 92023-0542   Phone/Fax: 619-632-0770

Profile: A music newsletter. Published by Imagination Station Communications. Issued 6 times a year. Circ: 1,000. Trim size: 8.5x11. Recycled paper; folded. 4 pages. Subscription cost: $10. Sample copy cost: $1. Writer's guidelines available with SASE.

Focus and Tips: *Take Note! Music Magazine* offers music news and information, career tips, lifestyle pieces, and practical how-to articles. It is looking for short, succinct, clear writing with positive viewpoints. If you choose to present a music-related problem such as music and substance abuse, be sure to offer positive steps for change.

Editorial Interests

Music, astrology, bodywork, the environment, feminism, gay and lesbian concerns, health, holistic health, inspiration, lifestyle, men's issues, natural health, new age, nutrition, parenting, politics, psychology, recovery, self-help, and social and world issues.

• *Nonfiction:* Positive articles, practical how-to pieces, profiles, features, and book, video, and music reviews. No length restrictions.

• *Illustrations:* 5x7 or smaller B/W prints. Artwork with environmentally conscious themes.

Submission Policy: Query with outline, writing samples, and resume. Include SASE. Accepts photocopies, IBM-compatible 3.5" HD disks, and faxes. No simultaneous submissions. Reports in 2 weeks. If accepted, expect publication in 2 months.

Terms and Payment: No payment. Offers advertising space in lieu of payment. Authors receive 2 copies of the issue.

Advertising: Accepts advertising. Contact P. J. Grimes.

Other Interests: Offers workshops and seminars in Music Media ConneXtion: How to Plug into the Press for Exposure Success. Held twice each year. For more information, contact P. J. Grimes.

Talking Leaves

Carolyn Moran, Editor, 1430 Willamette, Suite 367, Eugene, OR 97401   Phone: 503-342-2974, Fax: 503-343-3790

Profile: A thematic global journal of spiritual ecology. Published by Deep Ecology Education Project (DEEP), a nonprofit organization. Established in 1989. Issued quarterly. Circ: 8,000. Trim size: 8.5x11. Self cover; stapled. 48 pages. Subscription cost: $12. Sample copy cost: $4. Writer's guidelines and theme list available free.

Focus and Tips: *Talking Leaves* expresses and inspires the deep heart connection that must precede any meaningful change in how we treat the world. It serves as an educational tool, profiling projects and individuals whose actions make a positive and sustainable difference locally and globally. Distributed internationally, reaches readers in more that 23 countries. Prefers a heartfelt, journalistic style to academic writing—"make it personal."

Editorial Interests

Ecology and ecosystems, environment, feminism, folklore, gay and lesbian concerns, healing, holistic health, inspiration, magic, men's and women's issues, mysticism, mythology, politics, prayer, social and world issues, spirituality, witches, paganism, pantheism, shamanism, and indigenous worldviews.

• *Nonfiction:* Must relate to issue theme. Features, 1,500–3,000 words. Articles, 1,500 words. Interviews and profiles, 1,500–2,000 words. Essays, 800–1,200 words. Personal experiences, 1,000 words. Opinion and news pieces, 500 words. Reviews, 200–500 words. Filler, 200 words. Departments include World Rainforest Reports, Bioregionalism, and Indigenous Issues.

Submission Policy: Send complete manuscript. Include SASE. Prefers Macintosh Word disk submissions with hard copy. Accepts photocopies, computer printouts, and faxes. No simultaneous submissions. If accepted, expect publication within 1–4 months.

Terms and Payment: One-time rights. No payment. Authors receive 1 copy of the issue.

Advertising: Rates per page: B/W, $600. 10% discount for nonprofit organizations. Classifieds: $15 per word; $10 for non-profit organizations. Contact Hudson Dodd, 503-343-4089.

Other Interests: The Deep Ecology Education Project sponsors numerous conferences including The World Women's Conference for a Healthy Planet, held in Brazil; the International Conference for Environmental Education, held in Canada; and the Land, Air, Water conference at the University of Oregon Law School. Contact Carolyn Moran, 503-342-2974.

Tantra: The Magazine

Susana Andrews, Editor, P.O. Box 108, Torreon, NM 87061   Phone: 505-384-2292

Profile: A quarterly magazine devoted to the practice of Tantra sexuality and spirituality. Issued quarterly. Circ: 12,000. Trim size: 8.5x11. Glossy color cover; 55 lb. recycled paper; B/W inside; saddle stitched. 84 pages. Subscription cost: $18. Sample copy cost: $6. Writer's guidelines available with SASE.

Focus and Tips: *Tantra: The Magazine* was conceived to promote the discussion of Tantra, understood as the "expansion of consciousness toward transcendence," taken from the mystical teachings of Tibetan Buddhism, Hinduism, Sufism, Taoism, Shamanism, and Zen. Encourages Tantric expression through the fine arts including music, artwork, prose, and poetry. It seeks feature articles on Tantric history, philosophy, rituals, myths, mysteries, techniques, and lifestyles. Readers are spiritual seekers.

Editorial Interests

Tantra, sexuality, astrology, bodywork, cultural and ethnic viewpoints, feminism, folklore, healing and health, holistic and natural health, inspiration, lifestyle, meditation, men's issues, mysticism, mythology, new age, nutrition, philosophy, psychology, rebirthing, religion, self-help, spirituality, women's issues, and yoga.

• *Nonfiction:* Features, 3,000–4,000 words. Articles, 1,000–3,000 words. Interviews and profiles, 2,000–3,000 words. Essays and opinion pieces, 1,000 words. Personal experiences, 1,000–2,000 words. News items, 200–500 words. Reviews, 200–400 words. Filler, 200 words.

• *Illustrations:* Photos to accompany features.

Submission Policy: Query with outline and resume or send complete manuscript with cover letter and resume. Include SASE. Accepts photocopies, computer printouts, and IBM DOS disks. No simultaneous submissions. Reports in 6–12 months. If accepted, expect publication within 1–2 years.

Terms and Payment: One-time rights. No payment. Authors receive 1–3 copies of the issue; contributor's discount available for orders placed before press run.

Advertising: Rates: B/W full-page, $300; 4-color full-page, $600. Contact Colleen Mauro, 415-949-4240. List rental available: $75/M. Contact Alan Verdegraal, 505-384-2292.

Tarot News

Gloria Reiser, Editor, P.O. Box 561, Quincy, IL 62306-0561   Phone: 217-222-9082

Profile: A Tarot-related newsletter. Issued bimonthly. Circ: 125. Trim size: 8.5x11. Heavy bond cover; B/W; stapled. 10+

pages. Subscription cost: $15. Sample copy cost: $2.50. No writer's guidelines.

Focus and Tips: *Tarot News* is the newsletter of Tarot SIG, a special interest group of American Mensa. It is open, though, to all people interested in Tarot and strives to be a reader-participation forum.

Editorial Interests

Tarot, astrology, folklore, lifestyle, magic, meditation, metaphysics, mysticism, mythology, new age, occult, philosophy, psychic phenomenon, psychology, self-help, and spirituality.

• *Nonfiction:* Open to features, articles, interviews, profiles, essays, personal experiences, opinion pieces, news, reviews, and filler. No length restrictions.

Submission Policy: Send complete manuscript with cover letter. Include SASE. Accepts computer printouts and IBM WordPerfect disks. Simultaneous submissions okay. Reports in 2–4 months. If accepted, expect publication in 2 months.

Terms and Payment: One-time rights. No payment. Authors receive copies of the issue.

Advertising: Rates: B/W full-page, $50. Classified ads, $1 for 4-time placement. Contact Gloria Reiser, 217-222-9082.

Other Interests: Sister publications include *Somnial Times* and *Intuitive Explorations*.

Teaching Tolerance

Elsie Williams, Editorial Assistant, 400 Washington Avenue, Montgomery, AL 36104   Phone: 205-264-0286, Fax: 205-264-3121

Profile: A national educational journal promoting justice and diversity. Published by the nonprofit Southern Poverty Law Center. Established in 1991. Issued twice a year. Circ: 130,000. Trim size: 8.5x11. Glossy cover; full-color; saddle stitched. 64 pages. Subscription cost: Free. Sample copy cost: Free. Writer's guidelines available with SASE.

Focus and Tips: *Teaching Tolerance* is dedicated to helping pre-school, elementary, and secondary teachers promote tolerance and understanding between widely diverse groups of students. It seeks practical resources and techniques with classroom application and a national perspective where appropriate. Helpful sidebars such as how-to steps, resources lists, and short profiles are a plus. In addition, it is a reader's forum for the exchange of ideas, lesson plans, special projects, and other activities that enhance tolerance. Use a lively, simple, concise writing style that is both descriptive and reflective. Avoid jargon, rhetoric, and academic analysis.

Editorial Interests

Tolerance, education, gender equity, prejudice reduction, anti-bias, peace making, conflict resolution, community service, social action, cultural and ethnic issues, gay and lesbian concerns, and children's and teen issues.

• *Nonfiction:* Practical features with strong classroom focus, 1,000–3,000 words. Essays in the form of personal reflection, description of programs and activities, and how-to pieces, 400–800 words. Idea Exchange, classroom lesson plans and activities, 250–500 words.

Submission Policy: Prefers queries with outline. Accepts complete manuscripts with cover letter. Include SASE. Accepts photocopies, computer printouts, and Macintosh Microsoft Word or IBM-compatible submissions. No simultaneous submissions. Reports in 3 months. If accepted, expect publication in up to 9 months.

Terms and Payment: First North American serial rights. Pays on acceptance for features, $500–$2,500 per piece. Pays on publication for essays, $300–$800 per piece, and Idea Exchange, $100.

Advertising: List rental available. Contact Susan Anstrand at Names in the News, 415-989-3350.

Other Interests: The Southern Poverty Law Center makes available its representatives to lecture at conferences on tolerance issues. Contact Elsie Williams, 205-264-0286.

Temple Doors

Chrystine Star Eagle, Founder, 806 Emerald Wood Drive, Austin, TX 78745   Phone: 512-443-8482

Profile: A publication of the Star of Isis Mystery School. Published by the Star of Isis Mystery School. Issued twice a year. Circ: 100. Trim size: 8.5x11. Photocopied; stapled. 40 pages. Subscription cost: $25. Sample copy cost: $9. No guidelines.

Focus and Tips: *Temple Doors* reports on the doctrine of the Star of Isis Mystery School for its members. This doctrine "reveals the divine prism of mankind and promotes the transcendence of planetary consciousness." School members are "inner mystery" seekers, not "surface new agers." Accepts submissions from school members only.

Editorial Interests

Channeling, crystals, the environment, extraterrestrials, metaphysics, mysticism, mythology, occult, and spirituality.

• *Nonfiction:* Accepts articles about Star of Isis Mystery School doctrine by members only.

Terms and Payment: All rights.

Advertising: Accepts exchange ads. Contact Chrystine Star Eagle, 512-443-8482.

Other Interests: Affiliated with the Church of the Johannine Wellspring. Contact Chrystine Star Eagle for more information.

Thema

Virginia Howard, Editor, P.O. Box, 74109, Metairie, LA 70033-4109   Phone: 504-887-1263

Profile: A thematic journal of creative thought. Published by the Thema Literary Society. Issued 3 times per year. Circ: 300+. Trim size: 5.5x8.5. Heavy bond 2-color cover; B/W inside; perfect bound. 200 pages. Subscription cost: $16. Sample copy cost: $8. Writer's guidelines and theme list available with SASE.

Focus and Tips: *Thema* is designed to stimulate creative thinking. It appeals to the literate general public, creative writing instructors, and writing. Each issue centers around one theme; writers are advised to request themes, let ideas simmer, and let the theme guide them. Avoid "gratuitous bedroom/bathroom profanity, 'alternate' lifestyle, and romance."

Editorial Interests

Theme-related short stories and poetry, cultural and ethnic issues, inspiration, magic, parapsychology, psychic phenomenon, regional writing, relationships, seniors, and spirituality.

• *Fiction:* Short stories and genre fiction, 6,000 words. Short-short stories, 900–1,000 words. Poetry, 100 words.

Submission Policy: Send complete manuscript with cover letter specifying which target theme. Include SASE. Accepts photocopies and computer printouts. Responds on queries in 2 weeks, to manuscripts in 3 months after deadline for theme. If accepted, expect publication in 4 months.

Terms and Payment: One-time rights. Pays on acceptance. Short stories, $25. Short-short stories and poetry, $10. Authors receive 1 copy of the issue.

Third Force: Issues and Actions in Communities of Color

John Anner, Editor, 1218 East 21st Street, Oakland, CA 94606   Phone: 510-533-7583, Fax: 510-533-0923

Profile: A politics journal for people of color. Published by the Center for Third World Organizing. Established in 1984. Issued bimonthly. Circ: 3,000. Trim size: 8.5x11. Stapled. 36 pages. Subscription cost: $22. Sample copy cost: $4 on newsstand; free to potential contributors. Writer's guidelines available with SASE.

Focus and Tips: *Third Force* reports on grass-roots struggles and campaigns in communities of color throughout the country. Articles focus on the individuals involved in the struggle—those who are directly effected—not on experts. Avoid leftist rhetoric.

Editorial Interests

Social issues such as gangs, prison, and welfare, cultural and ethnic issues, the environment, feminism, gay and lesbian issues, healing, health, parenting, philosophy, politics, and seniors.

• *Nonfiction:* Features, articles, interviews, and profiles, 1,500–3,500 words. Essays, personal experiences, and opinion pieces, 1,000 words. News items, 500 words. Book reviews, 1,500 words.

Submission Policy: Query with outline. Include SASE. Accepts photocopies, computer printouts, faxes, and computer disks. Simultaneous submissions okay. Reports in 1 month. If accepted, expect publication in 2 months.

Terms and Payment: First North American serial rights. Pays on publication. $.08 per word. Authors receive a free 1-year subscription.

Advertising: Rates: B/W full-page, $450. List rental available. Contact John Anner, 510-533-7583.

Other Interests: For information about the Center for Third World Organizing, contact Francis Calpotura, 510-533-7583. Sponsors a conference for women entitled Weaving the Cloth of Resistance. Its goal is to unite women and involve them in community struggles. Held every 2 years in the Spring. Contact Rinku Sen, 510-533-7583.

Three Rivers Wellness Directory

James Dixon, Editor, P.O. Box 86054, Pittsburgh, PA 15221

Profile: A regional guide to holistic living services. Published by HLQ Associates. Issued annually. Circ: 10,000–15,000. Trim size: 8.5x11. Glossy color cover; B/W inside; saddle stitched. 50–80 pages. Subscription cost: $3.50. Sample copy cost: $3.50. No writer's guidelines.

Focus and Tips: *Three Rivers Wellness Directory* is a resource guide to services and issues of personal health care, global awareness, opportunities for self-sufficiency, and social responsibility in the Pittsburgh area. Its seeks practical, reference-oriented material that fosters personal responsibility and empowerment. "Address current problems, offer solutions, and include local resources available to readers." Especially interested in writers who can deliver articles with graphics, illustrations, or artwork. Avoid fiction and opinion pieces.

Editorial Interests

Health, holistic health, healing, natural health, social responsibility, the environment, lifestyle, metaphysics, self-help, and spirituality.

• *Poetry:* Wellness-related poetry.

• *Nonfiction:* How-to articles, up to 300 words. Accepts filler.

• *Illustrations:* Artwork, B/W photos, or cartoons to accompany articles.

Submission Policy: Send complete manuscript with cover letter. Include SASE. Accepts photocopies, computer printouts, and Macintosh disks. Simultaneous submissions okay. Reports in 4–6 months if interested.

Terms and Payment: Occasionally pays for article/illustration packages. Rates vary. Does not provide contributor's copies.

Advertising: Rates: B/W 2.25x2.75, $55. List rental available for local events. Contact Allen Goodman, Publisher.

Thresholds Quarterly

Laurel Fuller Clark, Senior Editor, HCR 1, Box 15, Windyville, MO 65783   Phone: 417-345-8411

Profile: A thematic educational and inspirational journal for members of the School of Metaphysics Associates (SOMA). Published by the School of Metaphysics. Issued quarterly. Circ: 2,500. Trim size: 7.5x10. Heavy bond cover; B/W; stapled. 28 pages. Subscription cost: $35. Sample copy cost: Free. Writer's guidelines available with SASE.

Focus and Tips: *Thresholds Quarterly* shares with SOMA members the results of research and promising developments in metaphysics, religion, spirituality, dreams, global consciousness, health and wellness, the arts, and intuition. Its mission is to help members to grow and develop spiritually. Looks for informative, innovative, uplifting pieces that raise consciousness and call for action to improve humanity. Stay away from any type of negative, depressing, or cynical outlooks.

Editorial Interests
Astrology, bodywork, cultural and ethnic issues, dreams, ecosystems and the environment, folklore, healing, holistic and natural health, inspiration, lifestyle, meditation, metaphysics, mysticism, mythology, new age, nutrition, parapsychology, parenting, philosophy, prayer, psychic phenomenon, psychology, relationships, interfaith religion, self-help, social and world issues, spirituality, and yoga.
- *Fiction:* Inspirational myths/fairy tales, children's stories, and humor, 1,000–2,000 words. Poetry, up to 1 page.
- *Nonfiction:* Features, articles, interviews and profiles, essays, and personal experiences, 1,000–2,000 words. Departments include Health, Arts, Business, Creative Writing, Education, and Religion.

Submission Policy: Query with outline or send complete manuscript with cover letter. Include SASE. Accepts photocopies and computer printouts. No simultaneous submissions. Responds to queries in 3 months, to manuscripts in 3–4 months. If accepted, expect publication in 3–12 months.

Terms and Payment: All rights. No payment. Authors receive up to 3 copies of the issue upon request.

Advertising: Accepts listings for resource directory. Contact Dr. Barbara Condron or Laurel Fuller Clark, 417-345-8411.

Other Interests: The School of Metaphysics sponsors an annual SOMA Conference, held in the Ozarks. Held July 4 and open to all SOMA members. Contact Dr. Barbara Condron, 417-345-8411, for SOMA membership information.

Time Pilot

Gary Bryant, Publisher, P.O. Box 2567, Bellingham, WA 98227   Phone: 206-733-7306

Profile: A new interactive newsletter set in the future. Published by The New Legends Publishing Group. Issued monthly. Circ: N/A. Trim size: 8.5x11. 2-color; folded. 6 pages. Subscription cost: N/A. Sample copy cost: N/A. Writer's guidelines available with SASE.

Focus and Tips: *Time Pilot* is an innovative newsletter with an imaginary publication date of 500 years in the future. Readers and contributors are asked to take an educated guess at how the people of Earth will actually be living in the 25th century. It is interactive: "readers submit news stories that they've created based on events and items published in previous issues." The newsletter's main goal is to "create a unique meeting place for a few forward thinking people."

Editorial Interests
Ecosystems, the environment, extraterrestrials, feminism, juvenile and teen issues, mythology, nutrition, parenting, philosophy, politics, psychology, and social and world issues.
- *Contents:* News stories, lifestyle features, ocean updates, science news, and views of history, all written as reactions to previously published material. News fiction, 300–500 words. Fictional interviews, 500–1,000 words. Letters, up to 200 words.

Submission Policy: Send complete manuscript with cover letter. Include SASE. Accepts photocopies, laser-quality computer printouts, and IBM–compatible computer disks. Simultaneous submissions okay. Responds to queries in 2 months, to manuscripts in 3 months. If accepted, expect publication in 2 months.

Terms and Payment: All rights. No payment. Authors receive a free one-year subscription.

Advertising: Rates: B/W full-page, $300. Contact Gary Bryant, 206-733-7306.

TRANS Quarterly

Lee Martin, Publisher, P.O. Box 121851, Nashville, TN 37212-1851   Phone: 615-292-4172

Profile: A regional new age magazine. Published by the TRANS Editors Group, a volunteer association. Issued quarterly. Circ: 4,000. Trim size: 8.5x11. Self cover; B/W; 70 lb. recycled paper; stapled. 24 pages. Subscription cost: $10. Sample copy cost: $3.

Focus and Tips: *TRANS Quarterly* aspires to be the voice of the alternative/transformational movement in the Mid-South (middle Tennessee, southern Kentucky, and northern Alabama). Serves as a forum of expression for readers interested in evolutionary transmutation of human consciousness through spiritual upliftment, peace, holistic healing, and Universal Love. Interested in uplifting pieces and informal writing styles; avoid negativity, hearsay, inaccuracy, dryness, and sensationalism.

Editorial Interests

New age, metaphysics, holistic health, bodywork, channeling, crystals, dreams, the environment, extraterrestrials, magic, meditation, mythology, nutrition, occult, psychic phenomenon, rebirthing, yoga, spiritual martial arts, geomancy, dowsing, and breathwork.

• *Fiction:* Short-short stories, up to 1,300 words. Book excerpts, up to 600 words. Poetry, up to 250 words.

• *Nonfiction:* Features, articles, interviews and profiles, and personal experiences, up to 1,300 words. Essays, up to 650 words. Opinion pieces, up to 900 words. News items and reviews, up to 325 words. Filler, up to 200 words.

Submission Policy: Send complete manuscript with cover letter and bibliography. Include SASE. Accepts photocopies, computer printouts, and IBM-compatible WordPerfect 5.0 or 5.1 disks. No simultaneous submissions. Responds to queries in 1 month, to manuscripts in 3 months. If accepted, expect publication in 2–3 months.

Terms and Payment: One-time rights. No payment. Authors receive 1 copy of the issue.

Advertising: Rates per page: B/W, $210. Contact Lee Martin, 615-292-4172.

Trends & Predictions Analyst

Patrick O'Connell, Editor/Publisher, 5610 Essex Drive NW, Albuquerque, NM 87114-4720   Phone: 505-898-3436

Profile: An update of paranormal happenings and reviews. Published by Patrick O'Connell Associates. Issued twice a year. Circ: 200. Trim size: 8.5x11. Photocopied. 6–10 pages. Subscription cost: $4. Sample copy cost: $2. No writer's guidelines.

Focus and Tips: *Trends & Predictions Analyst* reports on paranormal activity, UFO sitings, and predictions and prophecies on the weather, economy, and social trends and patterns. Regional focus is on the Southwestern United States.

Editorial Interests

Prophecies and predictions, near-death experiences, UFO abductions, end-time predictions, astrology, channeling, crystals, dreams, ecosystems, the environment, extraterrestrials, healing and health, holistic health, inspiration, magic, meditation, metaphysics, mysticism, natural health, new age, occult, parapsychology, prayer, psychic phenomenon, social and world issues, spirituality, and witches.

• *Nonfiction:* Features, 100–400 words. Articles, 400–800 words. Interviews and profiles, 100–300 words. Essays, 400 words. Personal experiences, 200–400 words. Opinion pieces and news items, 50–100 words. Reviews, 100–200 words. Filler, 50–100 words. Dowsing department, 100–200 words. Predictions column, 50–100 words.

Submission Policy: Call first to determine current interests. Then send complete manuscript with cover letter. Include SASE. Accepts photocopies, computer printouts, and Word for Windows, Word Star, or WordPerfect disks. Simultaneous submissions okay. Reports in 1–2 months. If accepted, expect publication in 2–6 months.

Terms and Payment: No payment. Authors receive up to 50 copies of the issue.

Advertising: Rates: B/W full-page, $100. List rental available: $.04 per name; 1,000 names minimum, 5,000 names maximum. Contact Patrick O'Connell, 505-898-3436.

Tricycle

Helen Tworkov, Editor, 163 West 22nd Street, New York, NY 10011-2401   Phone: 212-645-1143, Fax: 212-645-1493

Profile: A Buddhist journal. Published by Buddhist Ray, Inc. Issued quarterly. Circ: 48,000. Trim size: 8.5x11. Color cover; B/W inside; perfect bound. 112 pages. Subscription cost: $20. Sample copy cost: $10. No writer's guidelines.

Focus and Tips: *Tricycle* is an independent forum where Buddhists from different traditions can share ideas. All submissions must be strongly related to Buddhism in some way.

Editorial Interests

Buddhism, cultural and ethnic issues, the environment, meditation, philosophy, and social and world issues.

• *Fiction:* Occasionally accepts short stories and poetry of Buddhist interest.

• *Nonfiction:* Articles, interviews, profiles, essays, and personal experiences, up to 3,000 words. In the News section is open to information relevant to Buddhism. Assigns book reviews.

Submission Policy: Query first with outline for longer pieces and interviews or profiles. For shorter pieces, send complete manuscript with cover letter. Include SASE. Accepts photocopies, computer printouts, and Macintosh Microsoft Word 3.5" disks. No simultaneous submissions. Reports in 4–6 weeks. Publication time varies.

Terms and Payment: Rights vary. Pays on publication. Rates are negotiable. Authors receive copies of the issue.

Advertising: Rates: B/W full-page, $990; 4-color back cover, $1,500. List rental available on approval. $95/M. Contact Alexandra MacDonald, 212-645-1143.

Truth Seeker

Bonnie Lange, Editor, P.O. Box 2872, San Diego, CA 92112-2872   Phone: 619-239-9043

Profile: A journal of philosophical and religious thought. Established in 1873. Issued quarterly. Circ: N/A. Trim size: 8.5x11. Glossy color cover; B/W inside; saddle stitched. 40 pages. Subscription cost: $20. Sample copy cost: $5. Writer's guidelines available with SASE.

Focus and Tips: *Truth Seeker* is a forum for independent and free thought in the areas of religion, philosophy, and politics. Readers are those who choose to think for themselves, actually as well as potentially. "Let the *Truth Seeker* be successful in disseminating light and truth and in dispelling the fogs of superstition, bigotry, and error."

Editorial Interests

Philosophy, religion, politics, cultural and ethnic concerns, gay and lesbian interests, social and world issues, and women's issues.

• *Fiction:* Occasionally accepts short-short stories, up to 1,500 words, and poetry.

• *Nonfiction:* Articles, interviews, opinion pieces, and book reviews, up to 1,500 words.

Submission Policy: Send complete manuscript with cover letter. Single-space all material. Include SASE. Accepts photocopies, computer printouts, and IBM or Macintosh 3.5" or 5.25" disks. Simultaneous submissions okay if noted. Reports in 1–6 months. If accepted, expect publication in 2–6 months.

Terms and Payment: Authors retain rights. Pays on publication. $75 per 1–4 page articles. Authors receive 5 copies of the issue.

Advertising: Offers free advertising space for cause-oriented projects or products. Contact Bonnie Lange, 619-239-9043.

Turning the Tide

Michael Novick, Editor, P.O. Box 1990, Burbank, CA 91507   Phone: 310-288-5003, Fax: 818-848-2680

Profile: An anti-racist journal. Published by People Against Racist Terror, a nonprofit organization. Issued bimonthly. Circ: 7,500. Trim size: 11x14. Newsprint; folded. 24+ pages. Subscription cost: $10. Sample copy cost: $2. No writer's guidelines.

Focus and Tips: *Turning the Tide* is a journal of anti-racist activism, research, and education. It seeks material dedicated to opposing racism, sexism, and injustice. Avoid being too flowery or rhetorical. Instead, be hard-hitting and factual. Most, but not all, readers are from the Southern California region.

Editorial Interests

Anti-racism, social justice, Native Americans, Hawaiian sovereignty, prisons, the environment, feminism, gay and lesbian issues, lifestyle, men's issues, philosophy, politics, social and world issues, and women's issues.

• *Fiction:* Short-short stories and poetry, up to 1,000 words.

• *Nonfiction:* Features, articles, interviews, profiles, essays, personal experiences, opinion pieces, news items, and reviews, 1,000–2,500 words. Accepts filler.

Submission Policy: Query with outline. Include SASE. Accepts photocopies, computer printouts, faxes, and 3.5" IBM Microsoft Word double-density disks. Simultaneous submissions okay. Reports in 1–2 weeks. If accepted, expected publication in 2–4 months.

Terms and Payment: One-time rights. No payment. Authors receive 5 or more copies of the issue.

Turning Wheel

Susan Moon, Editor, P.O. Box 4650, Berkeley, CA 94704   Phone: 510-525-8596, Fax: 510-525-7973

Profile: The membership journal of the Buddhist Peace Fellowship. Published by the Buddhist Peace Fellowship, a nonprofit organization. Issued quarterly. Circ: 3,000. Trim size: 8.5x11. Self cover; B/W; saddle stitched. 48 pages. Subscription cost: $35. Sample copy cost: $5. No writer's guidelines.

Focus and Tips: *Turning Wheel* publishes material that promotes peace, social justice, and environmental awareness from a Buddhist perspective. Of special interest are articles about social change that are grounded in personal experience, that are helpful and encouraging to others, and that include some broad analytical perspective. Avoid academic styles, jargon, and flowery lyricism.

Editorial Interests

Buddhism, peace work, social justice, ecosystems, the environment, meditation, philosophy, politics, and spirituality.

• *Fiction:* Accepts short-short stories and poetry.

• *Nonfiction:* Features, articles, interviews, profiles, essays, personal experiences, opinion pieces, and reviews, 450–2,500 words.

Submission Policy: Send complete manuscript with cover letter. Include SASE. Accepts photocopies, computer printouts, and Macintosh disks. Simultaneous submissions okay if noted. Responds to queries in 1 month, to manuscripts in 3 months. If accepted, expect publication in 3 months.

Terms and Payment: One-time rights. No payment. Authors receive 2 copies of the issue.

Advertising: Rates: B/W full-page, $250. Contact Lewis Aframi, 510-525-8596.

Other Interests: Offers workshops, study groups, meetings, lectures, etc. Notification of events are sent to members of the Buddhist Peace Fellowship.

UFO Review

Timothy Green Beckley, Publisher, 11 East 30th Street, Suite 4R, New York, NY 10016   Phone: 212-685-4080

Profile: A UFO tabloid. Published by Global Communications. Issued quarterly. Circ: 100,000+. Trim size: Tabloid. Distributed nationally on newsstands. Sample copy cost: $5. Writer's guidelines available with SASE.

Focus and Tips: *UFO Review* is one of the many UFO/new age publications put out by Global Communications. It serves as a promotional vehicle for other GC products and features articles and timely findings on UFOs. Companion publications include *UFO Universe, Unsolved UFO Sightings, Unexplainable Universe*, and *Inner Light*.

Editorial Interests

UFOs and extraterrestrials.

• *Nonfiction:* Short articles. Accepts book excerpts for promotional purposes.

Submission Policy: Send complete manuscript with author biography and photo. Include SASE. Accepts photocopies and computer printouts. Allow 4–5 month lead-time.

Terms and Payment: One-time rights and reprint rights. Pays on publication. Articles, $25–$50.

Advertising: Rates: full-page, $600; half-page, $375; quarter-page, $250. Classified ads, $1 per word with a 20-word minimum. List rental available: $70/M. Contact Tim Beckley, 212-685-4080.

UFO Universe

Timothy Green Beckley, Publisher, 11 East 30th Street, Suite 4R, New York, NY 10016   Phone: 212-685-4080

Profile: A magazine of ufology. Published by Global Communications. Issued quarterly. Circ: 100,000+. Trim size: 8.5x11. Glossy cover; spot color; saddle stitched. Distributed nationally on newsstands. Sample copy cost: $5. Writer's guidelines available with SASE.

Focus and Tips: *UFO Universe* is one of the many UFO/new age publications put out by Global Communications. It is devoted to tales of close encounters, alien abductions, the philosophy of the Space Brothers, and strange events that science cannot explain. Avoid rehashed pieces, old UFO cases, and fiction. Companion publications include *Unsolved UFO Sightings, Unexplainable Universe, Inner Light*, and *UFO Review*.

Editorial Interests

UFOs, extraterrestrials, and related subjects.

• *Nonfiction:* Features that report recent case studies or focus on one aspect of the UFO enigma, 2,500–3,500 words. Accepts book excerpts for promotional purposes.

• *Illustrations:* B/W spot drawings, full-page illustrations, and cover art. Accepts B/W and color photographs.

Submission Policy: Send complete manuscript with author biography and photo. Include SASE. Accepts photocopies and computer printouts. Allow 4–5 month lead-time.

Terms and Payment: One-time rights and reprint rights. Pays on publication. Features, $100. Features with photos or artwork, $125. Shorter pieces, $50. Illustrations, $25–$50. Cover art, $200. Photos, $25.

Advertising: Rates: full-page, $500; half-page, $300; quarter-page, $200. List rental available: $70/M. Contact Tim Beckley, 212-685-4080.

Unexplainable Universe

Timothy Green Beckley, Publisher, 11 East 30th Street, Suite 4R, New York, NY 10016   Phone: 212-685-4080

Profile: A magazine of unusual phenomenon. Published by Global Communications. Issued quarterly. Circ: N/A. Trim size: 8.5x11. Glossy cover; spot color; saddle stitched. Distributed nationally on newsstands. Sample copy cost: $5. Writer's guidelines available with SASE.

Focus and Tips: *Unexplainable Universe* is one of the many UFO/new age publications put out by Global Communications. It focuses on unusual or psychic phenomenon such as sea monsters, life after death, ghosts, angels, mystical experiences, UFOs, and ancient mysteries. While similar, it is more new age in approach than its companion publication, *UFO Universe*. Other companion publications include *Unsolved UFO Sightings, Inner Light*, and *UFO Review*.

Editorial Interests

Psychic phenomenon, unusual experiences, parapsychology, extraterrestrials, folklore, mysticism, new age, and UFOs.

• *Nonfiction:* Hard-hitting features, 2,500–3,500 words. Accepts book excerpts for promotional purposes.

• *Illustrations:* B/W spot drawings, full-page illustrations, and cover art. Accepts B/W and color photographs.

Submission Policy: Send complete manuscript with author biography and photo. Include SASE. Accepts photocopies and computer printouts. Allow 4–5 month lead-time.

Terms and Payment: One-time rights and reprint rights. Pays on publication. Features, $100. Features with photos or artwork, $125. Shorter pieces, $50. Illustrations, $25–$50. Cover art, $200. Photos, $25.

Advertising: List rental available: $70/M. Contact Tim Beckley, 212-685-4080.

The Unexplained Magazine

J. Jensen, Editor, P.O. Box 16790, Encino, CA 91416-6790   Phone: 818-705-8865

Profile: A publication of psychic phenomenon. Issued bimonthly. Circ: 10,000. Perfect bound.
Focus and Tips: *The Unexplained Magazine* publishes articles on new age topics and unusual phenomenon. It prefers factual pieces with accompanying photographs. No fantasy.
Editorial Interests
Psychic and unusual phenomenon, new age, astrology, bodywork, channeling, crystals, extraterrestrials, healing, holistic health, magic, meditation, metaphysics, mysticism, natural health, occult, parapsychology, self-help, and spirituality.
• *Nonfiction:* Fact-based articles. Query for word length.
• *Illustrations:* Photos to accompany articles.
Submission Policy: Send complete manuscript with cover letter. Include SASE. Accepts photocopies, computer printouts, and ASCII disks. Simultaneous submissions okay. Responds to queries in 1 month, to manuscripts in 2 months. If accepted, expect publication in 6 months.
Terms and Payment: Pays $.05 per word.

The Unforgettable Fire

Jordan O'Neill, Editor, P.O. Box 388, Lyndhurst, NJ 07071

Profile: A newsletter of women's issues. Issued twice a year. Circ: 3,000. Trim size: 8.5x11. B/W; stapled. 30–40 pages. Subscription cost: $5. Sample copy cost: $2. Writer's guidelines available with SASE.
Focus and Tips: *The Unforgettable Fire* publishes writings by, for, and about women. Literary in nature, it is geared toward covering current social, political, and feminist issues. Materials should affirm women and women's cultures and beliefs and reflect multicultural perspectives whenever possible. While it does not exclude male writers, it is admittedly partial to women's work. Not interested in material that attacks race, specific creeds, sexual preference, gender, or disability. Avoid sending writing that contains any type of violence.
Editorial Interests
Women's issues, feminism, gay and lesbian concerns, inspiration, and social and world issues.
• *Fiction:* Short-short stories, up to 1,500 words. Poetry, up to 5 poems per submission.
• *Nonfiction:* Encourages essays, personal experiences, and opinion pieces, up to 1,500 words, as well as book reviews, 500–1,000 words. Accepts features, articles, interviews, and profiles, up to 1,500 words.
Submission Policy: Query with writing samples or send complete manuscript with cover letter and bibliography. Include SASE. Accepts photocopies and computer printouts. Simultaneous submissions okay. Reports in 3–6 weeks. If accepted, expect publication within 6 months.
Terms and Payment: Rights vary. No payment. Occasionally offers subscriptions or exchanges. Authors receive up to 3 copies of the issue.
Advertising: Rates: B/W full-page, $80; half-page, $40; third-page, $35. Classifieds, $.10 per word with a 20-word minimum. Contact Jordan O'Neill.

Unique Magazine

Robert Starky, Editor, 1147 Manhattan Avenue, Suite 43, Manhattan Beach, CA 90266   Phone/Fax: 818-845-2656

Profile: A magazine with an extraterrestrial focus. Issued quarterly. Circ: 30,000. Trim size: 8.5x11. Stapled. Subscription cost: $20. Sample copy cost: $4.95.
Focus and Tips: *Unique Magazine* is for "Earth-bound extraterrestrials." Its interests range from spirituality to the environment to the arts. Be unique, positive, and non-promotional. Avoid conspiracy theories, paranoia, and "scary stories."
Editorial Interests
Extraterrestrials, spirituality, the environment, the arts, animals, astrology, mysticism, and mythology.
• *Nonfiction:* Inspirational articles, unique interviews and profiles, and personal experiences, 2,000–3,000 words.
Submission Policy: Send complete manuscript with cover letter. Include SASE. Accepts computer printouts and faxes. No simultaneous submissions. Reports in 1 month. If accepted, expect publication in 3–6 months.
Terms and Payment: No payment.
Advertising: Accepts advertising. Contact Robert Starky, 818-845-2656.

Unity Magazine

Philip White, Editor, Unity Village, MO 64065   Phone/Fax: 816-524-3550

Profile: A magazine of metaphysical Christianity. Published by Unity School of Christianity. Established in 1889. Issued monthly. Circ: 120,000. Trim size: 5.5x8.5. Glossy color cover; 4-color; recycled paper; saddle stitched. 80 pages. Subscription cost: $10.95. Sample copy cost: Free. Writer's guidelines available with SASE.

Focus and Tips: *Unity* focuses on Christian metaphysics and successful living and serves those who have made Unity their primary path of spiritual growth. All quotes must be referenced with author, source, and page numbers.

Editorial Interests

Christian metaphysics, healing, holistic health, inspiration, meditation, philosophy, psychology, religion, and spirituality.

• *Nonfiction:* Features, 1,500 words. Articles, interviews, profiles, and personal experiences, 1,000–1,800 words. Essays, 800–1,200 words. Opinion pieces, 500–1,000 words. Reviews, 500 words. Filler, 250–500 words.

Submission Policy: Send complete manuscript with cover letter, bibliography, and resume. Include SASE. Accepts computer printouts and 3.5" computer disks. No simultaneous submissions. Reports in 1–3 months. If accepted, expect publication in 6–12 months.

Terms and Payment: First North American serial rights. Pays on acceptance. $.20 per word. Authors receive 4 copies of the issue.

Unsolved UFO Sightings

Timothy Green Beckley, Publisher, 11 East 30th Street, Suite 4R, New York, NY 10016   Phone: 212-685-4080

Profile: A magazine of ufology. Published by Global Communications. Issued quarterly. Circ: 100,000+. Trim size: 8.5x11. Glossy cover; spot color; saddle stitched. Distributed nationally on newsstands. Sample copy cost: $5. Writer's guidelines available with SASE.

Focus and Tips: *Unsolved UFO Sightings* is one of the many UFO/new age publications put out by Global Communications. It is devoted to tales of close encounters, alien abductions, the philosophy of the Space Brothers, and strange events that science cannot explain. While it does accept original articles, most material is reprinted from its companion publication, *UFO Universe*. Other companion publications include *Unexplainable Universe*, *Inner Light*, and *UFO Review*.

Editorial Interests

UFOs, extraterrestrials, and related subjects.

• *Nonfiction:* Features that report recent case studies or focus on one aspect of the UFO enigma, 2,500–3,500 words. Accepts book excerpts for promotional purposes.

• *Illustrations:* B/W spot drawings, full-page illustrations, and cover art. Accepts B/W and color photographs.

Submission Policy: Send complete manuscript with author biography and photo. Include SASE. Accepts photocopies and computer printouts. Allow 4–5 month lead-time.

Terms and Payment: One-time rights or second North American serial rights for reprints. Pays on publication. Original material: features, $100; features with photos or artwork, $125; shorter pieces, $50; illustrations, $25–$50; cover art, $200; photos, $25. Reprinted material, pays 50% of original price.

Advertising: List rental available: $70/M. Contact Tim Beckley, 212-685-4080.

Uptown Express

Sharon Ownchyld, Production Editor, 3406 Audubon Place, Houston, TX 77006   Phone: 713-520-7237

Profile: A new age magazine. Published by Up and Out Communications. Issued monthly. Circ: 32,000. Trim size: 8.5x11. 50 pages. Subscription cost: $12. Sample copy cost: Free. Writer's guidelines available with SASE.

Focus and Tips: *Uptown Express* is open to a variety of new age topics, especially self-help, spirituality, and holistic health and living.

Editorial Interests

New age, astrology, bodywork, channeling, crystals, cultural and ethnic concerns, dreams, ecosystems, the environment, folklore, gay and lesbian issues, healing, health, holistic health, inspiration, juvenile and teen issues, lifestyle, magic, meditation, men's issues, metaphysics, mysticism, mythology, natural health, nutrition, occult, parapsychology, parenting, politics, prayer, psychic phenomenon, psychology, rebirthing, recovery, regional issues, relationships, religion, self-help, seniors, social and world issues, spirituality, witches, women's issues, and yoga.

• *Nonfiction:* Features, articles on local issues and personalities, interviews with self-help authors, and personal experiences, 1,500–2,000 words.

Submission Policy: Send complete manuscript. Include SASE. Accepts photocopies, computer printouts, and Macintosh Pagemaker disks. Simultaneous submissions okay. Reports in several months. If accepted, expect publication in 1 month.

Terms and Payment: All rights. Will pay on occasion. Authors receive copies of the issue.

Advertising: Rates: B/W full-page, $1,058; 4-color full-page, $1,158. Contact Sharon Ownchyld.

Vegetarian Journal

Charles Stahler, Editor, P.O. Box 1463, Baltimore, MD 21203   Phone: 410-366-VEGE

Profile: A vegetarian magazine. Published by The Vegetarian Resource Group, a nonprofit organization that educates the pubic on vegetarianism and related issues. Issued bimonthly. Circ: 25,000. Trim size: 8.25x11. Glossy color cover; spot color inside; saddle stitched. 36 pages. Subscription cost: $20. Sample copy cost: $3. Writer's guidelines available with SASE.

Focus and Tips: *Vegetarian Journal* is a practical magazine for those interested in health, ecology, and ethics. All material must relate directly to vegetarianism. Seeks practical, scientific, and unique material that supports and informs individuals living a vegetarian lifestyle. Professionals are encouraged to respond: Nutrition articles must be written by a dietician or doctor; environment art pieces by a scientist. Not interested in graphic animal-abuse stories.

Editorial Interests

Vegetarianism, animal rights, ethics, lifestyle, cultural and ethnic issues, ecosystems, the environment, health, holistic health, natural health, nutrition, parenting, philosophy, politics, and social and world issues.

• *Nonfiction:* Articles on vegetarianism, nutritional articles by professionals, and environmental art articles by scientists, 2–3 manuscript pages.

Submission Policy: Query first with outline. Include SASE. No simultaneous submissions. Reports in 2 weeks. If accepted, expect publication in 6 months.

Terms and Payment: First North American serial rights. Pays on acceptance. Rates vary.

Advertising: List rental available.

Other Interests: Sponsors an annual Vegetarian Essay Contest for children 18 years and under. Deadline: May 1. Prize: $50 bond. Send an SASE for guidelines. Also Vegetarian Summer Gatherings at various locations during the Summer. Contact Charles Stahler.

Vegetarian Times

Toni Apgar, Editorial Director, 1140 Lake Street, Suite 500, Oak Park, IL 60303   Phone: 708-848-8100, Fax: 708-848-8175

Profile: A magazine of vegetarian cuisine. Published by Cowles Magazine Company. Issued monthly. Circ: 310,000. Trim size: 8.5x11. Glossy color cover; 4-color; saddle stitched. 120 pages. Subscription cost: $23.95. Sample copy cost: $4. Writer's guidelines available with SASE.

Focus and Tips: *Vegetarian Times* is an authority on healthful eating and a healthful lifestyle. It offers readers accurate, timely, thought-provoking information and tasty, healthful, attractive dishes. Contributions should be well-researched. Avoid "Why I Became a Vegetarian" stories and poetry.

Editorial Interests

Vegetarianism, holistic and natural health, nutrition, lifestyle, bodywork, cultural and ethnic issues, ecosystems, the environment, healing, and health.

• *Nonfiction:* Features, up to 4,000 words. Recipe articles, 400 word introduction with 6–8 recipes. Celebrity profiles and restaurant reviews, 200 words. News items, up to 500 words. Reviews of vegetarian cookbooks. Departments include Health by Choice and Answering Machine, 1,500 words.

Submission Policy: Query with outline and writing samples or send complete manuscript with cover letter and bibliography. Include SASE. Accepts photocopies, computer printouts, faxes, and WordPerfect or Microsoft Word disks. No simultaneous submissions. Reports in 1 month. If accepted, expect publication in at least 3 months.

Terms and Payment: All rights. Pays on publication. News pieces, $125–$150. Features and articles, rates vary. Authors receive 5 copies of the issue.

Advertising: Accepts advertising. List rental available.

Vegetarian Voice

Jennie Collura, Senior Editor, P.O. Box 72, Dolgeville, NY 13329   Phone: 518-568-7970, Fax: 518-568-7636

Profile: A vegetarian newsmagazine. Published by the North American Vegetarian Society (NAVS), a nonprofit organization. Issued quarterly. Circ: 9,000. Trim size: 8x10.5. Color cover; spot color inside; saddle stitched. 40 pages. Subscription cost: $18 including NAVS membership. Sample copy cost: $3. Writer's guidelines available with SASE.

Focus and Tips: *Vegetarian Voice* is dedicated to promoting the vegetarian way of life. It offers its vegetarian and non-vegetarian audience analysis of relevant issues including health, nutrition, and animal rights, as well as total-vegetarian recipes. Fresh ways to inspire and inform new and veteran vegetarians are welcome. Not interested in specific healing modalities such as acupressure or specific herbs. Do not send recipes that contain dairy products, eggs, or honey. Appreciates tight writing.

Editorial Interests

Vegetarianism, environment, holistic and natural health, healing, nutrition, new age, parenting, social and world issues, animal rights, and gardening.

• *Nonfiction:* Cover feature, 1,600 words. Articles, 400–1,600 words. Interviews and profiles, 1,200 words. News items, 100–400 words. Book and restaurant reviews, 800 words. Occasionally publishes essays and personal experience pieces.

Submission Policy: Query with outline or send complete manuscript with cover letter. Include SASE. Accepts photocopies, computer printouts, Macintosh MS Word or MacWrite 3.5" disks, and faxes. Simultaneous submissions okay if noted. Reports in 1 month. If accepted, expect publication within 3–6 months.

Terms and Payment: One-time rights. No payment. Authors receive copies of the issue.
Advertising: No advertising.
Other Interests: NAVS offers Vegetarian Summerfest, an annual 5-day conference on health, environment, animal rights, etc. Mid-July; location varies. Accommodations and total-vegetarian meals available. Contact NAVS, 518-568-7970.

Veggie Life

Margo Lemas, Editor, 1041 Shary Circle, Concord, CA 94518   Phone: 510-671-9852, Fax: 510-671-0692

Profile: A vegetarian journal. Published by EGW Publishing Co. Issued bimonthly. Circ: 200,000. Trim size: 8.5x11. Glossy color cover; full-color; saddle stitched. Subscription cost: $19.97. Sample copy cost: $2.95. Writer's guidelines available with SASE.
Focus and Tips: *Veggie Life* offers practical articles and recipes on meatless foods and cooking for those who embrace a vegetarian lifestyle. Avoid religious or dogmatic writing.
Editorial Interests
Vegetarianism, health, natural health, nutrition, lifestyle, and gardening.
• *Nonfiction:* Articles, 2–3 manuscript pages.
Submission Policy: Query with outline. Include SASE. Accepts photocopies, computer printouts, Macintosh computer disks, and faxes. No simultaneous submissions. Reports in 4–6 weeks. Publication time varies.
Terms and Payment: All rights. Payment varies.
Advertising: Accepts advertising.

Venture Inward

A. Robert Smith, Editor, 67th Street and Atlantic Avenue, Virginia Beach, VA 23451   Phone: 804-428-3588, Fax: 804-422-4631

Profile: A membership magazine based on the readings of Edgar Cayce. Published by Association for Research and Enlightenment, Inc., a nonprofit organization. Issued bimonthly. Circ: 35,000. Trim size: 8.5x11. Glossy color cover; 4-color; saddle stitched. Subscription included in membership. Writer's guidelines available with SASE.
Focus and Tips: *Venture Inward* seeks to inspire, challenge, and broaden the horizons of its readers in the areas of parapsychology, holistic health, and spiritual development. Read by members and potential members of the Association for Research and Enlightenment (A.R.E.), founded in 1931 by Edgar Cayce, the popular psychic. Avoid fiction, poetry, and preachy articles.
Editorial Interests
Psychic phenomenon, parapsychology, dreams, healing, holist health, meditation, metaphysics, mysticism, new age, philosophy, prayer, relationships, self-help, spirituality, and yoga.
• *Fiction:* Children's stories with a spiritual flavor or message, up to 1,500 words.
• *Nonfiction:* Features, articles, interviews, and profiles, 1,000–4,000 words. Essays and opinion pieces, up to 1,000 words. Turning points and personal mystical experiences, up to 1,000 words. Accepts book reviews. Considers guest writers for Viewpoint column.
Submission Policy: Send complete manuscript with cover letter. Include SASE. Accepts photocopies, computer printouts, Macintosh MS Word 3.5" disks, and faxes. Simultaneous submissions okay. Reports in 1–2 months. If accepted, expect publication within 6–12 months.
Terms and Payment: One-time rights. Pays on publication. $30–$300 per piece. Authors receive 2 copies of the issue.
Other Interests: A.R.E. is associated with Atlantic University and the Reilly School of Massotherapy. It sponsors a summer conference at Virginia Beach and other conferences year-round. For conference catalogue or more information, contact Rebecca Ghittino, 804-428-3588.

Village Voice

Editor, 36 Cooper Square, New York, NY 10003   Phone: 212-475-3300, Fax: 212-473-8944

Profile: A newspaper of progressive politics. Issued weekly. Circ: 160,000. Trim size: Tabloid. Newsprint; folded. 150 pages. Subscription cost: N/A. Sample copy cost: $1.
Focus and Tips: *Village Voice* offers commentary on politics, current social issues, and the arts with a progressive, distinctively leftist slant.
Editorial Interests
Politics, the arts, social and world issues, gay and lesbian interests, men's issues, and the occult.
• *Nonfiction:* Features, articles, interviews, profiles, essays, personal experiences, and opinion pieces, lengths vary.
Submission Policy: Query with outline. Call to check on interest and submit to appropriate editor. Accepts photocopies, computer printouts, and faxes. No simultaneous submissions.
Terms and Payment: Payment varies. Authors receive copies of the issue.
Other Interests: Internships available. Contact Frank Ruscitti, 212-475-3300.

Visions Magazine

Kate Joy Moser and Michael Moser, Co-publishers, 24 Kern Drive, Perkasie, PA 18944   Phone: 215-249-9190, Fax: 215-249-9193

Profile: A regional new age magazine. Established in 1988. Issued monthly. Circ: 15,000. Trim size: 8.5x11. Color cover; B/W inside; recycled paper; saddle stitched. 60 pages. Subscription cost: Free. Sample copy cost: Free. Writer's guidelines available with SASE.

Focus and Tips: *Visions Magazine* is an informational new age publication that reaches readers in Eastern Pennsylvania, New Jersey, and Delaware. Articles should reflect the magazine's interests and be informative and entertaining rather than technical or clinical. "Write personally, as though talking one-on-one with a reader." No promotional or advertorial pieces.

Editorial Interests

New age, regional issues, social justice, human rights, animal rights, children's rights, peace, stress management, gay and lesbian issues, healing, holistic health, inspiration, men's issues, metaphysics, psychology, spirituality, and women's issues.

• *Fiction:* Occasionally accepts short stories, no length restrictions.

• *Nonfiction:* Informative, educational, and entertaining articles, personal experiences, and opinion pieces, 750–1,000 words.

Submission Policy: Send complete manuscript with cover letter. Include SASE. Prefers IBM 3.5" or 5.25" disks with hard copy. Accepts photocopies and computer printouts. No simultaneous submissions. Reporting and publication times vary.

Terms and Payment: Authors retain rights. Credit requested for reprints. No payment. Authors receive 10 copies of the issues.

Advertising: Rates: B/W full-page, $400–$500; 4-color back cover, $600. Offers a 1% discount per month for consecutive months. Contact Kate Moser, 215-249-9190.

The Voice and The Vision

Jacalyn Mindell, Publisher, P.O. Box 4763, Topeka, KS 66604   Phone/Fax: 913-233-9066

Profile: A magazine exploring racial and social issues. Published by Content Communications. Issued quarterly. Circ: 1,000. Trim size: 8x10. Newsprint; stapled. 48 pages. Subscription cost: $19.95. Sample copy cost: $5. No writer's guidelines.

Focus and Tips: *The Voice and The Vision* serves as a guide to understanding issues of race, class, color, and ethnicity for a general audience that includes educators, business people, and the media. It is especially interested in subjects that are "off the beaten path, undercovered, or misunderstood." Prefers issue-oriented stories that include information that readers can apply to their own lives. Avoid mirroring mainstream media coverage.

Editorial Interests

Racial and ethnic issues, politics, psychology, relationships, and social and world issues.

• *Nonfiction:* Features, articles, interviews, profiles, essays, personal experiences, opinion pieces, news items, reviews, and filler. Word lengths should be based on subjects covered. Columns: Standpoint, 250–500 words; One Way or Another, 200–400 words.

Submission Policy: Send complete manuscript with cover letter, resume, and clips. Include SASE. Accepts photocopies, computer printouts, IBM-compatible disks, and faxes. Simultaneous submissions okay. Reports in 2 months. If accepted, expect publication in 3 months.

Terms and Payment: First North American serial rights. Pays on publication. Up to $75 per piece. Authors receive at least 2 copies of the issue.

Advertising: Rates: B/W full-page, $100. Contact Jacalyn Mindell, 913-233-9066.

Voices of Women

Lora Hall, Editor, 602 Woodbine Terrace, Towson, MD 21204   Phone: 410-337-5525, Fax: 410-339-7716

Profile: A resource guide for women. Issued quarterly. Circ: 20,000. Trim size: 10x16. Color cover; B/W newsprint inside; folded. 24 pages. Subscription cost: $15. Sample copy cost: $2. Writer's guidelines available with SASE.

Focus and Tips: *Voice of Women* seeks to empower women and inspire them to explore the female experience in our society, affirm feminine values, and offer networking opportunities. Its companion publication, *Baltimore Resources*, is a health and wellness newsmagazine. Writers are encouraged to call for topics of interest.

Editorial Interests

Women's issues, feminism, bodywork, cultural and ethnic issues, dreams, ecosystems, the environment, folklore, healing, health, holistic health, inspiration, lifestyle, meditation, mysticism, natural health, nutrition, parenting, philosophy, prayer, recovery, relationships, self-help, seniors, social and world issues, spirituality, witches, and yoga.

• *Nonfiction:* Women-empowering, research-based articles and personal experiences, 2,500 words and up.

Submission Policy: Query with outline and writing samples. Include SASE. Accepts photocopies, computer printouts, Macintosh disks, and faxes. Simultaneous submissions okay if competing markets are identified. Reports immediately. Publication time varies.

Terms and Payment: One-time rights. Pays on publication. $100–$150 per piece. Authors receive as many copies of the issue as requested.

Other Interests: Sponsors several conferences, expos, fairs, and weekend spirit circles. For more information, contact Lora Hall, 410-337-5525.

WE: Walk-ins for Evolution

Liz Nelson, Editor, P.O. Box 120633, St. Paul, MN 55112

Profile: A new age specialty newsletter. Published by WE Unlimited. Issued quarterly. Circ: N/A. Trim size: 8.5x11. Self cover; folded. 16–20 pages. Subscription cost: $12.50. Sample copy cost: $3.50. Writer's guidelines available with SASE.
Focus and Tips: *WE* is "a vehicle to assist walk-ins as they establish their own identities and paths. It serves as a connecting link to each other, the new age community, and those interested in the walk-in phenomenon." Focus is only on the walk-in and the walk-in phenomenon. No general new age material—only as it applies to walk-ins.
Editorial Interests
Walk-ins phenomenon.
• *Fiction:* Short stories and short-short stories, 600–9,000 words.
• *Nonfiction:* Features, interviews, and profiles, 900 words. Articles, 600 words. Essays, 200 words. Personal experiences, 300 words. Opinion pieces and reviews, 100 words. News items, 50 words. Filler, 25–50 words. Research pieces, 600–900 words. Channeled material, 600 words.
• *Illustrations:* Cartoons.
Submission Policy: Query first. Include SASE. Accepts photocopies and computer printouts. No simultaneous submissions. Responds to queries in 2 weeks, to manuscripts in 4–6 months. If accepted, expect publication in 1 month.
Terms and Payment: First World rights and reprint rights. No payment. Authors receive 5 copies of the issue.
Advertising: Rates: B/W, $100. Contact Liz Nelson.

Welcome Home

Laura Jones, Co-editor, 8310A Old Courthouse Road, Vienna, VA 22182   Phone: 703-827-5903, Fax: 703-790-8587

Profile: A publication for at-home mothers. Published by Mothers at Home, a nonprofit organization. Issued monthly. Circ: 15,000. Trim size: 6x9. Self cover; 2-color; saddle stitched. 32 pages. Subscription cost: $18. Sample copy cost: $2. Writer's guidelines available with SASE.
Focus and Tips: *Welcome Home* is for "the smart woman who has actively chosen to devote her exceptional skills and good mind to the nurturing of her family." It serves to put mothers in touch with mothers and depends on readers to fill its pages with humor, advice, information, and insights relevant to being a mother at home. Looks for upbeat, well-written, unique material, "different in topic, approach, or expression from what is currently available in other publications." Not interested in particular political or religious views. No attacks on mothers working outside the home.
Editorial Interests
Concerns of at-home mothers such as family life, health and safety, stress management, making money at home, maintaining professional skills, isolation, home management, parenting, marriage, the teen years, education, and support groups.
• *Poetry:* Poems on mothering and children, 8–20 lines.
• *Nonfiction:* Features on mothering and family life. Health and safety articles. Essays on public policy regarding families. Personal experience pieces on mothering. All 500–1,500 words. Short filler on family life, 500–600 words.
• *Illustrations:* Photos, cartoons, cover art, illustrations, borders, and filler art. Prefers pen-and-ink drawings.
Submission Policy: Send complete manuscript with cover letter, bibliography if appropriate, and author biography. Include SASE. Accepts computer printouts. Simultaneous submissions okay. Reports in 6 weeks. If accepted, expect publication in 1 year.
Terms and Payment: Authors retain rights. Pays on publication. First-time unsolicited pieces, gift payment of subscription or book. Subsequent features, $20 and gift subscription. Short poems, $15. Long poems, $20. Authors receive 3 copies of the issue.

Wheel of Dharma

Elson Snow, Editor, 1710 Octavia Street, San Francico, CA 94109

Profile: A Buddhist publication. Published by Buddhist Churches of America. Issued monthly. Circ: 13,000. Newsprint. 12 pages. Subscription cost: $5. Sample copy cost: Free. No writer's guidelines.
Focus and Tips: *Wheel of Dharma* is a religious publication of institutional and general feature articles on Mahayana Buddhism and Judo Shizhu. Sole focus is Buddhism—avoid comparative religion unless within Mahayana Buddhism.
Editorial Interests
Buddhism.
• *Nonfiction:* Features and essays on Buddhist history and social issues. No length restrictions. Accepts book reviews.

• *Illustrations:* Accepts photos and line drawings.
Submission Policy: Send complete manuscript with SASE. Accepts photocopies and computer printouts. No simultaneous submissions. Reports in 1 month. If accepted, expect publication in 2 months.
Terms and Payment: One-time rights. No payment. Authors receive 2 copies of the issue.

Whispering Wind Magazine

Jack Heriard, Editor, 8009 Wales Street, New Orleans, LA 70126   Fax: 504-246-2876

Profile: A Native American publication. Published by Written Heritage. Issued bimonthly. Circ: 8,500. Trim size: 8.5x11. Color and B/W; 60 lb. glossy paper; stapled. 40–60 pages. Subscription cost: $18. Sample copy cost: $5. Writer's guidelines available with SASE.
Focus and Tips: *Whispering Wind Magazine* explores Native American culture, history, arts, and related topics.
Editorial Interests
Native American culture, lifestyle, history, and folklore.
• *Nonfiction:* Articles and historical and cultural essays, up to 6,000 words. Personal experiences, 250 words. Book and music reviews, 100–150 words. Departments include Noteworthy, news relevant to Native Americans, 50–150 words.
Submission Policy: Send complete manuscript with cover letter and bibliography. Include SASE. Prefers IBM or ASCII computer disk submissions. Accepts photocopies, computer printouts, and faxes. No simultaneous submissions. Reports in 1 year. If accepted, expect publication in 1 year.
Terms and Payment: One-time rights. No payment. Authors receive 1–10 copies of the issue depending on article length.
Advertising: Rates: B/W full-page; $335; 4-color full-page, $835. Contact Darlene Heriard, 504-246-3742. List rental available. Contact Stan Madyda at D. J. Associates, 203-431-8777.
Other Interests: Sponsors a Native American art week.

Whole Earth Review

Ruth Kissane, Editor, P.O. Box 38, Salsolito, CA 94966   Phone: 415-332-1716, Fax: 415-332-3110

Profile: A publication of personal and social change. Published by the nonprofit Point Foundation. Issued quarterly. Circ: 40,000. Trim size: 8.5x11. B/W; perfect bound. 128 pages. Subscription cost: $20. Sample copy cost: $7. Writer's guidelines available with SASE.
Focus and Tips: *Whole Earth Review* offers tools and ideas for self-improvement and positive social transformation—environmentally, spiritually, emotionally, and physically. "Write about something that you love, and that others can use as a tool."
Editorial Interests
Self-help, social issues and change, bodywork, cultural and ethnic concerns, dreams, ecosystems, extraterrestrials, feminism, folklore, gay and lesbian issues, healing, health, holistic health, inspirational, children's and teen issues, magic, meditation, men's issues, metaphysics, mysticism, mythology, natural health, new age, nutrition, parenting, philosophy, politics, prayer, psychic phenomenon, psychology, recovery, regional issues, relationships, religion, seniors, spirituality, witches, women's issues, and yoga.
• *Fiction:* Short stories, short-short stories, drama, book excerpts, genre fiction, and poetry, no length restrictions.
• *Nonfiction:* Articles, interviews, profiles, personal experiences, opinion pieces, and news items, no length restrictions. Book, music, and video reviews, 150 words. Accepts jokes and cartoons.
Submission Policy: Send complete manuscript with cover letter. Include SASE. Accepts photocopies, computer printouts, Macintosh Word disks, and faxes. Simultaneous submissions okay. Reports in 6 weeks. Publication time varies.
Terms and Payment: Authors retain rights. Pays on publication. Rates vary. Authors receive copies of the issue.
Advertising: Accepts advertising. List rental available. Contact Reed Huegel, 415-332-1716.

Whole Life Times

Abigail Lewis, Editor, 21225 Pacific Coast Highway, Malibu, CA 90265   Phone: 310-317-4200, Fax: 310-317-4206

Profile: A newsmagazine of holistic living. Published by Whole World Communication, Inc. Issued monthly. Circ: 55,000. Trim size: 10.5x13.25. Color cover; B/W inside; stapled. 60 pages. Subscription cost: $26. Sample copy cost: $3. Writer's guidelines available with SASE.
Focus and Tips: *Whole Life Times* is a sophisticated, leading-edge publication that presents a holistic lifestyle to a broad audience. Especially interested in investigative reporting containing practical information. Stay away from opinion pieces and advertorials.
Editorial Interests
Holistic health, new age, astrology, cultural and ethnic issues, ecosystems, the environment, healing and health, magic, meditation, men's issues, metaphysics, mysticism, mythology, natural health, nutrition, occult, parapsychology, parenting, politics, psychic phenomenon, psychology, relationships, self-help, social issues, spirituality, witches, women's issues, and yoga.

• *Nonfiction:* Features, interviews, and profiles, 1,500–2,000 words.
Submission Policy: Query with outline and writing samples. Include SASE. Accepts photocopies, computer printouts, faxes, and Macintosh Microsoft Word disks. No simultaneous submissions. Reports in 1–2 month. If accepted, expect publication in 1–2 months.
Terms and Payment: First North American serial rights. Pays on publication. $.50 per word. Authors receive 3 copies of the issue.
Advertising: Accepts advertising. Contact Danielle Kidd, 310-317-4200.

Wholistic Alternatives

Dorothy Strain, 595 Seventh Avenue, Durango, CO 81301   Phone: 303-247-3260

Profile: An alternative lifestyle magazine. Published by the Center for Alternative Realities. Issued quarterly. Circ: 3,000. Trim size: 8.5x11. Newsprint; stapled. 28–30 pages. Subscription cost: $5. Sample copy cost: Free. Writer's guidelines available with SASE.
Focus and Tips: *Wholistic Alternatives* seeks articles on the metaphysical, alternative lifestyles and health care, and world religions. Not interested in fundamentalism or anything dealing in fear or guilt.
Editorial Interests
Metaphysics, lifestyles, Buddhism, Taoism, Christianity, astrology, bodywork, channeling, crystals, cultural and ethnic issues, dreams, ecosystems, the environment, extraterrestrials, feminism, gay and lesbian interests, healing, health, holistic health, inspiration, juvenile and teen issues, magic, meditation, men's issues, mysticism, mythology, natural health, new age, nutrition, occult, parapsychology, parenting, philosophy, psychology, regional issues, and social and world issues.
• *Nonfiction:* Features, articles, essays, and personal experiences. Considers interviews and profiles. Query for word length.
Submission Policy: Send complete manuscript with cover letter. Include SASE. Accepts photocopies, computer printouts, and Macintosh or IBM disks. Simultaneous submissions okay. Reports as soon as possible. If accepted, expect publication in 6 months.
Terms and Payment: All rights. No payment.
Advertising: Rates: Guide Listing, $45 per individual insertion; $30 each for 4 consecutive insertions. Contact Terry Brown, 303-247-3260.
Other Interests: Connected to the Four Corners Sanctuary, 595 Seventh Avenue, Durango, CO 81301. Will organize conferences, seminars, workshops, or retreats upon request. Contact Dorothy Strain, 303-247-3260.

The Wild Foods Forum

Vickie Shufer, Editor, P.O. Box 61413, Virginia Beach, VA 23462   Phone: 804-421-3929

Profile: A natural health, environmental newsletter. Published by Eco Images. Issued bimonthly. Circ: 1,000. Trim size: 8.5x11. Self cover; 60 lb. Ivory recycled offset paper; saddle stitched. Subscription cost: $15. Sample copy cost: $2. No writer's guidelines.
Focus and Tips: *The Wild Foods Forum* offers wild food enthusiasts information on wild edible plants, rare or poisonous plants, book reviews, upcoming events, and herbal folklore. Readers are educated and are interested and involved in outdoor activities. It is interested in material based on personal experiences using wild foods or unusual features on wild edible plants and related subjects. Avoid political issues and negative criticisms.
Editorial Interests
Wild foods and edible plants, ecosystems, the environment, folklore, health, lifestyle, natural health, and nutrition.
• *Nonfiction:* Features, 1,200–1,500 words. Articles, 500–1,200 words. Interviews and profiles, 500–1,000 words. Essays and personal experiences, 250–500 words. Opinion pieces and news items, 100–250 words. Reviews, 100–500 words. Filler, 50–200 words.
Submission Policy: Send complete manuscript with cover letter and short author biography. Include SASE. Accepts photocopies, computer printouts, and Macintosh disks. Simultaneous submissions okay. Responds to queries in 1 month, to manuscripts in 2 months. If accepted, expect publication in 6 months.
Terms and Payment: One-time rights. No payment. Offers free 1-year subscription. Authors receive 1 or more copies of the issue.
Advertising: Rates: B/W full-page, $85; half-page, $45; quarter-page, $25; business-card, $15. Classified ads, $.50 per word with a $5 minimum and a 50-word maximum. Contact Vickie Shufer, 804-421-3929.

Wildfire

Orville Burch, Executive Director, P.O. Box 9167, Spokane, WA 99201   Phone: 509-326-4505

Profile: A magazine of Native American and Earth-based cultures. Published by The Bear Tribe Medicine Society, a nonprofit education and communications organization. Issued twice a year. Circ: 12,000. Trim size: 8.5x11. B/W; saddle stitched. 75

pages. Subscription cost: $20 for 4 issues. Sample copy cost: $5. Writer's guidelines available with SASE.

Focus and Tips: *Wildfire* "blends the best of older traditions with the newest appropriate technology and self-discovery." Issues are thematic and embrace the beliefs and culture of Native Americans and other indigenous peoples. It looks for writing that is clear, honest, and well-grounded with natural, meaningful imagery. Connect feelings or concepts and create fresh viewpoints. Most material is written in-house or by authors with proven knowledge of issue themes.

Editorial Interests

Native American and indigenous cultures, the environment, Earth changes, holistic and natural health, healing, children's and teen issues, parenting, sexuality, spirituality, prophecy, self-sufficient living, extraterrestrials, and UFO reports.

• *Poetry:* Up to 55 lines.

• *Nonfiction:* First-person accounts of individuals or groups living in harmony with the environment and their spirits. How-to material. In-depth interviews. Book and product reviews. Word lengths vary.

Submission Policy: Nonfiction, query with outline. Poetry, send poems with cover letter. Include SASE. Accepts photocopies, computer printouts, and computer disks. Call to check on disk compatibility. Simultaneous submissions okay. Reports in 1–2 months.

Terms and Payment: One-time rights. No payment. Authors receive copies of the issue.

Advertising: Accepts advertising. List rental available; 30,000 names. Contact Orville Burch, 509-326-4505.

Willow Springs

Sarah Blain, Managing Editor, MS-1, E.W.U., Cheney, WA 99004-2496   Phone: 509-458-6429

Profile: A literary journal. Published by Eastern Washington University. Established in 1977. Issued twice a year. Circ: 1,000. Trim size: 5x9. Glossy color cover; B/W; perfect bound. 96 pages. Subscription cost: $8. Sample copy cost: $4.50.

Focus and Tips: *Willow Springs* is a forum of writing, art, and ideas. It welcomes the work of new and emerging authors and "strives to strike just the right balance between work you want to read and work you need to read." *Willow Springs* has received numerous grants and awards from the National Endowment for the Arts, Council of Literary Magazines and Presses, Editors' Choice, and the Pushcart Press. Not interested in genre fiction.

Editorial Interests

Literary writing.

• *Fiction:* Short stories, 10–30 double-spaced, typed pages. Short-short stories, 2–5 double-spaced, typed pages.

Submission Policy: Send complete manuscript with cover letter. Include SASE. Accepts photocopies. No simultaneous submissions. Reports in 6–12 weeks. If accepted, expect publication in 6 months.

Terms and Payment: First North American serial rights. Pays on publication. $15–$35 per piece. Authors receive 2 copies of the issue.

Advertising: Rates: B/W full-page, $125. List rental available. Contact Sarah Blain, 509-458-6429.

Windy City Times

Dan Perreten, Managing Editor, 970 West Montana, Chicago, IL 60614   Phone: 312-935-1974, Fax: 312-935-1853

Profile: A gay and lesbian newsweekly. Published by Sentury Publications. Issued weekly. Circ: 22,000. Trim size: 11x17. Newsprint; folded. 52 pages. Subscription cost: $120. Sample copy cost: Free. No writer's guidelines.

Focus and Tips: *Windy City Times* reports on issues of concern to the Chicago-area gay and lesbian community. Writers are advised to query with article ideas. Not interested in fiction or personal narratives.

Editorial Interests

Gay and lesbian issues, astrology, cultural and ethnic issues, feminism, health, lifestyle, politics, and women's issues.

• *Nonfiction:* Features, articles, interviews, profiles, and essays, 800–2,000 words. News items, 800–1,000 words. Opinion pieces, 800 words. Reviews, 600–800 words.

Submission Policy: Query first with outline and writing samples. Occasionally accepts unsolicited manuscripts with cover letter. Include SASE. Accepts photocopies, computer printouts, computer disks, and faxes. Simultaneous submissions okay. Reports in 1 month. If accepted, expect publication within 2–3 weeks.

Terms and Payment: One-time rights. Pays on publication. $50–$100 per piece. Authors receive 1–2 copies of the issue.

Advertising: Rates: B/W full-page, $900; 4-color full-page, $2,000. Contact Erin Nestor, 312-935-1790.

Winners

Sharon Boyd, Associate Editor, P.O. Box 38, Malibu, CA 90265

Profile: A magalog for retail outlets based on Master of Life concepts. Published by Valley of the Sun Publishing. Issued quarterly. Circ: 100,000. Trim size: 8.5x11. Glossy color cover; B/W inside; saddle stitched. 84 pages. Subscription cost: Free to retail buyers. Sample copy cost: $2. Writer's guidelines available with SASE.

Focus and Tips: *Winners* promotes mental, physical, and philosophical self-sufficiency. Dedicated to communicating Master of Life concepts, a personal philosophy of becoming all you are capable of being. Distributed free of charge to book and tape retail buyers. Most material is written in-house; on occasion will contract an outside writer. Interested only in articles that cross-market Valley of the Sun products, services, or seminars. Authors should be familiar with products and magazine.

Editorial Interests

Self-help, human potential, astrology, channeling, dreams, metaphysics, occult, and relationships.

• *Nonfiction:* Articles on Valley of the Sun products, services, or seminars, up to 3,500 words.

Submission Policy: Query with outline and 2 writing samples. Include SASE. Accepts photocopies and computer printouts. Simultaneous submissions okay if noted. Reports in 2 months. If accepted, expect publication in 1 year.

Terms and Payment: First North American serial rights. Pays on publication. $.05 per word. Authors receive copies of the issue upon request.

Advertising: Partial list rental available. Contact Jan Hale, 503-488-7880.

Other Interests: Valley of the Sun also publishes a line of self-help, metaphysical books. Sponsors Sutphen Seminars. Dates vary. For more information, write to Sutphen Seminars, P.O. Box 38, Malibu, CA 90265.

The Wise Woman

Ann Forfreedom, Editor, 2441 Cordova Street, Oakland, CA 94602   Phone: 510-536-3174

Profile: A journal of feminist issues. Established in 1980. Issued quarterly. Circ: N/A. Trim size: 8.5x11. Glossy cover; B/W; saddle stitched. 12–84 pages. Subscription cost: $15. Sample copy cost: $4. Writer's guidelines available with SASE.

Focus and Tips: *The Wise Woman* focuses on feminist issues, feminist spirituality, Goddess lore, and feminist witchcraft. Authors are advised to proofread all work thoroughly before sending. Avoid sexist or racist language, stereotypes, shallow treatment of subjects, oversimplifications, and common spelling errors.

Editorial Interests

Feminism, herstory, violence against women, the rising of women, feminist spirituality, witchcraft, metaphysics, mythology, politics, psychic phenomenon, social and world issues, and women's issues

• *Nonfiction:* Features, articles, interviews, profiles, essays, personal experiences, opinion pieces, news items, reviews, filler, and column. No length restrictions.

• *Illustrations:* Artwork and photographs.

Submission Policy: Query with brief outline or sample chapters. Include SASE. Accepts photocopies. Reporting time varies.

Terms and Payment: One-time, reprint, and microfilm rights. No payment. Authors receive 1 copy of the issue.

Advertising: Rates: B/W full-page, $40. Contact Ann Forfreedom, 510-536-3174 or 415-922-3837.

Woman of Power

Charlene McKee, Editor, P.O. Box 2785, Orleans, MA 02653   Phone: 508-240-7877

Profile: A magazine of feminism, spirituality, and politics. Published by Woman of Power, Inc., a nonprofit organization. Established in 1984. Issued quarterly. Circ: 23,000. Trim size: 8.5x11. Color glossy cover; B/W inside; saddle stitched. 88 pages. Subscription cost: $30. Sample copy cost: $8. Writer's guidelines available with SASE.

Focus and Tips: *Woman of Power* is an international quarterly honoring the work of women activists and visionaries. Of special interest is the role of women's personal and collective spiritual empowerment. All material should have a feminist, spiritual, and political focus and pertain to the theme of the issue. Past themes include Leadership, Relationships, Sacred Spaces, and The Living Earth. Upcoming themes include Tales of Empowerment, Money and Work, and Women in the 21st Century.

Editorial Interests

Astrology, cultural awareness, environment and ecosystems, gay and lesbian issues, holistic health, metaphysics, mythology, new age topics, occult, parapsychology, philosphy, politics, prayer, psychology, relationships, social issues, witches, and women's art and photography.

• *Nonfiction:* Accepts features, articles, interviews and profiles, essays, personal experiences, and opinion pieces, 5,000 words. Reviews, very short.

Submission Policy: Send complete manuscript with cover letter and bibliography. Include SASE. Accepts photocopies and computer printouts. Simultaneous submissions okay. Reports in 4–6 months.

Terms and Payment: One-time rights. No payment. Authors receive 2 copies of the issue; additional copies available at a 50% discount.

Advertising: Rates per page: B/W, $785. Contact Charlene McKee, 508-240-7877. 15% discounts offered to women-owned businesses, nonprofit organizations, and women artisans. List rental available; contact Pam Kiriaji, 508-240-7877.

Woman's Way: The Path of Empowerment

Lynn Marlow, Publisher/Editor, P.O. Box 19614, Boulder, CO 80308-2614   Phone/Fax: 303-530-7617

Profile: A magazine of women's empowerment. Issued quarterly. Circ: 6,000. Trim size: 8.5x11. 2-color cover; B/W inside;

saddle stitched. 12–28 pages. Subscription cost: $12. Sample copy cost: $3. Writer's guidelines available with SASE.

Focus and Tips: *Woman's Way* is dedicated to the self-discovery and self-expression of women. It supports women's creativity and self-expression by offering the space to read and write our life's experiences. Particularly interested in offering previously unpublished writers an opportunity to share their work. It welcomes personal experience pieces from a wide variety of women. Avoid theoretical material.

Editorial Interests

Women's issues, feminism, creativity, gay and lesbian issues, astrology, bodywork, healing, health, lifestyle, psychology relationships, self-help, social and world issues, and spirituality.

• *Fiction:* Short stories and short-short stories, up to 1,000 words. Poetry, 500 words.

• *Nonfiction:* Features and articles, 1,200–2,000 words. Interviews and profiles, 2,000–3,000 words. Essays, personal experiences, and opinion pieces, 1,000–2,000 words. News items, 1,000 words. Reviews, 500–1,000 words. Letters and journal excerpts.

Submission Policy: Send complete manuscript with cover letter. Include SASE. Accepts photocopies, faxes, and IBM or Macintosh disks. Simultaneous submissions okay. Responds to queries in 2–4 months, to manuscripts in 4–6 months. If accepted, expect publication in 3–6 months.

Terms and Payment: One-time rights. No payment. Authors receive 2 copies of the issue.

Advertising: Rates: B/W full-page, $140; half-page, $80; quarter-page, $50. Contact Lynn Marlow, 303-530-7617.

Women Artists News Book Review

Judy Seigel, Editor, 300 Riverside Drive, New York, NY 10025-5239   Phone: 212-666-6990

Profile: A journal of literary reviews. Published by Midmarch Arts Press. Issued annually. Circ: 5,000. Trim size: 8.5x11. Glossy cover; B/W; saddle stitched. 64 pages. Subscription cost: N/A. Sample copy cost: $5. Writer's guidelines available with SASE.

Focus and Tips: *Women Artists News Book Review* publishes book reviews on literature, the arts, and women's issues and interests, as well as relevant essays and poetry.

Editorial Interests

Women's issues, feminism, the arts, literature, crafts, poetry, cultural and ethnic issues, and gay and lesbian issues.

• *Poetry:* Must relate to artists or the arts.

• *Nonfiction:* Book reviews. Essays on artists or arts-related topics.

Submission Policy: Query with outline. Include SASE. Accepts photocopies and Macintosh Microsoft Word disks. No simultaneous submissions.

Terms and Payment: One-time rights. Pays only when there is grant money available. Authors receive 1–2 copies of the issue.

Advertising: Accepts advertising. Contact L. Hulkaver.

Women & Recovery

Sara Cole, Editor/Art Director, P.O. Box 151947, Cupertino, CA 95015   Phone: 408-865-0472, Fax: 408-996-8115

Profile: A forum for women involved in all types of recovery. Published by Need To Know Press. Established in 1984. Issued quarterly. Circ: 7,000. Trim size: 8.5x11. Glossy cover; B/W; saddle stitched. 48 pages. Subscription cost: $24. Sample copy cost: $5. Writer's guidelines available with SASE.

Focus and Tips: *Woman & Recovery* addresses women struggling to survive, thrive, and reclaim their bodies, minds, and spirits. Editorial viewpoint is feminist, yet unbiased. It encourages, supports, and informs women who are confronting physical, emotional, or spiritual challenges. Serves as an interactive forum for readers to share their experiences. Welcomes true personal stories that offer honest insights into recovery.

Editorial Interests

Recovery, women's issues, spirituality, feminism, gay and lesbian concerns, healing, health, inspiration, psychology, and self-help.

• *Poetry:* No length restrictions.

• *Nonfiction:* Personal experiences, interviews with industry professionals and visionaries, features and exposés on new programs and research, 1,000 words. Product or service evaluations, 300 words.

• *Illustrations:* B/W photos and illustrations reflecting some aspect of recovery. B/W single-box cartoon on political or humorous topics. B/W feminist comic strips addressing recovery.

Submission Policy: Send complete manuscript with cover letter and 10–20 word biography. Include SASE. Accepts photocopies, computer printouts, Macintosh computer disks, and faxes. Simultaneous submissions okay. Reports in 2 months. If accepted, expect publication within 2–12 months.

Terms and Payment: One-time rights. Personal experiences, interviews, and exposés, $50. Features and evaluations, $35. Poetry, $25–$35. Photos and illustrations, $50. Authors receive 2 copies of the issue. Additional copies, $5.

Advertising: Rates per page: B/W, $700. Contact Sara Cole, 408-865-0472.

Womyn's Press

J. R. David, Editor, P.O. Box 562, Eugene, OR 97440   Phone: 503-689-3974

Profile: An eclectic feminist newspaper. Established in 1970. Issued bimonthly. Circ: 2,000. Trim size: Tabloid. Newsprint; folded. 16 pages. Subscription cost: $8. Sample copy cost: $2. Writer's guidelines available with SASE.

Focus and Tips: *Womyn's Press* offers a forum for the voices of marginalized women and encourages contributions from the women most ignored by the mainstream press—old women, girls, women of color, poor women, working-class women, fat women, lesbians, Jewish women, and disabled women. It is more interested in presenting a diversity of viewpoints than in a "correct" political line, but avoid contributions that are "sexist/heterosexist, racist, anti-Semitic, classist, ageist, fatophobic, or ableist." Readers are largely feminists, centered on the West Coast, but reaching around the world.

Editorial Interests

Feminism, women's issues, cultural and ethnic issues, lesbian issues, and witches.

• *Fiction:* Short stories, short-short stories, drama, book excerpts, genre fiction, and poetry, up to 2,000 words.

• *Nonfiction:* Features, articles, interviews, profiles, essays, personal experiences, opinion pieces, news, and reviews, 2,000 words. Columns include Astrology, Car Repair, and Feminism in the Workplace.

Submission Policy: Query with writing samples or send complete manuscript with cover letter and bibliography. Include SASE. Accepts photocopies and computer printouts. Simultaneous submissions okay. Responds to queries in 1 month, to manuscripts in 1–3 months. If accepted, expect publication in 1–3 months.

Terms and Payment: Authors retain rights. No payment. Authors receive a free 1-year subscription.

Advertising: Rates: B/W full-page, $348 or $8 per column inch. Classified ads, $3 for the first 25 words and $.15 per word thereafter. Contact J. R. David, 503-689-3974.

The Word

Neil Avery, Editor-in-Chief, P.O. Box 180340, Dallas, TX 75218   Phone: 214-348-5006

Profile: A quarterly journal based on the works of Harold Percival. Published by The Word Foundation, Inc. Issued quarterly. Circ: N/A. Trim size: 8.5x11. Self cover; glossy paper; B/W; saddle stitched. 20 pages. Subscription cost: $15. Sample copy cost: $2.50. No writer's guidelines.

Focus and Tips: *The Word* seeks to introduce readers to the concepts of the author Harold W. Percival, especially his master work, "Thinking and Destiny."

Editorial Interests

The works of Harold Percival.

• *Nonfiction:* Features, up to 6,000 words. Articles, 4,000 words. Essays, 2,000 words. Reviews, 1,000 words.

Submission Policy: Query with outline or send complete manuscript with cover letter. Include SASE. Accepts computer printouts and Microsoft Word or WordPerfect disks. Reports in 1 month. If accepted, expect publication within 3–6 months.

Terms and Payment: One-time rights. No payment. Authors receive up to 10 copies of the issue.

World Rainforest Report

Randy Alfred, Editor, 450 Sansome Street, Suite 700, San Francisco, CA 94111   Phone: 415-398-4404, Fax: 415-398-2732

Profile: A membership newsletter for environmental activists. Published by Rainforest Action Network (RAN), a nonprofit global action group. Issued quarterly. Circ: 27,000. Trim size: 8.5x11. Recycled paper; stapled. 15 pages. Subscription/membership cost: $25. Sample copy cost: Free.

Focus and Tips: *World Rainforest Report* offers information pertinent to the world rainforest movement, particularly in South America, Southeast Asia, and Canada. It publishes action-oriented articles that provide solutions and alternatives. Study a sample copy for style and content. Subscription to *World Rainforest Report* includes membership in RAN and a subscription to *Action Alerts*, a monthly action-oriented news release.

Editorial Interests

Rainforests, ecosystems, the environment, rights of indigenous peoples, cultural and ethnic issues, politics, and social and world issues.

• *Nonfiction:* Articles, 75–900 words. Accepts reviews and news items for News & Notes.

Submission Policy: Send complete manuscript with cover letter. Include SASE. Accepts photocopies and computer printouts. No simultaneous submissions. Reporting time varies. Publication time varies.

Terms and Payment: First North American serial rights or reprint rights. No payment. Authors receive 1 copy of the issue.

Other Interests: Sponsors numerous activist-oriented conferences and workshops throughout the year.

Yoga Journal

Rick Fields, Editor, 2054 University Avenue, Berkeley, CA 94704   Phone: 510-841-9200

Profile: A national magazine of yogic practices. Issued bimonthly. Circ: 75,000. Trim size: 8.5x11. Glossy color cover; full color; saddle stitched. 60–68 pages. Subscription cost: $18. Sample copy cost: $3.95. Writer's guidelines available with SASE.

Focus and Tips: *Yoga Journal* covers a variety of fields and disciplines aimed at improving health and consciousness, while maintaining and emphasis on the practice and philosophy of yoga. It defines yoga broadly, as aspiring to union or communion with some higher power, greater truth, or deeper source of wisdom in addition to increased internal harmony.

Editorial Interests

Yoga, meditation, holistic health, bodywork, natural healing, nutrition, philosophy, transpersonal psychology, Eastern and Western spirituality, and social issues.

• *Nonfiction:* Features, interviews, and profiles, 1,000–5,000 words. Columns include Psychology, Meditation, Profile, Centering, Service, Well-Being, Food, Cooking, Bodywork, Open Forum, and Ecology, all 750–2,000 words. Accepts book reviews.

Submission Policy: Query with outline and clips or send complete manuscript with cover letter. Include SASE. Accepts photocopies and computer printouts. Simultaneous submissions okay. Reports in 3 months.

Terms and Payment: First North American serial rights. Pays on publication. Articles, $75–$600 per piece. Photos, $25 and up. Authors receive 2 copies of the issue.

Advertising: Accepts advertising. Contact Rick Fields, 510-841-9200.

BOOK PUBLISHERS: USING THE LISTINGS

Your research into the new age market can begin with a careful study of the listings that follow. The listings are divided into two groups: Publications, beginning on page 28, and Book Publishers, beginning on page 152. Both sections are organized in alphabetical order. For a complete index of all the publications and book publishers in the guide, turn to the Index of Publishers, on page 203.

Both the Publications and Book Publishers sections are preceded by a subject index of publishers listed alphabetically under various headings. Some are general categories of writing, others are topics specific to new age markets. Scan the subject headings for interests that match your own and you will find a list of likely markets. If your particular interests are not reflected, consider related subjects, or turn directly to the market listings for a complete assessment of editorial needs.

Our market listings are designed to help you make informed choices about the best opportunities for your work. The sample listing and outline that follow introduces the format and type of information presented under each subheading.

Health Communications, Inc.
Christine Belleris, Editorial Director, 3201 S.W. 15th Street, Deerfield Beach, FL 33431   Phone: 305-360-0909, Fax: 305-360-0034

1   **Profile:** Self-help books. Established in 1976. Titles: 30 per year; all nonfiction paperback. Average print run: 7,000. Binding: Otabind. Book catalogue available.
2   **Focus and Imprints:** Health Communications specializes in self-help books dealing with all of life's issues, from soulful enlightenment to personal growth and relationships. Prospective writers should make their message as clear as possible—don't bury it in jargon. "Include a thorough marketing study with the proposal, define the audience, list books similar to yours and their sales record, and describe how your book is unique." Avoid material that is autobiographical in nature unless it can provide a framework for others.
3   **Editorial Interests**
    • *Nonfiction:* Special interest in books with a positive, uplifting message such as self-help material, affirmations, mind-body-spirit connection, and personal growth. Topics include bodywork, crystals, cultural and ethnic concerns, dreams, feminism, folklore, healing, health, holistic and natural health, lifestyle, meditation, new age, parenting, psychology, relationships, spirituality, women's issues, and yoga.
4   **Recent Titles:** *Chicken Soup for the Soul* by Jack Canfield and Mark Victor Hanson. *Recovery of the Sacred* by Carlos Warter.
5   **Submission and Payment Policy:** Query first with outline and resume. Include SASE. Accepts photocopies and computer printouts. Simultaneous submissions okay. Responds to queries in 2–3 weeks, to manuscripts in 2–3 months. If accepted, expect publication in 9 months. Royalty, 20%.
6   **Other Interests:** Affiliated with U.S. Journal Training, Inc., which offers conferences on adolescence, relationships, and alternative methods of health and wellness. For more information, contact Gary Seidler, 3201 S.W. 15th Street, Deerfield Beach, FL 33431.

1. **Profile:** General description of the publisher including number of titles published per year and whether they are fiction or nonfiction, paperback or hardcover; the average print run; the type of book binding and printing press used; and the availability of a catalogue or booklist.
2. **Focus and Imprints:** The publisher's targeted interests, audience, and any philosophical, political, or stylistic guidance for writers interested in submitting their work. Additionally listed are imprints or book lines and their specific interests.
3. **Editorial Interests:** The fiction and nonfiction topics of concern to the publisher.
4. **Recent Titles:** Generally, two titles that are representative of the publisher's list.
5. **Submission and Payment Policy:** Details on how to approach the publisher: whether to query first of send complete manuscript; what to include with submissions, i.e., cover letter, resume, writing samples, marketing ideas, author biography, or outline; and acceptable submissions forms, i.e., photocopies, computer printouts, and disks, or fax submissions; and any special submissions restrictions. Also included are whether simultaneous submissions are accepted and the form of payment: royalty, flat fee, or advance.
6. **Other Interests:** Listed here are any school or organizational affiliations; the sponsorship of writing contests; and connections to conferences, workshops, seminars, retreats, or other programs.

BOOK PUBLISHER SUBJECT INDEX

ASTROLOGY
ACS Publications
A.G.S.
Grebner Books Publishing
Lampus Press
Libra Press
Llewellyn Publications
Nicolas-Hays, Inc.
T. Byron G. Publishing
Theosophical Publishing House
Valley of the Sun
Samuel Weiser Inc.
Whitford Press

BODYWORK
China Books & Periodicals
Grebner Books Publishing
Keats Publishing, Inc.
Metamorphous Press
Newcastle Publishing Company, Inc.
Pacific View Press
Rodmell Press
Sterling Publishing Co., Inc.
Wingbow Press

BUDDHISM
China Books & Periodicals
Parallax Press
Rodmell Press

BUSINESS
The Alternate Press
D.B.A. Books
First Editions
Miles River Press
New World Library

CHANNELING
Creativity Unlimited Press
Indelible Ink Publishing
Journal of Regional Criticism
Oughten House Publications
Telstar

CRYSTALS
Book World, Inc.
Brotherhood of Life, Inc.
Journal of Regional Criticism
Libra Press
Whitford Press

CULTURAL AND ETHNIC
Ability Work Shop Press
American Buddhist Movement
Arrowstar Publishing
Bandanna Books
Bear Tribe Publishing
Bliss Publishing Company
Blue Bird Publishing
Book Publishing Company
China Books & Periodicals
Civilized Publications
Council for Indian Education
Eagle's View Publishing
Harmony Books
In Print Publishing
New Mind Productions, Inc.
New Society Publishers
New World Library
North Star Press
Ox Head Press
Paragon House Publishing
Pogo Press, Incorporated
Read America!
Schiffer Publishing
Sierra Oaks Publishing Co.
Thunderbird Publications
Tilbury House Publishers
Charles E. Tuttle Company, Inc.

DREAMS
A.R.E. Press
Bear Tribe Publishing
Journal of Regional Criticism
New Spirit Press
Original Books
Ox Head Press
T. Byron G. Publishing
Whitford Press

ECOSYSTEMS
Bliss Publishing Company
Chelsea Green
Conservatory of American Letters
Human Potential Foundation Press
Kivaki Press
Parallax Press
Tide-Mark Press Ltd.

ENVIRONMENT
America West Publishers
Avery Publishing Group

Beacon Press
Beyond Words Publishing Inc.
Bliss Publishing Company
Ceres Press
Chelsea Green
Clear Light Publishers
Conservatory of American Letters
Countryman Press, Inc.
Crystal Clarity Publishers
Dawn Publications
Delphi Press
Human Potential Foundation Press
Island Meadow Farm Bookcraft
Michael Kesend Publishing, LTD.
Kivaki Press
More to Life Publishing
Naturegraph Publishers, Inc.
The New Dawn Publishing Co.
Silvercat Publications
The Sterling Publishing Co.
Third Side Press, Inc.
Tide-Mark Press Ltd.
Tilbury House Publishers
Waterfront Books
Whitman Publishing

EXTRATERRESTRIALS
A.G.S.
Athanor Press
Book World, Inc.
Brotherhood of Life, Inc.
Indelible Ink Publishing
International Guild of Advanced
  Sciences
New Spirit Press
Oughten House Publications
Thunderbird Publications
Whitford Press
Wild Flower Press

FEMINISM
Bandanna Books
Beacon Press
Conari Press
The Crossing Press
Delphi Press
Faber and Faber Publishers, Inc.
Harmony Books
New Society Publishers
Open Court Publishing Company
Parallex Press

Read America!
Sanguinaria Publishing
Third Side Press, Inc.
University of California Press
Wingbow Press

FICTION
American Buddhist Movement
Archives Publications
A.R.E. Press
Arrowstar Publishing
Bandanna Books
Book World, Inc.
Branden Books
Brotherhood of Life, Inc.
Brunswich Publishing Corporation
Center Press
Conservatory of American Letters
The Crossing Press
John Daniel & Company
Dawn Publications
Distinctive Publishing
Excalibur Publishing
Faber and Faber Publishers, Inc.
Fall Creek Press
Farrar, Straus and Giroux
Fithian Press
Hampton Roads Publishing Company
Harmony Books
Heaven Bone Press
Lighthouse Productions
Lindisfarne Press
Llewellyn Publications
MacMurray and Beck Inc.
Morning Glory Press
New Mind Productions, Inc.
Oughten House Publications
Ox Head Press
Perspectives Press
The Savant Garde Workshop
Sierra Oaks Publishing Co.
Superlove
Third Side Press, Inc.
Tilbury House Publishers
Traffic Light Press
Waterfront Books

FOLKLORE
Archives Publications
Bala Books, Inc.
Clear Light Publishers
Conservatory of American Letters

Council for Indian Education
Faber and Faber Publishers, Inc.
In Print Publishing
Jewish Lights Publishing
The New Dawn Publishing Co.
North Star Press
Ox Head Press
Paragon House Publishing
Sierra Oaks Publishing Co.
Tilbury House Publishers
Traffic Light Press
Whitman Publishing

GAY AND LESBIAN
Beacon Press
Chicago Review Press
The Crossing Press
Faber and Faber Publishers, Inc.
Mho & Mho Works
Read America!
Third Side Press, Inc.
University of California Press

HEALING
Asian Publishing
Avery Publishing Group
Blue Poppy Press
Book World, Inc.
Brotherhood of Life, Inc.
Creativity Unlimited Press
Dawn Publications
Hampton Roads Publishing Company
Harmony Books
Hay House
International Guild of Advanced
    Sciences
Jain Publishing Company
Keats Publishing, Inc.
Lampus Press
New Harbinger Publications
Newcastle Publishing Company, Inc.
Ox Head Press
Pacific View Press
Paradigm Publications
Pearl Publishing House
Rama Publishing Co.
Rodmell Press
Swan Raven & Company
Telstar
Thunderbird Publications
Tilbury House Publishers
Charles E. Tuttle Company, Inc.

Wild Flower Press
Wingbow Press

HEALTH
America West Publishers
Aslan Publishing
Bala Books, Inc.
Beyond Words Publishing Inc.
Blue Poppy Press
Branden Books
Center Press
Chicago Review Press
Clear Light Publishers
Contemporary Books, Inc.
Dawn Publications
Delta Sales Publishing
Dimi Press
Distinctive Publishing
Fithian Press
Hampton Roads Publishing Company
Harmony Books
Hay House
Hazelden Educational Materials
Health Communications, Inc.
Human Potential Foundation Press
Impact Publishers, Inc.
Keats Publishing, Inc.
Michael Kesend Publishing, LTD.
Kivaki Press
Libra Press
Lifetime Books
MacMurray and Beck Inc.
Metamorphous Press
The New Dawn Publishing Co.
New Harbinger Publications
New Mind Productions, Inc.
New World Library
Newmarket Press
Pacific View Press
Paradigm Publications
Prima Publishing
Rodmell Press
Silvercat Publications
Third Side Press, Inc.
University of California Press
Van Hoy Publishers
Whole Person Associates, Inc.

HOLISTIC HEALTH
Arcus Publishing Company
Avery Publications Group
Blue Poppy Press

INSPIRATIONAL—MYTHOLOGY

Ceres Press
Chicago Review Press
China Books & Periodicals
Creativity Unlimited Press
The Crossing Press
Element Books, Inc.
Hampton Roads Publishing Company
Hazelden Educational Materials
Jain Publishing Company
Kivaki Press
Libra Press
Lotus Light Publications
Paradigm Publications
Prima Publishing
Van Hoy Publishers
Whitman Publishing
Whole Person Associates, Inc.

INSPIRATIONAL
Aslan Publishing
Bell Tower
Blue Dove Press
Dawn Publications
DeVorss & Company
Health Communications, Inc.
In Print Publishing
Jewish Lights Publishing
Lifetime Books
Ox Head Press
Superlove
Theosophical Publishing House
Traffic Light Press
Waterfront Books

JUVENILE AND TEEN BOOKS
Bala Books, Inc.
Bandanna Books
Council for Indian Education
Dawn Publications
Island Meadow Farm Bookcraft
Lighthouse Productions
New Mind Productions, Inc.
Perspectives Press
Tilbury House Publishers
Traffic Light Press

LIFESTYLE
Beyond Words Publishing Inc.
Blue Bird Publishing
Civilized Publications
Countryman Press, Inc.
The Crossing Press

Distinctive Publishing
Elysium Growth Press
Grebner Books Publishing
Hartley & Marks
Health Communications, inc.
Michael Kesend Publishing, LTD.
Mills & Sanderson, Publishers
Morning Glory Press
Newmarket Press
Read America!
Silvercat Publications

MAGIC
A.G.S.
Brotherhood of Life, Inc.
Delphi Press
Journal of Regional Criticism
Llewellyn Publications
T. Byron G. Publishing
Whitford Press

MEDITATION
American Buddhist Movement
Bell Tower
Blue Dove Press
Hartley & Marks
Hazelden Educational Materials
Lampus Press
Omega Publications
Original Books
Oughten House Publications
Paragon House Publishing
Prima Publishing
Quest Books
Rodmell Press
Superlove
Traffic Light Press
Charles E. Tuttle Company, Inc.
Valley of the Sun
Van Hoy Publishers
Vedanta Press

MEN'S ISSUES
Bioenergetics Press
Delta Sales Publishing
Harmony Books
Mills & Sanderson, Publishers
Read America!
Swan Raven & Company
Whole Person Associates, Inc.
Wild Flower Press
Writer's Resources

METAPHYSICS
Ability Work Shop Press
America West Publishers
A.R.E. Press
Book World, Inc.
Cassandra Press, Inc.
Cosmic Concepts
Creativity Unlimited Press
Crystal Clarity Publishers
Hampton Roads Publishing Company
Human Potential Foundation Press
Illumination Arts, Inc.
Indelible Ink Publishing
Lampus Press
Libra Press
Mho & Mho Works
New Falcon Press
Omega Publications
Original Books
Oughten House Publications
Telstar
Theosophical Publishing House
Thunderbird Publications
Valley of the Sun
Vedanta Press
Samuel Weiser Inc.

MYSTICISM
Arkana
Bell Tower
Blue Dove Press
Book World, Inc.
Center Press
Cosmic Concepts
In Print Publishing
Lotus Light Publications
More to Life Publishing
Omega Publications
Pearl Publishing House
Vedanta Press

MYTHOLOGY
Arkana
Bala Books
Book World, Inc.
Cosmic Concepts
In Print Publishing
Indelible Ink Publishing
Journal of Regional Criticism
Lindisfarne Press
Nicolas-Hays, Inc.
Sierra Oaks Publishing Co.

T. Byron G. Publishing

NATIVE AMERICAN
Arrowstar Publishing
Bear Tribe Publishing
Book Publishing Company
Clear Light Publishers
Council Oak Publishing
Council for Indian Education
Eagle's View Publishing
Hampton Roads Publishing Company
Naturegraph Publishers, Inc.
Sierra Oaks Publishing Co.

NATURAL HEALTH
Cassandra Press, Inc.
Element Books, Inc.
Hazelden Educational Materials
Hohm Press
Keats Publishing, Inc.
Lotus Light Publications
McBooks Press
Prima Publishing
Sterling Publishing Co., Inc.
Charles E. Tuttle Company, Inc.
Van Hoy Publishers
Wingbow Press

NEW AGE
A.G.S.
Airo Press
Arcus Publishing Company
A.R.E. Press
Bear & Company Publishiong
Bear Tribe Publishing
Brotherhood of Life, Inc.
Cassandra Press, Inc.
Creativity Unlimited Press
The Crossing Press
Crystal Clarity Publishers
D.B.A. Books
DeVorss & Company
Distinctive Publishing
Excalibur Publishing
First Editions
Grebner Books Publishing
Hay House
Indelible Ink Publishing
International Guild of Advanced
    Sciences
Lampus Press
Lifetime Books

Lighthouse Productions
Llewellyn Publications
More to Life Publishing
New Falcon Press
Nicolas-Hays, Inc.
Oughten House Publications
Pearl Publishing House
Sterling Publishing Co., Inc.
Superlove
Swan Raven & Company
T. Byron G. Publishing
Telstar
Thunderbird Publications
Tilbury House Publishers
Traffic Light Press
Valley of the Sun
Samuel Weiser Inc.
Whitford Press
Whitman Publishing
Wild Flower Press

NUTRITION
America West Publishers
Avery Publishing Group
Bala Books, Inc.
Book Publishing Company
Ceres Press
Hohm Press
Jain Publishing Company
Keats Publishing, Inc.
McBooks Press
Morning Glory Press
Silvercat Publications
Whitman Publishing
Whole Person Associates, Inc.

OCCULT
A.G.S.
Athanor Press
Brotherhood of Life, Inc.
Conservatory of American Letters
Delphi Press
International Guild of Advanced
    Sciences
Llewellyn Publications
New Falcon Press
Ox Head Press
T. Byron G. Publishing
Telstar

PARAPSYCHOLOGY
Athanor Press

Cosmic Concepts
International Guild of Advanced
    Sciences
New Spirit Press
Sterling Publishing Co., Inc.

PARENTING
Avery Publishing Group
Beyond Words Publishing Inc.
Blue Bird Publishing
Branden Books
Civilized Publications
Conari Press
Contemporary Books, Inc.
Countryman Press, Inc.
Excalibur Publishing
Free Spirit Publishing
Hohm Press
Impact Publishers, Inc.
McBooks Press
Miles River Press
Morning Glory Press
New Harbinger Publications
New Society Publishers
Writer's Resources

PHILOSOPHY
Airo Press
American Buddhist Movement
Archives Publications
Arkana
Bandanna Books
Bear Tribe Publishing
Clear Light Publishers
Element Books, Inc.
Jewish Lights Publishing
Journal of Regional Criticism
Lindisfarne Press
The New Dawn Publishing Co.
New World Library
Nicolas-Hays, Inc.
Open Court Publishing Company
Paragon House Publishing
Pearl Publishing House
Quest Books
The Savant Garde Workshop
Superlove
Telstar
Theosophical Publishing House
Traffic Light Press
Charles E. Tuttle Company, Inc.
University of California Press

Vedanta Press
Samuel Weiser Inc.

POETRY
Airo Press
Center Press
Conservatory of American Letters
Creativity Unlimited Press
John Daniel & Company
Fithian Press
Heaven Bone Press
Island Meadow Farm Bookcraft
Journal of Regional Criticism
Mortal Press
New Native Press
New Spirit Press
Telstar
Tilbury House Publishers

POLITICS
America West Publishers
Bliss Publishing Company
Branden Books
Fithian Press
Lindisfarne Press
New Society Publishers
Pacific View Press
University of California Press

PRAYER
Jewish Lights Publishing
North Star Press
Rama Publishing Co.
Traffic Light Press

PSYCHIC PHENOMENON
A.R.E. Press
Athanor Press
Cassandra Press, Inc.
Conservatory of American Letters
Crystal Clarity Publishers
New Spirit Press
Valley of the Sun

PSYCHOLOGY
Airo Press
Archives Publications
Arkana
Aslan Publishing
Beyond Words Publishing Inc.
Conari Press
Delta Sales Publishing

Distinctive Publishing
Element Books, Inc.
Free Spirit Publishing
Grebner Books Publishing
Hartley & Marks
Hay House
Hohm Press
Human Potential Foundation Press
Impact Publishers, Inc.
Lampus Press
Lifetime Books
Lindisfarne Books
Metamorphous Press
Mho & Mho Works
Mills & Sanderson, Publishers
New Falcon Press
New Harbinger Publications
New Mind Productions, Inc.
Newcastle Publishing Company, Inc.
Nicolas-Hays, Inc.
Open Court Publishing Company
Silvercat Publications
Sterling Publishing Co., Inc.
Samuel Weiser Inc.

RECOVERY
Ability Work Shop Press
Aslan Publishing
Hazelden Educational Materials
Jewish Lights Publishing
Lifetime Books
Mho & Mho Works
Mills & Sanderson, Publishers
New World Library
Newcastle Publishing Company, Inc.
Rama Publishing Co.

RELATIONSHIPS
Ability Work Shop Press
Blue Bird Publishing
Civilized Publications
Conari Press
Free Spirit Publishing
Hartley & Marks
Health Communications, Inc.
Impact Publishers, Inc.
MacMurray and Beck, Inc.
Metamorphous Press
New Harbinger Press
The Savant Garde Workshop
Whole Person Associates, Inc.

RELIGION
Airo Press
Arkana
Austin and Winfield Publishers
Bala Books, Inc.
Beacon Press
Blue Dove Press
Element Books, Inc.
Fithian Press
Hohm Press
Jain Publishing Company
Lindisfarne Press
Lotus Light Publications
Mho & Mho Works
More to Life Publishing
New Falcon Press
New Mind Productions, Inc.
Omega Publications
Open Court Publishing Company
Original Books
Paragon House Publishing
Pearl Publishing House
Quest Books
Rama Publishing Co.
Theosophical Publishing House
Writer's Resources

SELF-HELP
Ability Work Shop Press
Airo Press
American Buddhist Movement
Amherst Media Publications
Arcus Publishing Company
Aslan Publishing
Avery Publishing Group
Bear & Company Publishing
Beyond Words Publishing Inc.
Blue Bird Publishing
Blue Poppy Press
Ceres Press
Civilized Publications
Contemporary Books, Inc.
Creativity Unlimited Press
Crystal Clarity Publishers
DeVorss & Company
Delta Sales Publishing
Dimi Press
Distinctive Publishing
Eagle's View Publishing
Element Books, Inc.
Fall Creek Press
Free Spirit Publishing

Hampton Roads Publishing Company
Hartley & Marks
Hay House
Health Communications, Inc.
Hohm Press
Impact Publishers, Inc.
Libra Press
Lifetime Books
Lotus Light Publications
Metamorphous Press
More to Life Publishing
The New Dawn Publishing Co.
New Falcon Press
New Harbinger Publications
New Mind Productions, Inc.
New Society Publishers
New World Library
Newcastle Publishing Company, Inc.
Newmarket Press
Rama Publishing Co.
Silvercat Publications
Superlove
Third Side Press, Inc.
Upper Access, Inc.
Valley of the Sun
Waterfront Books
Writer's Resources

SENIORS
Distinctive Publishing
Fithian Press
North Star Press

SOCIAL AND WORLD ISSUES
Ability Work Shop Press
Archives Publications
Bliss Publishing Company
Blue Bird Publishing
Cosmic Concepts
Faber and Faber Publishers, Inc.
Free Spirit Publishing
Hay House
Miles River Press

New Society Publishers
Open Court Publishing Company
Prima Publishing
The Savant Garde Workshop
University of California Press

SPIRITUALITY
America West Publishers
American Buddhist Movement
A.R.E. Press
Arkana
Bear & Company Publishing
Bear Tribe Publishing
Bell Tower
Blue Dove Press
Cassandra Press, Inc.
Center Press
Clear Light Publishers
Conari Press
Cosmic Concepts
Council Oak Publishing
Dawn Publications
Fall Creek Press
Grebner Books Publishing
Hazelden Educational Materials
Health Communications, Inc.
Heaven Bone Press
Illumination Arts, Inc.
Indelible Ink Publishing
Jewish Lights Publishing
Lindisfarne Press
More to Life Publishing
The New Dawn Publishing Co.
New Mind Productions, Inc.
New Spirit Press
Newcastle Publishing Company, Inc.
Nicolas-Hays, Inc.
North Star Press
Omega Publications
Oughten House Publications
Paragon House Publishing
Parallax Press
Quest Books

Rama Publishing Co.
Theosophical Publishing House
Threshold Books
Thunderbird Publications
Vedanta Press
Samuel Weiser Inc.
Wild Flower Press
Writer's Resources

WITCHES
Delphi Press
Faber and Faber Publishers, Inc.
International Guild of Advanced
   Sciences

WOMEN'S ISSUES
Branden Books
Chicago Review Press
Conari Press
Contemporary Books, Inc.
The Crossing Press
Delphi Press
Harmony Books
MacMurray and Beck Inc.
Miles River Press
Mills & Sanderson, Publishers
Morning Glory Press
North Star Press
Swan Raven & Company
Third Side Press, Inc.
Whole Person Associates, Inc.
Wild Flower Press
Wingbow Press
Writer's Resources

YOGA
Archives Publications
Jain Publishing Company
Lotus Light Publications
Original Books
Rodmell Press
Van Hoy Publishers

Ability Work Shop Press

Eldon Braun, Editor, 1601 Old Bayshore, No. 260, Burlingame, CA 94133   Phone: 415-692-1715, Fax: 415-692-8997

Profile: Self-help books. Titles: 4 per year; all nonfiction paperback. Average print run: 5,000. Binding: Perfect bound.
Focus and Imprints: Ability Work Shop Press publishes nonfiction books on improving conditions for which the author preferably has a following or at least a passion.
Editorial Interests
• *Nonfiction:* Self-help books in the areas of education reform, cultural and ethnic issues, ecosystems, the environment, healing, health, holistic health, inspiration, metaphysics, nutrition, parapsychology, parenting, psychology, recovery, relationships, seniors, social and world issues, and spirituality.
Submission and Payment Policy: Contact publisher for submission guidelines. Considers book packaging and subsidy publishing. Royalty, 10%.

ACS Publications

Maritha Pottenger, Editorial Director, 408 Nutmeg, San Diego, CA 92103   Phone: 619-297-9203

Profile: Publishes astrology-related nonfiction. An imprint of Astro Communications Services, Inc. Established in 1973. Titles: 4–6 per year; all nonfiction paperback. Average print run: 3,000. Binding: Perfect bound. Book catalogue available.
Focus and Imprints: ACS Publications seeks astrology books that emphasize personal power and responsibility rather than determinism. Make it practical and helpful with down-to-earth applications. "Avoid causal language that implies planets make things happen. Focus instead on choice, human responsibility, and power."
Editorial Interests
• *Nonfiction:* Astrology.
Recent Titles: *The Book of Jupiter* by Marilyn Waram. *Astro Essentials* by Maritha Pottenger.
Submission and Payment Policy: Query with outline. No unsolicited manuscripts. Include SASE. Accepts photocopies and computer printouts. Simultaneous submissions okay. Reports in 1–2 months. If accepted, expect publication in 1–2 years. Royalty, 10%.

A.G.S.

Collaboration Editor, Box 460313, San Francisco, CA 94146   Phone: 415-285-8799, Fax: 415-285-8790

Profile: Co-publisher of astrology and other new age titles. A division of Blue Wood Books. Titles: 6 per year; all nonfiction; hardcover and paperback. Average print run: 5,000. Binding: Varies. Book catalogue available.
Focus and Imprints: A.G.S. focuses primarily on astrology, though it is open to a variety of related and new age titles. Deals mostly in self-publishing and co-publishing relationships with writers.
Editorial Interests
• *Nonfiction:* Interests include astrology, channeling, crystals, cultural and ethnic issues, dreams, ecosystems, the environment, extraterrestrials, folklore, lifestyle, magic, metaphysics, mythology, new age, occult philosophy, and social and world issues.
Recent Titles: *The Astrological Cookbook* by Rana Birkmeier.
Submission and Payment Policy: Query first with outline. Include SASE. Accepts photocopies and computer printouts. Simultaneous submissions okay. Reports in 1 month. If accepted, expect publication in 9–12 months. Seeks publishing collaborations, either self-publishing or co-publishing.

Airo Press

David Webb, Managing Editor, 2165 B East Francisco Boulevard, San Rafael, CA 94901

Profile: Uplifting self-help material. A division of Uma Silbey, Inc. Titles: 1 per year; nonfiction paperback. Average print run: 10,000. Press: Web. Binding: Perfect bound. Book catalogue not available.
Focus and Imprints: Airo Press specializes in self-help books that nurture and promote a feeling of togetherness.
Editorial Interests
• *Nonfiction:* Self-help books in the areas of psychology, philosophy, religion, astrology, bodywork, channeling, crystals, cultural and ethnic issues, dreams, extraterrestrials, feminism, folklore, healing, health, holistic health, inspiration, lifestyle, meditation, metaphysics, mysticism, natural health, new age, parenting, prayer, recovery, relationships, Eastern and Western religion, social and world issues, spirituality, and yoga.
Recent Titles: *Enlightenment on the Run* by Uma. *Complete Crystal Guidebook* by Uma.
Submission and Payment Policy: Query first with outline. Include SASE. Accepts Macintosh disks. Simultaneous submissions okay. Reports in 1 week. Publication times varies. Royalty, 5%.

The Alternate Press

Wendy Priesnitz, Editor, 272 Highway 5, RR 1, St. George, ON N0E 1N0 Canada

Profile: Homeschooling books. Titles: 5 per year; all nonfiction paperback. Average print run: 2,000. Book catalogue available.
Focus and Imprints: The Alternate Press focuses solely on books for the homeschooling and home-based business market. It also publishes *Natural Life*, a monthly newsmagazine of holistic living.
Editorial Interests
• *Nonfiction:* Interested only in homeschooling topics and home business operation.
Recent Titles: *School Free* by Wendy Priesnitz.
Submission and Payment Policy: Query first with outline, writing samples, and resume. No unsolicited manuscripts. Include SASE. Accepts computer printouts and IBM text files of Microsoft Word disks. Reports in 1 month. Publication time varies. Royalty negotiated on an individual basis.

America West Publishers

George Green, President, P.O. Box 3300, Bozeman, MT 59772   Phone: 406-585-0700, Fax: 406-585-0703

Profile: Nonfiction on political and spiritual themes. Titles: 10 per year; all nonfiction paperbacks. Average print run: 5,000. Book catalogue available.
Focus and Imprints: American West publishes and/or distributes a main line of titles on political, economic, and social conspiracies as well as spiritual and metaphysical fare. To be considered, book proposals should explain why the submission is important and unique in content and approach, how it will benefit readers, and what will make it marketable.
Editorial Interests
• *Nonfiction:* Books on socio-political conspiracies, alternative health, the environment, survival, preparedness, spiritual and religious history, prophecy, new science, Native American studies, meditation, education, gardening, and UFO cases.
Recent Titles: *Using the Whole Brain* by Ronald Russell. *Mass Dreams of the Future* by Chet Snow and Helen Wambach.
Submission and Payment Policy: Query with a 300–400 word description of the book, 3 sample chapters, and author resume. Include SASE. Accepts photocopies, computer printouts, and computer disks. Simultaneous submissions okay. Reports in 1–2 months. If accepted, expect publication in 6 months. Royalty, 5–10%; advance, $250–$500.

American Buddhist Movement

Marian Valchar, Vice President, 301 West 45th Street, 6th Floor, New York, NY 10036   Phone: 212-489-1075

Profile: Books on Buddhism. Titles: 20 per year; all nonfiction; 10 hardcover; 10 paperback. Average print run: 1,000. Binding: Saddle stitched. Book catalogue not available.
Focus and Imprints: American Buddhist Movement publishes fiction and nonfiction on Buddhism, Daoism, Asian studies, and related topics. Avoid any type of vulgarity.
Editorial Interests
• *Fiction:* Fiction and poetry reflecting or exemplifying Buddhist philosophy and spirituality.
• *Nonfiction:* Interests include Buddhism/Daoism, meditation, Asian studies, positive thinking, networking, computer/databases/InterNet, bodywork, channeling, crystals, cultural and ethnic concerns, ecosystems, the environment, feminism, healing, health, holistic health, inspiration, lifestyle, metaphysics, mysticism, natural health, nutrition, philosophy, psychic phenomenon, psychology, recovery, relationships, self-help, social and world issues, spirituality, and yoga.
Recent Titles: *Consumer Direct Marketing* by Sunny O'Neil. *Introduction to C'Han* by Nelson Cai.
Submission and Payment Policy: Prefers complete manuscripts with cover letter. Accepts queries with outline, writing samples, and resume. Include SASE. Accepts photocopies, computer printouts, and IBM disks. Simultaneous submissions okay. Reports in 3 months. Royalty, 50%; advance, 50%.
Other Interests: Affiliated with the Association of American Buddhists. Sponsors a writing contest entitled Buddhism in American for manuscripts exploring Buddhism, Zen, Tibetan Buddhism, social action, and Tantra. For more information on the Association or contest guidelines, contact Dr. Kevin O'Neil, Publisher, 212-489-1075.

Amherst Media Publications

Richard Lynch, Editor, 155 Rand Street, Suite 300, Buffalo, NY 14207   Phone: 716-874-4450, Fax: 716-874-4508

Profile: Photography books. Titles: 10 per year; all nonfiction paperback. Average print run: 5,000. Binding: Notch. Book catalogue available.
Focus and Imprints: Amherst Media Publications lists how-to books on photography, videography, astronomy, and imaging, as well as equipment buyer's guides, repair manuals, and art photography books. Writers should have a clear idea of their audience and avoid infusing a great deal of personal material that does not relate directly to the manuscript topic. Accepts short fiction for its New Writing Award contest.

Editorial Interests
• *Nonfiction:* Self-help/how-to books in the areas of photography, videography, astronomy, and imaging. Consumer's guides and equipment repair manual. Art books.
Recent Titles: *The Basic Camcorder Guide* by Steve Bryant. *Video Sex* by Kevin Campbell.
Submission and Payment Policy: Query first with outline and 3 sample chapters. Include SASE. Accepts photocopies, computer printouts, and computer disks. No simultaneous submissions. Responds to queries in 1 month, to manuscripts in 2 months. If accepted, expect publication in 1 year. Book contracts are negotiated on an individual basis.
Other Interests: Sponsors an annual New Writing Award contest for short fiction. Requires a $10 reading fee to enter. Deadline, December, 31. Send an SASE for guidelines. Also offers New Writing Workshops correspondence courses that are developed individually for each writer. For more information, contact Richard Lynch. Is affiliated with The Book Doctor, which offers agent and editorial services. Contact Sam Meade, Box 1812, Amherst, NY 14226-7812.

Archives Publications

Phil Wycliff, Publisher, 334 State Street, Los Altos, CA 94022   Phone: 800-373-1897, Fax: 415-941-1773

Profile: Social history, archaeology, and equestrian arts. Titles: 10 per year; fiction and nonfiction; hardcover and paperback. Average print run: 10,000. Press: Sheet fed or web. Book list available.
Focus and Imprints: Archives Publications is interested in informative nonfiction books in the areas of archaeology, social history, and equestrian-related topics as well as vivid novels. Fiction must be riveting on the first read—no clichés or romance novels. Preference is given to works set in or exploring North California or Canadian British Columbia region.
Editorial Interests
• *Fiction:* Vivid novels on equestrian topics, archaeology, Irish or Celtic culture and folklore, spirituality, ethics, and sexuality.
• *Nonfiction:* Interests include archaeology, social history, and equestrian topics, as well as lifestyle, magic, men's issues, mysticism, mythology, natural health, nutrition, occult, parenting, philosophy, psychology, regional issues, spirituality, witches, women's issues, and yoga.
Submission and Payment Policy: Query first with outline. No unsolicited manuscripts. Include SASE. Accepts photocopies, computer printouts, and Macintosh ASCII disks. Reports in 1 month. Considers co-publishing ventures. Royalty, 5–15%; advance, $1,000–$5,000.

Arcus Publishing Company

Editor, 752 Broadway, P.O. Box 228, Sonoma, CA 94022   Phone: 707-996-9529, Fax: 707-996-1738

Profile: Self-help nonfiction. A division of Iris Influences, Inc. Established in 1983. Titles: 1 per year; nonfiction paperback. Average print run: 5,000. Perfect bound. Book list available.
Focus and Imprints: Arcus Publishing Company is dedicated to publishing beautiful, innovative, useful, insightful, and timeless books for personal growth. It seeks inspiring, ground-breaking themes in the field of self-help. Prefers a practical how-to format to books that are purely personal experience in nature.
Editorial Interests
• *Nonfiction:* Interested in practical self-help/how-to and personal growth books in the areas of astrology, bodywork, cultural and ethnic issues, dreams, the environment, feminism, folklore, gay and lesbian concerns, healing, health, holistic health, inspiration, lifestyle, meditation, men's issues, metaphysics, mysticism, mythology, natural health, and new age.
Recent Titles: *A Change of Heart* by Meryn Callander and Jon Travis. *Artist of the Spirit* by Mary Carroll Nelson.
Submission and Payment Policy: Query first with outline. Include SASE. Accepts photocopies, computer printouts, and faxes. Simultaneous submissions okay. Reports in 3 months. If accepted, expect publication in 1 year. Royalty.

A.R.E. Press

Jon Robertson, Editor-in-Chief, 68th Street and Atlantic Avenue, Box 656, Virginia Beach, VA 23451-0656
Phone: 804-428-3588, Fax: 804-422-6921

Profile: Hardcover and trade paperback books related to the spiritual principles of Edgar Cayce. A division of the Association for Research and Enlightenment. Titles: 14 per year; 2 fiction; 12 nonfiction; 4 hardcover; 10 paperback. Average print run: 5,000. Book catalogue and writer's guidelines available.
Focus and Imprints: A. R. E. Press dedicates its list to the exploration of the philosophy of psychic Edgar Cayce and related themes. All book proposals must be based on or compatible with the material in the Cayce psychic readings. Prefers material about the successful application of Edgar Cayce's spiritual principles, as opposed to the academic or analytical perspective. Any work identified as occult will be rejected.
Editorial Interests
• *Fiction:* Uplifting fiction that is spiritual or metaphysical and is compatible with the Cayce philosophy.
• *Nonfiction:* Books on or compatible with Cayce spiritual principles on the subjects of astrology, dreams, healing, health,

holistic health, inspiration, meditation, metaphysics, mysticism, new age, parapsychology, philosophy, psychic phenomenon, psychology, self-help, spirituality, and reincarnation.

Recent Titles: *Facing Myself: Reflections from Past Lives, Dreams and Psychic Readings* by Jennifer Borchers. *Spiritual Lessons of Learning to Love* by Lin Cochran.

Submission and Payment Policy: Request guidelines before submitting. Accepts queries with outline, synopsis, and 2 sample chapters. No unsolicited manuscripts. Include SASE. Accepts computer printouts. Simultaneous submissions okay. Reports in 2 months. If accepted, expect publication in 18 months. Royalty, 10–15%; advance, up to $2,000.

Other Interests: The Association for Research and Enlightenment sponsors conferences on Cayce principles throughout the country. For more information contact the Association at Box 595, Virginia Beach, VA 23451 or call 804-428-3588.

Arkana

David Stanford, Senior Editor, 375 Hudson Street, New York, NY 10014   Phone: 212-366-2000

Profile: Nonfiction books on spirituality and religion. A division of Penguin USA. Titles: 10 per year; all nonfiction. Average print run: Varies. Book catalogue available.

Focus and Imprints: Arkana acquires high-quality nonfiction titles on spirituality, philosophy, psychology, and religion. Material must be submitted through an agent.

Editorial Interests

• *Nonfiction:* Interests include spirituality, philosophy, psychology, and religion, specifically women's spirituality, mythology, Zen Buddhism, and Christian mysticism.

Recent Titles: *Zen and the Art of Making a Living* by Lawrence Boldt. *The Healing Path* by Marc Barasch.

Submission and Payment Policy: Accepts material only when submitted through a literary agent. Offers a royalty.

Arrowstar Publishing

John Bell, Editor, 100134 University Park Station, Denver, CO 80210-0134   Phone: 303-231-6599

Profile: Native American and Native Alaskans titles. Established in 1983. Titles: 5 per year; all nonfiction paperbacks. Average print run: 100–5,000. Book catalogue available.

Focus and Imprints: Arrowstar Publishing is an American Indian nonprofit organization publishing books that improve the social and economic conditions of Native Americans and Alaska Native communities. All authors are of Native American heritage.

Editorial Interests

• *Fiction:* Novels dealing with Native American concerns.

• *Nonfiction:* Documentary-type books on Native American culture and issues.

Recent Titles: *Motorcycle Sex* by Gregory Frazier. *How to Enroll in an Indian Tribe* by Morning Star.

Submission and Payment Policy: Query first with outline. Include SASE. Accepts photocopies and computer printouts. Responds to queries in 1 month, to manuscripts in 6 weeks. If accepted, expect publication in 6 months. Pays a royalty.

Aslan Publishing

Dawson Church, Editor, P.O. Box 108, Lower Lake, CA 95457   Phone: 707-995-1861, Fax: 707-995-1814

Profile: Self-help trade titles. A division of Atrium Publishers Group. Titles: 5 per year; all nonfiction paperbacks. Binding: Perfect bound. Book catalogue available.

Focus and Imprints: Aslan Publishing's list consists primarily of trade-oriented nonfiction on self-development, psychology, spirituality, business, and health. Presently, it is not accepting new manuscripts in order to focus on its distributorship, Atrium Publishers Group.

Editorial Interests

• *Nonfiction:* Interests include self-help, healing, health, holistic health, inspiration, parenting, psychology, recovery, relationships, and spirituality.

Recent Titles: *Fritjof Capra in Conversation with Michael Toms* by Michael Toms. *Man with No Name* by Wally Amos.

Submission and Payment Policy: Not currently accepting submissions.

Athanor Press

Bruce Schaffenberger, Managing Editor, 5550 Franklin Boulevard, Suite 101, Sacramento, CA 95820-4742
Phone/Fax: 916-424-4355

Profile: Books on the paranormal. Titles: 2 per year; nonfiction. Average print run: 5,000. Binding: Perfect bound. Book catalogue available.

Focus and Imprints: Athanor Press specializes in nonfiction books that explore ghost and UFO sitings and other paranormal events. Material should be well documented. Avoid injecting personal philosophy into the manuscript. Try to report on the subject objectively.

Editorial Interests
• *Nonfiction:* Interests include the occult, parapsychology, psychic phenomenon, extraterrestrials, ghosts, monsters, and sacred sites.

Recent Titles: *National Directory of Haunted Places* by Dennis William Hauck. *UFO Manual* by Alan Ecurb.

Submission and Payment Policy: Send complete manuscript with cover letter, bibliography, and resume. Include SASE. Accepts photocopies, computer printouts, faxes, and IBM Word for Windows disks. Simultaneous submissions okay. Reports in 3–6 months. If accepted, expect publication in 6–12 months. Considers subsidy and co-publishing ventures. Flat fee, $300–$1,000.

Austin and Winfield Publishers

Robert West, Editor-in-Chief, P.O. Box 2590, San Francisco, CA 94126   Phone: 415-981-5144, Fax: 415-981-6313

Profile: Scholarly books. Titles: 30 per year; all nonfiction; hardcover and paperback. Average print run: 500. Book catalogue available.

Focus and Imprints: Austin and Winfield Publishers acquires scholarly books on law, policy, and the social sciences. Imprints include Catholic Scholars Press, International Scholars Publications, Christian Universities Press, and Jewish Scholars Press. For consideration, submit a concise, accurate, and thorough proposal. Avoid optimism.

Editorial Interests
• *Nonfiction:* Scholarly monographs and dissertations textbooks.

Recent Titles: *Gerome Carlin: Lawyers on Their Own. Challenges of a Changing America* by Ernest Myers.

Submission and Payment Policy: Send a book proposal, curricula vitae, and writing samples. Include SASE. Accepts photocopies, computer printouts, and faxes. Simultaneous submissions okay. Reports in 1 month. If accepted, expect publication in 1 year. Contracts are negotiated on an individual basis.

Avery Publishing Group

Managing Editor, 120 Old Broadway, Garden City Park, NY 11040   Phone: 516-741-2155

Profile: Self-help, alternative health books. Titles: 35 per year; all nonfiction; 3 hardcover; 32 paperback. Average print run: 5,000–10,000. Binding: Perfect bound. Book catalogue available.

Focus and Imprints: Avery Publishing Group lists nonfiction self-improvement and alternative health titles.

Editorial Interests
• *Nonfiction:* Interests include holistic health, healing, the environment, parenting, healthy cooking, nutrition, sexuality, business, and self-help.

Recent Titles: *The Vegetarian Journal's Guide* by Vegetarian Resource Group. *Sharks Don't Get Cancer* by I. William Lane and Linda Comac.

Submission and Payment Policy: Query with outline. Include SASE. Accepts photocopies and computer printouts. Simultaneous submissions okay. Reports in 2 weeks. If accepted, expect publication in 8–12 months.

Bala Books, Inc.

Philip Gallelli, Director, 12520 Kirkham Court, Suite 7, Poway, CA 92064   Phone: 619-679-9080, Fax: 619-679-6908

Profile: Adult and children's books on East Indian culture. Book list available.

Focus and Imprints: Bala Books focuses on aspects of East Indian lifestyle and culture as well as Vaishaua/Hindu religion.

Editorial Interests
• *Fiction:* Children's stories, retellings, picture books, and activity books for ages 4–11 that reinforce East Indian spirituality, mythology, and folklore.
• *Nonfiction:* East Indian culture, customs, cooking, health practices, nutrition, mythology, and Vaishaua/Hindu beliefs.

Recent Titles: *Lord Krishna's Cuisine: The Art of Indian Vegetarian Cooking* by Yamuna Devi. *A Gift of Love: The Story of Sudama the Brahman* by Yogeswara Das.

Submission and Payment Policy: Query first with outline, 2 sample chapters, and resume. Include SASE. Accepts photocopies, computer printouts, and Macintosh Microsoft Word, Pagemaker, or QuarkXPress disks. Reports in 1–6 months. Publication time varies. Payment negotiated on an individual basis.

Bandanna Books

Sasha Newborn, Editor/Publisher, 319-B Anacapa Street, Santa Barbara, CA 93101   Phone: 805-962-9915, Fax: 805-564-3278

Profile: Humanist literary classics and translations. Titles: 3 per year; 1 fiction; 2 nonfiction; all paperback. Average print run:

1,500. Press: Offset. Binding: Perfect bound. Book list available.

Focus and Imprints: Bandanna Books specializes in classics in literature and history as well as language books, with an emphasis on humanist principles. It publishes reprints, new translations, and occasionally the work of a new author. It markets to high-school and college-aged readers and designs its books to help readers become thinking, independent citizens. Bandanna Books does not tolerate sexism and is not open to religion. Avoid fantasy, metaphysical speculation, or spiritualism and the supernatural. Its *Little Humanist Classics* series offer classic works in philosophy, literature, or history from the Greeks to the 19th century. It also publishes a list of language books looking at new approaches in language learning.

Editorial Interests

• *Fiction:* Non-sexist adolescent-to-adult growth stories that apply as equally to women as to men.

• *Nonfiction:* New translations of humanist classics from any age or culture. Language books. General interests include humanism, cultural and ethnic issues, feminism, children's and teen issues, philosophy, self-help, and women's issues.

Recent Titles: *Benigna Machiavelli* by Charlotte Perkins Gilman. *Sappho, the Poems* edited by Sasha Newborn.

Submission and Payment Policy: Query first with outline and 2 sample chapters. Include SASE. Accepts photocopies and computer printouts. Simultaneous submissions okay. Reports in 2 months. If accepted, expect publication in 1 year. Royalty, 10%.

Other Interests: Offers print brokering, book design, typesetting, and editing services through its affiliate, Words Worth of Santa Barbara. Bandanna Books considers entering into co-publishing ventures for books that spark interest.

Beacon Press

Editor, 25 Beacon Street, Boston, MA 02108   Phone: 617-742-2110, Fax: 617-723-3097

Profile: Scholarly nonfiction. A division of the Unitarian Universalist Association, a nonprofit organization. Established in 1854. Titles: 50 per year; all nonfiction; 35 hardcover; 15 paperback. Average print run: 4,000. Book catalogue available.

Focus and Imprints: Beacon Press supports a list of high-quality scholarly nonfiction books, many of which address topics of urgent public concern and encourage open discussion. Publishes several well-known authors such as Cornel West, Rosemary Radford Ruether, and Thich Nhat Hanh.

Editorial Interests

• *Nonfiction:* The environment, feminism, gay and lesbian issues, and religion.

Recent Titles: *Race Matters* by Cornel West. *The Measure of Our Success* by Marian Wright Edelman.

Submission and Payment Policy: Query first with outline, 2 sample chapters, and resume. Include SASE. Accepts photocopies and computer printouts. Simultaneous submissions okay. Reports in 3–4 months.

Bear & Company Publishing

Barbara Hand Clow, Editor, P.O. Box 2860, Santa Fe, NM 87504   Phone: 505-983-5968, Fax: 505-989-8386

Profile: New age books. Established in 1982. Titles: 12 per year; 1 fiction; 11 nonfiction; 2 hardcover; 9 paperback. Average print run: 5,000. Binding: Perfect bound. Book catalogue available.

Focus and Imprints: Bear & Company is dedicated to awakening the consciousness of individuals by addressing their spiritual needs, intellectual growth, and emotional exploration in ways that are sensitive to the environment and all forms of life. Books deal with new thought, new age, and spirituality.

Editorial Interests

• *Nonfiction:* Interests include uplifting, informative books on spirituality, Native American spirituality, Creation spirituality, astrology, bodywork, channeling, cultural and ethnic concerns, ecosystems, the environment, extraterrestrials, feminism, folklore, gay and lesbian concerns, healing, health, holistic health, magic, meditation, men's issues, metaphysics, mysticism, mythology, natural health, new age, parapsychology, philosophy, politics, psychic phenomenon, psychology, recovery, relationships, self-help, social and world issues, and women's issues.

Recent Titles: *World War II: Population in the Biosphere at the End of the Millennium* by Michael Tobias. *Emerald River of Compassion* by Rowena Pattee Kryder.

Submission and Payment Policy: Query first with outline and 2 sample chapters, or send complete manuscript with cover letter and author biography. Include SASE. Accepts photocopies, computer printouts, and ASCII disks. Simultaneous submissions okay. Reports in 2–6 weeks. If accepted, expect publication in 1 year. Writer's contracts vary.

Bear Tribe Publishing

Orville Burch, Executive Director, P.O. Box 9167, Spokane, WA 99209   Phone: 509-326-6561, Fax: 509-326-1713

Profile: Native American nonfiction. Titles: 1–2 per year; nonfiction paperback. Average print run: 20,000. Book catalogue available.

Focus and Imprints: Bear Tribe Publishing seeks to pass on the teachings and philosophies of Sun Bear, founder and medicine chief of the Bear Tribe, a worldwide, multiracial tribe bounded by belief and action, not geography. It publishes nonfiction books about Native American's and Native American philosophy. Seeks out and assists Native American authors. Proceeds go to support the Bear Tribe Medicine Society, a nonprofit education and spiritual organization. Avoid writing about "philosophies unless you have lived them—not interested in viewpoints, but in experience." Also publishes *Wildfire Magazine*.

Editorial Interests
• *Nonfiction:* General nonfiction and biographies on Native American philosophy, spirituality, practices, and history. Related topics include crystals, dreams, the environment, feminism, folklore, healing, holistic and natural health, lifestyle, men's issues, mysticism, mythology, new age, nutrition, self-help, social and world issues, and women's issues.

Recent Titles: *Dreaming With the Wheel* by Wabun Wind, Jun Bear, and Shawodese. *Return to Creation* by Manitonquat.

Submission and Payment Policy: Query first with outline, 3 sample chapters, and writing samples. Include SASE. Accepts photocopies and computer printouts. No simultaneous submissions. Reports in 2–3 months. If accepted, expect publication in 8–10 months. Payment negotiated on an individual basis.

Bell Tower

Toinette Lippe, Editorial Director, 201 East 50th Street, New York, NY 10022   Phone: 212-572-2041, Fax: 212-572-2662

Profile: Inspirational fiction and nonfiction. A division of Harmony Books. Titles: 6 per year; 1 fiction; 5 nonfiction; 3 hardcover; 3 paperback. Book list available.

Focus and Imprints: Bell Tower offers fiction and nonfiction books that "nourish the soul, illuminate the mind, and speak directly to the heart."

Editorial Interests
• *Fiction and Nonfiction:* Books of inspiration and companionship that help people in their spiritual lives. Interests include meditation, mysticism, and spirituality.

Recent Titles: *The Alchemy of Illness* by Kat Duff. *Sharing Silence* by Gunilla Norris.

Submission and Payment Policy: Query first with 2 sample chapters. Include SASE. Accepts photocopies and computer printouts. Simultaneous submissions okay. Reports in 1 week. If accepted, expect publication in 1 year. Royalty; advance.

Beyond Words Publishing Inc.

Julie Livingston, Managing Editor, 4443 NE Airport Road, Hillsboro, OR 97123   Phone: 503-647-5109, Fax: 503-647-5114

Profile: Growth-oriented books for adults and children. Established in 1983. Titles: 6–8 per year; 2 fiction; 6 nonfiction; 4 hardcover; 4 paperback. Average print run: 1,500. Press: Sheet-fed or web. Binding: Smythe or perfect bound. Book catalogue available.

Focus and Imprints: Beyond Words Publishing lists gift/coffee table books with nature-related and indigenous themes; self-help books on personal growth, parenting, business success; and fiction for children. Avoid personal or autobiographical stories and anthropomorphic animal characters. Book lines include *The Earthsong Collection*, coffee table books with a conscience, and *Kids Books by Kids*.

Editorial Interests
• *Fiction:* General and Native American children's books, picture books, legends, and folktales.
• *Nonfiction:* Nature photography, creativity, life management, self-help, personal growth, psychology, health, holistic and natural health, lifestyle, nutrition, parenting, relationships, spirituality, and women's issues.

Recent Titles: *Men, Women, and Relationships* by Dr. John Gray. *Raising a Son* by Do and Jeanne Elium.

Submission and Payment Policy: Query with outline, 3 sample chapters, and resume. Identify potential audience for the book and offer pertinent marketing information. Include SASE. Accepts photocopies, computer printouts, Macintosh disks, and faxes. Simultaneous submissions okay. Responds to queries in 3 months, to manuscripts in 4–5 months. If accepted, expect publication in 1 year. Royalty, 10% of net.

Bioenergetics Press

R. Schenk, President, Box 9141, Madison, WI 53715   Phone: 608-255-4028, Fax: 608-251-0658

Profile: Books on gender issues. Titles: 1 per year; paperback. Book catalogue available.

Focus and Imprints: Bioenergetics Press publishes books concerning gender issues, including men's issues books.

Editorial Interests
• *Nonfiction:* Books on gender-related issues and men's interests.

Recent Titles: *On Sex and Gender* by Roy Schenk.

Submission and Payment Policy: Query with outline. Include SASE. Accepts faxes. Reports in 1 month. If accepted, expect publication in 2–3 months.

Bliss Publishing Company

Stephen Clouter, Publisher, P.O. Box 920, Marlboro, MA 01752   Phone: 508-779-2827

Profile: Nonfiction publisher. Titles: 2 per year; all nonfiction paperback. Average print run: 2,000. Binding: Sewn or perfect bound. Book catalogue available.

Focus and Imprints: Bliss Publishing Company is a small publisher of nonfiction with a particular interest in New England regional titles and music books.

Editorial Interests

• *Nonfiction:* Interests include New England regional issues, music, cultural and ethnic concerns, ecosystems, the environment, politics, and social and world issues.

Recent Titles: *On the Child's River* by Ron McAdow.

Submission and Payment Policy: Query with outline, 2–3 sample chapters, table of contents, and author biography. Include SASE. Accepts photocopies and computer printouts. Simultaneous submissions okay. Reports in 4–6 weeks. If accepted, expect publication within 1 year. Payment negotiable.

Blue Bird Publishing

Cheryl Gorder, Publisher, 1739 East Broadway, No. 306, Tempe, AZ 85282   Phone: 602-831-6063, Fax: 602-831-1829

Profile: Educational and home schooling material. Titles: 6 per year; all nonfiction paperbacks. Binding: Perfect bound. Book catalogue available.

Focus and Imprints: Blue Bird Publishing lists resource guides and self-help books on home schooling, parenting, and social issues. "Be clear and concise." Avoid fiction and children's books.

Editorial Interests

• *Nonfiction:* Educational, self-help, and resource books on parenting, curriculum for home schooling families, home business operation, multicultural and social issues, relationships, and lifestyle.

Recent Titles: *Expanding Your Child's Horizons* by Art Attwell. *Home Education Resource Guide* by Don Hubbs.

Submission and Payment Policy: Query first with outline and 2 sample chapters. Include SASE. Accepts photocopies and computer printouts. Simultaneous submissions okay. Reports in 2 months. If accepted, expect publication in 6–12 months. Considers subsidy publishing ventures. Payment varies.

Blue Dove Press

Jeff Blom, Publisher, 10141 Maya Linda Road, Suite 107, San Diego, CA 92126   Phone: 619-271-0490, Fax: 619-271-5695

Profile: Spiritual and inspirational books. Titles: 12 per year; all nonfiction; 6 hardcover; 6 paperback. Average print run: 2,500. Binding: Perfect or case bound. Book catalogue available.

Focus and Imprints: Blue Dove Press publishes books by and about saints of all the world's religions, on scripture of all religions, and on other spiritually uplifting topics. Not interested in recovery or 12-step-oriented books.

Editorial Interests

• *Nonfiction:* Lives of saints from all religions, inspirational material, meditation, mysticism, and spirituality.

Recent Titles: *In Quest of God* by Swami Ramdas. *1008 Undeniable Truths* by Andrew Williams.

Submission and Payment Policy: Query with outline and 1 sample chapter. Include SASE. Accepts photocopies, computer printouts, faxes, and computer disks. Simultaneous submissions okay. Responds to queries in 1 month, to manuscripts in 6 weeks. Royalty, 8%; advance, $250–$1,000.

Blue Poppy Press

Bob Flaws, Editor, 1775 Linden Avenue, Boulder, CO 80304   Phone: 303-447-8372, Fax: 303-447-0740

Profile: Nonfiction books on acupuncture and oriental medicine. Established in 1981. Titles: 9 per year; all nonfiction; 1 hardcover; 8 paperback. Average print run: 1,000. Perfect bound. Book catalogue available; publishes 2 per year.

Focus and Imprints: Blue Poppy Press specializes in books on acupuncture and oriental medicine for both the professional and lay reader. Its *Great Masters Series* publishes translations of preeminent Chinese medical classics.

Editorial Interests

• *Nonfiction:* Acupuncture and oriental medicine.

Recent Titles: *A New American Acupuncture* by Mark Seem. *Imperial Secrets of Health and Longevity* by Bob Flaws.

Submission and Payment Policy: Query with outline, 1–2 sample chapters, and resume. Include SASE. Accepts photocopies, computer printouts, and faxes. No simultaneous submissions. Reports in 1 month. If accepted, expect publication in 4–6 months. Final manuscripts must be submitted in both hard copy and disk format, either 3.5" or 5.25" ASCII or WordPerfect 5–6.0. Pays 10–15% royalty.

Other Interests: Affiliated with the Council of Oriental Medical Publishers, 1775 Linden Avenue, Boulder, CO 80304. Authors participate in and lead numerous workshops throughout the United States, Europe, Australia, and New Zealand. For more information, contact Honorahee Wolfe, 303-447-8372.

The Book Publishing Company

Cynthia Holzatfel, Managing Editor, P.O. Box 99, Summertown, TN 38483   Phone: 615-964-3571

Profile: Vegetarian cookbooks and health-related material. Titles: 12 per year; all nonfiction paperback. Average print run: 5,000. Perfect bound. Book catalogue available.
Focus and Imprints: The Book Publishing Company offers a line of nonfiction on health and lifestyle with an emphasis on vegetarian cookbooks and writings by Native American authors.
Editorial Interests
• *Nonfiction:* Vegetarianism, vegetarian cookbooks, nutrition, and books on Native American history and culture written by Native Americans.
Recent Titles: *The Uncheese Cookbook* by JoAnn Stepaniak. *The Almost No-Fat Cookbook* by Bryanna Clark Grogan.
Submission and Payment Policy: Query first with outline, sample chapters, and writing samples, or send complete manuscript with cover letter. Include SASE. Accepts photocopies and computer printouts. Simultaneous submissions okay. Reports in 2 months. If accepted, expect publication in 1 year. Royalty or flat fee.

Book World, Inc.

Barbara DeBolt, Editor, 9666 East Riggs Road, No. 194, Sun Lakes, AZ 85248   Phone: 602-895-7995

Profile: New age books. Established in 1992. Titles: 12 per year; paperback fiction and nonfiction. Average print run: Varies. Binding: Perfect bound. Book catalogue available.
Focus and Imprints: Formerly the Southwest Publishing Company of Arizona, Book World, Inc. is a small, independent publisher of new age and metaphysical books with uplifting, positive messages. New to its publishing interests are the *Blue Star Books* line of mail-order titles and *Book World Today*, a newsletter for authors, independent publishers, and booksellers. "Avoid the negative and concentrate on the positive."
Editorial Interests
• *Fiction:* Inspirational fiction and fantasy with new age and Native American themes.
• *Nonfiction:* Interested in new age topics: channeling, crystals, dreams, extraterrestrials, healing, meditation, metaphysics, mysticism, mythology, philosophy, psychic phenomenon, and spirituality.
Recent Titles: *Homecoming of the Alien Heart* by B. Lambert. *Crazy Horse, The Boy* by Edward Heisel.
Submission and Payment Policy: Query with outline and 3 sample chapters, or send complete manuscript with cover letter. Include SASE. Accepts photocopies and computer printouts. Simultaneous submissions okay if noted. Reports in 2–6 months. If accepted, expect publication in 2–3 years. Royalty, 10%.
Other Interests: Sponsors the Book World Today Writers Conference for authors, independent publishers and booksellers. Held in Phoenix, Arizona. For more information, contact Barbara DeBolt, 602-895-7995.

Branden Books

Adolfo Caso, Editor, 17 Station Street, Box 843, Brookline V., MA 02147   Phone/Fax: 617-734-2045

Profile: Hardcover and paperback fiction and nonfiction. Titles: 15 per year; 2 fiction; 13 nonfiction; 10 hardcover; 5 paperback. Average print run: 3,000. Book list available.
Focus and Imprints: Branden Books publishes a variety of titles, primarily nonfiction with a focus on biographies.
Editorial Interests
• *Fiction:* Historical fiction.
• *Nonfiction:* Interests include biographies, reference books, African American issues, health and women's issues, the military, music, parenting, politics, religion, and philosophy.
Recent Titles: *Mary Dyer* by Ruth Plimpton. *Fighting Men* by John Zubritsky.
Submission and Payment Policy: Query first in the form of a 1–2 paragraph description of the book. No unsolicited manuscripts. Include SASE. Accepts computer printouts and WordPerfect disks. No simultaneous submissions. Reports in 1 week. If accepted, expect publication in 6–10 months. Royalty, 10%.

Brotherhood of Life, Inc.

Richard Buhler, President, 110 Dartmouth SE, Albuquerque, NM 87106-2218   Phone: 505-873-2179, Fax: 505-873-2423

Profile: Nonfiction new age and metaphysical books. Established in 1969. Titles: 4 per year; all nonfiction paperback. Average print run: 2,000+. Binding: Perfect bound. Book catalogue available.
Focus and Imprints: Brotherhood of Life is a nonsectarian publisher interested in cutting-edge, metaphysical books on a variety of topics related to the new age/new consciousness movement.
Editorial Interests
• *Nonfiction:* Interests include metaphysics, new age, Tantra, shamanism, I Ching, gems, crystals, vibrational healing, ancient

wisdom, spiritism, lost civilizations, UFOs, magic, astrology, bodywork, channeling, dreams, the environment, folklore, holistic health, meditation, mysticism, mythology, occult, parapsychology, prayer, psychic phenomenon, rebirthing, spirituality, witches, and yoga.

Recent Titles: *The Giants of Gaia* by Nicholas R. Mann and Marcia Sutton, Ph. D. *Aghora II: Kundalini* by Robert E. Svoboda.

Submission and Payment Policy: Query with outline and 3 sample chapters. Include SASE. Accepts photocopies, computer printouts, and computer disks. Simultaneous submissions okay. Reports in 2 months. If accepted, expect publication in 6–8 months. Royalty, 10–15%.

Brunswick Publishing Corporation

Marianne Salzmann, Publisher, or Walter J. Raymond, Editor, Route 1, Box 1A1, Lawrenceville, VA 23868
Phone: 804-848-3865

Profile: A co-publishing/subsidy press. Titles: 15–20 per year; 20% fiction; 80% nonfiction; 70% hardcover; 30% paperback. Average print run: 500–5,000. Press: Offset. Binding: Smythe sewn, case bound, perfect bound, or paper bound. Book announcement sheets available.

Focus and Imprints: Brunswick Publishing Corporation operates primarily as a co-publisher, working with authors to produce their books. It is open to manuscripts that may not be profitable enough for commercial publishers to handle and works of value that may have limited appeal due to their unique character and esoteric subject matter. Encourages writers to approach commercial publishers before contracting with Brunswick. "We want books published by our company to benefit the reader—in other words, to make a difference." Avoid "trashy" mass market paperback material. Does not consider fanatical hate literature or pornographic material.

Editorial Interests

• *Fiction and Nonfiction:* Considers all topics, styles, and genres. It is more important that the writer "be focused on what they want their book to accomplish."

Recent Titles: *The Women's Song Still Not Heard* by Frances Louise Drew. *Exploring Inner Space* by Robert Fletcher Smith.

Submission and Payment Policy: Request and review Statement of Philosophy and Purpose. Send complete manuscript with cover letter, resume, clips, and any relevant information. Include SASE. Accepts photocopies and computer printouts. Simultaneous submissions okay. Responds to queries in 1 week, to manuscripts in 1 month. If accepted, expect publication in 1 year. Co-publishing agreement: Publishes a pilot edition of 500 copies. Author and publisher share costs and profits on a 60/40 basis respectively. Subsequent editions are shared on a 50/50 basis. Brunswick will occasionally subsidize publishing costs for works of particular merit.

Cassandra Press, Inc.

Gurdas, CEO, P.O. Box 150868, San Rafael, CA 94915   Phone: 415-382-8507, Fax: 415-382-7758

Profile: New age nonfiction. Titles: 4–6 per year; all nonfiction. Average print run: Varies.

Focus and Imprints: Cassandra Press publishes metaphysical and new age nonfiction titles.

Editorial Interests

• *Nonfiction:* New age, metaphysics, astrology, channeling, crystals, extraterrestrials, healing and health, holistic health, mysticism, natural health, nutrition, occult, parapsychology, psychic phenomenon, self-help, and spirituality.

Recent Titles: *Health Secrets from the Ancient World* by John Heinerman, Ph.D. *Spiritual Nutrition and the Rainbow Diet* by Gabriel Cousens.

Submission and Payment Policy: Query with outline and 2 sample chapters or send complete manuscript with cover letter, bibliography, and resume. Include SASE. Accepts photocopies and computer printouts. Simultaneous submissions okay. Reports in 2–3 months. Royalty.

Center Press

Gabriella Caine, Editor, Box 16452, Encino, CA 91416-6452

Profile: Literary fiction, poetry, and nonfiction. Titles: 6 per year; 3 hardcover; 3 paperback. Average print run: 5,000. Book catalogue not available.

Focus and Imprints: Center Press publishes a variety of literary fiction, poetry, and eclectic nonfiction. The manuscripts it publishes are acquired primarily through its Masters Literary Award writers contest, a quarterly writing contest in operation since 1981. Manuscripts are judged and awarded by three anonymous literary professionals. Writers are encouraged to "write what your heart tells you, take classes and workshops, join professional clubs and organizations, and love your craft." Its imprints include the Universal Science Press.

Editorial Interests

• *Fiction:* Short stories, vignettes, novel excerpts, or stage or screenplay excerpts, up to 5,000 words. Accepts all styles and genres. Prefers current material with literary merit.

• *Poetry:* Poems or song lyrics, 5 pieces maximum totaling no more that 150 lines. Accepts all poetic forms and styles. Prefers a clear, fresh voice, discipline, natural rhythm, and individuality.

• *Nonfiction:* Essays, editorials, journalistic or photojournalistic pieces or excerpts, up to 5,000 words. Demonstrate social consciousness or offer educational and cultural enrichment. Welcomes humor and satire. Interests include health, mysticism, and philosophy.

Recent Titles: *The 60s: Literature of Rebellion,* collected essays. *Spacion* by Evan Adar

Submission and Payment Policy: Send for Masters Literary Award guidelines before submitting. Submit complete manuscript or poetry with $10 entry fee and resume or brief biography. Entries must be received within predetermined deadlines, either March 15, June 15, September 15, or December 15 to be considered. Do not send originals; manuscripts are not returned. Include SASE for notification of award results. Accepts photocopies and computer printouts. Simultaneous submissions okay. Reports in 8–16 weeks. If accepted, expect publication in 1 year. Quarterly awards, $250. Yearly Grand Prize, $1,500. Center Press retains a one-time option on publication rights to all winning manuscripts.

Other Interests: Sponsors the Whiz Bang Waiter's Workshops and Write On, writer's conferences with quality facilitators. For more information, contact Gabriella Caine, Box 16452, Encino, CA 91416-6452.

Ceres Press

David Goldbeck, Editor/Publisher, P.O. Box 87, Woodstock, NY 12498   Phone/Fax: 914-679-5573

Profile: How-to books on holistic health and environmental issues. Established in 1977. Titles: 1 per year; nonfiction; paperback. Average print run: 5,000. Binding: Perfect bound. Book catalogue available.

Focus and Imprints: Named after the Greek goddess of grain, Ceres Press publishes books on natural foods, health and nutrition, and the environment. Use query to "educate us about and interest us in the subject of the book."

Editorial Interests

• *Nonfiction:* How-to and self-help books for adults and children on holistic health and nutrition, natural foods and cooking, vegetarianism, and the environment.

Recent Titles: *Clean and Green* by Annie Berthold-Bond. *The Smart Kitchen* by David Goldbeck.

Submission and Payment Policy: Query first with outline and 1 sample chapter. No unsolicited manuscripts. Include SASE. Accepts photocopies and computer printouts. Simultaneous submissions okay. Reports in 2 weeks. If accepted, expect publication in 1 year. Royalty and advance; rates negotiable.

Chelsea Green

Jim Schley, Editor-in-Chief, P.O. Box 428, No. 205, Gates-Briggs Building, White River Junction, VT 05001
Phone: 802-295-6300, Fax: 802-295-6444

Profile: Nonfiction books on sustainable living. Established in 1984. Titles: 6 per year; all nonfiction; 1 hardcover; 5 paperback. Average print run: 10,000. Press: Sheetfed and web. Binding: Perfect and case bound. Book catalogue available.

Focus and Imprints: Chelsea Green publishes books about nature and the environment that focus specifically on practical ecology, renewable energy, and sustainable approaches to agriculture and shelter. Looks for authors who "look at the future with hope, and with an acute sense of the practical" and can share "their own knowledge and experience to show us how we can begin, right now, to live sustainably." Not interested in fiction, poetry, or new age writing.

Editorial Interests

• *Nonfiction:* Practical books on sustainable living, organic gardening, ecology, and the environment.

Recent Titles: *Solar Gardening* by Leandre and Gretchen Poisson. *The Contrary Farmer* by Gene Logsdon.

Submission and Payment Policy: Query with outline, 1 sample chapter, and clips. Include SASE. Accepts photocopies. No simultaneous submissions. Reports in 1–2 months. If accepted, expect publication in 1–3 years. Offers advance and royalty; terms negotiable.

Chicago Review Press

Amy Teschner, Editor, 814 North Franklin, Chicago, IL 60201   Phone: 312-337-0747, Fax: 312-337-5985

Profile: Nonfiction books. Titles: 15 per year; all nonfiction; hardcover and paperback. Average print run: 5,000–7,500. Binding: Perfect bound. Book catalogue available.

Focus and Imprints: Chicago Review Press is open to publishing a variety of nonfiction titles, including those of regional Midwestern United States interest and children's activity books. Writers are encouraged to research this company before submitting material. It does not publish fiction, poetry, or any type of self-help nonfiction.

Editorial Interests

• *Nonfiction:* Interests include children's activity books, cultural and ethnic issues, feminism, gay and lesbian concerns, health, holistic health, juvenile and teen issues, natural health, nutrition, parenting, politics, regional Midwestern affairs, seniors, social and world issues, and women's issues.

Recent Titles: *The Mole People: Life In the Tunnels Beneath New York City* by Jennifer Toth. *Midwest Gardens* by Pamela Wolfe.
Submission and Payment Policy: Query first with outline. Include SASE. Accepts photocopies and computer printouts. Simultaneous submissions okay. Reports in 1–2 months. If accepted, expect publication in 1 year. Royalty, 7.5% on paperbacks. Offers a modest advance.

China Books & Periodicals

Wendy K. Lee, Editor, 2929 24th Street, San Francisco, CA 94110   Phone: 415-282-2994, Fax: 415-282-0994

Profile: Chinese culture and history titles. Titles: 4–6 per year; fiction and nonfiction. Average print run: 5,000. Book catalogue available.
Focus and Imprints: China Books & Periodicals specializes in books relating to China and Chinese culture, cooking, arts, health practices, and religion. Study catalogue for style and content before submitting.
Editorial Interests
• *Fiction:* Accepts fiction written in Chinese by Chinese writers. No English-language novels.
• *Nonfiction:* Books about or relating in some way to Chinese culture. Special interest in health books on Tai Chi, Qigong, and acupuncture. Other interests include travel guides, feminism, folklore, healing, mythology, nutrition, philosophy, Chinese and East Asian regions, social and world issues, and Buddhism and Taoism.
Recent Titles: *I Can Read That!: A Traveler's Guide to Chinese Characters* by Julie Mazel Sussman. *Biking Beijing* by Diana Kingsbury.
Submission and Payment Policy: Query first with outline, 1–3 sample chapters, writing samples, and resume. Include SASE. Accepts photocopies, computer printouts, faxes, and DOS or Macintosh disks. Simultaneous submissions okay. Responds to queries in 1 month, to manuscripts in 2–3 months. If accepted, expect publication in 6–12 months. Considers subsidy and co-publishing ventures. Royalty varies.

Civilized Publications

Jackie Turner, Office Manager, 2023 South Seventh Street, Philadelphia, PA 19148   Phone: 215-339-0061, Fax: 215-339-0449

Profile: Self-help books for African Americans. Titles: 1 nonfiction paperback per year. Average print run: 10,000. Binding: Perfect bound. Book flyers available.
Focus and Imprints: Civilized Publications devotes its list to self-help material aimed at African Americans for the purpose of "rebuilding the Black family and civilizing Black mothers and fathers." Not accepting the work of new authors until 1996.
Editorial Interests
• *Nonfiction:* African-American self-help books on the family, cultural concerns, lifestyle, men's issues, parenting, psychology, recovery, relationships, and women's issues.
Recent Titles: *The Black Man's Guide* by Shahrazad Ali. *Are You Still a Slave?* by Shahrazad Ali.
Submission and Payment Policy: Not accepting submissions until 1996. Authors may query with book ideas. Reports in 1 week.

Clear Light Publishers

Harmon Houghton, Publisher, 823 Don Diego, Santa Fe, NM 87501   Phone: 505-989-9590, Fax: 505-989-9519

Profile: Books celebrating the human spirit. Titles: 15 per year; 3 fiction; 12 nonfiction; all hardcover. Average print run: 5,000. Binding: Cloth bound. Book catalogue available.
Focus and Imprints: Clear Light Publishers select books that reflect the beauty of the natural world and pay tribute to people who have maintained and passed on their traditions. It focuses primarily on Native American art and culture, Western folklore, and the environment.
Editorial Interests
• *Fiction and Nonfiction:* Interests include Native American and Western American culture, the environment, folklore, healing, holistic health, inspirational material, philosophy, politics, and spirituality.
Recent Titles: *Brave Are My People* by Frank Waters. *Stone Time* by T. H. Watkins.
Submission and Payment Policy: Query with outline and 2 sample chapters. Include SASE. Accepts photocopies and computer printouts. Simultaneous submissions okay. Reports in 3 months. If accepted, expect publication in 1 year. Royalty, 10% of net; advance, 50% of expected royalty.

Conari Press

Mary Jane Ryan, Executive Editor, 1144 65th Street, Suite B, Emeryville, CA 94608   Phone: 510-596-4040, Fax: 510-654-7259

Profile: Nonfiction books on women's issues and psychology. Established in 1987. Titles: 12 per year; all nonfiction; 2 hardcover; 10 paperback. Average print run: 10,000. Book catalogue available.

Focus and Imprints: Conari Press is a small, independent press that publishes primarily in the area of women's issues and personal growth. Welcomes quality books that will make a difference in people's lives, not "simplistic, jargonistic self-help" books. Offer "hope, humor, encouragement, and deep insight into what ails us and what might transform us." Study catalogue to see if your material is appropriate for this press. Not interested in recovery, childhood sexual abuse, or incest issues.
Editorial Interests
• *Nonfiction:* Interests include women's issues, feminism, parenting, psychology, relationships, and spirituality.
Recent Titles: *The Woman's Book of Courage* by Sue Patton Thoele. *True Love: How to Make Your Relationship Sweeter, Deeper and More Passionate* by Daphne Rose Kingma.
Submission and Payment Policy: Query first with outline and sample chapters. Include SASE. Accepts photocopies and computer printouts. Simultaneous submissions okay. Reports in 2 months. If accepted, expect publication in 6 months to 2 years. Offers a royalty; contracts negotiated on an individual basis.

Conservatory of American Letters

Robert W. Olmsted, President, P.O. Box 298, Thomaston, ME 04861   Phone: 207-354-0998

Profile: Literary fiction and nonfiction. Titles: 7 per year; 4 fiction; 3 nonfiction; 7 hardcover; 7 paperback. Average print run: 1,000. Press: Offset. Binding: cloth and perfect bound. Book catalogue available.
Focus and Imprints: Conservatory of American Letters publishes literary fiction, nonfiction, poetry collections, and drama. Poetry is released under its Northwood Press imprint. Its Dan River Press imprint lists fiction and books on Maine history. Encourages writers to write well and identify a market. "We're a small press. Don't submit to us and expect large press treatment."
Editorial Interests
• *Fiction:* Poetry, fiction, and drama. No restrictions on content.
• *Nonfiction:* Interests include the environment and ecosystems, folklore, lifestyle, occult, parapsychology, psychic phenomenon, psychology, rebirthing, relationships, witches, and yoga.
Recent Titles: *The Betheaden Road* by Sheldon Webster. *Moses Rose* by William Raiwbolg.
Submission and Payment Policy: Request guidelines before submitting. Include SASE. Accepts photocopies, computer printouts, and faxes. No simultaneous submissions. Reports in 2–8 weeks. If accepted, expect publication in 1 year. Royalty, 10%; advance, $250–$500.
Other Interests: Sponsors the Northwoods Journal Fall Poetry Contest. For guidelines or more information, contact Roy Schwartzman, 207-354-0998. Holds the annual Just Another Writer's Conference in the late summer. Contact Debbie Benner for more information, 207-354-0998.

Contemporary Books Inc.

Nancy Crossman, Editor, 180 North Stetson, Two Prudential Plaza, Suite 1200, Chicago, IL 60601-6790   Phone: 312-782-9181

Profile: Trade nonfiction. Titles: 30–40 per year; all nonfiction. Average print run: 10,000. Book catalogue available.
Focus and Imprints: Contemporary Books' adult nonfiction trade list is comprised of self-help/how-to books, cookbooks, and women's health and childcare titles.
Editorial Interests
• *Nonfiction:* How-to, women's health, and cookbooks.
Recent Titles: *Nature Abhors a Vacuum* by Catherine Henmner. *Dear Miss Demeanor* by Mary Mitchell.
Submission and Payment Policy: Query first with outline, 2–3 sample chapters, a description of author's qualifications, and any applicable artwork. Include SASE. Accepts photocopies and computer printouts. Simultaneous submissions okay. Considers book packaging, subsidy publishing, and co-publishing ventures. Payment is negotiated on an individual basis.

Cosmic Concepts

George W. Fisk, President, 2531 Dover Lane, St. Joseph, MI 49085   Phone: 616-428-2792, Fax: 616-983-5220

Profile: Fiction and nonfiction promoting spiritual enlightenment and planetary unity. Titles: 1 per year; paperback. Average print run: 3,000. Book list available.
Focus and Imprints: Cosmic Concepts seeks to produce books for all ages that will enhance spiritual enlightenment and planetary unity. "In accord with these goals, believing that the Creator is moving through all humanity, Cosmic Concepts is open to reviewing manuscripts from other countries and other cultures."
Editorial Interests
• *Fiction and Nonfiction:* Spiritually enlightened books on metaphysics, mysticism, mythology, parapsychology, and social and world issues.
Recent Titles: *The White Stone* by Alcot Allison. *Your Life and Love Beyond Death* by David Hyatt.
Submission and Payment Policy: Query first with outline, 3 sample chapters, and resume. No unsolicited manuscripts.

Include SASE. Reports in 1–2 months. If accepted, expect publication in 9–24 months. Royalty, 8%; advance, $500.
Other Interests: Affiliated with The Academy of Religion and Psychical Research. For more information contact, Boyce Batey, P.O. Box 614, Bloomfield, CT 06002-0614. Sponsors SFFI Great Lake Retreats at Olivet College, MI.

Council for Indian Education

Hap Gilliland, Editor, 3209 Grand Avenue, Billings, MT 59102   Phone: 406-252-7451

Profile: Native American books for children. Titles: 6 per year; 5 fiction; 1 nonfiction; all paperback. Average print run: 1,500. Binding: Perfect bound. Book catalogue available.
Focus and Imprints: Council for Indian Education publishes children's books about Native American life and culture. Material must be fast-starting high-interest. Be sure stories are culturally accurate for the particular tribe and period of history. No vulgarity or downgrading of any culture. Accepts bilingual books.
Editorial Interests
• *Fiction:* Historical and contemporary fiction on Native American life and culture for primary grades K–4, middle grades 4–8, and advanced grades, 8–12/Adult.
• *Nonfiction:* How-to books on Native American crafts and skills. Factual, information books on Native American life and history. Gear toward primary grades K–4, middle grades 4–8, or advanced grades, 8–12/Adult.
Recent Titles: *Remember My Name* by Sara Banks. *Kamacke and The Medicine Bead* by Jerry Cunnyngham.
Submission and Payment Policy: Query with outline and 3 sample chapters, or send complete manuscript with cover letter. Include SASE. Do not submit manuscripts between June 1 and October 1. Accepts photocopies and computer printouts. Simultaneous submissions okay . Responds to queries in 2 months, to manuscripts in 6 months. If accepted, expect publication in 1 year. Considers co-publishing ventures. Royalty, 10% of wholesale price.

Council Oak Publishing

Sally Denison, Editor, 1350 East 15th Street, Tulsa, OK 74120   Phone: 918-587-6454

Profile: Native American spirituality. Titles: 8 per year; all nonfiction.
Focus and Imprints: Council Oak Publishing focuses solely on Native American spirituality.
Editorial Interests
• *Nonfiction:* Native American spirituality.
Recent Titles: *Cherokee Festival of Days* by Joyce Sequichie Hifler. *Secret Native American Pathways* by Thomas E. Mails.
Submission and Payment Policy: Query first with outline. Include SASE. No unsolicited manuscripts. Reporting time varies. Royalty.

Countryman Press, Inc.

Helen Whybrow, Editor-in-Chief, P.O. Box 175, Woodstock, VT 05091   Phone: 802-457-1049, Fax: 802-457-3250

Profile: General trade titles. Established in 1973. Titles: 20 per year; 5 fiction; 15 nonfiction; 5 hardcover; 15 paperback. Average print run: 4,000. Binding: Notch. Book catalogue and writer's guidelines available.
Focus and Imprints: Countryman Press is a trade publisher of mysteries and New England regional, recreational, and environmental nonfiction. Its book lines include *Foul Play*, mystery books; *Backcountry*, recreational guides to regional areas; and *Countryman*, nature-related and general nonfiction. Authors are encouraged to do some research into the market and competition. Avoid trendy subjects, personal memoirs, and self-help/new age titles. Not interested in children's or young adult books.
Editorial Interests
• *Fiction:* Crime and suspense mysteries. No true crime, romance, or supernatural themes.
• *Nonfiction:* Guidebooks on biking, walking, hiking, and skiing in New England; how-to books on gardening, herbs, and herbalism; nature and environmental books; U.S. travel and recreation guides; country living books; and general nonfiction.
Recent Titles: *Perennials for the Backyard Gardener* by Patricia Turcotte. *The New Complete Guide to Beekeeping* by Roger A. Morse.
Submission and Payment Policy: Query first outline, market analysis, and resume. No unsolicited manuscripts. Include SASE. Accepts photocopies and computer printouts. Simultaneous submissions okay. Reports in 1 month. If accepted, expect publication in 2 years. Royalty, 7.5–10%; advance, $1,000.

Creativity Unlimited Press

Rochelle Ann, Owner, 30819 Casilina, Rancho Palos Verdes, CA 90274   Phone: 310-541-4844

Profile: Self-help books and tapes. A division of the Creativity Learning Institute. Titles: 1 per year; nonfiction paperback. Average print run: 2,000. Binding: Perfect bound. Book catalogue available.

Focus and Imprints: Creativity Unlimited Press is a small publisher of self-help/how-to books and tapes on personal growth, enlightenment, health, and new age topics. It accepts poetry collections for its annual poetry competition. "Humor is important—be personal."

Editorial Interests

• *Nonfiction:* Self-help/how-to material on new age concepts, enlightenment, channeling, past lives, healing, holistic health, and metaphysics. Interests include self-hypnosis tapes and programs.

Recent Titles: *Time Travel: Do-It-Yourself Past Life Regression Handbook* by Shelley Stockwell. *Denial Is Not a River In Egypt: Overcome Depression, Addiction, and Compulsion* by Shelley Stockwell and Barbara McNurun.

Submission and Payment Policy: Query first with outline. Include SASE. Accepts photocopies and computer printouts. Simultaneous submissions okay. Reports in 2 months. If accepted, expect publication in 1 year. Foreign rights available. Flat fee, rates negotiable.

Other Interests: Sponsors the Creativity Unlimited Press Annual Poetry Competition for easy-to-read, humorous, heartfelt poetry. Requires a $4 submission fee for 5 poems. Send an SASE for guidelines. Also sponsors conferences and workshops in hypnosis training, enlightenment, self-esteem, and overcoming addictions and compulsions. Send an SASE for information.

The Crossing Press

Editor, 97 Hangar Way, Watsonville, CA 95076   Phone: 408-722-0711, Fax: 408-722-2749

Profile: Fiction and nonfiction that "celebrates life." Established in 1972. Titles: 35 per year; 7 fiction; 28 nonfiction; primarily paperback. Average print run: 5,000. Book catalogue and writer's guidelines available.

Focus and Imprints: The Crossing Press publishes "Books for Life," an eclectic list of books that "help find the answers, pose new questions, offer new solutions, explore other cultures and lifestyles, help fill our minds, hearts, and stomachs, and take a poke at our funny bones." Also seeks books that give voice to the challenges of life's changes.

Editorial Interests

• *Fiction:* Women's interests, gay and lesbian interests, Native American stories, erotica, inspirational, and humor. No romances or adventure stories that stress the macho male hero.

• *Nonfiction:* Interests include new age, feminism, women's issues, alternative health, gay and lesbian issues, cookbooks, astrology, bodywork, crystals, cultural and ethnic concerns, dreams, the environment, folklore, healing and health, lifestyle, magic, meditation, men's issues, metaphysics, mysticism, mythology, nutrition, occult, parapsychology, parenting, philosophy, psychic phenomenon, rebirthing, recovery, relationships, self-help, seniors, social and world issues, spirituality, witches, women's issues, and yoga.

Recent Titles: *O Mother Sun! A New View of the Cosmic Feminine* by Patricia Monaghan. *Sex, Violence & Power in Sports: Rethinking Masculinity* by Michael A. Messner and Donald E. Sabo.

Submission and Payment Policy: Query with outline and 2 sample chapters. Include SASE. Accepts photocopies and computer printouts. Simultaneous submissions okay. Reports in 1–2 months. Publication time varies.

Crystal Clarity Publishers

Jay Steven Levin, Publisher/Editor, 424B Henderson, Graces Valley, CA 95945   Phone: 916-272-3293, Fax: 916-272-2181

Profile: Self-help and metaphysical books. Titles: 5–10 per year; all nonfiction; hardcover and paperback. Average print run: 5,000–10,000. Book catalogue not available.

Focus and Imprints: Crystal Clarity Publishers offers a line of self-help and metaphysical books for both the gift and trade markets. Its *Dawn* book line lists books on nature awareness

Editorial Interests

• *Nonfiction:* Metaphysical, self-help, the environment, inspirational, lifestyle, meditation, mysticism, mythology, new age, occult, parapsychology, parenting, philosophy, prayer, psychic phenomenon, psychology, relationships, religion, spirituality, and yoga.

Recent Titles: *The Rubayat of Orua Khayajain* by Pararnahanda Yogananda.

Submission and Payment Policy: Query with outline and 3 sample chapters. Include SASE. Accepts photocopies, computer printouts, and faxes. Simultaneous submissions okay. Reporting time varies. If accepted, expect publication in 1–3 months. Payment is negotiable on an individual basis.

Other Interests: Affiliated with the Aranda World Brotherhood Village. For more information, contact Jay Steven Levin, 916-272-3293.

John Daniel & Company

John Daniel, Publisher, P.O. Box 21922, Santa Barbara, CA 93121   Phone: 805-962-1780

Profile: Literary fiction and nonfiction. A division of Daniel & Daniel, Publishers, Inc. Titles: 4 per year; 2 fiction; 2 nonfiction; 1 hardcover; 3 paperback. Average print run: 2,000. Press: Offset.

Focus and Imprints: John Daniel & Company seeks well-written poetry and prose of literary quality. Not interested in genre fiction. Its imprint, Fithian Press, is devoted to co-publishing ventures.

Editorial Interests

• *Fiction:* Literary fiction and short story and poetry collections.

• *Nonfiction:* Memoirs and essays, all of literary merit.

Recent Titles: *The Tall Uncut* by Pete Fromm. *Winter Return* by John Espey.

Submission and Payment Policy: Query with outline or send complete manuscript with cover letter. Include SASE. Accepts photocopies and computer printouts. Simultaneous submissions okay. Responds to queries in 1 month, to manuscripts in 2 months. If accepted, expect publication in 1 year. Open to co-publishing arrangements through its Fithian Press imprint. Royalty, 10% of net.

Dawn Publications

Glenn Hovemann, Editor, 14618 Tyler Foote Road, No. 49, Nevada City, CA 95959   Phone: 916-292-3482, Fax: 916-292-4258

Profile: Nonfiction books on health and the environment and children's fiction. Titles: 4–6 per year; all nonfiction; hardcover and paperback. Book list available.

Focus and Imprints: Dawn Publications is dedicated to helping people experience a sense of unity and harmony with all life. Its titles intend to foster a deeper sensitivity and appreciation for the natural world. It is also open to health-related material and other themes that are helpful and inspiring, including those with more explicitly spiritual content.

Editorial Interests

• *Fiction:* Inspirational children's fiction, particularly those with nature themes, that uplift and engage but don't preach.

• *Nonfiction:* Nature awareness books that show nature's power to enliven the human soul. Health and healing books that help people grow physically, mentally, and spiritually. Inspirational books on spiritual themes.

Recent Titles: *Quest for Life: A Handbook for People with Life-Threatening Illnesses* by Petrea King. *Journey to the Heart of Nature* by Joseph Cornell.

Submission and Payment Policy: Children's fiction: send complete manuscript with cover letter stating the intended age of the audience. Nonfiction: send complete manuscript with cover letter, or query with outline, table of contents, and 2 sample chapters. If appropriate, enclose samples of artwork or illustrations. Include SASE. Accepts photocopies and computer printouts. Simultaneous submissions okay. Reports in 1–2 months. If accepted, expect publication in 1 year.

D.B.A. Books

Diane Bellavance, Owner, 323 Beacon Street, Boston, MA 02116   Phone: 617-262-0411

Profile: Self-help business books. Titles: 3 per year; all nonfiction paperback. Average print run: 5,000. Press: Lithograph. Binding: Saddle stitched. Book catalogue available.

Focus and Imprints: D.B.A. Books is a privately owned publisher of books on how to launch and operate home-based new age businesses.

Editorial Interests

• *Nonfiction:* How-to/self-help books on new age business operation.

Recent Titles: *Advertising and Public Relations for a Small Business* by Diane Bellavance. *Bookkeeping for a New Age Business* by Diane Bellavance.

Submission and Payment Policy: Query with outline and 1 sample chapter. Include SASE. Accepts photocopies and computer printouts. No simultaneous submissions. Reports in 1 month. If accepted, expect publication in 4 months. Royalty: 7%.

Delphi Press

Karen Jackson, President, P.O. Box 267990, Chicago, IL 60626

Profile: Nonfiction books on pagan spirituality. Titles: 8–10 per year; all nonfiction paperback. Average print run: 2,500–4,500. Book catalogue available.

Focus and Imprints: Delphi Press offers a small list of titles centered around pagan spirituality, goddess worship, magic, and witchcraft. No channeled books.

Editorial Interests

• *Nonfiction:* Interests include paganism, the environment, feminism, magic, men's issues, metaphysics, occult, psychology, sexuality, spirituality, witches, and women's issues.

Recent Titles: *Cauldron of Change* by De-anna Alba. *Wildman, Earth and Stars* by Daniel Corey.

Submission and Payment Policy: Query with outline and 3 sample chapters, or send complete manuscript with cover letter. Include SASE. Accepts photocopies. Simultaneous submissions okay. Responds to queries in 1–2 months, to manuscripts in 2–3 months. If accepted, expect publication in 8–18 months. Considers co-publishing ventures. Royalty, 10% of net.

Delta Sales Publishing

Dick Bathurst, President, 4195 Chino Hills Parkway, Suite 520, Chino Hills, CA 91709 Phone: 800-393-9737, Fax: 909-393-9856

Profile: Self-help books. Titles: 5 per year; all nonfiction; 4 hardcover; 1 paperback. Average print run: 5,000. Binding: Perfect bound. Book catalogue available.
Focus and Imprints: Delta Sales Publishing focuses on nonfiction self-help books in the area of business and leadership. "Be brief, specific, and explain the market."
Editorial Interests
• *Nonfiction:* Self-help books on leadership, management, general business practices, creativity, golf, health, men's issues, and psychology.
Recent Titles: *Passionate Leadership* by Tony Vercillo. *Stretching for Golf* by Bill Wallace and Dave Coter.
Submission and Payment Policy: Query first with outline, 2 samples chapters, and resume. Include SASE. Accepts photocopies and computer printouts. Simultaneous submissions okay. Reports in 3–4 weeks. If accepted, expect publication in 6 months. 25% co-publishing contracts. Royalty, 10%; advance negotiable. Also works on a sliding scale based on volume sold.

DeVorss & Company

Arthur Vegara, Editor, 1046 Princeton Drive, Marina del Rey, CA 90292 Phone: 213-870-7478, Fax: 310-821-6290

Profile: Self-help books. Titles: 8 per year; all paperback. Average print run: 3,000. Binding: Perfect bound.
Focus and Imprints: DeVorss & Company devotes its list to inspirational, self-help, and metaphysical nonfiction.
Editorial Interests
• *Nonfiction:* Self-help and metaphysical books in the areas of channeling, dreams, the environment, healing, health, holistic health, meditation, mysticism, new age, occult, prayer, psychology, recovery, and spirituality.
Recent Titles: *Workhealing* by Charles Mallory. *Life on the Line* by Rory Elder.
Submission and Payment Policy: Query with outline, 2 sample chapters, and resume. Include SASE. Accepts photocopies, computer printouts, and Quark XPress disks. No simultaneous submissions. Reports in 2 months. If accepted, expect publication in 6 months. Royalty, 10%.

Dimi Press

Dick Lutz, President, 3820 Oak Hollow Lane SE, Salem, OR 97302 Phone: 503-364-7698, Fax: 503-364-9727

Profile: Health-related and anthropology books with wide appeal. Titles: 1 per year; nonfiction. Average print run: 2,000. Press: Offset. Binding: Perfect bound. Book catalogue and writer's guidelines available.
Focus and Imprints: Dimi Press is a small, independent publisher of books and cassettes. It seeks practical, hands-on how-to books on health issues and anthropology for a lay audience. Material should be crisp and well-written. Not interested in regional titles, fiction, poetry, or first-person accounts. Authors should have some credentials in their area of interest and must be able to promote their books. "Tell me who will buy your book and why you are qualified to write it."
Editorial Interests
• *Nonfiction:* Practical how-to/self-help books on health issues that affect a large population such as headaches, arthritis, insomnia, and depression. Anthropology books for lay readers about interesting subcultures.
Recent Titles: *Feel Better! Live Longer! Relax* by Richard L. Lutz. *Komodo, the Living Dragon* by Dick Lutz and J. Marie Lutz.
Submission and Payment Policy: Query first with outline, author qualifications, and market analysis. Include SASE. Accepts photocopies, computer printouts, computer disks, and faxes. Simultaneous submissions okay. Responds to queries in 2 months, to manuscripts in 4 months. Publication time varies. Considers co-publishing ventures. Royalty, generally 10% of retail and 5% on direct-mail sales. First-time authors not eligible for advance.

Distinctive Publishing

Alan Erdlee, Publisher, 1888 NW 21st Street, Pompano Beach, FL 33069 Phone: 305-975-2413, Fax: 305-972-3949

Profile: A variety of self-help and new age titles. Titles: 25–30 per year; all nonfiction; 10% hardcover; 90% paperback. Average print run: 2,000–5,000. Book catalogue available.
Focus and Imprints: Distinctive Publishing lists a variety of nonfiction titles, primarily self-help and how-to but including new age, biography, psychology, lifestyle, and children's books. Its subsidiary, Author's Advantage, offers a range of writing, editing, and publishing services.
Editorial Interests
• *Nonfiction:* Self-help and how-to books on health, holistic health, lifestyle, men's issues, new age, nutrition, parenting and the family, psychology, recovery, relationships, seniors, social issues, and women's issues. Also interested in exposés, biographies, and children's books.
Recent Titles: *Life in the Trash Lane* by Mel Levine. *Caregivers Mission* by Steven Ross.

Submission and Payment Policy: Query with resume or send complete manuscript with cover letter, resume, and clips. Include SASE. Accepts photocopies and computer printouts. Simultaneous submissions okay. Reports in 2 months. If accepted, expect publication in 6–12 months. Royalty, 6–15%.

Other Interests: Offers manuscript assessment, editorial, ghostwriting, rewriting, submission assistance, and self-publishing services through the Author's Advantage subsidiary. For brochure, write to Author's Advantage, P.O. Box 17868, Plantation, FL 33318-7868, or call 305-968-5372.

Eagle's View Publishing

Denise Knight, Editor, 6756 North Fork Road, Liberty, UT 84310   Phone: 801-393-4555

Profile: Culture-specific how-to books. Titles: 6 per year; all nonfiction paperback. Average print run: 5,000–10,000. Book catalogue available.

Focus and Imprints: Eagle's View Publishing has specific interests in how-to craft and beading books and Native American and frontier history and living. Focus on these topics only when submitting to this company.

Editorial Interests

• *Nonfiction:* Interests include crafts, beading, Native American history, and frontier history and living.

Recent Titles: *Techniques of Beading Earrings* by Deon DeLang. *Techniques of North American Indian Beading* by Monte Smith.

Submission and Payment Policy: Query first with outline and 1–2 sample chapters or send complete manuscript with cover letter. Include sample craft projects. Include SASE. Accepts photocopies, computer printouts, and Macintosh disks. Simultaneous submissions okay. Reports in 6–12 months. If accepted, expect publication in 1–2 years.

Element Books, Inc.

Del Riddle, Managing Director, 42 Broadway, Rockport, MA 01966   Phone: 508-546-1040, Fax: 508-546-9882

Profile: General trade books with a emphasis on self-help. A division of Element Books, LTD. Titles: 75 per year; all nonfiction; 10 hardcover; 65 paperback. Average print run: 10,000–15,000. Book catalogue available.

Focus and Imprints: Element Books is a general trade publisher in the areas of self-help/psychology, alternative medicine, philosophy, and world religions. Writers should send detailed queries or book proposals that are professionally presented. "You must be a good writer—a good idea is not enough."

Editorial Interests

• *Nonfiction:* Interests include self-help, psychology, religion, holistic and natural health, bodywork, cultural and ethnic concerns, dreams, ecosystems, the environment, feminism, folklore, healing, health, inspiration, meditation, metaphysics, mysticism, mythology, nutrition, parapsychology, parenting, philosophy, politics, prayer, psychic phenomenon, relationships, social and world issues, spirituality, women's issues, and yoga.

Submission and Payment Policy: Query first with outline, 2 sample chapters, writing samples, and resume. Include SASE. Accepts photocopies and computer printouts. Simultaneous submissions okay. Responds to queries in 2 months, to manuscripts in 3–5 months. If accepted, expect publication in 9–12 months. Book contracts are negotiated on an individual basis.

Elysium Growth Press

Iris Bancroft, Editor, 700 Robinson Road, Topanga, CA 90290   Phone: 310-455-1000, Fax: 310-455-2007

Profile: Books for nudists/naturalists. A division of EGL Enterprises, Inc., a nonprofit organization. Titles: 5 per year; all nonfiction; hardcover and paperback. Average print run: 5,000. Press: Sheetfed. Binding: Perfect or Smythe bound. Book catalogue available.

Focus and Imprints: Elysium Growth Press specializes in books about nude recreation and travel for nudists and naturalists. Seeks qualified writers only in the field of nudism. Does not accept sexually oriented material.

Editorial Interests

• *Nonfiction:* Material on nudism, naturalist lifestyles, self-help material, clothing-optional travel and recreation, and psychology and sociology as it relates to nudism. Welcomes nudist photography.

Recent Titles: *International Nude Travel Guide 1994/95* by International Naturist Federation. *Nudist Society* by Dr. William Hartman.

Submission and Payment Policy: Query first with outline and 2 sample chapters. No unsolicited manuscripts. Include SASE. Accepts photocopies, computer printouts, and Macintosh Microsoft Word 4.0 or 5.1 disks. Simultaneous submissions okay. Reports in 2 months. If accepted, expect publication in 1–2 years. Considers book packaging and co-publishing ventures. Royalty, 10%.

Excalibur Publishing

Sharon Good, 434 Avenue of the Americas, Suite 790, New York, NY 10011   Phone/Fax: 212-777-1790

Profile: Nonfiction new age and art books. Titles: 2 per year; both nonfiction paperbacks. Average print run: 2,000. Binding: Perfect bound. Book catalogue available.

Focus and Imprints: Seeking "books for life and art," Excalibur Publishing supports a small line of new age nonfiction, books on the performing arts, and parenting and children's books. It is open to adult and children's fiction submissions for its Excalibur Book Award contest.

Editorial Interests

• *Nonfiction:* Interests include new age, performing arts, parenting, and self-help books for children.

Recent Titles: *Practical Parenting for the 21st Century* by Julie A. Ross. *A Singer's Manual of Spanish Lyric Diction* by Nico Castel.

Submission and Payment Policy: Query first. Include SASE. Accepts photocopies. Simultaneous submissions okay. Reports in 3 months. If accepted, expect publication in 1 year. Offers a standard royalty.

Other Interests: Accepts full-length fiction and nonfiction submission for its Excalibur Book Award contest. Winners receive a book contract and cash prizes. Requires a $25 application fee. Send an SASE for guidelines to Excalibur Book Award, 434 Avenue of the Americas, Suite 790, New York, NY 10011.

Faber and Faber Publishers, Inc.

Editorial Assistant, 50 Cross Street, Winchester, MA 01890   Phone: 617-721-1427

Profile: Trade fiction and nonfiction. A division of Faber and Faber, Ltd. Book catalogue available.

Focus and Imprints: Faber and Faber is a well-known publisher of high-quality adult trade fiction and nonfiction.

Editorial Interests

• *Fiction:* Literary fiction. No genre or mass market fiction.

• *Nonfiction:* Memoirs of literary figures, gay and lesbian interests, feminism, folklore, social and world issues, witches, music, and pop culture.

Recent Titles: *What Is Told* by Askold Melnyczuk. *Battlefield* by Peter Svenson.

Submission and Payment Policy: Query first with outline, 3 sample chapters, and resume. No unsolicited manuscripts. Include SASE. Accepts photocopies and computer printouts. Simultaneous submissions okay. Reports in 3 months. If accepted, expect publication in 1 year.

Fall Creek Press

Helen Wirth, Editor-in-Chief, P.O. Box 1127, Fall Creek, OR 97438   Phone: 503-744-0938

Profile: Short-story anthologies. Titles: 2 per year; all fiction paperback. Average print run: 3,000. Binding: Trade paper. Book list and writer's guidelines available.

Focus and Imprints: Fall Creek Press publishes anthologies of original short stories, specifically, nondogmatic spiritual fiction. Its singular and continuing series is *VeriTales*, short stories for the evolving spirit. "Through a well-developed and forward-moving story line, the reader is sensitized to an opportunity for personal choice that opens the door to spiritual growth. If a writer finds our guidelines appealing and enjoys a personal and intense editorial dialogue geared to both excellence of writing and the process of spiritual growth, he or she will probably enjoy working with us."

Editorial Interests

• *Fiction:* Short spiritual fiction with substance. Up to 9,000 words. Any theme is acceptable.

Recent Titles: *VeriTales: Ring of Truth* edited by Helen Wirth. *VeriTales: Beyond the Norm* edited by Helen Wirth.

Submission and Payment Policy: Request and follow writer's guidelines. Accepts queries and complete manuscripts. Include SASE. Reports on 1 month. If accepted, expect publication in 3 months to 3 years. Pays a royalty with advance plus one free copy of the book. Discounts available on additional copies.

Farrar, Straus and Giroux

Jonathan Gallassi, Editor-in-Chief, 19 Union Square West, New York, NY 10003   Phone: 212-741-6900

Profile: High-quality literary books. Titles: 80 per year; fiction and nonfiction; hardcover and paperback. Average print run: 10,000. Book catalogue available.

Focus and Imprints: Farrar, Straus and Giroux publishes a distinguished list of literary fiction and nonfiction for children, young adults, and adult readers. Its paperback imprints—Hill and Wang, The Noonday Press, and North Point Press—offer special-interest books on politics and history, among others. Its juvenile imprints, Sunburst Books and Ariel Fiction, carry fiction and nonfiction for young readers.

Editorial Interests

• *Fiction and Nonfiction:* Well-written literary material.

Recent Titles: *The Bird Artist* by Howard Norman. *One Art—The Letters of Elizabeth Bishop* by Ian Frasier.

Submission and Payment Policy: Query with outline and 1 sample chapter. Include SASE. Accepts photocopies and computer printouts. Simultaneous submissions okay. Reports in 1 month. If accepted, expect publication in 1 year. Royalty.

First Editions

Sophia Tarila, Owner/Founder, P.O. Box 2578, Sedona, AZ 86339   Phone: 602-282-9574, Fax: 602-282-9730

Profile: New age marketing references. Titles: 8 per year; all nonfiction paperback. Book catalogue available.
Focus and Imprints: First Editions specializes in new age marketing references. Its primary reference, *New Marketing Opportunities*, is a comprehensive trade directory for the new age/metaphysical marketplace in the U.S. and Canada. It also publishes a bimonthly newsletter, *New Age Marketing Opportunities*, that offers timely marketing possibilities. Not interested in fiction, poetry, or biographies.
Editorial Interests
• *Nonfiction:* New age business and marketing material; self-empowerment/self-help information; and sacred sites.
Recent Titles: *New Marketing Opportunities, 3rd Edition* edited by Sophia Tarila. *Flyers that Work* by Sophia Tarila.
Submission and Payment Policy: Query first. Include SASE. Reports in 1 month. If accepted, expect publication in 1 year. Considers co-publishing ventures. Payment varies. Offers royalty with advance or flat fee.
Other Interests: Sponsors New Age Marketing workshops and seminars on publishing, marketing, and flyer development. For more information, contact Sophia Tarila, 602-282-9574.

First Glance Books

Rodney Grisso, Editor, P.O. Box 960, Cobb, CA 95426   Phone: 707-928-1994, Fax: 707-928-1995

Profile: Cookbooks and children's books. Titles: all nonfiction; hardcover and paperback. Average print run: 25,000. Binding: Perfect bound.
Focus and Imprints: First Glance specializes in nonfiction books for children, cookbooks, and illustrated gift and coffee table books. It is always on the look out for unusual, new, fresh concepts.
Editorial Interests
• *Nonfiction:* Children's books, cookbooks, and gift books.
Submission and Payment Policy: Query first with outline or send complete manuscript with cover letter. Include SASE. Accepts photocopies and computer printouts. Simultaneous submissions okay. Reports in 2 weeks. If accepted, expect publication in 6 months. Considers co-publishing ventures. Royalty with advance or flat fee depending on material.

Fithian Press

John Daniel, Publisher, P.O. Box 1525, Santa Barbara, CA 93102   Phone: 805-962-1780, Fax: 805-962-8835

Profile: General trade books. An imprint of Daniel & Daniel Publishers, Inc. Titles: 35–40 per year; fiction and nonfiction; 15% hardcover; 85% trade paperback. Average print run: 1,000–1,500. Press: Web. Book catalogue available.
Focus and Imprints: Fithian Press is an independent small-press publisher of contemporary fiction, poetry, memoirs, and general nonfiction. Its goal is "to bring good books into the world and thereby introduce good writers to good readers." Specializes in experimental fiction and poetry. It does not consider genre fiction or violent material.
Editorial Interests
• *Fiction:* Contemporary and experimental fiction and poetry.
• *Nonfiction:* General nonfiction, memoirs and biographies, books of California-regional interest, health, politics, seniors, and Judaica.
Recent Titles: *Torn by the Issues* edited by Stephen Maguire and Bonnie Wren. *The Great Limbaugh Con* by Charles Kelly.
Submission and Payment Policy: Query first with outline, 1–2 sample chapters, and table of contents. Include SASE. Accepts photocopies and computer printouts. Simultaneous submissions okay. Reports in 6 weeks. If accepted, expect publication in 9–12 months. Considers book packaging, subsidy publishing, and co-publishing ventures.

Free Spirit Publishing

Liz Salzmann, Editorial Assistant, 400 First Avenue North, No. 616, Minneapolis, MN 55401
Phone: 612-338-2068, Fax: 612-337-5050

Profile: Self-help books for children. Titles: 12 per year; 1–2 fiction; 10 nonfiction; 2 hardcover; 10 paperback. Average print run: 5,000. Perfect bound. Book catalogue available.
Focus and Imprints: Free Spirit Publishing specializes in self-help and psychology books for or about children. Books should foster character development in children and show children involved in social action and community interests. Not interested in religious material or poetry.
Editorial Interests
• *Fiction:* Character-building stories and picture books.

• *Nonfiction:* Self-help books for or about children on issues of mental and emotional health, cultural and ethnic concerns, lifestyle, parenting, psychology, relationships, and social and world issues.
Recent Titles: *Stick Up for Yourself* by Gershen Kaufman and Lev Arfael. *Safe at School* by Carol Silverman Saunders.
Submission and Payment Policy: Query first with outline, sample chapters, and author biography or resume. Include SASE. Accepts photocopies and computer printouts. Simultaneous submissions okay. Reports in 3 months. If accepted, expect publication in 1 year. Open to book packaging, subsidy publishing, and co-publishing ventures. Royalty; advance.

Grebner Books Publishing

Bernice Grebner, Editor, 5137 North Montclair Avenue, Peoria Heights, IL 61614   Phone: 309-685-6306

Profile: New age books. Titles: 1 per year; nonfiction paperback.
Focus and Imprints: Grebner Books Publishing lists a variety of new age and new enlightenment titles that focus on the balance of body, mind, and spirit.
Editorial Interests
• *Nonfiction:* Interests include new age, body-mind-spirit, astrology, astronomy, bodywork, the environment, lifestyle, psychology, and spirituality.
Recent Titles: *A Day of Your Birth. ABC Astrology and Astronomy.*
Submission and Payment Policy: Query first with outline. Include SASE. Accepts photocopies. No simultaneous submissions. Reports in 1–2 weeks. Publication time varies.

Hampton Roads Publishing Company, Inc.

Frank DeMarco, Chief Editor, 891 Norfolk Square, Norfolk, VA 23502   Phone: 804-459-2453, Fax: 804-455-8907

Profile: Inspirational fiction and self-help metaphysics. Titles: 12–20 per year; 1–4 fiction; 16 nonfiction; 1 hardcover; 12–20 paperback. Average print run: 5,000. Press: Offset. Binding: Perfect bound. Book catalogue available.
Focus and Imprints: Hampton Roads concentrates on the area of metaphysics, in particular self-help metaphysics—"metaphysics the reader can do something with to help transform his or her life." Also welcomes books on alternative medicine and cutting-edge material that links two established fields and offers new ways of structuring thought and experience. Considers fiction, but avoid anything that is too "new age-y."
Editorial Interests
• *Fiction:* Quality, inspirational fiction with a strong metaphysical bent.
• *Nonfiction:* Metaphysical self-help, alternative medicine, Native American spirituality, astrology, channeling, dreams, healing and health, holistic and natural health, meditation, mysticism, new age, nutrition, parapsychology, psychic phenomenon, psychology, and relationships.
Recent Titles: *Using the Whole Brain* by Ronald Russell. *Mind Trek* by Joe McMoneagle.
Submission and Payment Policy: Query first. Include SASE. Accepts photocopies, computer printouts, and WordPerfect disks with hard copy. Simultaneous submissions okay. Reports in 2 weeks. If accepted, expect publication in 6–18 months. Offers standard writing contract.

Harmony Books

Editor, 201 East 50th Street, New York, NY 10022   Phone: 212-572-6179

Profile: High-quality fiction and nonfiction. An imprint of the Crown Publishing Group, a division of Random House. Book catalogue available.
Focus and Imprints: Harmony Books' high-quality list includes books on women's issues, health and healing, alternative business, erotica and contemporary, literary fiction.
Editorial Interests
• *Fiction:* Erotica and literary fiction.
• *Nonfiction:* Interests include health and healing, women's issues, cultural and ethnic issues, feminism, meditation, men's issues, new age, relationships, self-help, social and world issues, spirituality, and yoga.
Recent Titles: *Journey Into Healing* by Deepak Chopra, M.D. *No Night Is Too Long* by Barbara Vine.
Submission and Payment Policy: Query first with outline and 2 sample chapters. Include SASE. Accepts photocopies. No simultaneous submissions. Reporting times varies. If accepted, expect publication in 1 year.

Hartley & Marks

Sue Tauber, Editorial Director, P.O. Box 147, Point Roberts, WA 98281   Phone: 206-945-2017, Fax: 604-738-1913

Profile: High-quality self-help books. Titles: 6–10 per year; all nonfiction paperback. Average print run: 5,000. Book catalogue available.

Focus and Imprints: Hartley & Marks publishes quality self-help and how-to trade paperbacks in the areas of health, relationships, ecobuilding, meditation, practical crafts, and lifestyle. No cookbooks or decorative craft books. "We invite authors who are experts in their fields to submit innovative techniques and methods useful to the educated lay reader." Not interested in theoretical "idea" books, personal accounts, or metaphysical material. Willing to work with academic writers to help them adapt their writing style for a wide readership. Looks for manuscripts with clarity, simplicity of style, good organization, and originality. Avoid patronizing the reader, academic jargon and/or presentation.

Editorial Interests

• *Nonfiction:* Practical self-help and how-to books in the areas of health, holistic and natural health, family and relationships, practical psychology, meditation, lifestyle, parenting, and seniors' concerns.

Recent Titles: *The Whole Way to Allergy Relief & Prevention* by Jacqueline Krohn, M.D. *The Long Distance Grandmother: How to Stay Close to Distant Grandchildren* by Dr. Selma Wassermann.

Submission and Payment Policy: Query first with outline and author biography stating qualifications. Include SASE. Accepts computer printouts. Simultaneous submissions okay if noted. Reports in 1–2 months. If accepted, expect publication in 7–9 months. Payment policy varies. Offers royalty with advance.

Hay House

Jill Kramer, Editorial Director, P.O. Box 6204, Carson, CA 90749-6204   Phone: 310-605-0601, Fax: 310-605-5313

Profile: New age self-help books. Titles: 12 per year; all nonfiction; 2 hardcover; 10 paperback. Average print run: Varies. Book catalogue available.

Focus and Imprints: Hay House has established a list of positive self-help and psychology books on a variety of new age and health-related topics. The common thread throughout its titles is the "attempt to heal the planet in some fashion." Writers should study competitive books and not submit anything too similar to what is already on the market. Avoid material that is negative, too "far-fetched," or too technical or scholarly. Aim material at a mainstream audience.

Editorial Interests

• *Nonfiction:* Interests include new age, self-help, angels, astrology, bodywork, channeling, crystals, dreams, ecosystems, the environment, extraterrestrials, feminism, gay and lesbian concerns, healing, health, holistic health, inspirational material, lifestyle, meditation, men's issues, metaphysics, mysticism, mythology, natural health, nutrition, parapsychology, parenting, psychic phenomenon, psychology, recovery, relationships, seniors, social and world issues, spirituality, women's issues, and yoga.

Recent Titles: *Losing Your Pounds of Pain* by Doreen Virtue, Ph. D. *Your Companion to 12-Step Recovery* by Robert Odom.

Submission and Payment Policy: Query with 3 sample chapters and resume, or send complete manuscript with cover letter, resume, and clips. Include SASE. Accepts photocopies and computer printouts. Simultaneous submissions okay. Reports in 3 weeks. If accepted, expect publication in 1 year. Payment is negotiated on an individual basis.

Hazelden Educational Materials

Linda Peterson, Manager, 15251 Pleasant Valley Road, Center City, MN 55012   Phone: 612-257-4010, Fax: 612-257-2195

Profile: Recovery and health-related nonfiction. A division of the Hazelden Foundation, a nonprofit organization. Titles: 80 per year; all nonfiction paperback. Average print run: 10,000. Binding: Perfect bound and saddled stitched. Book catalogue available.

Focus and Imprints: Hazelden Educational Materials specializes in books that explore the prevention of and recovery from chemical dependency and additions as well as books on how-to establish and maintain a healthy lifestyle. It discourages the submission of autobiographical works, poetry, and art.

Editorial Interests

• *Nonfiction:* Interests include chemical and substance abuse; prevention and recovery issues for children, teens, and adults; holistic and natural health; healthy lifestyles; inspirational material; meditation; spirituality; and women's issues.

Recent Titles: *Winning a Day at a Time* by John Lucas.

Submission and Payment Policy: Query with outline and 2 sample chapters. Include SASE. Accepts photocopies and computer printouts. Simultaneous submissions okay. Reports in 2 months. If accepted, expect publication in 8–12 months. Royalty, 7–9%.

Health Communications, Inc.

Christine Belleris, Editorial Director, 3201 S.W. 15th Street, Deerfield Beach, FL 33431   Phone: 305-360-0909, Fax: 305-360-0034

Profile: Self-help books. Established in 1976. Titles: 30 per year; all nonfiction paperback. Average print run: 7,000. Binding: Otabind. Book catalogue available.

Focus and Imprints: Health Communications specializes in self-help books dealing with all of life's issues, from soulful enlightenment to personal growth and relationships. Prospective writers should make their message as clear as possible—

don't bury it in jargon. "Include a thorough marketing study with the proposal, define the audience, list books similar to yours and their sales record, and describe how your book is unique." Avoid material that is autobiographical in nature unless it can provide a framework for others.

Editorial Interests
• *Nonfiction:* Special interest in books with a positive, uplifting message such as self-help material, affirmations, mind-body-spirit connection, and personal growth. Topics include bodywork, crystals, cultural and ethnic concerns, dreams, feminism, folklore, healing, health, holistic and natural health, lifestyle, meditation, new age, parenting, psychology, relationships, spirituality, women's issues, and yoga.
Recent Titles: *Chicken Soup for the Soul* by Jack Canfield and Mark Victor Hanson. *Recovery of the Sacred* by Carlos Warter.
Submission and Payment Policy: Query first with outline and resume. Include SASE. Accepts photocopies and computer printouts. Simultaneous submissions okay. Responds to queries in 2–3 weeks, to manuscripts in 2–3 months. If accepted, expect publication in 9 months. Royalty, 20%.
Other Interests: Affiliated with U.S. Journal Training, Inc., which offers conferences on adolescence, relationships, and alternative methods of health and wellness. For more information, contact Gary Seidler, 3201 S.W. 15th Street, Deerfield Beach, FL 33431.

Heaven Bone Press
Steve Hirsch, Editor, P.O. Box 486, Chester, NY 10918   Phone: 914-469-9018, Fax: 914-469-7880

Profile: Spiritual and ecological fiction and nonfiction. Titles: 4 per year. Average print run: 2,500. Press: Offset. Binding: Saddle stitched. Book flyers available.
Focus and Imprints: Heaven Bone Press publishes fiction, nonfiction, and poetry collections that focus on spiritual, esoteric, ecological, erotic, and literary topics. Avoid end-line rhyming poetry and religious "psychobabble." It also publishes *Heaven Bone Magazine*, a journal of fiction and poetry reviews.
Editorial Interests
Buddhism, astrology, channeling, crystals, cultural and ethnic issues, dreams, ecosystems, the environment, extraterrestrials, feminism, folklore, meditation, metaphysics, mysticism, mythology, parapsychology, philosophy, politics, psychic phenomenon, psychology, social and world issues, spirituality, witches, women's issues, and yoga.
• *Fiction:* Short stories, 6,000 words. Novellas and novel excerpts. Non-rhyming poetry.
• *Nonfiction:* Memoirs and travel journals.
Recent Titles: *Red Bracelets* by Janine Pommy Vega. *Down with the Move* by Kirpal Gordon.
Submission and Payment Policy: Query first with outline, 2 sample chapters, and writing samples, or send complete manuscript with cover letter. Submit up to 8 poems per submission. Include SASE. Accepts photocopies, computer printouts, and 3.5" Macintosh or PC ASCII or Microsoft Word disks. No simultaneous submissions. Responds to queries in 3 weeks, to manuscripts in up to 7 months. If accepted, expect publication in up to 18 months. Considers co-publishing ventures. Pays in copies unless otherwise arranged.
Other Interests: Sponsors an annual International Chapbook Competition for poetry collections of up to 30 pages. Contact Steve Hirsh, 914-469-9018. Also offers a weekend workshop, Digging in the Dirt: Toward a New Visionary Poetics. Contact Mary Rutkovsky Ruskin, c/o My Retreat, P.O. Box 1077, Lincoln Road, South Fallsburgh, NY 12779, 914-436-7455.

Hohm Press
Regina Sara Ryan, Managing Editor, P.O. Box 2501, Prescott, AZ 86302   Phone: 602-778-9189, Fax: 602-717-1779

Profile: Health and nutrition books. Established in 1946. Titles: 6–12 per year; all nonfiction paperbacks. Average print run: 6,000. Binding: Perfect bound. Book catalogue available.
Focus and Imprints: Hohm Press concentrates on health-related, growth-oriented, and self-help books and tapes as well as translations of religious poetry and original texts. Material should be sound and well-researched. No "channeled" material. "Tell us in your query letter what contacts you have that would help marketing your book. Describe your book and outline it."
Editorial Interests
• *Nonfiction:* Health-related issues; solid, natural healing; herbal approaches to nutrition; psychology and self-help; childbirth and parenting; translations of religious poetry and original texts; solid spirituality of great world religions and original material by recognized teachers of great spiritual traditions: Buddhism, Christianity, Sufism, Hinduism, and Judaism.
Recent Titles: *Ten Essential Herbs* by Lalitha Thomas. *Crazy As We Are: Rumi Poems* translated by Nevit O. Ergin.
Submission and Payment Policy: Query first with detailed outline and marketing strategy. Include SASE. Accepts photocopies and computer printouts. Simultaneous submissions okay. Responds to queries in 2–3 months, to manuscripts in 3–6 months. If accepted, expect publication in 1 year. Royalty, 8%.

Home Education Press
Helen Hegener, Managing Editor, P.O. Box 1083, Tonasket, WA 98855   Phone/Fax: 509-486-1351

Profile: Books for homeschooling families. Titles: 3–4 per year; all nonfiction paperback. Average print run: 1,500. Binding: Perfect bound. Book catalogue available.
Focus and Imprints: Home Education Press is a leading publisher of homeschooling materials. Its materials combine a common sense approach to education with a real commitment to families who opt to teach their children at home. In addition to its list of resource books, Home Education Press publishes *Home Education Magazine*. Writers should be familiar with the homeschooling market.
Editorial Interests
• *Nonfiction:* Homeschooling resources and booklets on any topic pertaining to at-home education such as testing and assessments, learning disabilities, homeschooling and the public schools, careers and colleges, and research.
Recent Titles: *Good Stuff* by Rebecca Rupp. *I Learn Better by Teaching Myself* by Agnes Leistico.
Submission and Payment Policy: Query first with outline, 1–2 sample chapters, and writing samples. No unsolicited manuscripts. Include SASE. Accepts photocopies, computer printouts, faxes, and Microsoft Word disks. No simultaneous submissions. Reports in 1 month. If accepted, expect publication in 1 year. Royalty, 10%.

Human Potential Foundation Press

Bob Teets, Managing Editor, P.O. Box 52, Terra Aha, WV 26764   Phone/Fax: 304-789-5951

Profile: Nonfiction alternative science books. A division of Human Potential Foundation, Inc., a nonprofit foundation. Titles: 2 per year; all nonfiction paperback. Average print run: 1,500. Binding: Perfect bound. Book catalogue not available.
Focus and Imprints: Human Potential Foundation Press lists new science, psychology, and metaphysics books with typically small press runs. Prefers material that is science-based.
Editorial Interests
• *Nonfiction:* Alternative science, ecosystems, the environment, healing, health, holistic health, meditation, metaphysics, natural health, philosophy, and psychology.
Recent Titles: *Spirit Releasement Therapy* by Dr. William J. Baldwin, D.DS., Ph, D.
Submission and Payment Policy: Query first with outline and resume. Include SASE. Accepts computer printouts and DOS or ASCII disks. Simultaneous submissions okay. Responds to queries in 3 months, to manuscripts in 6 months. If accepted, expect publication in 1 year. Open to co-publishing ventures. Payment policy varies.

Illumination Arts, Inc.

Alison McIntosh, Vice President, P.O. Box 1865, Bellevue, WA 98009   Phone: 206-822-8015, Fax: 206-827-1213

Profile: Children's fiction with spiritual themes. Titles: 1 per year; fiction hardcover. Average print run: 10,000. Binding: Case bound. Book catalogue not available.
Focus and Imprints: Illumination Arts acquires illustrated children's books in which adventures and spiritual concepts are blended with full-color, inspiring artwork. Writers should develop short, simple, uplifting or enlightening story lines. Open-minded and fun-loving stories preferred. "Nothing silly or too fantastic." Avoid didactic, preachy materials, doctrines and dogmas, and strong opinions.
Editorial Interests
• *Fiction:* Inspirational and enlightening children's books with metaphysical and spiritual content.
Recent Titles: *All I See Is Part of Me* by Chara M. Curtis. *How Far to Heaven?* by Chara M. Curtis.
Submission and Payment Policy: Send complete manuscript with cover letter and sample illustrations. No originals. Include SASE. Accepts photocopies and computer printouts. Simultaneous submissions okay. Responds to queries in 1 month, to manuscripts in 1–2 months. If accepted, expect publication in 1–2 years. Royalty; advance. First-time authors receive royalty only. Rates negotiable.

Impact Publishers, Inc.

Freeman Porter, Senior Editor, 874 Via Esteban, P.O. Box 1094, San Luis Obispo, CA 93406-1094
Phone: 805-543-5911, Fax: 805-543-4093

Profile: Popular psychology books and children's fiction. Titles: 6 per year; all nonfiction paperback. Average print run: 5,000. Binding: Perfect bound. Book catalogue and writer's guidelines available.
Focus and Imprints: Impact Publishers specialize in popular psychology books written by professionals in the areas of personal growth, relationships, families, communities, health, aging, and children. Encourages writers to "read our catalogue and author's guidelines, be sure your work fits our list, and be sure you have the credentials we require, such as an advanced degree and experience in human services." Its *Little Imp Books* line lists children's fiction and nonfiction.
Editorial Interests
• *Fiction:* Children's fiction that models self-esteem, creativity, individuality, responsibility, and emotional and social growth.
• *Nonfiction:* Adult and children's nonfiction on personal growth, families, communities, aging, health, children's issues, par-

enting, men's issues, psychology, self-help, and women's issues.

Recent Titles: *Growing Beyond Emotional Pain* by John Preston, Psy. D. *Getting Off the Merry-Go-Round* by Carla Perez, M.D.

Submission and Payment Policy: Query first with outline, 2 sample chapters, and resume. Include SASE. Accepts photocopies and laser-quality computer printouts. Simultaneous submissions okay if noted. Reports in 3 months. If accepted, expect publication in 1 year. Royalty, 10% of net; offers an advance.

In Print Publishing

Tomi Keitlen, Publisher/Editor, 65 Verde Valley School Road, Suite F-2, Sedona, AZ 86351

Phone: 602-284-1370, Fax: 602-284-0534

Profile: Metaphysical books and audio and video cassettes. Titles: 4 per year; all nonfiction paperback. Average print run: 3,500–5,000. Binding: Perfect bound. Book catalogue available.

Focus and Imprints: In Print Publishing lists nonfiction books and cassettes for a general audience. Considers metaphysical books, Native American themes, and books about overcoming difficulty.

Editorial Interests

• *Nonfiction:* Interests include metaphysics, Native American issues, folklore, inspiration, mysticism, mythology, new age and parapsychology.

Recent Titles: *In the Kingdom of the Dalai Lama* by A. T. Steel. *In Search of Grace: Documented Case of Murder and Reincarnation* by Dr. Bruce Goldberg.

Submission and Payment Policy: Query with outline, 3 sample chapters, and resume. No unsolicited manuscripts. Include SASE. Accepts photocopies and faxes. Simultaneous submissions okay. Reports in 1 month. If accepted, expect publication in 5–8 months. Royalty, 6–8%; advance, generally $500.

Indelible Ink Publishing

Judi Pope, Editor, P.O. Box 33, Eastsound, WA 98280   Phone/Fax: 206-376-6081

Profile: New age books. Titles: 2–3 per year. Average print run: 5,000. Binding: Perfect bound.

Focus and Imprints: Indelible Ink Publishing lists books dedicated to the evolution of consciousness, including new age titles and material on Native American spirituality. It also publishes *Wolf Lodge Journal*, a magazine of Native American wisdom.

Editorial Interests

• *Nonfiction:* Interests include new age, Native American and indigenous wisdom, alchemy, channeling, UFOs, men's issues, metaphysics, mysticism, mythology, relationships, spirituality, and women's issues.

Submission and Payment Policy: Query or send complete manuscript. Include SASE. Accepts photocopies, computer printouts, and Macintosh disk. Considers co-publishing ventures. Payment varies.

Other Interests: Affiliated with the Wolf Lodge, a nonprofit educational organization of indigenous spirituality. It operates a teaching lodge, medicine lodge, and ceremonial lodge. For more information, contact Judi Pope, 206-376-6081.

International Guild of Advanced Sciences

Thor Templar, President, 255 North El Cielo Road, Suite 565, Palm Springs, CA 92262   Phone: 619-327-7355, Fax: 619-327-7355

Profile: Alternative, new age titles. Titles: 45 per year; all nonfiction hardcover. Book catalogue and guidelines available.

Focus and Imprints: Not a traditional publishing house, International Guild of Advanced Sciences will print and help distribute ready-made, fully edited book manuscripts. This organization does not provide editing, design, and layout services. Instead, it operates as an output service or vanity press, printing the camera-ready material prepared and deemed ready for publication by the author. It also offers limited marketing services. Writers are advised to study guidelines before entering into a publishing contract. It is open to alternative subject matter, primarily new age and occult themes.

Editorial Interests

• *Nonfiction:* Open to all new age topics including occult, new science, witchcraft, UFOs, healing, herbs, alternative thought, astrology, channeling, crystals, dreams, holistic health, magic, mysticism, parapsychology, psychic phenomenon, rebirthing, spirituality, and translations of ancient occult texts.

Recent Titles: *Holy Devas* by Paul V. Beyerl. *Psionic Combat* by Charles Cosimano.

Submission and Payment Policy: Query with outline and 2 sample chapters. Include SASE. Accepts camera-ready manuscript pages only. Simultaneous submissions okay. Reports in 1 month. Books are printed within 90 days. Writers are required to pay a $75 copyrighting fee, plus $30 membership fee to the International Guild of Advanced Sciences. Authors receive $1–$4 per book sold.

Island Meadow Farm Bookcraft

Barbara Berst, Editor, 295 Sharpe Road, Anacortes-Fidalgo Island, WA 98221

Profile: Adult nonfiction and poetry collections for children. A division of J & JR Publishing. Titles: 2 per year; all nonfiction paperback. Average print run: 2,000. Binding: Perfect bound or pamphlet.
Focus and Imprints: Formerly National Lilac Publishing, Island Meadow Farm Bookcraft publishes collections of poetry for children, with an essence of connection to nature and humanity. Themes must center around living in the Pacific Northwest. It accepts writing only from authors who reside in this region. Poems will be compiled in an annual anthology. It is also interested in adult titles on sustainable living. No sexist or fundamentalist language.
Editorial Interests
• *Poetry:* Current, rhyming children's poetry with a connection to nature and the Pacific Northwest region. Prefers short poems, up to 1 page.
• *Nonfiction:* Sustainable agriculture and organic farming, multi-age education books, and books on blending male–female surnames.
Submission and Payment Policy: Contact publisher for specific submission guidelines. Pays $10 per published poem.

Jain Publishing Company

M. K. Jain, Editor-in-Chief, P.O. Box 3523, Fremont, CA 94539   Phone: 510-659-8272, Fax: 510-659-0501

Profile: Practical guidebooks with general market appeal. Titles: 15 per year; all nonfiction; 5 hardcover; 10 paperback. Average print run: 3,000. Binding: Perfect bound. Book catalogue available.
Focus and Imprints: Jain Publishing Company acquires nonfiction titles with a practical orientation that can safely be marketed to the general trade market. It welcomes books that lend themselves to illustration. Its imprint, Asian Humanities Press, publishes books on Eastern religions, philosophies, and approaches to health and well-being. Ideal submissions are clearly written, cleanly presented, and well-focused with a practical, understandable approach. Not interested in biographical or first-person accounts or extreme viewpoints that generate unnecessary controversies.
Editorial Interests
• *Nonfiction:* Practical guides, handbooks, and self-help books on Eastern religion, the environment, healing, health, holistic health, inspirational, meditation, natural health, nutrition, psychology, recovery, and yoga. Up to 80,000 words.
Recent Titles: *The Little Book of Inspiration* by Jim Beggs. *The Psychology of Enlightenment* by Guruder Shree Chitrabhana.
Submission and Payment Policy: Query first with outline and resume. Include SASE. Accepts photocopies, computer printouts, and IBM or Macintosh 3.5" Microsoft Word or WordPerfect disks. Simultaneous submissions okay. Reports in 2 months. If accepted, expect publication in 1–2 years. Pays royalty or flat fee; rates negotiable.

Jewish Lights Publishing

Editor, P.O. Box 237, Sunset Farm Offices, Route 4, Woodstock, VT 05091   Phone: 802-457-4000, Fax: 802-457-4004

Profile: Books for spiritual seekers of all faiths. A division of LongHill Partners, Inc. Titles: 12 per year; all nonfiction; 6 hardcover; 6 paperback. Book catalogue available.
Focus and Imprints: Jewish Lights Publishing lists nonfiction books for people of all faiths and backgrounds on the essence of seeking meaning and spirituality in life. Not interested in fiction or biographies.
Editorial Interests
• *Nonfiction:* Interested in spirituality, the environment, folklore, inspirational material, philosophy, prayer, recovery, and women's issues.
Recent Titles: *The Book of Words* by Lawrence Kushner. *Lifecycles* by Debra Orenstein.
Submission and Payment Policy: Query first with outline and 2 sample chapters. Include SASE. Accepts photocopies and computer printouts. Simultaneous submissions okay. Responds to queries in 4 months, to manuscripts in 6 months. Publication time varies.

Journal of Regional Criticism

Joseph A. Uphoff, Jr., Editor-in-Chief, 1025 Garner Street, D, Space, 18, Colorado Springs, CO 80905-1774

Profile: Poetry and arts- and math-related theory. Titles: 2 per year; 1 fiction; 1 nonfiction; paperback. Average print run: 20. Xeroxed material. Binding: Perfect bound. Book catalogue not available.
Focus and Imprints: Journal of Regional Criticism is open to theoretical works for art and mathematics as well as poetry. Avoid trends, slang, and obscene or profane language—these "are not a substitute for good writing and interesting material." "Editors are not rejecting your ability when they reject your work. Keep looking for the appropriate opportunity to publish." Currently not encouraging submissions due to a backlog.
Editorial Interests
• *Poetry:* Surrealistic poems.
• *Nonfiction:* Mathematical theory for the arts, Tarot, astrology, channeling, crystals, dreams, extraterrestrials, magic, mythology, and philosophy.

Recent Titles: *A Message From the Ruins. The Great American Art Auction.*
Submission and Payment Policy: Query first with resume. Include SASE. Accepts photocopies and computer printouts. Simultaneous submissions okay. Reporting time varies. If accepted, expect publication in 1 month.

Keats Publishing, Inc.

Nathan Keats, Publisher, 27 Pine Street, New Canaan, CT 06840   Phone: 203-966-8721, Fax: 203-972-3991

Profile: Alternative health care. Established in 1971. Titles: 15 per year; all nonfiction; 6 hardcover; 9 paperback. Book catalogue available.
Focus and Imprints: Keats Publishing is well-established in the health and nutrition field, particularly in the realm of alternative and preventative medicine. In addition to its book list, the *Good Health Guide* series publishes pamphelts summarizing the latest information on a range of health topics. These are sold internationally and translated into six languages. Keats also publishes *Health News & Review*, a quarterly tabloid dedicated to promoting healthier lifestyles.
Editorial Interests
• *Nonfiction:* Alternative health care and medicine, holistic and natural health, healing, astrology, bodywork, ecosystems, the environment, lifestyle, new age, nutrition, self-help, women's issues, and yoga.
Recent Titles: *The Complete Book of Water Therapy* by Dian Dincin Buchman. *Round-the-World Cooking at The Natural Gourmet* by Debra Stark.
Submission and Payment Policy: Query with outline. Include SASE. Accepts photocopies and computer printouts. No simultaneous submissions. Reports in 2 months. If accepted, expect publication in 1 year. Royalty with advance or flat fee.

Michael Kesend Publishing, LTD.

Judy Wilder, Editor, 1025 Fifth Avenue, New York, NY 10028   Phone: 212-249-5150, Fax: 212-249-2129

Profile: Nonfiction books on outdoor activities. Book catalogue available.
Focus and Imprints: Michael Kesend Publishing specializes in guidebooks on travel and a variety of outdoor activities and sports. Within that arena, it is interested in books or subjects that are unique or have little competition in their fields. Does not publish fiction.
Editorial Interests
• *Nonfiction:* Guidebooks on travel, outdoor sports and activities, camping, hiking, mountain biking, walking, health, lifestyle, and animal and pet care.
Recent Titles: *Essential Guide to Hiking in the United States* by Charles Cook. *Art Walks in New York* by Harrison and Rosenfeld.
Submission and Payment Policy: Query first with outline, 3 sample chapters, resume, and book synopsis. No unsolicited manuscripts. Include SASE. Accepts photocopies and computer printouts. No simultaneous submissions. Reports in 6 weeks. If accepted, expect publication in 18 months. Considers book packaging, subsidy publishing, and co-publishing ventures. Royalty, 6%. Advance, 6%. Flat fees negotiated.

Kivaki Press

Kevin Groves, Editorial Assistant, 585 East 31st Street, Durango, CO 81301   Phone: 303-385-1767, Fax: 303-385-1974

Profile: Books on the environment and holistic living. Titles: 6–8 per year; all nonfiction. Average print run: 2,500. Book catalogue and writer's guidelines available.
Focus and Imprints: Kivaki Press acquires nonfiction titles in the areas of holistic health, environmental restoration, and community renewal. Not interested in fiction or children's books.
Editorial Interests
• *Nonfiction:* Holistic health, ecological and environmental restoration, gardening, recycling, community renewal, and the semiotics of nature, place, and culture.
Recent Titles: *Sacred Land, Sacred Sex* by Dolores La Chapelle. *Look to the Mountain* by Dr. Gregory Cajete.
Submission and Payment Policy: Query first with outline. Include SASE. Accepts Macintosh disks and faxes. Offers a generous royalty.
Other Interests: Kivaki Press is a member of the Rocky Mountain Publishers Association.

Lampus Press

Arthur Graham, 19611 Antioch Road, White City, OR 97503

Profile: New age psychology books. Book list available.
Focus and Imprints: Lampus Press is dedicated to publishing books that clarify the ideas and principles of esoteric psychology and "the Ageless Wisdom," as presented by Bailey, Blavatsky, and Roerich.

Editorial Interests
• *Nonfiction:* Specific interests include The Seven Rays, esoteric psychology, esoteric astrology, chakras, healing, meditation, metaphysics, and the new age.
Recent Titles: *Psychology Types and the Seven Rays* by Kurt Abraham. *Introduction to the Seven Rays* by Kurt Abraham.
Submission and Payment Policy: Query with outline. Include SASE. Accepts photocopies and computer printouts. Simultaneous submissions okay. Payment varies.
Other Interests: Affiliated with the School for the Study of the Seven Rays, which offers a correspondence course on the Seven Rays. For more information, contact Kurt Abraham, 19611 Antioch Road, White City, OR 97503.

Libra Press

Dr. Loretta Kurban, Editor, 4328 North Lincoln, Chicago, IL 60618   Phone: 312-478-2410

Profile: Health-related nonfiction. Titles: 5 per year; all nonfiction paperback. Average print run: 1,000. Binding: Perfect bound. Book list available.
Focus and Imprints: Libra Press is a small publisher of nonfiction books on health-related and spiritual topics. Most material is written in-house.
Editorial Interests
• *Nonfiction:* Health, spirituality, astrology, crystals, holistic health, metaphysics, occult, self-help, women's issues, and numerology.
Recent Titles: *Famous Women* by Dr. Loretta Kurban. *Face and Body Language* by Michael J. Kurban.
Submission and Payment Policy: Query first with outline. Include SASE. No simultaneous submissions. Reports in 1 month.
Other Interests: Affiliated with the Hyperactive Child Institute. Sponsors health and spiritual classes. For more information, contact Dr. Loretta Kurban, 312-478-2410.

Lifetime Books

2131 Hollywood Boulevard, Suite 305, Hollywood, FL 33020   Phone: 305-925-5242, Fax: 305-925-5244

Profile: Inspirational self-help books. An imprint of Fell Publishing, Inc. Titles: 20 per year; all nonfiction; hardcover and paperback. Average print run: 5,000–10,000. Binding: Perfect bound. Book catalogue available.
Focus and Imprints: Lifetime Books publishes a list of inspirational nonfiction primarily in the how-to/self-help genre. Authors should consider how their book will be marketed and where it would be sold, then "convince the publisher that it should be published." Encourages writers to research competitive books on the market. If the topic has been covered in many different ways, try to find a new topic. Not interested in fiction or children's books.
Editorial Interests
• *Nonfiction:* Inspirational how-to and self-help books concerning business, speechmaking, cooking, cultural and ethnic concerns, dreams, extraterrestrials, feminism, gay and lesbian issues, healing, health and holistic health, lifestyle, magic, men's issues, natural health, new age, nutrition, parenting, philosophy, politics, psychology, recovery, regional issues, relationships, seniors, social and world issues, and women's issues.
Recent Titles: *How to Make a Great Presentation in Two Hours* by Frank Paolo.
Submission and Payment Policy: Query with outline and 3 sample chapters, or send complete manuscript with cover letter, chapter outline, and author biography. Include SASE. Accepts photocopies and computer printouts. Simultaneous submissions okay. Reports in 3–6 months. If accepted, expect publication in 1 year. Pays a royalty.

Lighthouse Productions

M. Mathiesen, President, P.O. Box 7885, Santa Cruz, CA 95060   Phone: 408-423-8580, Fax: 408-423-0131

Profile: Electronic or computer accessible books on any topic. Titles: 100 per year; fiction and nonfiction. Average print run: 10,000. Book catalogue available.
Focus and Imprints: Lighthouse Productions acquires a variety of fiction and nonfiction that is computer readable and publishable in electronic format. Avoid heavily opinionated, political, or religious material.
Editorial Interests
• *Fiction and nonfiction:* Considers all topics. Especially open to science fiction, science and educational books for children in kindergarten through college, and materials for home study. Specific interests include astrology, channeling, cultural and ethnic issues, dreams, ecosystems, the environment, extraterrestrials, feminism, folklore, healing and health, holistic health, inspirational material, lifestyle, magic, meditation, men's issues, metaphysics, mysticism, mythology, natural health, new age, nutrition, occult, parapsychology, parenting, philosophy, prayer, psychic phenomenon, psychology, rebirthing, recovery, regional issues, relationships, self-help, seniors, social and world issues, and yoga.
Recent Titles: *The Interactive Yellow Pages* by M. Mathiesen. *The Penetrators* by M. Mathiesen.
Submission and Payment Policy: Query first with outline, 3–5 sample chapters, and writing samples. Include SASE. Accepts

computer submissions in .TXT or ASCII format. Reports in 1 month. If accepted, expect publication in 1 month. Offers a 3.5% royalty or $3.50 per book fee. Advance, $5,000.
Other Interests: Associated with The Electronic Publisher's Association, which offers seminars and training material. Contact M. Mathiesen, P.O. Box 7885, Santa Cruz, CA 95060.

Lindisfarne Press
Christopher Bamford, Editor, R.R. 4, Box 94 A-1, Hudson, NY 12534   Phone: 518-851-9155, Fax: 518-851-2047

Profile: Titles on spiritual transformation. A division of the nonprofit Anthroposophic Press. Titles: 6 per year; all nonfiction paperback. Average print run: 3,000. Binding: Smythe sewn. Book catalogue available.
Focus and Imprints: Lindisfarne Press strives to publish books that "contribute to a renewed understanding of humanity, nature, the cosmos, and the divine as a single, complex, evolving, interpenetrated spiritual being."
Editorial Interests
• *Nonfiction:* Interests include philosophy, psychology, spirituality, religion, Christianity, new science, literature, astrology, dreams, ecosystems, feminism, meditation, metaphysics, mysticism, mythology, occult, politics, prayer, and economics.
Recent Titles: *The Life of the Soul: Elements of a Spiritual Psychology* by Georg Kuhlewind. *The Planets Within: The Astrological Psychology of Marsilio Fincino* by Thomas More.
Submission and Payment Policy: Query with outline and resume. No unsolicited manuscripts. Include SASE. Accepts photocopies and computer printouts. Simultaneous submissions okay. Reports in 2 months. If accepted, expect publication in 1 year. Royalty, 5% and up.

Llewellyn Publications
Nancy J. Mostad, Acquisitions Manager, P.O. Box 64383, St Paul, MN 55164   Phone: 612-291-1970, Fax: 612-291-1908

Profile: Mass market, trade, and workbooks on new age sciences. Division of Llewellyn Worldwide, Ltd. Titles: 60 per year; all nonfiction paperback. Average print run: 5,000. Book catalogue and writer's guidelines available.
Focus and Imprints: Llewellyn is a specialty publisher in what is generally called "New Age" sciences. Emphasizes practical, how-to, and self-help material in the areas of new age, occult, and metaphysics. Llewellyn aims its products at a general audience of lay readers. Prefers books with strong mail-order potential as well as general bookstore appeal. Avoid first-person stories or biographical materials. Open to working with new writers, Llewellyn looks for books with long shelf-lives and authors with whom they can develop lasting relationships. Writers are advised to send for the company's extensive guidelines.
Editorial Interests
• *Fiction:* Entertaining, educational fiction reflecting true occult principles, from astrology to Zen, including parapsychology, mythology, and witchcraft.
• *Nonfiction:* Areas of interests include new age, occult, magick, self-improvement, self-development, self-awareness, spiritual science, alternative technologies, nature, religion and lifestyles, spiritist and mystery religions, divination, UFOs and unexplained phenomena, and Tantra.
• *Illustrations:* Requires authors to provide as many original illustrations as possible to accompany manuscripts. Submit, sketches and diagrams with instructions or professional-quality high-contrast B/W photos.
Recent Titles: *Create Your Own Joy* by Elizabeth Jean Rogers. *The Pagan Family* by Ceisiwr Serith.
Submission and Payment Policy: Query first with outline, 2 sample chapters, and resume. Include SASE. Accepts photocopies and computer printouts. Simultaneous submissions okay. Reports in 2 weeks. If accepted, expect publication in 1 year. Royalty, 10%.

Lotus Light Publications
Nirankar Agarwal, Administrative Assistant, 1100 Lotus Drive, Silver Lake, WI 53170   Phone: 414-889-8561, Fax: 414-889-8591

Profile: Books on alternative health issues. A division Lotus Brands, Inc. Titles: 15 per year; all nonfiction; 1–2 hardcover; 13–14 paperback. Average print run: 5,000. Book catalogue available.
Focus and Imprints: Lotus Light Publications offers books on alternative health including Ayurveda and Sri Aurobindo's integral yoga books. Imprints include Lotus Press and Arcana Publishing.
Editorial Interests
• *Nonfiction:* Interests include Ayuredic medicine, mysticism, Hindu religion, alternative health, holistic and natural health, self-help, and yoga.
Recent Titles: *Ayurvedic Beauty Care* by Melanie Sachs. *Lost Secrets of Ayurvedic Acupuncture* by Dr. Frank Ross.
Submission and Payment Policy: Query first with outline. Include SASE. Responds to queries in 2 months, to manuscripts in 3 months. If accepted, expect publication in 12–18 months. Royalty.

MacMurray and Beck Inc.

Frederick Ramey, Executive Director, P.O. Box 150717, Lakewood, CO 80215   Phone: 303-239-9688, Fax 303-239-0828

Profile: General-interest fiction and nonfiction. Titles: 8 per year; 2 fiction; 6 nonfiction; all hardcover. Average print run: 6,000. Binding: Case bound. Book catalogue available.

Focus and Imprints: MacMurray and Beck publishes a list of fiction and nonfiction that reflects the intertwining of life's relationships. Writers should submit concise, saleable proposals that define clearly why their books should be published. Special preference is given to writers from the West. Not interested in poetry, science fiction, or new age topics.

Editorial Interests

• *Fiction:* Eccentric literary fiction. Send fiction submissions to Greg Michalson, Fiction Editor, 8201 East Highway W.W., Columbia, MO 65201. Phone: 314-882-4474, Fax: 314-884-4671.

• *Nonfiction:* Health and women's titles.

Recent Titles: *Confessions of a Healer* by O.T. Bonnett. *Stygo* by Laura Hendrie.

Submission and Payment Policy: Query first with outline and 3 sample chapters. Include SASE. Accepts photocopies and computer printouts. Simultaneous submissions okay. Reports in 3 months. Publication time varies. Royalty with advance.

McBooks Press

Alex Skutt, Publisher, 908 Steam Mill Road, Ithaca, NY 14850   Phone: 607-272-2114, Fax: 607-273-6068

Profile: Health-related books and nonfiction of regional interest. Distributed by Atrium Publishers Group. Established in 1980. Titles: 2 per year; all nonfiction paperback. Average print run: 5,000. Press: Offset. Binding: Perfect bound. Book catalogue available.

Focus and Imprints: McBooks Press seeks practical nonfiction books on health and related issues, as well as books with New York State regional interest. No fiction or children's books. It is interested in exploring new publishing technologies such as CD ROM.

Editorial Interests

• *Nonfiction:* Practical, useful books on natural health, vegetarianism, nutrition, parenting, and New York State regional issues.

Recent Titles: *Vegetarian Pregnancy* by Sharon Yntema. *From Blood to Verdict* by Deborah Homsher.

Submission and Payment Policy: Query first with outline. No unsolicited manuscripts. Include SASE. Accepts photocopies, computer printouts, and computer disks, preferably Macintosh. Simultaneous submissions okay. Reports in 2 months. If accepted, expect publication in 18 months. Open to subsidy and co-publishing ventures. Offers royalty and advance; amounts vary.

Metamorphous Press

Nancy Wyatt-Kelsey, Acquisitions Editor, P.O. Box 10616, Portland, OR 97210-0616   Phone: 503-228-4972

Profile: Self-help nonfiction. Established in 1984. Titles: 8 per year; all nonfiction paperback. Average print run: 2,000–5,000. Binding: Perfect bound. Book catalogue available.

Focus and Imprints: Metamorphous Press specializes in nonfiction on neurolinguistic programming, bodywork, and other related self-help topics and techniques.

Editorial Interests

• *Nonfiction:* Neurolinguistic programming, enneagram, bodywork technologies, education, business and sales, health and fitness, psychology, relationships, and self-help.

Recent Titles: *Enneagram and NLP* by Linden and Spalding. *Sales on the Line* by Sharon Drew Morgen.

Submission and Payment Policy: Query with outline. Include SASE. Accepts photocopies, computer printouts, and IBM WordPerfect disks. Simultaneous submissions okay. Reports in 10 days. If accepted, expect publication in 6–12 months. Royalty 10% of net.

Mho & Mho Works

Sharon Worth, Editor, Box 33135, San Diego, CA 92163   Phone: 619-280-3488

Profile: Lists a variety of alternative nonfiction. Division of The R.A. Fessenden Educational Fund. Titles: 1–2 per year; 1 nonfiction; 1 hardcover; 1 paperback. Average print run: 5,000. Press: Coldtype. Binding: Perfect or case bound. Book catalogue available.

Focus and Imprints: Mho & Mho Works publishes an interesting, eclectic list of nonfiction titles encompassing such topics as sexuality, disability, and broadcasting. The best way to ascertain its needs is to read some of its titles. No "dull, boring, immature, gutless writings."

Editorial Interests
• *Nonfiction:* Interests include media and broadcasting, family therapy, sexuality, disability, recovery, Eastern religion, gay and lesbian issues, metaphysics, and psychology.
Recent Titles: *The Blob that Ate Oaxaca and Other Travel Tales* by Carlos Amantea. *And Other Voyages* by Robin Magowan.
Submission and Payment Policy: Query first with outline and 3–5 sample chapters. Include SASE. Accepts photocopies, computer printouts, and WordPerfect 4.1 disks. Simultaneous submissions okay. Responds to queries in 1 month, to manuscripts in 3 months. If accepted, expect publication in 6–12 months. Subsidy publishing services are available. Payment is negotiated on an individual basis.

Miles River Press
Libby Schraeder, Marketing Coordinator, 1009 Duke Street, Alexandria, VA 22314   Phone: 703-683-1500, Fax: 703-683-0827

Profile: Nonfiction trade books. Titles: 11 per year; all nonfiction paperback. Average print run: 5,000. Binding: Perfect bound. Book announcements available.
Focus and Imprints: Miles River Press publishes a variety of anthologies on business management and organizational change.
Editorial Interests
• *Nonfiction:* Anthologies on organizational change, parenting, social and world issues, and women's issues.
Recent Titles: *Participation Works: Business Cases from Around the World* by James P. Troxel, General Editor. *Transforming Leadership* by John Adams, General Editor.
Submission and Payment Policy: Query with outline. Include SASE. Accepts photocopies and faxes. No simultaneous submissions. Reports in 1–2 months. If accepted, expect publication in 6–9 months. Offers royalty and advance. Rates vary depending on book and number of authors involved.

Mills & Sanderson, Publishers
Jan Anthony, Publisher/Managing Editor, 41 North Road, Suite 201, Bedford, MA 01730
Phone: 617-275-1410, Fax: 617-275-1713

Profile: Adult nonfiction family problem-solving books. Established in 1986. Titles: 6–7 per year; all nonfiction paperback. Average print run: 2,000. Binding: Perfect bound. Book catalogue available.
Focus and Imprints: Mills & Sanderson seeks and publishes nonfiction books that enhance the quality of life for their readers. Advises writers to study guidelines before submitting. Not interested in journals or serialized columns "converted" to book form or in antagonistic approaches to therapy.
Editorial Interests
• *Nonfiction:* Lifestyle, men's issues, psychology, recovery, and women's issues.
Recent Titles: *My Child Needs Special Services* by Nancy O. Wilson. *Understanding the Trauma of Childhood Psycho-Sexual Abuse* by Elizabeth Adams.
Submission and Payment Policy: Prefers a query first with outline, 2–3 sample chapters, writing samples, and resume. Accepts complete manuscripts with cover letter, bibliography, resume, and clips. Include SASE. Accepts photocopies and computer printouts. Simultaneous submissions okay. Reports in 2 months. If accepted, expect publication in 1 year. Considers book packaging and co-publishing ventures. Royalty, 12.5% of net; advance, $1,000.

More to Life Publishing
Kim Michaels, President, P.O. Box 92, Emigrant, MT 59027   Phone: 406-333-4513

Profile: Contemporary titles with a spiritual dimension. Titles: 3 per year; all nonfiction paperbacks. Average print run: 1,500. Binding: Perfect bound. Book catalogue not available.
Focus and Imprints: More to Life Publishing lists books on contemporary subjects with a distinct spiritual angle. It seeks informative material that provides new perspectives on issues based on spiritual insights. Reading their recent titles is the best way to judge if a manuscript is suitable for this publisher. Not interested in fiction or material about psychic energies.
Editorial Interests
• *Nonfiction:* Informative, inspirational exposés and self-help books on the environment, holistic health, metaphysics, mysticism, new age, philosophy, politics, psychology, religion, and spirituality.
Recent Titles: *Forbidden Questions About Abortion* by Kim Atman.
Submission and Payment Policy: Query first with outline. Include SASE. Accepts photocopies, computer printouts, and Macintosh disks. Simultaneous submissions okay. Reports in 1 month. Payment is negotiated on an individual basis.

Morning Glory Press
Jeanne Lindsay, Editor, 6595 San Haroldo Way, Buena Park, CA 90620   Phone: 714-828-1998, Fax: 714-828-2049

Profile: Special interest books for teenagers. Established in 1977. Titles: 4 per year; 2 fiction; 2 nonfiction; hardcover and paperback. Average print run: 5,000. Binding: Perfect bound. Book catalogue available.

Focus and Imprints: Morning Glory Press specializes in fiction and nonfiction for teens dealing with teenage pregnancy and parenting. Its titles are marketed to schools, libraries, and social service agencies. Be aware of the special focus and audience. "Our books are usually purchased for pregnant teens. Readability level should be accessible." Avoid highly academic language. Morning Glory Press also publishes a quarterly newsletter, *PPT Express*, for professionals who work with pregnant teens and teenage parents.

Editorial Interests

• *Fiction:* Themes relating in some way to pregnant/parenting teens.

• *Nonfiction:* Books for school-age parents on feminism, pregnancy and health issues, childbirth, parenting, lifestyle, nutrition, relationships, self-help and women's issues, and adoption from the perspective of the birth family.

Recent Titles: *Too Soon for Jeff* by Marilyn Reynolds. *Teen Dads: Rights, Responsibilities and Joys* by Jeanne Warren Lindsay.

Submission and Payment Policy: Send manuscript with cover letter. Include SASE. Accepts photocopies and computer printouts. Simultaneous submissions okay. Reports in 3 months. If accepted, expect publication in 5 months. Royalty, 10%.

Mortal Press

Terry James Mohaupt, Publisher, 2315 North Alpine Road, Rockford, IL 61107-1422   Phone: 815-399-8432

Profile: Poetry and fine arts. A division of Mortal Communications Group. Established in 1975. Titles: 2 per year; 1 fiction; 1 nonfiction; 1 hardcover; 1 paperback. Average print run: 250. Book list available.

Focus and Imprints: Mortal Press publishes literary volumes of poetry and fine art. Seeks high-quality poetry. "Right now, it's discouraging to send rejections to all the unprofessional submitters. We don't have the staff to try to decipher illegible handwriting."

Editorial Interests

• *Poetry:* Quality poems with professional presentations.

Recent Titles: *No Lover Ever Dies* by Morpheus. *Can You Hear My Trembling Soul?* by T. J. Mohaupt.

Submission and Payment Policy: Query with writing samples and resume or send complete poems with clips. Include SASE. Accepts photocopies, laser-quality printouts, and Macintosh, Microsoft Word, or WriteNow disks. Responds to queries in 1 month; to manuscripts in 1–3 months. If accepted, expect publication in 1 year. Payment is negotiable, within accepted industry standards.

Naturegraph Publishers, Inc.

Barbara Brown, Editor, 3543 Indian Creek Road, Happy Camp, CA 96039   Phone: 916-493-5353, Fax: 916-493-5240

Profile: Nonfiction books on the environment. Established in 1946. Titles: 2–3 per year; nonfiction; paperback. Average print run: 2,500. Press: Sheet fed. Binding: Perfect bound. Book catalogue available.

Focus and Imprints: Since 1946, Naturegraph Publishers has been publishing "books for a better world" on nature and the environment. Be sure ideas are appropriate before querying—this company receives many ill-suited submissions.

Editorial Interests

• *Nonfiction:* Nature, natural history, the environment, Native American life and culture, wildlife, and gardening.

Recent Titles: *Wisdom of Nature* by Dagton Foster. *Wildlife and Plants of the Cascades* by Charles Yocom and Vinson Brown.

Submission and Payment Policy: Query first with outline. Include SASE. Accepts photocopies and computer printouts. Simultaneous submissions okay. Reports in 1 month. If accepted, expect publication in 18 months. Royalty, 8–10% of wholesale.

The New Dawn Publishing Co.

Geraldine Bennett, Owner, 20526 County Route 59, Dexter, NY 13634-9743   Phone: 315-639-6764

Profile: Self-help and self-improvement books. Titles: 3 per year; all fiction paperback. Average print run: Varies. Binding: Perfect and spiral bound. Book catalogue available.

Focus and Imprints: The New Dawn Publishing Co. is a small press offering a list of self-improvement books for children and adults. Not interested in material that is disrespectful of any race or group of people.

Editorial Interests

• *Fiction:* Stories for children that foster self-esteem, self-discipline, respect for others, and spiritual awareness.

• *Nonfiction:* Adult and juvenile self-improvement and inspirational books on the environment, folklore, healing, holistic and natural health, metaphysics, mysticism, mythology, parapsychology, philosophy, psychic phenomenon, spirituality, and women's issues.

Recent Titles: *Opening the Door to Your Inner Self/My Lessons* by Geraldine M. P. Bennett. *The Witch of Burchard Street* by John D. Blacké.

Submission and Payment Policy: Query first with outline and 3 sample chapters. Include SASE. Accepts computer printouts, faxes, and Word for Windows disks. No simultaneous submissions. Responds to queries in 3 months, to manuscripts in 3–6 months. If accepted, expect publication in 1–2 years.

New Falcon Press

Nicholas Tharcher, Editor, 1739 East Broadway Road, Suite 1-277, Tempe, AZ 85282   Phone: 602-246-3546

Profile: Trade paperbacks on metaphysics and the occult. A division of J.W. Brown, Inc. Titles: 15 per year; 3–4 fiction; 11 nonfiction; all paperback. Average print run: 3,000–5,000. Binding: Perfect bound. Book catalogue available.
Focus and Imprints: New Falcon Press specializes in books on metaphysics, the occult, religion, and psychology. It prefers works based on personal experiences. Avoid arrogance.
Editorial Interests
• *Fiction:* Books dealing with occult and science fiction themes.
• *Nonfiction:* Special interest in personal experiences. Topics include astrology, bodywork, channeling, dreams, the environment, extraterrestrials, gay and lesbian concerns, inspirational pieces, magic, meditation, men's issues, metaphysics, mysticism, mythology, new age, occult, parapsychology, philosophy, psychic phenomenon, psychology, religion, self-help, seniors, social and world issues, spirituality, witches, women's issues, and yoga.
Recent Titles: *Game of Life* by Timothy Leary. *Pathworkings of Allister Crowley* by Allister Crowley.
Submission and Payment Policy: Prefers receiving the complete manuscript with author biography. Accepts a query with 3 sample chapters. Include SASE. Accepts photocopies and computer printouts. Simultaneous submissions okay. Reports in 2–4 months. If accepted, expect publication in 1 year. Considers subsidy publishing ventures. Payment negotiable.

New Harbinger Publications

Kirk Johnson, Senior Editor, 5674 Shattuck Avenue, Oakland, CA 94609   Phone: 510-652-0215, Fax: 510-652-5472

Profile: Self-help and psychology books. Titles: 10–15 per year; all nonfiction; hardcover and paperback. Average print run: 10,000. Book catalogue and writer's guidelines available.
Focus and Imprints: New Harbinger Publications seeks self-help and psychology books in the areas of health and family issues. Its books are designed to allow readers the maximum use with a minimum of research—more time using techniques and less trying to understand them. Strongly suggests that writers send for guidelines before submitting work. This publisher is willing to work closely with authors to help them shape their books into useful, workbook format. Prefers practical, how-to material with broad appeal. Avoid using a narrative style.
Editorial Interests
• *Nonfiction:* Books designed to help people help themselves. Interests include psychology, family issues, health and healing, bodywork, the environment, feminism, gay and lesbian concerns, holistic and natural health, lifestyle, meditation, men's issues, nutrition, parenting, recovery, relationships, and women's issues.
Recent Titles: *Couple Skills: Making Your Relationships Work* by Matthew McKay, Patrick Fanning, and Kim Paleg. *The Postpartum Survival Guide* by Ann Dunnewald and Diane Sanford.
Submission and Payment Policy: Query with outline and 2 sample chapters. Include SASE. Accepts photocopies, computer printouts, and IBM WordPerfect disks. Simultaneous submissions okay. Responds to queries in 1–2 months, to manuscripts in 3–4 months. If accepted, expect publication in 1 year. Royalty, 12% of net; advance, up to $2,000.

New Mind Productions, Inc.

Armiya Nu'man, Publisher, 116 Van Nostrand Avenue, Jersey City, NJ 07305   Phone: 201-434-1939, Fax: 201-434-0321

Profile: African-American literature. Established in 1979. Titles: 4–5 per year; fiction and nonfiction; all paperback. Average print run: 2,000–5,000. Binding: Perfect bound or saddle stitched. Book catalogue available.
Focus and Imprints: New Mind Productions is interested primarily in literature oriented to the African-American experience. Most of its material has a psychological or religious focus. Avoid writing that degrades the human character.
Editorial Interests
• *Fiction:* Interested in children's fiction that promotes self-awareness, story-based activity books, and fictionalized accounts of true experiences.
• *Nonfiction:* Material of African-American interest aimed at human development. Topics of interest include Islam, symbolism, freemasonry, cultural and ethnic concerns, the environment, healing, health, inspirational material, children's and teen issues, meditation, men's issues, metaphysics, natural health, nutrition, parenting, philosophy, prayer, psychic phenomenon, psychology, relationships, self-help, social and world issues, spirituality, and women's issues.
Recent Titles: *Chains and Images of Psychological Slavery* by Dr. Na'im Akbar. *What Every American Should Know About Islam and the Muslims* by Armiya Nu'man.
Submission and Payment Policy: Query with outline, 2 sample chapters, and resume. Include SASE. Accepts photocopies,

computer printouts, and Macintosh disks. Simultaneous submissions okay. Reports in 2 months. If accepted, expect publication in 6–12 months. Royalty, 10–15%.

New Native Press

Thomas Rain Crowe, Publisher, P.O. Box 661, Cullowhee, NC 28723   Phone: 704-293-9237

Profile: Poetry translations. Titles: 3 per year; all poetry collections; all paperback. Average print run: 500. Press: Offset. Binding: Perfect bound. Book list available.
Focus and Imprints: New Native Press is a small independent publisher of poetry collections. Emphasis is placed on translations into English.
Editorial Interests
• *Poetry:* Open to all subjects. Prefers translations.
Recent Titles: *Against Information* by John Lane. *Night Sun: An Initiation Trilogy* by Thomas Rain Crowe.
Submission and Payment Policy: Query with outline and 2–3 writing samples. Include SASE. Accepts photocopies and computer printouts. Simultaneous submissions okay. Reports in 3 weeks. If accepted, expect publication in 1 year. No payment. Authors receive copies of their books to market and sell individually.
Other Interests: New Native Press is affiliated with Fern Hill Records, a spoken-word label that releases collaborations of music and the spoken word. For more information, contact John Rain Crowe, 704-293-9237.

New Society Publishers

T. L. Hills, Editor, 4527 Springfield Avenue, Philadelphia, PA 19143   Phone: 215-382-6543

Profile: Self-help books that promote social change. A division of the New Society Educational Foundation, a nonprofit, worker-controller organization. Titles: 12–14 per year; all nonfiction paperback. Average print run: 2,300. Press: Sheet fed and web. Binding: Library. Book catalogue and writer's guidelines available.
Focus and Imprints: New Society Publishers is committed to fundamental social change through nonviolent action. The aim of its books is to motivate readers to "take control of their lives and change the way things are." Emphasis is always on inspirational, motivational, and skill-oriented material. Not interested in books that merely stress what is wrong in the world— provide constructive, practical information. Does not publish fiction or poetry. Read guidelines before submitting.
Editorial Interests
• *Nonfiction:* Interests include nonviolent action, social justice, sustainable living, activists manuals, social organizing tools, group dynamics, conflict resolution, world relations, economics, education, cultural and ethnic issues, the environment, feminism, health, children's issues, lifestyle, men's issues, parenting, philosophy, politics, relationships, self-help, social and world issues, and women's issues.
Recent Titles: *In the Tiger's Mouth* by Katrina Shields. *Teaching Young Children in Violent Times* by Diane E. Levin.
Submission and Payment Policy: Send for guidelines and proposal outlines. Query first with sample chapter, table of contents, and book proposal. No unsolicited manuscripts. Include SASE. Accepts photocopies, computer printouts, and computer disks. Simultaneous submissions okay. Reports in 1 month. Publication time varies. Royalty, 10% of net payable twice a year.

New Spirit Press

Ignatius Graffeo, Editor, 82-34 138 Street, No. 6F, Kew Gardens, NY 11435   Phone: 718-847-1482

Profile: Poetry chapbooks. An imprint of The Poet Tree. Titles: 16 per year; all paperback. Average print run: 250. Press: Laser xerox. Binding: Stapled. Book catalogue not available.
Focus and Imprints: New Spirit Press publishes poetry chapbooks only, as part of its monthly New Spirit Chapbook Contest. It seeks well-written material with "universal appeal, thematic unity, and cohesion." Welcomes the use of "clever metaphor, imaginative but conceivable imagery, a connection to the mythological, and poems that are classical yet current in subject matter." Advises authors to send for and study writer's guidelines and recently published chapbooks. No profanity, gratuitous violence, perversion, pornography, or graphic horror. Avoid greeting card verse and "cascade" style poetry. Affiliations include The Poet Tree, a self-publishing poetry chapbook series, and I.O.T.A. Press, a cooperative publishing enterprise.
Editorial Interests
• *Poetry:* High-quality poetry chapbooks. Subject matter includes dreams, the environment, extraterrestrials, folklore, metaphysics, mysticism, mythology, new age, occult, parapsychology, psychic phenomenon, and spirituality.
Recent Titles: *Green Snake Riding* by Lois Marie Harrod. *What Death Would Be Without Us* by Arthur Nahill.
Submission and Payment Policy: Send up to 30 poems, preferably camera-ready, with a brief author biography. Include SASE. $10 reading fee. Accepts photocopies. Simultaneous submissions okay. Responds to queries in 2 weeks, to manuscripts in 2 months. If accepted, expect publication in 2 months. No payment: Contest winners receive 50 copies of book plus 10% of reprints over 200 copies.

New World Library

Marc Allen, Publisher, 58 Paul Drive, San Rafael, CA 94903 Phone: 415-472-2100, Fax: 415-472-6131

Profile: New age nonfiction books and cassettes of a self-help nature. An imprint of Whatever Publishing, Inc. Titles: 20 per year; all nonfiction; 2 hardcover; 18 paperback. Average print run: 7,500. Binding: Perfect bound. Book catalogue available.
Focus and Imprints: New World Library offers nonfiction books and cassettes that uplift, heal, and help improve the quality of life. Imprints include *Amber-Allen Publishing*, health and personal growth books, and *Wildcat Canyon Press*, women's issues. It is not interested in poetry, fiction, or children's books.
Editorial Interests
• *Nonfiction:* Interests include personal growth, business, prosperity, Native American and African American issues, health and holistic healing, cultural and ethnic issues, inspiration, meditation, new age, parenting, philosophy, psychology, recovery, self-help, spirituality, and business prosperity.
Recent Titles: *Creating Affluence* by Deepak Chopra. *Creative Visualization* by Shakti Gawain.
Submission and Payment Policy: Query with outline, 1 sample chapter, and resume. Include SASE. Accepts photocopies, computer printouts, and faxes. Simultaneous submissions okay. Reports in 1–2 months. If accepted, expect publication in 1 year. Royalty, 12–16% of net; advance is negotiable.

Newcastle Publishing Company, Inc.

Alfred Saunders, Editor-in-Chief, 13419 Saticoy, North Hollywood, CA 91605 Phone: 213-873-3191, Fax: 818-780-2007

Profile: Self-help trade paperbacks. Titles: 12 per year; all nonfiction paperback. Average print run: 3,000–5,000. Binding: Perfect bound. Book catalogue available.
Focus and Imprints: Newcastle Publishing Company concentrates on "pop" psychology trade books dealing with self-healing. Authors are encouraged to "check the bookshelves. Don't duplicate what is already out there—find a new twist."
Editorial Interests
• *Nonfiction:* Interests include self-help/self-healing, spirituality, psychology, astrology, bodywork, healing, health, holistic health, inspirational material, magic, meditation, metaphysics, mysticism, mythology, nutrition, occult, psychic phenomenon, rebirthing, relationships, seniors, women's issues, and yoga.
Recent Titles: *The Live Your Dreams Workbook* by Joyce Chapman. *Expressions on Healing* by Sandra Graves.
Submission and Payment Policy: Query with outline, 3 sample chapters, and resume. Include SASE. Accepts photocopies, computer printouts, faxes, and IBM or Macintosh disks. Simultaneous submissions okay. Responds to queries in 6–8 weeks, to manuscripts in 3 months. If accepted, expect publication in 10 months. Royalty, 8%.

Newmarket Press

Grace Farrell, Assistant Editor, 18 East 48th Street, New York, NY 10017 Phone: 212-832-3575, Fax: 212-832-3629

Profile: Nonfiction trade books. A division of Newmarket Publishing and Communications. Titles: 20 per year; all nonfiction; 5 hardcover; 15 paperback. Book catalogue available.
Focus and Imprints: Newmarket Press publishes a variety of nonfiction hardcover and paperback books for adults and children, with a special concentration on self-help and performing arts/film books. Imprints include Newmarket Pictorial Moviebooks and Medallion Books for Young Readers.
Editorial Interests
• *Nonfiction:* Adult and juvenile self-help and special-interest books on health, inspiration, lifestyle, magic, men's issues, nutrition, parenting, psychology, relationships, women's issues, film, and the performing arts.
Recent Titles: *Discovering Great Music* by Roy Hemming. *The Male Stress Syndrome* by Georgia Witlein.
Submission and Payment Policy: Query first with outline and resume. Include SASE. Accepts photocopies and computer printouts. Simultaneous submissions okay. Reports in 2 weeks. Publication time varies.

Nicolas-Hays Inc.

B. Lundsted, Publisher, Box 612, York Beach, ME 03910 Phone: 207-363-4393, Fax: 207-363-5799

Profile: Esoteric nonfiction trade titles. Distributed by Samuel Weiser. Titles: 2 per year; all nonfiction paperback. Average print run: 5,000. Trade paperback. Book catalogue available.
Focus and Imprints: Nicolas-Hays publishes esoterica relating to music, Jungian psychology, oriental philosophy, and spiritual development. Seeks nonfiction titles that are seriously concerned with subject matter. No poetry, novels, or new age fiction. Nicolas Hays titles are distributed by Samuel Weiser and are included in the Weiser book catalogue.
Editorial Interests
• *Nonfiction:* Astrology, dreams, extraterrestrials, healing, health, holistic health, inspiration, magic, meditation, men's issues, metaphysics, mysticism, mythology, natural health, new age, occult, parapsychology, philosophy, psychic phenomenon, psy-

chology, recovery, relationships, non-Christian religion, self-help, spirituality, witches, women's issues, and yoga.

Recent Titles: *Tarot and Individuation* by Dr. Irene Gad. *Beginner's Guide to Jungian Psychology* by Robin Robertson.

Submission and Payment Policy: Query with outline, sample chapters, and resume, or send complete manuscript with cover letter, bibliography, and resume. Include SASE. Accepts photocopies and computer printouts. Simultaneous submissions okay. Reports in 2–3 months. If accepted, expect publication in 18 months. Pays 15% royalty with advance.

North Star Press

Corinne Dwyer, Editor, P.O. Box 451, St. Cloud, MN 56302-0451   Phone: 612-253-1636

Profile: Nonfiction books on women's interests and regional titles. Titles: 6–8 per year; all fiction paperback. Average print run: 2,000. Binding: Perfect bound. Book catalogue available.

Focus and Imprints: North Star Press devotes much of its list to books on women's issues and women's spirituality. It also publishes books about Finnish culture and regional Midwest and Minnesota-related issues by area authors. Not interested in children's books, cookbooks, or self-help titles.

Editorial Interests

• *Nonfiction:* Women's issues and spirituality including meditation, prayer, dreams, the environment, and folklore. Finnish culture and people. Midwestern U.S. regional issues with emphasis on Minnesota history and towns.

Recent Titles: *Beginning in Triumph* by Edith Mucke. *Hellroaring* by Peter Leschak.

Submission and Payment Policy: Query first with 1 sample chapter. Include SASE. Accepts photocopies and computer printouts. Simultaneous submissions okay. Responds to queries in 1 month, to manuscripts in 3 months. If accepted, expect publication in 1 year. Considers subsidy publishing and co-publishing ventures. Royalty, 10% of net.

Omega Publications

Abi'l-Khayr, Manager, RD 1, Box 1030E Darrow Road, New Lebanon, NY 12125   Phone: 518-794-8181, Fax: 518-794-8187

Profile: Books on Sufism. A division of the Sufi Order in the West. Established in 1977. Titles: 2–3 per year; all nonfiction; hardcover and paperback. Average print run: 2,400. Book catalogue available.

Focus and Imprints: Omega Publications is a publisher and distributor of books and tapes related to the subject of Sufism. Past titles covered dreamwork, dances, walking meditation, and practical wisdom for developing self-control or cultivating personality.

Editorial Interests

• *Nonfiction:* Translations of texts by the ancient Sufis and notable works on Sufism published in French, German, or Spanish. Interests include Sufi-related meditation, metaphysics, mysticism, and spirituality.

Recent Titles: *The Call of the Dervish* by Pir Vilayat Inayat Khan. *The Soul Whence and Whither* by Hazrat Inayat Khan.

Submission and Payment Policy: Query with 1 sample chapter. No unsolicited manuscripts. Include SASE. Accepts photocopies and 3.5" or 5.25" IBM-compatible disks. Simultaneous submissions okay. Reports in 1 month. Publication time varies. Considers co-publishing ventures. Royalty, 10% of net.

Open Court Publishing Company

Edward Roberts, Assistant Editor, 332 South Michigan Avenue, Suite 2000, Chicago, IL 60604
Phone: 312-939-1500, Fax: 312-939-8150

Profile: Scholarly nonfiction exploring philosophy and psychology. A division of Carus Corporation. Titles: 18 per year; all nonfiction; hardcover and paperback. Average print run: 1,500–2,000 paperback; 500 cloth. Press: Offset. Binding: Perfect bound or cloth bound. Book catalogue available.

Focus and Imprints: True to the vision of its founder, philosopher Paul Carus, Open Court Publishing Company values writing that promotes philosophical debate. Most titles fall under the categories of philosophy, psychology, and comparative and Eastern religion. Its book lines include the *Dreamcatcher* series, personal stories of discovery, healing, recovery, and inner development and the *Reality of the Psyche* series, books on Jungian psychology. "Summarize the thesis of your manuscript in a page or less. If we can't tell what the book is about by reading your cover letter or outline, we're not likely to read the entire manuscript to find out."

Editorial Interests

• *Nonfiction:* Scholarly writing on philosophy, feminist thought, religious studies, comparative religion, Eastern thought, social issues, education, and Jungian psychology. Also interested in personal stories of discovery, healing, and inner development.

Recent Titles: *Jungian Analysis* edited by Murray Stein. *Solitude: A Philosophical Encounter* by Philip Koch.

Submission and Payment Policy: Query with outline, 3 sample chapters, and resume. Include SASE. Accepts photocopies and computer printouts. No simultaneous submissions. Responds to queries in 1 month, to manuscripts in 3–4 months. If accepted, expect publication in 1–3 years. Royalty, 10% and up; advance, $1,000 and up.

Original Books

M. Wurmbrand, Editor, Box 2948, Torrance, CA 90509   Phone: 310-539-7015, Fax: 310-377-0511

Profile: Translation from ancient languages. Titles: 2–3 per year. Average print run: 2,000–4,000. Book catalogue available.
Focus and Imprints: Original Books publishes translations of books originally written in ancient languages such as Chinese, Sanskrit, Tibetan, and Greek. It considers translations only; no original material.
Editorial Interests
• *Nonfiction:* Translations of original writings on dreams, holistic health, meditation, metaphysics, philosophy, religion, and yoga.
Recent Titles: *The Primordial Breath* translated by Jane Huang. *The Interpretation of Dreams* translated by Robert J. White.
Submission and Payment Policy: Query with outline. Include SASE. Accepts photocopies and computer disks. Reports in 2 months. Royalty: 10%.

Oughten House Publications

Ariane An-Rah, Director of Programs, P.O. Box 2008, 1560 Holmes Street, Building D, Livermore, CA 94551-2008
Phone: 510-447-2332

Profile: New age books. Titles: 10 per year; all paperback. Writer's and submission guidelines available.
Focus and Imprints: Oughten House Publications is dedicated to publishing fiction and nonfiction on new age and ascension transformational spirituality.
Editorial Interests
• *Fiction:* New age novels portraying spiritual transformation.
• *Nonfiction:* Interests include new age, ascension spirituality, channeling, extraterrestrials, meditation, metaphysics, and mysticism.
Recent Titles: *The Crystal Stair* by Eric Klein. *An Ascension Handbook* by Tony Stubbs.
Submission and Payment Policy: Send SASE for writer's and submission guidelines before submitting. No unsolicited manuscripts. Accepts photocopies and computer printouts. Simultaneous submissions okay. Reports in 9 months. If accepted, expect publication in 1 year.
Other Interests: Plans to establish a writing contest for works related to ascension and spirituality. For more information, contact Ariane An-Rah, 510-447-2332.

Ox Head Press

Don Olsen, Editor, Route 3, Box 136, Browerville, MN 56438   Phone: 612-594-2454

Profile: Creative, inspirational fiction in miniature format. Titles: 3 per year; all fiction; hardcover and paperback. Average print run: 300–400. Book catalogue not available.
Focus and Imprints: Ox Head Press looks for highly creative, unique short fiction to be published as miniature books. Welcomes illustrations for books and notecards. "We like to be surprised."
Editorial Interests
• *Fiction:* Creative, unusual stories, 400 words. Open to any topic including cultural and ethnic themes, dreams, folklore, healing, and some occult subjects.
Recent Titles: *Fishing* by Joy Harjo. *Findings* by Ursula LeGuin.
Submission and Payment Policy: Send complete manuscript with cover letter. Include SASE. Accepts photocopies and computer printouts. Simultaneous submissions okay. Reports immediately. If accepted, expect publication in 1 year. Royalty: paperback, 10%; hardcover, 20%.

Pacific View Press

Pam Zumwalt, President, P.O. Box 2657, Berkeley, CA 94702   Phone: 510-849-4213, Phone: 510-843-5835

Profile: Nonfiction books of Pacific Rim and Asian interest. Titles: 4 per year; all nonfiction; 2 hardcover; 2 paperback. Average print run: 5,000. Book catalogue not available.
Focus and Imprints: Pacific View Press concentrates on books about Pacific Rim businesses, Asian studies and affairs, Chinese medicine, and bodywork. The best way to assess a manuscript's suitability is to "take a look at what we've published and see if your project fits in."
Editorial Interests
• *Nonfiction:* Interests include Pacific Rim business, Asian/Chinese traditional healing, Asian current affairs and history, bodywork, the environment, health, politics, and social and world issues.
Recent Titles: *Treating AIDS with Chinese Medicine* by Mary Kay Ryan and Arthur Shattuck. *China: Business Strategies for the '90s* by Arne De Keijzer.

Submission and Payment Policy: Query first with outline. Include SASE. Accepts photocopies, computer printouts, and Microsoft Word, WordPerfect, or ASCII disks. Simultaneous submissions okay. Reports in 1 month. If accepted, expect publication in 18 months. Open to considering book packaging, subsidy publishing, or co-publishing ventures. Royalty, 10% of net.

Paradigm Publications

Bob Felt, Publisher, 44 Linden Street, Brookline, MA 02146   Phone: 617-738-4664, Fax: 617-738-4620

Profile: Nonfiction books on Oriental medicine. A division of Redwing Book Company, Inc. Titles: 4 per year; all nonfiction; 3 hardcover; 1 paperback. Average print run: 2,000. Book catalogue available.
Focus and Imprints: Paradigm Publications focuses solely on professional, technical books in the area of Oriental medicine. Manuscripts must comply with University standards. Avoid "sloppy epistemological approaches."
Editorial Interests
• *Nonfiction:* Oriental medicine textbooks.
Recent Titles: *Chinese Acupuncture* by George Solvié de Morant. *Clinical Applications of Japanese Acupuncture* by Stephen Birch.
Submission and Payment Policy: Query with outline, 2–4 sample chapters, and resume, or send complete manuscript with bibliography, resume, and translation methodology. Include SASE. Accepts computer printouts and DOS and Unix disks. Simultaneous submissions okay. Responds to queries in 3–6 months, to manuscripts in 6–12 months. If accepted, expect publication in 2 years. Royalty, 10–15% of net; advance, up to 10%.

Paragon House Publishing

Marybeth Tregarthen, Production Manager, 370 Lexington Avenue, New York, NY 10017   Phone: 212-953-5950

Profile: Books on philosophy and religion. Established in 1982. Titles: 50 per year; all nonfiction; hardcover and paperback. Average print run: 10,000. Binding: Perfect bound, cloth and paper. Book catalogue available.
Focus and Imprints: Paragon House Publishing offers a collection of titles on philosophy, religion, culture, and criticism. It caters to a mainly academic audience.
Editorial Interests
• *Nonfiction:* Interests include religion, philosophy, culture, the environment, feminism, folklore, inspirational material, meditation, metaphysics, mysticism, mythology, new age, prayer, social and world issues, spirituality, women's issues, and yoga.
Recent Titles: *Against All Hope* by Herman Langbein. *Nature's Web* by Peter Marhall.
Submission and Payment Policy: Query first with outline, 2 sample chapters, and author biography. Include SASE. Accepts photocopies and computer printouts. Simultaneous submissions okay. Reports in 6 weeks. If accepted, expect publication in 2 years. Royalty.

Parallax Press

Arnold Kotler, Editor-in-Chief, 850 Talbot Avenue, Albany, CA 94706   Phone: 510-525-0101, Fax: 510-525-7129

Profile: Nonfiction books on Buddhism. Titles: 10 per year; all nonfiction; 1 hardcover; 9 paperback. Average print run: 2,500. Binding: Perfect bound. Book catalogue available.
Focus and Imprints: Parallax Press specializes in Buddhist books that integrate mindful awareness and social responsibility. All material must relate to socially engaged Buddhism. No poetry.
Editorial Interests
• *Nonfiction:* Socially engaged Buddhism including eco-spirituality, eco-feminism, and the practice of nonviolence.
Recent Titles: *Love in Action* by Thich Nhat Hanh. *Thinking Green!* by Petra Kelly.
Submission and Payment Policy: Query with outline and 2–3 sample chapters. Include SASE. Accepts photocopies, computer printouts, and Macintosh disks. Simultaneous submissions okay. Responds to queries in 3 months, to manuscripts in 6 months. If accepted, expect publication in 2 years. Open to subsidy and co-publishing ventures. Offers royalty and advance.
Other Interests: Affiliated with The Community of Mindful Living, a nonprofit organization. Contact Therese Fitzgerald, 510-527-3751, for more information. Sponsors Reflective Writing: Mindfulness and the War with novelist Maxine Hong Kingston, a series of ongoing writing workshops for veterans and families. For more information, contact Michael Gardner, CML, P.O. Box 7355, Berkeley, CA 94707, 510-527-3751.

Pearl Publishing House

Shaikh Muhammad Al-Akili, Publisher, P.O. Box 28870, Philadelphia, PA 19151   Phone: 215-877-4458, Fax: 215-877-7439

Profile: Books on Islam and Sufism. Titles: 4 paperbacks per year. Average print run: 10,000. Binding: Perfect bound. Book catalogue available.
Focus and Imprints: Pearl Publishing House specializes in classic Islamic and Sufi books and related titles.

Editorial Interests
• *Nonfiction:* Islamic and Sufi books. Related areas of interest include healing, health, holistic health, inspiration, mysticism, new age, nutrition, parapsychology, philosophy, prayer, psychology, and spirituality.
Recent Titles: *Medicine of the Prophet* by Muhammad Al-Akili. *Dictionary of Dream Interpretation* by Muhammad Al-Akili.
Submission and Payment Policy: Query with outline, writing samples, and resume. Include SASE. Accepts photocopies and IBM disks. Call before submitting computer disks. No simultaneous submissions. Reports in 3–6 months. If accepted, expect publication in 6–12 months. Considers co-publishing ventures. Royalty, 10–15%.

Perspectives Press

Pat Johnston, Publisher, P.O. Box 90318, Indianapolis, IN 46290-0318

Profile: Books on infertility and adoption. Book catalogue and writer's guidelines available.
Focus and Imprints: Perspectives Press focuses exclusively on infertility, adoption, and closely related reproductive health and child welfare issues in books for children and adults. Its purpose is to promote understanding of these issues and to educate those who face them, as well as professionals in the field and the general public. It seeks to foster understanding between adoptees, adoptive parents, and birthparents. Prefers manuscripts from writers who are personally or professionally involved in the field, especially submissions from infertile persons, adoptees, birthparents, and adoptive parents. Material should be research-based, open, engaging, and free of jargon.
Editorial Interests
• *Fiction:* Fiction and picture books for preschool and elementary-age children on issues of adoption, single parent adoption, donor insemination, donor embryo, and surrogacy. Stories should be racially and ethnically inclusive and respectful of birthparents.
• *Nonfiction:* Nonfiction for adults in the form of decision-making material, books dealing with issue-related parenting concerns, books to share with others to help explain infertility or adoption issues, and special programming or training manuals. 40,000 words and up. Nonfiction for children from preschoolers through young adults on issues of adoption, single parent adoption, donor insemination, donor embryo, and surrogacy.
Recent Titles: *Flight of the Stork* by Anne C. Bernstein, Ph.D. *Sweet Grapes: How to Stop Being Infertile and Start Living Again* by Jean and Michael Carter.
Submission and Payment Policy: Query first with outline, table of contents, market and audience analysis, resume, and author biography. May send complete manuscript with resume and author background for picture book submissions. Include SASE. Reports in 2 months.

Pogo Press, Incorporated

Leo J. Harris, Vice President, Four Cardinal Lane, St. Paul, MN 55127   Phone/Fax: 612-483-4692

Profile: Trade paperbacks on the arts and popular culture. Established in 1986. Titles: 3 per year; all paperback. Book catalogue available.
Focus and Imprints: Pogo Press is a small press that publishes books with a regional emphasis, devoted primarily to the arts, history, breweriana, and popular culture.
Editorial Interests
• *Nonfiction:* Interests include the arts, popular culture, history, and Minnesota regional issues.
Recent Titles: *Minnesota's Literary Visitors* by John T. Flanagan. *Between Two Cultures: Kiowa Art from Fort Marion* by Moira F. Harris.
Submission and Payment Policy: Query first with outline. Include SASE. Reports in 1 month. If accepted, expect publication in 8 months. Payment is negotiable.

Prima Publishing

Jennifer Basye Sander, Senior Editor, P.O. Box 1260, Rocklin, CA 95677   Phone: 916-786-0426, Fax: 916-786-0488

Profile: General nonfiction trade books. Imprint of Prima Communications, Inc. Established in 1984. Titles: 200 per year; all nonfiction; 30 hardcover; 170 paperback. Average print run: 10,000+. Book catalogue available.
Focus and Imprints: Prima publishes a wide variety of high-quality nonfiction trade books. Writers approaching this company should be as professional as possible and prepare by reading recent Prima titles. Do not submit glossy picture books. Prima's imprints include *Prima Computer Books, Secrets of the Games*—video and computer games, and *Paradise Family Guides*—travel books.
Editorial Interests
• *Nonfiction:* Interests include health, holistic and natural health, meditation, social and world issues, business, travel, cookbooks with emphasis on vegetarianism, and parenting.
Recent Titles: *The Tao of Money* by Ivan Hoffman. *The Healing Power of Food* by Michael T. Murray, M.D.

Submission and Payment Policy: Query first with outline. Include SASE. Accepts photocopies and high-quality computer printouts. Simultaneous submissions okay. Responds to queries in 1 month; to manuscripts in 3 months. If accepted, expect publication in 1 year. Royalty, 15% of actual gross receipts on paperback books.

Quest Books

Brenda Rosen, Senior Editor, 306 West Geneva Road, Wheaton, IL 60187   Phone: 708-665-0130, Fax: 708-665-8791

Profile: Books on theosophical philosophy. A division of the Theosophical Society in America, a nonprofit organization. Titles: 12 per year; all nonfiction; 6 hardcover; 6 paperback. Average print run: 7,000. Book catalogue available.
Focus and Imprints: Quest Books' sole focus is on nonfiction trade paperbacks that speak either explicitly or implicitly to some aspect of theosophical philosophy. Writing should be well-researched, well-written, and engaging to the reader. Not interested in fiction, poetry, children's books, or books based on channeling or personal psychic impressions.
Editorial Interests
• *Nonfiction:* Theosophical philosophy and related topics: universal philosophical and religious principles, world religious traditions, meditation, spiritual ecology, transpersonal psychology, new science, men's and women's spirituality, Native American spirituality, mysticism, mythology, parapsychology, the environment, and holistic health and healing.
Recent Titles: *Dialogues with a Modern Mystic* by Andrew Harvey and Mark Matousek. *Spiritual Parenting* by Steven M. Rossman, Ph.D.
Submission and Payment Policy: Query first with outline, 1 sample chapter, and resume. Include SASE. Accepts photocopies and computer printouts. Simultaneous submissions okay. Responds to queries in 1 month, to manuscripts in 2 months. If accepted, expect publication in 12–18 months. Royalty, 10%; advance, $1,500–$5,000.
Other Interests: Affiliated with the Theosophical Society in America. Contact John Algeo, President, 708-668-1571, for information about the society.

Rama Publishing Co.

Richard Aschwanden, Editor/Publisher, P.O. Box 793, Carthage, MO 64836-0793   Phone: 417-358-1098

Profile: Self-help spirituality. Titles: 1–2 per year; nonfiction paperback. Average print run: 2,000. Press: Offset. Binding: Perfect bound. Book catalogue available.
Focus and Imprints: Rama Publishing seeks books that focus on the physical, mental, and spiritual regeneration of humankind. All material should have a self-help angle with an eternal rather than worldly perspective. Gear writing toward that which is specifically related to physical and spiritual health. "We are here through the will of God. Its is up to each of us as individuals to discover what our own purpose is." Avoid violence and prejudice.
Editorial Interests
• *Nonfiction:* Books with a self-help perspective on bodywork, ecosystems, the environment, healing, health, holistic health, inspiration, natural health, nutrition, parenting, prayer, recovery, relationships, Christianity, exercise, humanism as religion, and homeschooling.
Submission and Payment Policy: Prefers complete manuscript with cover letter. Accepts a query with outline. Include SASE. Accepts photocopies and computer printouts. Simultaneous submissions okay. Responds to queries in 4 weeks, to manuscripts in 6–8 weeks. If accepted, expect publication in 3 months. Payment negotiated on an individual basis.

Read America!

Roger Hammer, Editor/Publisher, 3900 Glenwood Avenue, Golden Valley, MN 55422
Phone: 612-374-2120, Fax: 612-593-5593

Profile: Specializes in biographies. An imprint of The Place in the Woods. Titles: 1 per year; nonfiction paperback. Average print run: 1,000. Press: Offset. Binding: Perfect bound. Book catalogue available.
Focus and Imprints: Read America! seeks biographies that feature the achievements of American minorities: African Americans, women, Hispanic Americans, Native Americans, Asian Americans, and people with disabilities.
Editorial Interests
• *Nonfiction:* Biographies of minorities. Interests include cultural and ethnic issues, feminism, gay and lesbian issues, lifestyle, men's issues, seniors, social and world issues, spirituality, and women's issues.
• *Illustrations:* Artwork to accompany manuscript.
Submission and Payment Policy: Query first with outline and 1 sample chapter, or send complete manuscript with cover letter. Include SASE. Accepts photocopies, computer printouts, and faxes. No simultaneous submissions. Reports in 2 weeks. If accepted, expect publication in 6 months. Offers $10 flat fee per printed piece. Purchases all rights, terms negotiated.

Rodmell Press

Donald Moyer, Publisher, 2550 Shattuck Avenue, Suite 18, Berkeley, CA 94704   Phone: 510-841-3123, Fax: 510-841-3191

Profile: Books on yoga and meditation. Titles: 2–3 per year; nonfiction paperback. Average print run: 8,000–10,000. Press: Sheet fed. Book catalogue available.
Focus and Imprints: Rodmell Press is a publisher of books on yoga and Buddhist practices as they relate to health and fitness, mediation, and women's health.
Editorial Interests
• *Nonfiction:* Yoga, Buddhism, Zen Buddhism, meditation, holistic health and fitness, women's health, bodywork, healing, mysticism, nutrition, parenting, philosophy, self-help, and spirituality.
Recent Titles: *Back Care Basics* by Mary Pullig Schatl, M.D. *Relax and Renew* by Judith Lasater, Ph.D., P.T.
Submission and Payment Policy: Query first with outline. Include SASE. Accepts photocopies and computer printouts. Simultaneous submissions okay. Reports in 2–3 months. If accepted, expect publication in 18–24 months. Royalty; advance.

Sanguinaria Publishing

Selma Miriam, Partner, 85 Ferris Street, Bridgeport, CT 06605   Phone: 203-576-9168

Profile: Feminist-related material. Titles: 1 nonfiction paperback title every 3 years. Average print run: 5,000. Binding: Perfect bound. Book catalogue available.
Focus and Imprints: Sanguinaria Publishing specializes in nonfiction feminist books, especially cookbooks and humor.
Editorial Interests
• *Nonfiction:* Feminist-related cookbooks and humor.
Recent Titles: *The Perennial Political Pallet* by The Bloodroot Collective.
Submission and Payment Policy: Query with outline. No unsolicited manuscripts. Include SASE. Accepts photocopies and computer printouts. Simultaneous submissions okay. Reports in 1 month. If accepted, expect publication in 1 year. Royalty, 12%.

The Savant Garde Workshop

Artemis Smith, Artistic Director, P.O. Box 1650, Six Union Street, Sag Harbor, NY 11963-0060   Phone: 516-725-1414

Profile: Literary fiction. Titles: 3 per year; all paperback. Average print run: Varies. Binding: Perfect bound. Book catalogue not available. Writer's guidelines and policies available with SASE.
Focus and Imprints: The Savant Garde Workshop is "interested in evaluating only literary or art works, in any medium, of extreme originality and humanistic/futuristic content." Prefers to work with established authors. Writers are advised to send for guidelines and publishing statement before submitting their work to this organization.
Editorial Interests
• *Fiction:* Quality novels, plays, poetry. Topics of interest include philosophy, relationships, and social and world issues.
Recent Titles: *OI or A Machine Called Skeets* by Artemis Smith. *Bottomfeeder: A Fishhk Story* by Mark Spitzer.
Submission and Payment Policy: Query first with outline. Include SASE. Accepts photocopies, computer printouts, and ASCII disks. No simultaneous submissions. Responds to queries in 1 month, to manuscripts in 6 months. If accepted, expect publication in 2 years. Detailed payment policy set forth in "Public Notice" guidelines.

Schiffer Publishing

Peter Schiffer, Owner, 77 Lower Valley, Atglen, PA 19310   Phone: 610-593-1777, Fax: 610-593-2002

Profile: Craft and collectibles books. Titles: 100–115 per year; all nonfiction; hardcover and paperback. Average print run: N/A. Book catalogue available.
Focus and Imprints: Schiffer Publishing specializes in books on arts and crafts, hobbies, and collectibles. It focuses both on specific artisans and general categories. Its Whitford Press imprint publishes new age books.
Editorial Interests
• *Nonfiction:* Books on arts and crafts, ethnic and cultural arts and crafts, antiques and collectibles, and military aviation crafts and history.
Recent Titles: *PEZ Collectibles* by Richard Geary. *Horse Carving with Tom Wolfe* by Tom Wolfe.
Submission and Payment Policy: Query first with outline and sample photos where applicable. Include SASE. No unsolicited manuscripts. Reports as soon as possible. If accepted, expect publication in 6–9 months. Royalty.

Sierra Oaks Publishing Co.

Stephanie Morris, Managing Editor, 1370 Sierra Oaks Court, Newcastle, CA 95658-9791   Phone/Fax: 916-663-1474

Profile: Native American children's books. Titles: 3 per year. Average print run: 10,000. Binding: Perfect bound. Book catalogue available.
Focus and Imprints: Sierra Oaks Publishing Company specializes in authentic children's books about Native American litera-

ture, history, and culture. Its books are designed to emphasize the role Native Americans played and continued to play in American society. Publishes the works of Native Americans only.

Editorial Interests
• *Fiction and Nonfiction:* Children's books about Native American myths, legends, history, and culture.
Recent Titles: *American Indians As Cowboys* by Clifford Trafzer. *Where Indians Live* by Nashone.
Submission and Payment Policy: Query first with outline. Include SASE. Accepts photocopies, computer printouts, faxes, and Microsoft Word or Works disks. Simultaneous submissions okay. Reports in 1 month. If accepted, expect publication in 1 year. Pays a flat fee; payment varies according to book size.

Silvercat Publications

R. Outlaw, Editor, 4070 Goldfinch Street, Suite C, San Diego, CA 92103   Phone: 619-299-6774, Fax: 619-299-9119

Profile: Nonfiction lifestyle books. Titles: 4–6 per year; all nonfiction paperbacks. Average print run: 3,000–5,000. Book catalogue available.
Focus and Imprints: Silvercat Publications gives editorial priority to nonfiction titles addressing consumer and quality-of-life concerns. It seeks fairly mainstream self-help books—it is not a publisher of spiritual, occult, or metaphysical material. "We are not a 'new age' publisher, per se. We want material that will interest 'old age' readers as well, especially those who are willing to better their own lives. We try to keep our feet planted on the cement." Open to working with both new and established writers. Not interested in inspirational stories or fiction.
Editorial Interests
• *Nonfiction:* Practical self-help books on consumer affairs, lifestyle, the environment, health, nutrition, parenting, psychology, and relationships. Prefers shorter manuscripts of 30,000–60,000 words.
Recent Titles: *A Quick Guide to Food Safety* by Robert Goodman. *Moving: A Complete Checklist and Guide for Relocation* by Karen G. Adams.
Submission and Payment Policy: Query with outline and 1–2 sample chapters. Include SASE. Prefers MS-DOS ASCII files on 3.5" or 5.25" disks with hard copy. Simultaneous submissions okay. Reports in 1–2 months. If accepted, expect publication in 1 year. Considers book packaging arrangements. Royalty, 12–15% of net; advance, varies.

Sterling Publishing Co., Inc.

Charles G. Nurnberg, Senior Vice President, 387 Park Avenue South, New York, NY 10016
Phone: 212-532-7160, Fax: 212-213-2495

Profile: Nonfiction trade titles. Titles: 200 per year; all nonfiction; 50 hardcover; 150 paperback. Average print run: 7,500. Binding: Perfect bound. Book catalogue available.
Focus and Imprints: Sterling Publishing Co. is an international press with an extensive current and back list of nonfiction trade titles, including a line of new age books.
Editorial Interests
• *Nonfiction:* Interests include psychology, the environment, new age, astrology, bodywork, crystals, dreams, extraterrestrials, healing, health, holistic and natural health, meditation, mythology, nutrition, occult, parapsychology, psychic phenomenon, and witches.
Recent Titles: *Dictionary of Dream Symbols* by Erik Ackroyd. *Rainbow Medicine* by Wolf Moondance.
Submission and Payment Policy: Query first with a detailed outline and at least 10 sample illustrations. Include SASE. Accepts photocopies, computer printouts, and faxes. Simultaneous submissions okay. Reports in 1 month. If accepted, expect publication in 6–8 months. Royalty, 10%. Advance commensurate with book.

Superlove

Editor, 2128 Watauga Avenue, Orlando, FL 32812-5113   Phone: 407-894-1773

Profile: Self-help books. Book catalogue not available.
Focus and Imprints: Superlove publishes fiction and nonfiction on "real philosophy, truth, and new view." Most material is self-help and educational in nature. "Make sure it has mass appeal and value."
Editorial Interests
• *Fiction and Nonfiction:* Self-help, education, inspiration, meditation, new age, philosophy, and yoga.
Recent Titles: *Diamond Rainbow* by Superlove. *Musical Monkeys* by Superlove.
Submission and Payment Policy: Query first with outline. Include SASE. Accepts IBM-compatible disks. Reports in 6 weeks. If accepted, expect publication in 6 months. Payment is negotiable.

Swan•Raven & Company

Brian Crissey, Publisher, 33350 N.E. Old Parrett Mt. Road, Newberg, OR 97132   Phone: 503-538-0264, Fax: 503-538-8485

Profile: Nonfiction new age books. An imprint of Blue Water Publishing, Inc. Titles: 6 per year; all nonfiction. Average print run: 5,000. Book catalogue available.

Focus and Imprints: Swan•Raven & Company publishes new age and new thought books and tapes with themes that explore "the sacred message between the otherworld and our world." Its sister imprint, Wild Flower Press, publishes a book line dedicated to ufology.

Editorial Interests

• *Nonfiction:* Interests include new age, rituals and healings, indigenous wisdom, women and health, natural health, men's and women's issues, and future speculations.

Recent Titles: *Ritual: Power, Healing, and Community* by Maildoma Patrice Somé. *Human Robots & Holy Mechanics: Reclaiming Our Souls in a Machine World* by David T. Kyle.

Submission and Payment Policy: Query first with outline, 3 sample chapters, resume, and market analysis. Include SASE. Accepts computer printouts. Simultaneous submissions okay. Royalty varies depending on author's experience.

T. Byron G. Publishing

Tom, Editor, Box 26, Angels Camp, CA 95222

Profile: New age books. Titles: 1 per year; nonfiction paperback. Average print run: 2,000. Binding: Perfect bound. Distributed by Samuel Weiser.

Focus and Imprints: T. Byron G. Publishing will consider co-publishing relationships with authors of books on a variety of new age topics. It prefers logical examination to "fanciful" writing. "Be exoteric, not esoteric." Its Mini Novel Publishing imprint publishes "mini" novels, books that take less than an hour to read.

Editorial Interests

• *Nonfiction:* New age titles in the areas of astrology, dreams, ecosystems, the environment, magic, metaphysics, mythology, occult, philosophy, Tarot, and cosmology.

Submission and Payment Policy: Query with outline and 1–2 sample chapters or writing samples. Include SASE. Accepts photocopies, computer printouts, and 3.5" disks. Simultaneous submissions okay. Reports in 1 month. Publication time varies. Open to co-publishing ventures only.

Telstar

Kathleen Lee Mendel, President, P.O. Box 65656-566, Lubbock, TX 79464   Phone: 206-578-2072

Profile: Spiritually uplifting poetry collections. Titles: 6 per year; all poetry paperback. Average print run: 200. Binding: Spiral bound. Book list available.

Focus and Imprints: Telstar seeks to acquire poetry that touches the soul with clarity and vision. "Speak with a universal voice." Not interested in "work that lacks a reason for being."

Editorial Interests

• *Poetry:* Poems and collections with spiritual substance and vision. Interests include channeling, crystals, dreams, folklore, healing, inspiration, meditation, metaphysics, mysticism, mythology, new age, occult, parapsychology, philosophy, prayer, and spirituality.

Recent Titles: *Substance and Shadow* by John Marrs. *Back to the Blanket* by Waterhawk Sorenson.

Submission and Payment Policy: Query first with outline, writing samples, and resume, or send complete poems with cover letter, author biography, and clips. Include SASE. Accepts photocopies, computer printouts, and computer disks. No simultaneous submissions. Responds to queries in 3 months, to manuscripts in 6–9 months. If accepted, expect publication in 9 months. Royalty, 15%.

Theosophical Publishing House

Brenda Rosen, Editor, 306 West Geneva Road, Wheaton, IL 60187   Phone: 708-665-0130

Profile: Books on metaphysics, philosophy, and spirituality. A division of the Theosophical Society in America. Book catalogue available.

Focus and Imprints: Along with its imprint, Quest Books, the Theosophical Publishing House publishes nonfiction trade books that address theosophical philosophy as well as Native American spirituality. Writing should be well-researched, well-written, and engaging to the reader. Not interested in fiction, poetry, children's books, or books based on channeling or personal psychic impressions.

Editorial Interests

• *Nonfiction:* Interests include theosophical philosophy, Native American spirituality, metaphysics, astrology, comparative religion, inspiration, meditation, mysticism, spirituality, yoga, reincarnation, vegetarianism, and science.

Recent Titles: *Chakras* by Led Beader. *Native Healer* by Bobby Lake.

Submission and Payment Policy: Query first with outline or send complete manuscript with cover letter. Include SASE.

Accepts computer disks.

Third Side Press, Inc.

Midge Stocker, Publisher, 2250 West Farragut, Chicago, IL 60625-1802   Phone: 312-271-3029, Fax: 312-271-0459

Profile: Feminist and lesbian literature. Titles: 4 per year; 2 fiction; 2 nonfiction; 2 hardcover; 2 paperback. Average print run: 3,000. Press: offset. Binding: Perfect bound. Book catalogue available.
Focus and Imprints: Third Side Press publishes feminist literature, including lesbian fiction and women's nonfiction from a feminist perspective. Primary interest is in the field of women's health.
Editorial Interests
• *Fiction:* Lesbian novels, defined as novels written by a lesbian that include at least one major character who is lesbian.
• *Nonfiction:* Books on feminism, women's health, nutrition, holistic and natural health, cultural and ethnic issues, the environment, metaphysics, philosophy, politics, psychology, recovery, and self-help.
Recent Titles: *On Lill Street* by Lynn Kanter. *Confronting Cancer, Constructing Change* edited by Midge Stocker.
Submission and Payment Policy: Send complete manuscript. Include SASE. Accepts photocopies and computer printouts. Simultaneous submissions okay. Responds to queries in 1 month, to manuscripts in 2–4 months. If accepted, expect publication in 18 months. Offers royalty contract.

Threshold Books

Tom Goldberg, Managing Editor, 139 Main Street, Room 403, Brattleboro, VT 05301   Phone: 802-254-8300, Fax: 802-257-2779

Profile: Books on Sufism. Titles: 3 per year. Average print run: 4,000. Binding: Sewn. Book catalogue available.
Focus and Imprints: Interested in all aspects of Sufism, Threshold Books seeks translations of spiritual classics from the Sufi tradition. It plans to publish *Threshold*, a "journal/catalogue" which will serve the many readers interested in Sufism.
Editorial Interests
• *Nonfiction:* Translations of Sufi classics and by Sufi masters, particularly the strongest works of poetry.
Recent Titles: *Signs of the Unseen* by Jelaluddin Rumi. *Awakened Dreams* by Ahmet Hilmi.
Submission and Payment Policy: Query first with 2 sample chapters. Poetry, submit 10 translations per submission. Include SASE. Accepts computer printouts. Simultaneous submissions okay. Reports in 3 months. If accepted, expect publication in 6–12 months. Royalty, 7%.

Thunderbird Publications

Karen Degenhart, Publisher, P.O. Box 35, Idaho Springs, Co 80452   Phone: 303-567-4210

Profile: New age books. Titles: 2 per year; all nonfiction paperback. Average print run: 300. Perfect bound. Book list available.
Focus and Imprints: Thunderbird Publications is a small, independently owned press currently publishing the works of its publisher only, but with plans to expand. Its interests include new age books and personal spiritual journeys as well as Native American consciousness, UFOs, and conspiracy theories. "Please write first—I mainly publish myself, but could branch out in the future."
Editorial Interests
• *Nonfiction:* Personal spiritual experiences, new age, Native American, UFOs, astrology, channeling, crystals, cultural and ethnic concerns, dreams, ecosystems, the environment, extraterrestrials, folklore, healing, inspiration, lifestyle, magic, meditation, metaphysics, mysticism, mythology, natural health, occult, parapsychology, philosophy, politics, prayer, psychic phenomenon, psychology, relationships, religion, self-help, social and world issues, spirituality, and women's issues.
Recent Titles: *A Medicine Story: The Return to Native American Consciousness* by Karen Degenhart. *Beautiful Simplicity: The Journey into a Hidden Reality* by Karen Degenhart.
Submission and Payment Policy: Query first with outline and 1 sample chapter. Include SASE. Accepts photocopies and computer printouts. Simultaneous submissions okay. Reports immediately. Considers book packaging, subsidy publishing, and co-publishing ventures. Payment negotiable.
Other Interests: Connected with the Starlight Medicine Society, a club for people interested in Native American traditions, UFOs, and government secrets. Contact Karen Degenhart, 303-567-4210.

Tide-Mark Press Ltd.

Scott Kaeser, Editor, P.O. Box 280311, East Hartford, CT 06128   Phone: 203-289-6363. Fax: 203-289-3654

Profile: Calendars and environmental topics. Titles: 40 per year. Average print run: 8,000. Press: Sheetfed. Binding: Saddle stitched.
Focus and Imprints: Primarily a publisher of calendars, Tide-Mark Press plans to expand its list to include books on conservation and wildlife. It is currently looking for unique ideas for upscale-image calendars. No dog or cat calendars. "Calendars

should be more than just twelve pictures."
Editorial Interests
• *Nonfiction:* Informative, unique calendar ideas. Environmental, conservation, and wildlife books.
Recent Titles: *Herbal Calendar* by Lynn Hartman, artwork by Jonathan Green. *Desk Diary on Writers and Writing* by Helen Sheehy and Leslie Stainton.
Submission and Payment Policy: Send a brief proposal, preferably with samples of artwork. Include SASE. Accepts photocopies, computer printouts, DOS or WordPerfect disks, and faxes. Simultaneous submissions okay. Reports in 2 months. If accepted, expect publication in 1 year.

Tilbury House Publishers

Jennifer Elliot, Associate Publisher, 132 Water Street, Gardiner, ME 04345   Phone: 207-582-1899, Fax: 207-582-8227

Profile: Children's and adult nonfiction. Titles: 12 per year; all nonfiction; hardcover and paperback. Average print run: 3,000–10,000. Book catalogue available.
Focus and Imprints: Tilbury House Publishers seeks children's books on multicultural themes that promote diversity and tolerance as well as general nonfiction for adult. It accepts poetry collections from established authors only. Look at its catalogue and back list before considering this company. "No Fluffy-the-Dog-type manuscripts."
Editorial Interests
• *Nonfiction:* Multicultural children's books. Adult titles in the areas of body-mind connection, healing through dance, bodywork, cultural and ethnic issues, dreams, ecosystems, the environment, feminism, folklore, gay and lesbian issues, healing, health, holistic health, meditation, men's issues, natural health, new age, nutrition, parenting, philosophy, politics, prayer, psychology, rebirthing, Maine regional issues, relationships, social and world issues, women's issues, and yoga.
Recent Titles: *Talking Wolves* by Margie Night. *Women's Worlds/Women's Stories* by Louise Edgerly.
Submission and Payment Policy: Query first with outline or send complete manuscript or several chapters with cover letter. Include SASE. Accepts photocopies, computer printouts, and faxes. Simultaneous submissions okay if noted. Reports in 6 weeks. If accepted, expect publication in 1–2 years.

Traffic Light Press

Al Stone, Editor 2406 Newport Court, Fort Collins, CO 80526   Phone: 303-221-5534

Profile: New age, spiritual, and multicultural books. Titles: 3 per year; 2 fiction; 1 nonfiction; all paperback. Average print run: 1,000. Binding: Spiral or perfect bound.
Focus and Imprints: Traffic Light Press seeks interesting eclectic adult nonfiction on new age topics, Eastern religious practices, and spiritual. It also publishes Navaho children's books. "Be patient—this is a one-person operation."
Editorial Interests
• *Fiction:* Books for and about Navaho children.
• *Nonfiction:* Interests include Tai Chi, cultural and ethnic issues, folklore, inspiration, meditation, mysticism, mythology, new age, philosophy, prayer, Western regional issues, Eastern religion, social and world issues, and spirituality.
Recent Titles: *Vermillion Sky.*
Submission and Payment Policy: Query or send complete manuscript. Include SASE. Accepts photocopies, computer printouts, ASCII or WordPerfect disks, and faxes. Simultaneous submissions okay. Reports in 4–6 weeks. If accepted, expect publication in 6–12 months. Profits are divided: one-half to charity, one-quarter to publisher, and one-quarter to author.

Charles E. Tuttle Company, Inc.

Michael Kerber, General Manager, 153 Milk Street, Boston, MA 02109   Fax: 617-951-4045

Profile: Fiction and nonfiction books of Asian interest. Titles: 18 per year; 2 fiction; 16 nonfiction; 4 hardcover; 14 paperback. Average print run: 3,000. Book catalogue available.
Focus and Imprints: Charles E. Tuttle Company is a leading publisher of books on Japan and other Asian countries. It is currently expanding its list to include books on body, mind, and spirit.
Editorial Interests
• *Nonfiction:* Body, mind, spirit, Japan and Asian countries, Buddhism, Taoism, healing, health, meditation, natural health, philosophy, and women's issues.
Recent Titles: *A Woman's Book of Yoga* by Louise Taylor. *The Everyday Meditator* by Osho.
Submission and Payment Policy: Query first with outline. Include SASE. Accepts photocopies, computer printouts, and DOS Microsoft Word 5.5 disks. Simultaneous submissions okay. Responds to queries in 3 months, to manuscripts in 12 months. If accepted, expect publication in 18 months. Royalty, 6%; advance.

Twin Peaks Press

Helen Hecker, Editor, P.O. Box 129, Vancouver, WA 98666   Phone: 206-694-2462, Fax: 206-696-3210

Profile: Nonfiction. Titles: 12 per year; all nonfiction. Average print run: 10,000. Press: Web. Binding: Perfect bound. Book catalogue not available.
Focus and Imprints: Twin Peaks Press is open to all subjects and categories of nonfiction.
Editorial Interests
• *Nonfiction:* All topics, subjects, and styles.
Submission and Payment Policy: Query with outline. Accepts photocopies and computer printouts. Simultaneous submissions okay. Reports only if interested. Publication time varies. Contracts and payment negotiated on an individual basis.

University of California Press

Editor, 2120 Berkeley Way, Berkeley, CA 94720   Phone: 510-642-4247, Fax: 510-643-7127

Profile: Academic and trade books. Titles: 190 per year; nonfiction and translations; hardcover and paperback. Average print run: Varies. Book catalogue available.
Focus and Imprints: University of California Press deals in both the academic and trade markets. Content and writing style should appeal to both a scholarly and lay audience. It is currently looking for material on subjects with intellectual merit—history, the humanities, and social sciences among others. Scientific or technical material is not considered. Study its catalogue to glean its interest, audience, and style.
Editorial Interests
• *Nonfiction:* Interests include feminism, gender studies, gay and lesbian studies, health, Western history and culture, philosophy, politics, religious studies, and social sciences.
Recent Titles: *Unbearable Weight* by Susan Bordo. *Living Downtown* by Paul Groth.
Submission and Payment Policy: Prefers a query with outline, 2 sample chapters, and resume. Accepts complete manuscripts with cover letter and resume. Include SASE. Accepts photocopies and computer printouts. Simultaneous submissions okay. Reports in 2–6 weeks. Publication time varies. Considers co-publishing ventures. Royalty.

Upper Access Inc.

Gay Mullett,Editor, P.O. Box 457, One Upper Access Road, Hinesburg, VT 05461   Phone: 800-356-9315

Profile: Self-help nonfiction. Titles: 2 per year; all nonfiction; hardcover and paperback. Book catalogue available.
Focus and Imprints: Upper Access publishes a line a nonfiction aimed at improving the quality of life. It also distributes a variety of small-press titles.
Editorial Interests
• *Nonfiction:* Open to all topics that address quality-of-life issues.
Recent Titles: *Herbs of the Earth* by Mary Carse. *Letters from the Other Side* by Mary White.
Submission and Payment Policy: Query first with outline. Include SASE. Accepts photocopies, computer printouts, WordPerfect and DOS disks, and faxes. Simultaneous submissions okay. Reports in a few days.
Other Interests: Upper Access is a member of the Vermont Book Publishers association.

Valley of the Sun

Sharon Boyd, Editor, Box 38, Malibu, CA 90265   Phone: 818-706-0961, Fax: 818-706-3606

Profile: Self-help books. Titles: 4 per year; all nonfiction paperback. Average print run: 5,000–10,000. Press: Web. Binding: Perfect bound. Book catalogue available.
Focus and Imprints: Valley of the Sun specializes in self-help and metaphysical books for a general audience. Polished, professional queries and writing samples will get noticed. No fiction.
Editorial Interests
• *Nonfiction:* Interests include self-help, metaphysics, astrology, bodywork, dreams, healing, health, holistic health, inspiration, meditation, natural health, new age, nutrition, occult, parapsychology, philosophy, psychic phenomenon, psychology, relationships, and spirituality.
Recent Titles: *How to Believe in Nothing and Set Yourself Free* by Michael Misita. *Fifty Spiritually Powerful Meditations* by Margaret Rogers.
Submission and Payment Policy: Query first with outline and 1–2 sample chapters. Include SASE. No unsolicited manuscripts. Reports in 1 month. If accepted, expect publication in 9–12 months. Royalty.
Other Interests: Sponsors Sutphen Seminars. For more information, contact Jan Hale, 503-488-7880.

Van Hoy Publishers

Jay Yasgur, Editor, P.O. Box 925, Greenville, PA 16125   Phone: 412-588-7339

Profile: Homeopathic titles. Titles: 1–2 per year; all nonfiction; hardcover and paperback. Average print run: 1,000–2,000. Book list available.

Focus and Imprints: Van Hoy Publishers offers a small list of books on homeopathic medicine. It is also interested in autobiographical material.

Editorial Interests

• *Nonfiction:* Homeopathic medicine, autobiography, health, holistic and natural health, meditation, new age, yoga, and T'ai Chi.

Recent Titles: *Homeopathic Materia Medica for Nurses* edited by Jay Yasgur. *A Dictionary of Homeopathic Medical Terminology* edited by Jay Yasgur.

Submission and Payment Policy: Query first with outline and 2–3 sample chapters. Include SASE. Accepts photocopies, computer printouts, and computer disks. Reports in 1–2 months. If accepted, expect publication in 2–3 years. Pays a royalty or flat fee.

Vedanta Press

Robert Adjemian, Manager, 1946 Vedanta Place, Hollywood, CA 90068   Phone: 213-465-7114, Fax: 213-465-9568

Profile: Nonfiction books on Vedanta philosophy. Titles: 1 per year; paperback. Average print run: 2,000. Book catalogue available.

Focus and Imprints: As its name suggests, Vedanta Press focuses on books exploring Vedanta philosophy as taught by Ramakrishna, Vivekananas, and Pradhavananda, which teaches that real human nature is divine and advocates searching for the God within. Most material is written in-house, but is open to receiving "the great book." Avoid submissions that are psychic in orientation, drug-related, astrology-based, or "weird."

Editorial Interests

• *Nonfiction:* Vedanta philosophy, meditation, metaphysics, mysticism, philosophy, and spirituality.

Recent Titles: *Concordance to the Gospel of Sri Ramakrishna* by Katharine Whitmarsh. *Living Wisdom* by Vrajaprava.

Submission and Payment Policy: Query with outline or send complete manuscript with resume. Include SASE. Accepts photocopies and computer printouts. Simultaneous submissions okay. Responds to queries in 1–2 months, to manuscripts in 2 months. If accepted, expect publication in 4 months. No payment.

Other Interests: Affiliated with the Vedanta Society of Southern California, 1946 Vedanta Place, Hollywood, CA 90068.

Waterfront Books

Sherrill Musty, Editor, 85 Crescent Road, Burlington, VT 05401   Phone/Fax: 802-658-7477

Profile: Special-interest books for children. Titles: 2–3 per year; fiction and nonfiction; hardcover and paperback. Average print run: 5,000. Book catalogue available.

Focus and Imprints: Waterfront Books publishes children's fiction and nonfiction on special and sensitive subjects such as sexual abuse, death, disease and illness, disabilities, and empowerment. "Be inspirational, not powerless." Send for guidelines to ascertain interests.

Editorial Interests

• *Fiction:* Inspirational, empowering children's books and stories based around difficult life issues.

• *Nonfiction:* Self-help books for children on issues of death, illness and recovery, disabilities, sexual abuse, etc.

Recent Titles: *What's a Virus Anyway* and *Changing Families* by Fassler and McQueen.

Submission and Payment Policy: Query first with outline or send complete manuscript with cover letter. Include SASE. Accepts photocopies and computer printouts. Simultaneous submissions okay. Reports in 2 months. If accepted, expect publication in 1 year. Royalty, 15% of net.

Samuel Weiser Inc.

Eliot Stearnes, Editor, Box 612, York Beach, ME 03910   Phone: 207-363-4393, Fax: 207-363-5799

Profile: New age nonfiction trade titles. Titles: 20 per year; all nonfiction; 2 hardcover; 18 paperback. Average print run: 5,000. Trade paperback. Book catalogue available.

Focus and Imprints: Samuel Weiser specializes in new age books relating to oriental philosophy and all facets of the secret and hidden teachings. Its titles are intended "to help many different people find the path that is right for them." Appreciates submissions that are well-researched, footnoted, and referenced. Author's background is important—"explain what you do or teach." Not interested in material on witches or goblins, poetry, or general books that are better sent to a mass-market, nonspecialist house.

Editorial Interests
• *Nonfiction:* New age, astrology, dreams, healing, holistic health, inspiration, magic, meditation, men's issues, metaphysics, mysticism, mythology, natural health, occult, parapsychology, philosophy, psychology, recovery, religion, self-help, spirituality, women's issues, yoga, kabbalah, tarot, and oriental philosophy.
Recent Titles: *Mysticism* by Bruno Borchert. *Tarot of the Spirit* by Pamela Eakins.
Submission and Payment Policy: Query with outline, sample chapters, and resume, or send complete manuscript with cover letter, bibliography, clips, and resume. Include SASE. Accepts photocopies, computer printouts, and faxes. Simultaneous submissions okay. Reports in 2–3 months. If accepted, expect publication in 18 months. Pays a royalty with advance.

Whitford Press

Ellen Taylor, Editor, 77 Lower Valley, Atglen, PA 19310   Phone: 610-593-1777, Fax: 610-593-2002

Profile: New age books. A division of Schiffer Publishing. Titles: 5 per year; all nonfiction paperback. Average print run: N/A. Binding: Perfect bound. Book catalogue available.
Focus and Imprints: Whitford Press publishes new age books.
Editorial Interests
• *Nonfiction:* Interested in books on the new age, astrology, crystals, dreams, extraterrestrials, magic, metaphysics, witches, and divining.
Recent Titles: *Green Magic* by Morwyn. *Sweet Mythtery of Life* by Robert Asprin.
Submission and Payment Policy: Query first with outline. Include SASE. No unsolicited manuscripts. Reporting and publication time varies. Royalty.

Whitman Publishing

William Dows, Editor, P.O. Box 280038, Lakewood, CO 80228   Fax: 303-987-1911

Profile: General nonfiction trade books. 50% subsidy publishing. Titles: 6 per year; all nonfiction; 5 hardcover; 1 paperback. Average print run: 3,000. Book catalogue available.
Focus and Imprints: Whitman Publishing lists a variety of nonfiction trade books. Authors are advised to evaluate if there is truly a potential market for their work. " If the writing is good and the subject interesting, anything, short of pornography, is acceptable for editorial review." Will subsidize a book if the market is deemed too narrow for a fully financed trade book endeavor.
Editorial Interests
• *Nonfiction:* Topics include the environment, folklore, health, holistic health, men's issues, new age, nutrition, and self-help.
Recent Titles: *Light and Well-Being* by John O'The. *Healing Power of the Mind* by Harold Ickes.
Submission and Payment Policy: Query with outline, sample chapters, writing samples, and resume. Include SASE. Accepts photocopies and computer printouts. Simultaneous submissions okay. Reports in 1 month. If accepted, expect publication in 6–8 months. Payment is negotiated on an individual basis. Subsidy: full pay back before royalties.

Whole Person Associates, Inc.

Susan Gustafson, Editor, 210 West Michigan, Duluth, MN 55802-1908   Phone: 218-727-0500, Fax: 218-727-0505

Profile: Stress management. Titles: 20 per year; all nonfiction paperback. Average print run: 5,000. Press: Offset. Binding: Perfect bound. Book catalogue available.
Focus and Imprints: Whole Person Associates publishes books and audio and video tapes on stress management and wellness promotion with a whole person perspective designed specifically for trainers, consultants, and educators who work with groups. Materials are meant to promote group participation, such as structured exercises on stress management. Books are sold by direct mail. Its Pfeifer-Hamilton imprint lists regional titles.
Editorial Interests
• *Nonfiction:* Books and tapes on stress management, wellness, health, holistic health, men's issues, nutrition, relationships, seniors, and women's issues.
Recent Titles: *Working with Women's Groups* by Louis Eberhardt. *Working with Groups from Dysfunctional Families* by Cheryl Hetherington.
Submission and Payment Policy: Prefers a query with outline and 1–2 sample chapters. Accepts complete manuscript with cover letter. Include SASE. Accepts photocopies and computer printouts. Reports in 1 month. If accepted, expect publication in 18 months. Royalty.
Other Interests: Affiliated with the National Wellness Association.

Wild Flower Press

Brian Crissey, Publisher, P.O. Box 726, Newberg, OR 97132   Phone: 503-538-0264, Fax: 503-538-8485

Profile: Books on ufology and spirituality. An imprint of Blue Water Publishing, Inc. Titles: 6 per year; all nonfiction. Average print run: 5,000. Book catalogue available.

Focus and Imprints: Wild Flower Press specializes in nonfiction books on ufology that transcend the split between UFOs and metaphysics and blend the psychic and the spiritual. Its sister imprint Swan•Raven & Company publishes a list of general new age titles.

Editorial Interests

• *Nonfiction:* Accounts of UFO experiences, encounters, and phenomenon such as speculated extraterrestrial origins of Christianity, time-traveling UFOs, or how to survive alien abductions.

Recent Titles: *Close Extraterrestrial Encounters* by Richard J. Boylan. *Visitors From Time: The Secret of the UFOs* by Marc Davenport.

Submission and Payment Policy: Query first with outline, 3 sample chapters, resume, and market analysis. Include SASE. Accepts computer printouts. Simultaneous submissions okay. Royalty varies depending on author's experience.

Wingbow Press

Randy Fingland, Editor, 7900 Edgewater Drive, Oakland, CA 94621   Phone: 510-632-4700, Fax: 510-632-1281

Profile: Health and women's studies. A division of Bookpeople. Titles: 1 per year; nonfiction paperback. Average print run: 3,000.

Focus and Imprints: Wingbow Press publishes women's studies and health-related nonfiction. Gear material toward a broad, general-interest audience.

Editorial Interests

• *Nonfiction:* Women's issues, feminism, health, healing, natural and alternative health, and bodywork.

Recent Titles: *Heart of the Goddess* by Hallie Iglehart Austin. *Your Healing Hands* by Richard Gordon.

Submission and Payment Policy: Query first with outline. Include SASE. Accepts photocopies, computer printouts, IBM disks, and faxes. Simultaneous submissions okay. Reports in 4–6 weeks. If accepted, expect publication in 2 years. Considers co-publishing ventures. Royalty, 7–10%.

Writer's Resources, Inc.

Elizabeth Gould, Editor, 15 Margaret's Way, Nantucket, MA 02554   Phone: 508-325-0041, Fax: 508-325-0667

Profile: Writer's guidebooks and books on awareness. Titles: 2 per year; nonfiction paperback. Average print run: 4,000. Binding: Perfect bound. Book catalogue not available.

Focus and Imprints: Specializing in market guides for freelance writers, Writer's Resources is expanding its interests to include how-to books that promote self-awareness, individual and group empowerment, and responsibility. Works should be well-grounded in experience, and offer ways to enhance life spiritually, emotionally, and physically. Be practical and use a conversational tone. Levity is encouraged. No violence, sexism, racism, etc. "If you can describe your book using the words 'how-to,' we want to see it." No fiction or poetry.

Editorial Interests

• *Nonfiction:* How-to; self-help; relationships; health; juvenile and teen issues; parenting, religion, spirituality, and philosophy as they apply to day-to-day life; social issues; men's issues as they relate to parenting, family, and committed partnerships; and women's issues.

Recent Titles: *The Guide to Religious and Inspirational Magazines* edited by Elizabeth Gould and Livia Fiordelisi. *New Choices for Writers* edited by Elizabeth Gould.

Submission and Payment Policy: Query first with outline, 2–3 sample chapters, and marketing plan detailing who would buy the book and why. No unsolicited manuscripts. Include SASE. Accepts photocopies and computer printouts. Simultaneous submissions okay. Reporting and publication time varies. Royalty.

GLOSSARY

Advance: Form of payment where author is given a portion of the final fee prior to publication of the book.

All rights: Ownership rights contracted to a publisher. Allows use of manuscript anywhere and in any form without consent of the author.

Assignment: Commissioning a manuscript by an editor for a predetermined fee.

B/W: Black and white; refers to photographs, slides, and illustrations.

Bibliography: A list of the books, articles, and other sources referred to in a text or consulted by the author in its production.

Bimonthly: Published every two months.

Book packaging: A company organizes the production of a book and hires the necessary professionals to get it written, printed, and sold to a publisher.

Byline: A line at the beginning of an article crediting the author.

Circulation: Average number of copies of a publication sold per printing.

Clips: Samples of a writer's published work.

Contributor's copies: Copies of the issue in which the writer's work appears.

Copyedit: Closely editing a manuscript for grammar, punctuation, style, and mechanics.

Copyright: The exclusive legal right to copy, publish, and sell written works, music, photographs, and illustrations.

Co-publishing: Joint publishing venture wherein the author and publisher share costs.

Cover letter: A brief business letter accompanying a complete manuscript. (see *How to Write a Cover Letter,* p. 13)

Deadline: Due date for the submission of a complete manuscript.

Disk submissions: Manuscripts submitted on computer diskette.

Dot-matrix printout: Computer printout where the individual characters are composed of a pattern of dots.

Essay: Analytic or interpretive article written from a limited or personal point of view.

Feature: Often a lead article of human interest rather than news.

Fiction: An invented story of the imagination.

Filler: Short items used to fill a page: jokes, puzzles, short facts.

First North American serial rights: The right to publish an article or story for the first time in North America.

Flat Fee: Form of payment where author is given a one-time fee.

Genre: A category of fiction characterized by a specific format, style, or content such as romance, mystery, or fantasy.

Glossy prints: Photographs printed on a shiny finish as opposed to a matte finish.

Imprint: The name under which a publisher issues books or book lines.

In-house: Material written by a publication's staff, usually departments or columns.

International Reply Coupon (IRC): Coupon exchangeable in any foreign country for postage on a single-rate, surface-mailed letter.

Kill fee: Percentage of an agreed upon fee that is paid to a writer for a completed assigned article that has been canceled.

Lead: The beginning of an article.

Lead time: Time between the acquisition of a manuscript and its publication.

Letter-quality printout: A computer printout that looks typewritten.

Manuscript: A handwritten or typewritten document.

N/A: Abbreviation for "not available."

Nonfiction: Literature based in fact not invention.

Novella: A work of fiction falling in length between a short story and a novel.

One-time rights: The right to publish a piece one time.

Outline: A summary covering the main points of a manuscript under headings and subheadings.

Payment on acceptance: Payment for an article or story is made upon the editor's decision to publish it.

Payment on publication: Payment for an article or story is made on or following its publication.

Personal-experience piece: An article based on the author's experience.

Proofread: The reading and correction of a manuscript's errors, usually spelling, punctuation, and typographical.

Quarterly: Published four times a year in regular intervals.

Query: A business letter written to interest an editor in an article or book idea. (see *How to Write a Query Letter*, p. 12)

Reprint: A subsequent printing of an article in a different publication or format.

Reprint rights: The right to publish an article or story that has previously appeared in another publication. Also called Second rights.

Resume: A short account of one's professional and educational qualifications and publishing credits.

Royalty: Form of payment where the author is given a percentage of the profits from the sale of the book.

SAE: Self-addressed envelope.

SASE: Self-addressed, stamped, envelope.

Self cover: A publication that uses the same interior and exterior paper.

Serial: A story published in parts at intervals.

Simultaneous submission: Submitting the same article or story to more than one magazine or book publisher at a time.

Slant: A particular approach to an article or book that will appeal to a specific readership.

Slush pile: Describes a back log of unsolicited manuscripts.

Solicited manuscript: A manuscript specifically requested by an editor.

Staff written: Written by the publication's staff; usually columns or departments.

Subsidy publishing: A method of publishing whereby the author pays a publisher to produce a book.

Synopsis: A brief summary of a fictional piece.

Tabloid: A style of newspaper that is half the size of an ordinary newspaper and contains news in a condensed fashion.

Transparencies: Color slides.

Trim size: The height and width of a publication.

Unsolicited manuscript: Any manuscript not specifically assigned by an editor.

Word count: Refers to the approximate number of words in manuscript.

World rights: The right to publish a manuscript anywhere in the world.

Writer's guidelines: Editorial objectives and specifications provided by editors for writers.

Writing samples: Examples of a writer's unpublished work often sent with a query.

INDEX OF PUBLISHERS